Books, Music, and Videos by Rama - Dr. Frederick Lenz

Books

Lifetimes: True Accounts of Reincarnation (1979, 2011)
Total Relaxation: The Complete Program for Overcoming Stress, Tension, Worry, and Fatigue (1980, 2011)
Surfing the Himalayas (1994, 2016)
Snowboarding to Nirvana (1997, 2016)
Insights: Tantric Buddhist Reflections on Life (1994)
The Enlightenment Cycle (2002, 2016)*
On the Road with Rama (2002)*
Zen Tapes (2002)*
Insights: Talks on the Nature of Existence (2003)*
Tantric Buddhism (2003)*
How to Meditate (2004)*
The Lakshmi Series (2007, 2016)*

Music

Atlantis Rising*   Surfing the Himalayas
Canyons of Light   Occult Dancer
Cayman Blue   Mandala of Light
Ecologie   Retrograde Planet*
Ecstasy*   Mystery School
Enlightenment   Techno Zen Master
Light Saber   Tantra*
Samadhi*   Urban Destruction*
Samurai*   Zen Master

Videos

Tantric Buddhism with Rama (1993)*
Cayman Blue and Canyons of Light (1997)*

Rama Meditation Society

* Audio formats of these books, selected music, and videos are available from the Rama Meditation Society - Resource Library site: www.ramameditationsociety.org

The Frederick P. Lenz Foundation for American Buddhism

For more information about the legacy of Dr. Frederick Lenz, please visit The Frederick P. Lenz Foundation for American Buddhism site: www.fredericklenzfoundation.org

The Lakshmi Series

Frederick Lenz

MYSTIC BUDDHA PUBLISHING HOUSE

THE LAKSHMI SERIES

Published by

Mystic Buddha Publishing House

www.MysticBuddha.com

First Edition Published 2007 by

The Frederick P. Lenz Foundation for American Buddhism

Second Edition, 2016

ISBN 978-0-9972431-2-3

Library of Congress Control Number: 2016908069

Categories: Religion & Spirituality, Buddhism, Meditation

Photo of Rama - Dr. Frederick Lenz by Greg Gorman

This book is dedicated to Rama – Dr. Frederick Lenz and to the principles of American Buddhism he cherished, embodied, and tirelessly taught.

"I come into the world to be of service to beings who seek knowledge, empowerment, enlightenment; who seek to grow, evolve, develop; who want to have more fun with their lives and experience the profundity of being; who want to become more conscious in their short time in an incarnate form. I'm a teacher."

– Rama - Dr. Frederick Lenz

FOREWORD

I am a student of Enlightenment and Rama was my teacher. His teachings merge the ancient wisdom of the East with practical life in the West.

In the 1980s, the Lakshmi years, I sat with hundreds of students in beautiful Beverly Hill's theaters, listening to Rama, and experiencing the light energy that filled the room. I also traveled to the Anza-Borrego desert, traversing the night, meditating under the stars, and listening to Rama as he taught with energy and words.

This book, The Lakshmi Series, includes all of the teachings from the Lakshmi years, directly from Rama, and it is a treasure! Rama's words are here for you, and the energy lines that he used to teach are also here. I can't explain how that happens, it is part of the magic and mystery of studying with an enlightened teacher. Each time you read this book, you will learn something new, something that will expand your awareness.

— Lynne Miller, M.A.
Founder of Integrated Meditation Studies, Co-Founder
of the San Diego Dharma Center

TABLE OF CONTENTS

INTRODUCTION

In 1980, Rama - Dr. Frederick Lenz taught classes in meditation from the living room of his San Diego home. In early 1981, he formed his first, formal teaching center and called it Lakshmi, after the Indian goddess of beauty, harmony, and prosperity. As Dr. Lenz expanded his classes to Los Angeles and San Francisco, the number of students formally enrolled in the Lakshmi program quickly grew from 18 to over 800. The house in San Diego was replaced by large university lecture halls and public auditoriums that held over a thousand people.

To assist the spiritual progress of his growing numbers of students, in 1982 and 1983 Dr. Lenz recorded a series of 28 lectures called *The Lakshmi Series*. This set of teachings comprises a comprehensive foundation for self-discovery. The talks cover a wide variety of topics including meditation, the four principal Hindu yogas, the Buddhist paramitas of purity and humility, spiritual absorption, nirvana, the subtle physical body, spiritual teachers, dreaming, tantric mysticism, and others.

These teachings reflect Dr. Lenz's wide range of knowledge of spiritual traditions, and while he later began to focus on Buddhist teachings, particularly Zen Buddhism and Tantric Buddhism, he often referred to his early teachings as "the basics which everyone should know."

Dr. Lenz saw how difficult it was for Westerners to learn meditation and self-discovery in the twenty-first century due to the breadth of knowledge available, and the fact that many, if not all, of the classical textbooks were written hundreds or thousands of years ago in Sanskrit, Chinese, Japanese, or Tibetan.

In *The Lakshmi Series*, Dr. Lenz touches upon all these teachings and restructures them, breathing life into the classics while bringing them into the here and now.

"My interest is the essence of these teachings," he stated, "not so much what's happened with them historically or the books that have been written about them, detailing them, or the descriptions of people who have had experiences in the monasteries or experiences living a more secular life. Rather, my interest is the essence of the teaching – the Way, as it were."

Thus, in *The Lakshmi Series*, Dr. Lenz brings forth these ancient teachings and aligns them with the modern world to succinctly present their essence – the path of modern self-discovery.

The Lakshmi Series

INTRODUCTORY AND INTERMEDIATE MEDITATION

Meditation is the art of life. All of life is meditation. Meditation is not simply a practice. It is an experience, an awareness, a way of perceiving and also a way of life. All of life, from the personal point of view, is dependent upon our perception. When we can perceive life as it really is, then no emotional cloud or discordant melody from the world can distract us from our own original, perfect being. If we trace life back to its source, we find perfection.

Life itself, in essence, is light and consciousness. Beyond this world and other worlds, beyond time and space and dimension, beyond what we call duality, is God. God is not a person. God does not have a history. God does not have a future. God is beyond definition. We can say that your perception of this world is God. We can say that this world is God, that perception, this world, and you who are having the perception are all part of God. As a matter of fact, there's nothing that isn't God.

When we think of God, normally we have an apprehension of a celestial being. We think of a big person who lives in heaven. God is not particularly personal. God is existence. Try to redefine the word through your experiences in meditation. Let us just say that there is an all-powerful force or energy that creates all, sustains all, and draws all back into it again. This is God. It is beyond intelligence, beyond analysis.

Now, in meditation what we do is something original. We experience God. That is to say, we experience that essence of existence from which we have come forth, which sustains us and to which we will eventually return. From the point of view of meditation, there is nothing that is not God. When we meditate, we are participating in a spiritual experience. We are seeing that life is not perhaps as we thought, but a little bit different – vastly different.

The results of meditation vary. It depends upon many, many different things. Have you meditated in your past lives? How hard are you trying to meditate? How long have you been meditating in this life, or are you just starting? How old are you? In what condition is your psyche? What kind of influences do you have around you? What are the people like that you associate with – your family, friends, acquaintances, people you work with or study with? All of these people have fields of energy and through your association with them, you touch those energy fields and they enter into you, as does your energy field touch and affect everyone in your life.

All of these things affect us. Our past affects us, our present affects us, even our future can affect us. We live in a relative world of time and space. We're born and we die. The space in-between we call life. The space on the other side of life we call death. We've developed a very complex filing system for existence. We see things in terms of good or bad. We feel happiness, joy, pain, loss, guilt, remorse -- very few people are happy in this world. Most are miserable. Even in their so-called happiness, they're unhappy because compared to what real happiness can be, the transitory happiness that most human beings experience is ephemeral; it does not last and it's so short of complete ecstasy, of God consciousness, of true being, that it's almost pitiful.

You as a human being are capable of so much more than you realize. You are capable of being consciously eternal. You are not a body, a mind, or a group of perceptions. You're not a history or a future, or even a present. If you can look beyond the physical and the mental, you'll see that that essence which we call God, that perfect reality that is within all things and sustains and nurtures all things and transforms all things, that essence is you.

At the moment you're suffering from what we call maya. Maya is illusion. Maya is a Sanskrit word that suggests that we have forgotten. We're suffering from temporary amnesia. We've forgotten the purpose of life, how to live life. We've forgotten what we are. You could be the son or the daughter of a very, very rich person, a great king, but if you were wandering in a strange land and you had amnesia, you might think yourself an impoverished beggar. If, one day, you were able to remember that you were the daughter or son of a king and if you were able to return to your land, your poverty would fall away. You would be reinstated to your rightful place. In life, most of us have forgotten. We've forgotten what our rightful place is. Our rightful place is to merge our awareness with the perfect being of existence. Anything short of that is frustration.

We live in a world of wars and war's alarms, of famines, of oppression. While there are many wonderful people in this world, you'll notice one curious fact about them – they all suffer, they all die, and sometimes those who are the nicest seem to suffer the most. There is an end to suffering. There is a way beyond limitation. The way is meditation. When you meditate, you take charge of your life. You bring your conscious awareness to a new high point, where the vista, the view, is beyond any horizon. To do this you're going to have to go through a lot of changes. We're discussing, in other words, the fact that you are going to become perfect. Perfect awareness. There's a definite way to do this. There is a training program that you will go through, and it's delightful. It's absolutely beautiful.

When you meditate, you feel joy, harmony, peace, stillness, ecstasy, laughter, certainty, courage, strength, awareness, and immortality. In the beginning you will feel these things vaguely, a distant knocking at your castle door, but then, as time goes on, they will no longer be vague but strong and certain. In the beginning you will only feel these emotions during meditation, but as time goes on you will feel these emotions and have these perceptions constantly.

We're going to alter the structure of our beings together. We are going to not only modify but also totally change what we are. This is the possibility and inevitability that meditation offers us. The practice of meditation is an ancient practice. It's been practiced in many lands, for many lifetimes. You may have practiced it before, but I feel it is best in the beginning to not worry too much about the past or the future, or even the present – to approach the study for the first time. You should always feel, each time you sit down to meditate, no matter how many times you've meditated before, that this is your first meditation. You have no idea what will happen or what won't happen. Only by meditating will you find out.

How do you meditate in the beginning? What is the process? To start with, there are some very basic considerations – time, place, condition, things like that. These are easy to learn. In the beginning, it's good to set a time for meditation. I recommend that you meditate two times a day, in the morning and in the evening. In the morning, after you wake up, you should take a shower and then meditate. Select a corner in your room for a meditation table. Put a rug down in front of it, perhaps, to sit on while you meditate, or a chair if you prefer sitting in a chair. You need to sit up straight, though. Have a pretty table with some candles on it. Candlelight is much easier to meditate by than incandescent light. It's nice to keep flowers on a meditation table. Flowers are beautiful. They just bring a nicer aura of energy into our awareness; they elevate our consciousness as all things of beauty do. If you can burn incense, it will add to the ambience, the flavor of the meditation. While you can certainly meditate without a special table or candles in attractive candleholders, without incense, without flowers, these things help; they aid us in our journey. They make the journey happier and they make the journey more pleasant.

Sit down to meditate. Sit up straight. If you're an absolute beginner, have a watch or clock handy. Set a minimum time that you will sit and meditate. In the beginning I recommend 15 minutes, if you're just starting. You'll sit and meditate for 15 minutes regardless of what happens or does not happen, and then at the end of 15 minutes, if you'd like to sit longer, you can. Or you can run off to work or school to start your day. But certainly, always sit for at least 15 minutes. Then as time goes on, you'll find that you'll add time. Fifteen minutes will go by and the meditation will just start to be fun. Then you'll sit for another five minutes or another 10 minutes.

After about a month of meditation, you should work up to a half an hour a day. Then after three or four months of meditation, sit for 45 minutes a day. When you reach 45 minutes a day per session, stop at that level for a while. If you're sitting and meditating and you go over that time, that's fine, but average about 45 minutes per session twice a day, after about four months of meditation. After a year or so of meditation, bring that up to an hour twice a day.

What do you do with the time when you meditate? What are you supposed to be doing as you're sitting there? Are you just sitting there being quiet? Are you thinking of things? What's really going on? How does this whole meditation thing work?

There are a number of approaches to meditation. We're trying to go into a house and there are many different doors that we can pass through. Once we pass through the door and we're in the house, we forget about the door. We can come in the front door, the back door, or the side door. It really doesn't matter which door – whichever is handy. The following approaches, which I'm going to outline, are only doorways. They are ways in. Once you're actually meditating, it's not necessary to follow the ways in.

I recommend the following practice for the first year or two or three. Each meditation session, when you sit down, relax for a moment, and consider what you're doing. As you sit for just a moment, before you start, take a deep breath and relax. Then sit up nice and straight, either in a cross-legged position on a rug, on the floor, or in a chair. Close your eyes, and repeat AUM. AUM is a mantra. Mantras are powerful sounds which, when repeated, help clear our mind and bring us into a deeper state of meditation. Whenever you chant a mantra, you should chant it lovingly and beautifully. The sound has tremendous power. It activates our psychic consciousness; it creates a response.

To begin with, chant AUM four or seven times, or as many times as you would like, but four or seven is a good figure. Always elongate the mantra. Chant AUM as follows – (Rama demonstrates). When you repeat AUM, the second part of the mantra, that is to say the "mmm" should be much longer than the "Au." Try and sustain the mantra for as long as you can, but don't overdo it. Chant the mantra a number of times. As you do, focus your full awareness upon it. This is the beginning of your meditation session. Now, after you've chanted AUM, let's say seven times, open your eyes. Now it's necessary to practice concentration for several minutes. This is a very, very important step in your meditation session each day.

I recommend that you concentrate on a yantra. A yantra is a visual design that has been specially formulated to aid you in meditation. Yantras are available in metaphysical bookstores or you can order them from Lakshmi. If you place one in a clear frame and keep it on your meditation table, it will help you in your concentration practice. If you don't have a yantra, you can use a candle flame, but I recommend a yantra.

Focus your attention on the central dot in the yantra. Look at the geometric design, which is the yantra, but now focus on the central point, the dot in the center, or the triangle in the center. Just for a minute or two, focus your attention on it very intensely. Look at nothing else, think of nothing else. It's not necessary to think thoughts about the dot, or about the yantra or the triangle, simply observe it, but do so with intensity. When thoughts come in and out of your mind, ignore them. Focus all your awareness on the dot or triangle in the center of the yantra. Then, after doing this for just two or three minutes, when your mind begins to get a little bit tired, look at the entire yantra without focusing on any one part. As you look at the geometric design of the yantra, you'll notice that it will appear to move. The lines will appear to merge and change. When this occurs, it's not simply eye fatigue, but rather you're beginning to see into another plane of awareness.

Begin your meditation session sitting down, chanting AUM a number of times, sitting up nice and straight, then for a minute or two focusing on the dot in the center of the yantra or the triangle, holding your attention on it. Then after doing that for a minute or two, looking at the entire geometric design of the yantra, and in a more relaxed fashion just gazing at it. Now close your eyes again and listen, listen to the stillness of eternity.

The wind of existence is blowing all around you. All you have to do is listen to hear it. The truths of eternity are ready to be revealed to you, truths that will free you from unhappiness, that will bring joy and beauty into your life, and completion, but you have to listen to them. The truths of eternity speak very, very softly and can only be heard when your mind becomes calm and quiet and still. Meditation is a practice of detaching and then stopping ourselves from thinking; our thoughts are interruptions in the flow of awareness. Think of a lake without any ripples. Now a lot of rocks are thrown into it, and there are waves and ripples everywhere. Consciousness, in its highest aspect, awareness, is perfect and formless, but thought and perception create lots of waves and waveforms in awareness itself.

What you will be doing in meditation is learning to stop thought. This is done in a number of stages. The first stage is simply to ignore thought, to become conscious as you're sitting there meditating that there is something beyond thought. To feel yourself as being separate, in other words, to sit and think and perceive that you are not your thoughts, that you are rather the person who is listening to the thoughts. Your thoughts are like birds. Birds come into the sky and we see them. Then they fly by and they're gone. The sky, which is the element through which they travel, remains the same. The sky was there before the birds came; it was there while they passed through and while they left.

We want to know what our self is. We are the sky. Our thoughts are the birds that come and go. You can enjoy the birds and their beauty, but it is the sky that endures, that lasts. If the birds squawk and make too much noise, we can't hear the stillness of the sky, the sound of the wind. If the birds are angry and attack us, we have a terrible problem.

We're learning for a while to perceive existence in separate phases. One phase is to see that we are not our thoughts. As you sit with your eyes closed in meditation, try and feel what is beyond thought and sense that you're separate from thought.

Then, the second stage, after you've become somewhat accomplished, after meditating for several months, is to begin to eliminate negative thoughts. You've learned to practice detachment – now you can pay no attention to your thoughts, even though they whirl by, but now you want to actually change thought. In meditation, when you have happy thoughts, creative thoughts, thoughts of good things you can do or be or become, let them come. When you have unhappy thoughts, frustrating thoughts, anger, fears, jealousies, things like that, just don't let those thoughts inside you. The angry birds are flying around your house – you're simply going to close the door and not let those critters in. If a beautiful, happy bird comes, then you can let the bird inside and play with it, but you must practice discrimination.

Discrimination means keeping the negative and unhappy thoughts away and allowing the pretty thoughts to come inside you. Then a day comes when we don't worry about whether the birds are nice or ferocious. We leave the house behind. We go up into the sky ourselves, like the birds. We fly among them and then we fly beyond them, into space and into eternity. We leave them all behind. Eventually in meditation, you'll learn to go beyond thought. You'll leave the body and mind and this world behind. You'll go beyond time, space, and all relative conditions and you'll fly through eternity, perfectly free. You'll merge with God, that basic awareness of existence – total joy, total happiness and total completion.

How the heck do you keep those nasty birds away? Well, consider it this way, as "a" way. There are many. One of the things that you can do is practice meditating on the heart chakra. There are many, many ways to meditate. This is only one of them, but it's one of my favorites and it's quite good for the first few years of your meditative practice.

We have a body, but we also have a subtle body, a body of energy that looks like our physical body, if you could see it. The subtle physical body, which is approximately the same size as our physical body, is made up of energy, of light, a light that vibrates at a very, very high rate so that the human physical eyes can't see it. When you develop your psychic vision after some meditation, you will be able to see the subtle physical of others, or perhaps of yourself. At first you'll see it as an aura, a light that seems to appear around someone, but eventually you can see the whole subtle physical.

Just as your physical body is composed of tissue, organs, bones and different parts, so your subtle physical body has many different parts. There are seven primary centers, junctions, within the subtle physical body. They run from the base of the spine to the crown of the head. These are called the seven chakras. When you meditate and focus your attention on any one of the chakras, it will open a doorway into a specific world, another dimensional plane. Each chakra leads to a different floor in the building.

For the first few years, it's most beneficial to meditate on the heart chakra. The heart chakra, called the anahata chakra in Sanskrit, is located in the center of the chest, dead center. It's not in the exact location of the physical heart but rather more to the center. If you focus your attention on the center of your chest while you're meditating for the first few minutes, you'll feel a warm and tingling sensation. The heart chakra takes you into the plane of beauty, humility, purity, and love. As you focus your attention on this area, you'll begin to feel your thoughts slowing down. You'll begin to feel your mind becoming calm and quiet. Even if there are lots of birds flying around, even if you have lots of thoughts, they'll become distant. They won't bother you. You'll hear the birds flying above you, screaming and cawing in the distance; you'll be down at the beach, sitting and meditating, but they won't affect you. You'll go so deep within yourself that you won't even notice them.

While you're meditating, after you've focused on the yantra, focus your attention on the center of the chest and gently begin to meditate. Pay no attention to your thoughts, let the birds come and go. Don't try and stop them, if you're a beginner, but rather just focus your awareness on the center of the chest. Relax, sit up straight, and let go. Meditation is letting go. Not letting go to your thoughts – they're in the distance – but letting go to something deep within you, releasing your deeper self, which will actually meditate for you.

Focus your awareness on the heart chakra. As you do, you'll feel your consciousness shifting. You may feel different perceptions of energy in different parts of your body. Pay no attention to them. Let them come and go, like our friends the thought birds. Just keep focusing on the center of the chest, not too hard, not too aggressively, but gently.

As you begin to meditate, as you sit there and the thoughts become quieter, you'll begin to become conscious. Don't think about it, those are just more birds you're inviting in to scree and caw and create more problems for you. If you do start to think about your experiences while meditating, don't become upset. Again, just ignore thought. Sit there very passively but happily, feeling. Meditation is feeling. You're trying to feel what lies beyond the doorway of existence. You may not be able to see it or touch it yet, but with your heart, with your love, you can feel it.

As you sit there and meditate on the heart center, feel love, feel joy. You can actually create these emotions in many, many different ways. Just meditating on the heart center, focusing your attention in the area of the center of the chest will help this process. You have to help yourself to your higher emotions. Consciously begin to feel love. Start by feeling love for a friend, or an experience, anything that you like – love for God, love for yourself – and let that love circulate. Let that emotion pass through you. Focus on it for a while. Then you'll find your thoughts will become quieter. You can let go of that emotion. You can even stop focusing on the center of the chest once the meditation begins to go.

You're in the river. If you're in the current of the river, you don't have to do a thing. The current of the river will take you where you want to go, but if you're on the banks of the river, there's no movement, no motion. Focusing on the heart center, feeling love, thinking beautiful thoughts gets you into the river. Then, as you meditate, you'll find that consciousness itself will move you beyond time, space, and condition into a larger, vaster, more beautiful state of awareness. Once you enter into that state of awareness, you'll start to know things. Knowledge will come to you of this life and that which is beyond this life. This knowledge comes from God. You're accessing eternity. You're plugging yourself into that source which is all light, all beauty, and all perfection.

As you meander down the river of consciousness, at times you'll get stuck on the bank. You'll find that you're thinking a lot of thoughts, the birds are becoming annoying again; they're screeching and cawing and you've forgotten that you should be meditating. You're so busy thinking about what you're going to do tomorrow or what you did yesterday, or you'll be worrying that you don't have enough money to pay your bills or that someone doesn't love you or just something's not right, that you'll become upset and you'll stop meditating. Everyone does this again and again, don't be disturbed by this, but thinking about the things of this world is not going to help you. The world is always in a state of transition, and thinking about it isn't going to solve any problems. Instead, forgetting about everything for a while and looking at something that is perfect will help you deal with the world better.

You need to regain your perspective on life. You're down in the valley and the valley is filled with smog. You can't see too well, but if you go up on top of a very high mountain, you have a point of view, you have a vision, you can see. Then when you go back into the valley, you can remember that vision and it will help you. When we meditate, we're going beyond the smog to the top of the mountain, to a point of clarity. Clarity is stillness. You need to stop all those thoughts. All the birds must become silent eventually. As you meditate more and more deeply, this will happen automatically, by itself.

After you've meditated for 15 or 20 minutes or half an hour, an hour, whatever the time limit you've set for yourself, at the end of the meditation, chant AUM again. Repeat the mantra seven times, or as many times as you like. Chanting a mantra at the beginning of your meditation helps you to clear the mind and takes you deep within the self. Chanting the mantra at the end of meditation helps you seal the meditation. It helps you bring the awareness of the meditation down into your daily life.

After meditation, it's important to offer the meditation to eternity. It's a good idea to bow and offer your meditation to God, to that stillness and perfection that is existence, and just feel that you're giving your meditation away. Then sit quietly, for just a minute or two. Very often you won't be aware of how good a meditation you did and how much benefit you've received from it until several minutes after the meditation. While you're meditating it seems that you're working away and not much is happening sometimes. You don't realize how high you've gone until afterwards, but there's a period of time right after your meditation session in which you have to be a little bit careful. If you start to think a lot of thoughts and become very active, you can prevent some of the meditative awareness that you have worked so hard to receive from coming into your mind.

For a few minutes, sit quietly, or if you need to do something, do so, but remain meditative. If it's the morning and you've just finished your morning meditation, then take a couple of minutes to just walk around the house, do a few dishes, organize things, but keep the mind quiet. Stay in a happy state. You might like to read a meditation book or a spiritual book of some type. Something written by myself or Ramakrishna, something about Buddha, something about Christ, about Yogananda, about any spiritual teacher or written by them – something that will elevate you. If you give yourself a few minutes, you'll find that you'll absorb the meditation. Then suddenly the mind becomes clear. The world is shiny and luminous; you're seeing correctly.

It's a good idea to avoid eating for an hour or two before you meditate. If you try and meditate on a full stomach, you'll find that it's difficult to meditate because you're just too heavy. You feel your body too much. Try to wear clean, comfortable clothing, and always be physically clean before you meditate. Try to take a shower or a bath. If you can't, if it's an evening meditation and you don't have time, at least wash your hands and face. You need to bring a sense of purity and cleanliness to your meditative practice.

There are some other things you can do during meditation to help facilitate the practice. There are many methods or ways of meditating. Now we're moving more from basic meditation, which I've just described, to more of an intermediate meditation level.

In intermediate meditation you have a number of choices. At this point you should be used to meditating twice a day. In the morning, before you start your day, this is your most important meditation. The morning meditation clears the mind. While you may be a little bit sleepy after you've just gotten up, the mind is not yet filled with impressions. After you've started your day and you've been out in the world, it's harder to meditate. When you first wake up, all the birds are quiet and they've been sleeping. They're not too active yet and they may make a few sounds, but once they've been up for a while, they're chirping away and active, and it's harder to quiet them down. In the beginning of the day, meditate.

It doesn't really matter what time you get up, but whenever you do get up, set aside enough time before you have to leave the house to have a good meditation, and then remain for a few minutes and just enjoy the feelings afterwards. Doing this will clear your mind and put you into a very sharp and aware state of consciousness so that you'll do a good job and have a good day. Then, around the end of the day when you come home, you'll be tired and you will have picked up a lot of different energies from the world. It's a good time to relax for a while, and before dinner have another meditation.

Sunset is a good time. At sunset a doorway between the worlds opens up. It's a very powerful and easy time to meditate. You may meditate again for another half an hour. Clear the day away and return to a very beautiful and clear state of awareness. As you meditate day after day, twice a day or three times, if you like, you'll find that the awareness of meditation will begin to creep into your daily life. You'll be sitting at the office or talking with a friend, exercising, going to the movies, or having some type of experience, but you'll notice that you're high, your mind is clear, you're at peace with yourself. You're feeling joy for no apparent reason, simply because joy is and you are.

But now it's time, now that you've gotten this practice a little bit together, to start to work on refining your meditative level. To do this you need to intensify the practice. Try some of the following methods. When you're meditating, after you've started to meditate and you've meditated on the yantra or a candle flame, instead of meditating on the heart center, now instead, simply try feeling gratitude. Sit and feel grateful to existence or to eternity or to life because you are, because your life is good, because you're meditating and if you're meditating, that means that your life is going to continue to become more beautiful, you'll become happier and clearer and more aware. Feel grateful for the people you love, for the beauty of the day or evening. If you can't feel grateful, if you're discouraged or depressed, then think of the fact that things could be a lot worse than they are, and you should be grateful that things are not worse because believe me, no matter how bad things may seem, they can always get a lot worse.

Just start gratitude. Create it. Gratitude is a bird that soars very, very high, and you can get on its back and fly with it, way above the clouds. Gratitude is a good method.

Try will power. When your thoughts come and you're trying to stop them, simply say "No." Learn the mantra, "No." N-O. Every time a thought comes in your mind, say "No." Just repeat the thought, 'No.' This is the method endorsed, in a sense, by Sri Ramakrishna, the great spiritual teacher from many years ago. He said that when you have a thorn stuck in your foot, you can take another thorn to help you get the first one out, and then throw both away.

In this case, as you sit there and you're trying to make your thoughts quiet, you're using one thought to negate another. Every time a thought comes, whether it's beautiful or not so beautiful, just think 'No.' Don't let it happen, push it away. Then once you've done that, push the thought of no thought away.

The inner cry is a very good way to meditate. As you're sitting there in meditation, just cry inwardly to God, to that source, to your spiritual teacher if you have one, to a particular god or goddess, a celestial being in a higher plane that you're drawn to. As you sit and meditate, reach with your whole being. Cry like a child, not with tears or unhappiness, but just reach. For example, if you were meditating with your whole being on Lakshmi, the goddess of light and beauty, you might repeat her name. You might, with your whole being, just say, "Lakshmi, Lakshmi, Lakshmi" silently inside yourself. If you do this with great intensity just for a few minutes, it will bring your heart out, and the power of your love will attract a higher reality to you.

Try the inner cry. Cry to God, cry to your spiritual teacher, if you have one. Cry to a favorite god or goddess or whatever you consider noble and divine. If you do that just for a couple of minutes with your whole being, just like a child who so badly wants a cookie is going to say, "Oh, Mom, pleeeease can I have a cookie? Pleeease?" The child wants that cookie more than anything else. If you feel that you want eternity and light more than anything else in your meditation – just for a few minutes, you don't have to go on and on – you'll break through the barrier of the mind. You'll go beyond it. Then just sit quietly and feel, and you'll see that light will enter your consciousness and fill your meditation.

These, then, are a few ways that you can progress a little further. Practice them at different times – the inner cry, when you reach with your whole being to eternity; willpower, when you're just saying, "No," when you reject thought; focusing, of course, on the heart chakra and feeling love and gratitude; detachment, simply ignoring thought and having nothing to do with it, not thinking of the thought or no thought.

Try to be creative in your meditation. Don't get hung up or stuck. Try meditating outside on a nice day. Meditate with your friends if you like, but try and have at least your morning meditation to yourself. Don't meditate with anyone else. Because when you meditate with others, there will be lots of different energies around, and you're trying to center in on the stillness of existence. You have enough birds flying through your own mental sky creating a disturbance without picking up those of others.

There are many different mantras that you can use when you meditate. I have several favorites. I like Aum, of course, which is the most powerful of all mantras, but I also like Lakshmi's mantra. Lakshmi is a celestial being who lives in a higher plane of existence, another world. Her mantra is "Sring." S-R-I-N-G. When you chant it, it brings beauty and light into your consciousness. Someday you might try starting your meditation with Sring instead of Aum. Chant Sring as follows – (Rama demonstrates chanting Sring). Try chanting Sring for five minutes and see what happens. You'll find that your whole consciousness will fill with light.

Another time you might try Kali's mantra. Kali, of course, is another celestial being. She offers very fast spiritual progress through intensity. Her mantra is "Kring." K-R-I-N-G. When you chant Kring, chant it very intensely and sharply. (Rama demonstrates chanting Kring.) When you chant Kring, you'll feel power entering your being. Only chant Kring, though, when you're in a high meditation. While you can chant Aum and Sring and most other mantras at the beginning of your meditation, or any time you like, Kring will only really work when you're already in a meditative state. You would chant Kring towards the end of your meditation a few times very intensely and then sit and meditate for a few more minutes.

These are a few different mantras that you can use. Experiment – see how they feel.

An advanced way to meditate, of course, is to focus on your teacher. If you have a spiritual teacher and you focus on them during meditation, then you access the light that flows through them. For example, I am a liberated teacher. After many lifetimes of meditation, I've reached a point where I can no longer be separated from meditation. I'm always in the state of meditation, or you could say I am meditation itself.

A person who meditates with me, even though they may be thousands of miles away, focuses their attention on me. If they think of me, if they chant my name a few times or just in some way focus on me, then they'll connect inwardly, psychically, with me. Well, "me" is light, to be honest with you. That's about all there is inside me anymore. When you focus on me that light will be drawn into you. You're not taking anything away from me. It's not my light to begin with, in a sense; it's the light of God and the light of eternity. Take all you want. This is how real spiritual teaching takes place.

You can focus on myself or on any spiritual teacher. Spiritual teachers who have left the body, who are no longer on earth can help you too. I'm on earth now, but I won't always be here. When I leave the body someday, I can help people just as effectively if they focus upon me.

You can focus on Jesus or Buddha or Krishna, Ramakrishna, Lao Tsu, Yukteswar, Yogananda, Vivekenanda, any of the great spiritual teachers who have lived, or on a living teacher, and draw light from them, energy from them. This is a more advanced way. You see, what we really have to teach you in meditation can't be expressed in words. These instructions will to help you get started, but to be honest, deeper meditation can only be learned from a teacher.

When I sit with my students and meditate with them, I channel the kundalini, the energy, directly into them. I bring them to plane after plane of consciousness. What they would do in 100 years of meditation, I can do in an hour with them. This is how meditation is learned in its advanced stages. Regardless of whether you're working with a teacher or not, everyone must meditate each day on their own and do their daily meditations.

As you do your daily meditations, your life will change. A new power and energy will enter your life. Most people change between age zero and four. Then around age four or five the personality begins to become structured and our growth slows down. The older we get, the less we change. When we meditate we become perpetually young. We make the personality structure more pliant.

Each time you meditate you hold the possibility of completely changing your life in one meditation. If you meditate with your whole heart and your whole soul, with your whole being, you will become light itself. You will not only see and feel God, existence, eternity, Nirvana, samadhi, but you will become quite happy, very humble, and pure, and yet you'll deal with the world very effectively. Your mind will become razor sharp. Your memory and retention will be superb. New talents and abilities will develop. Your artistic nature will begin to unfold. In other words, you'll start to grow again. You'll become younger each day yet wiser. You'll develop a good sense of humor so that you can laugh at yourself, which you need to do in this world. You'll be able to look at both the beauties and the horrors of life and accept them with an equal mind. You'll love more and be kinder to those around you.

Meditation is existence. When we meditate, all we're simply doing is letting go and allowing ourselves to dissolve back into that which we really are. Our amnesia is fading away and we're consciously becoming the source again. We're merging with life and light. When you meditate deeply, you'll see beyond life and death. You'll see that you can't die and you can't be reborn. You are existence itself.

Learn to meditate, practice and don't get frustrated. It will take you years to learn to meditate perfectly but every time you try, you're growing. It's not as if you have to learn to meditate perfectly to make progress. Even your first, most basic attempt will bring you something. In the beginning your experiences may be sporadic. Nothing will seem to be happening. It is! You must be patient.

Try to find a teacher of meditation and meditate at least once a week in a group with people who meditate a little better than you do. It's good to meditate in a group every week. It will inspire you to keep meditating and if you have a teacher, even if the teacher isn't really advanced but even just a little more advanced than you, then you'll grow, develop, and learn. Also, meditation is sharing. You learn to share your experiences with others. As you develop more and more, you'll learn a new language that other people who meditate speak.

There are a few things that you can do that will help you in your meditation. If you become a vegetarian it will make it easier to meditate. Eating meat, fish, and birds, things like that, makes it harder to meditate. The consciousness of animals is very restless, very aggressive. You are affected by the food that you eat. Everything has a vibration, and the flesh of animals has a very unruly vibration. It makes it harder to stop thought. If you give up meat, fish, birds, and things like that, you'll find that it's much easier to meditate. It's also much healthier and less expensive. Human beings were not always carnivores. Originally they were vegetarians until the Ice Age. You can eat eggs – they have a good pure consciousness – for protein. Dairy products are fine, vegetables, pastas, all kinds of things, there's lots of worlds to explore in vegetarian cuisine that will help.

It's important not to move while you meditate. Sometimes when you're sitting there meditating you may find yourself swaying. As the prana current and the kundalini and different energies begin to move through you, you'll feel yourself moving and rocking. Keep the body still at all times, otherwise that energy will be lost as it expresses itself through the physical. Whereas if you keep very, very still you'll find that that energy will just take you higher in meditation.

Never expect anything from a particular meditation. Don't try and meditate a certain way. Once you've gotten started, once you've chanted the mantra a few times and practiced concentration on the yantra or a candle flame and meditated maybe for a few minutes on your heart center, or tried gratitude or willpower, all these different methods just to get you into the stream, then just let go and let the meditation take you wherever it would like to. Be free in your awareness and free in your love. Relax and let it happen. Remember you have lots of help. God is meditating in you and through you. The beneficent forces of existence are glad to help you. You can focus on me or any spiritual teacher. We're glad to help you. You've got lots of help. All you need.

Try to read books about meditation, but not so many that they get confusing. You know, there are so many different viewpoints and ways to meditate that you can begin to wonder which is best. There is no best way. It's just what works for you at the time. Ultimately you won't use any techniques. One day you'll stop using the yantras and the mantras. You'll just be able to sit and instantly stop thought. As soon as you do, the curtain of reality parts and you are lost in the immortal rapture of existence. You will see perfection in everything. You will see that there is no time, there is no space. All there is – is light. Death is no threat. Life is no threat. All there is – is perpetual joy, perpetual existence, perpetual oneness with the source. You'll see this not only in your meditation but also in your work, your service to others, your lifestyle, your play, and everything that you do.

Don't try to be someone. Be yourself. This is what meditation should teach you. Oh, you'll learn the great truths of eternity and infinity. You'll learn to be perfect. You'll overcome your jealousies, your depressions, and your fears. Don't try and force it, these things will happen gradually, on their own.

Just meditate each day in the morning and the evening and maybe for a few minutes at noon – that's a nice time. Whenever you like, be free and be open, and trust. Trust that life is guiding you and showing you every step that is necessary to learn to be perfect. Have faith in yourself. You'll come through OK. Have faith in existence. Try to find a spiritual teacher who can teach you the more advanced things. Practice what I've told you every day and your life will be beautiful. You will see beauty in all things. You'll learn to accept the transitory nature of existence of the body and the mind happily because you'll see eternity in everything – both in this world, in the other worlds and beyond the worlds, in the void and nirvana. Meditate with feeling and with love and then take your realizations from meditation and give them to others.

Don't preach about meditation, but as you change and grow, as you love more, as you become kinder and more sensitive, help people. Help the world in any way that you want to. Do something with all that good energy and you'll find, as I have found, that the more light you give and spread, the more you share, the more you will evolve, the closer to God you will be, until one day you'll be like I am, you can't tell yourself from God. There is no difference anymore. You become existence. You've merged with the source. You've gone back. Yet you'll still be a person with eternity expressing itself through you as a person, or in its absolute form, you will be dissolved into the ecstasy of nirvana. You'll go back and forth as long as you're in this world and then some day, of course, you'll go beyond this and all other worlds.

So good luck, do well. You will.

PURITY AND HUMILITY

PURITY

Tonight I'd like to talk to you just a little bit about purity and its importance in the inner life. Purity is meditation. When you meditate, purity radiates through you. Purity is light. Not just an ordinary light that we see in the physical universe, but a transcendental light. Without purity it's impossible to realize God. To realize God means to see your own eternality in all things, in all places, at all times.

We have a lot of different ideas about what self-realization is, what God consciousness is, but in order to go beyond ideas to direct realization of that which is and will always be, it's essential to have a great deal of purity. The easiest place to see purity at work is in nature. When you go for a walk in the woods or out to the desert or by the ocean, when you look at flowers, it's very easy to get a sense of that which is pure.

Purity is something that comes from another world. It really doesn't exist, per se, in this physical world. It's a radiance or a light that stems from eternity and enters into the physical, into this world of transformation and change. It's very fragile when it takes physical manifestation. It's very, very strong in its original aspect.

Unless you have a great deal of purity, it's difficult, if not impossible, to retain higher spiritual energy, or we might say, it's difficult, if not impossible, to stay in a higher consciousness. Beyond this world, beyond this earth, beyond this life, there's something that is immortal, perfect, and shining. I call it eternity. You pick your own name. That existence has always been and will always be. Without any awareness of that existence, your life is extremely empty. The greater your awareness of that existence, the more complete your life is. Your life is incomplete without that awareness, no matter what you have or what you do, because it is your own body.

As you become more conscious of your body, which is eternity, a sense of ease, a fullness beyond description, occurs. In deep meditation we see nothing but purity. In deep meditation thought stops, action stops, time stops. The world stops, and we become consciously one with eternity. That is to say, anything that separates us from that still perfection, which is reality, which is what they call

God and truth and nirvana, falls away. All obstructions fall away. At that point, one becomes immortal, in the sense that one sees that one has always been immortality itself.

You can no longer be on the wheel of death and rebirth because the wheel has dissolved. The wheel was but a manifestation of eternity. When the sun rises, the darkness vanishes. With absorption in eternity, all thoughts, actions and ideas, all consequences, all former births and future deaths, vanish. These are mere ideas in the eye of the beholder. Very few people, as you know, are conscious of the deeper strata of eternity. The primary reason is either because they lack purity or they lack motivation. It's essential to have both.

Purity is receptivity, the ability to sit and wait patiently, for as long as necessary, for the coming of the light. Keeping a vigil from lifetime to lifetime, waiting. Purity means lack of hatred, lack of jealousy, lack of fear, lack of any volatile, antagonistic energy. It is the absence of greed, the absence of lust, the absence of anything that can stain consciousness. Greed, fear, lust, hate, jealousy, these are all part of reality too. They exist, but they are partialities. They are small bundles of consciousness wrapped tightly. They are barbs on which you can injure yourself, volatile energies which serve as separations between yourself and perfect stillness, an end to suffering, an end to salvation, an end to realization.

Have what you will, do what you shall, without the realization of eternity, without living in that eternal consciousness, you are alone, separate, fixated, unhappy, incomplete. Human beings become so obsessed with partialities that they miss eternity. It's what we call penny wise but pound foolish. We're so busy trying to perfect our desires and the things that matter and sustain us in this world that we don't see what really is, but these things, no matter how we bring them to perfection, don't last. Accumulate vast sums of money today and feel better, but tomorrow you'll die and it's all gone away. Perfect your friendships and your relationships, but then tomorrow someone will forget you. Someone else will die, and it's all gone away. Do what you will, succeed at what you shall, but these are all temporary bulwarks, shortstops against existence itself.

To think that fulfilling yourself in this world will create eternal fulfillment is absurd. We think this way, and we feel this way, because we lack purity. Purity is the ability to see dharma, truth, in its manifold forms, both in the field of action, which we call this world, the physical world, the field of manifestation, and in and through the subtle physical worlds, in any plane or any loka. To develop purity is essential then, just for your own peace of mind. Otherwise you'll go through this world like a mad person, howling and screaming and cursing, never satisfied, never happy. You'll go howling, screaming, yelling, and kicking from lifetime to lifetime. It doesn't end with death – it should be so simple. It goes on and on and on.

To run away from life and from desire is impossible because you are life and you have desire. Rather, not to fight against desire, not to condemn yourself because you have lust or you have jealousy or fears, rather to accept that this is part of your physical condition, which is transitory. To see that these aspects or qualities are not really indigenous to what you are is a beginning. To be able to discriminate and see that, 'I am not the body, I am not the mind, I am not the hatred, I am not the desire, I am not the passion, I am not the fear,' is a beginning. But still, these can only be ideas in the mind, mere abstractions. You have to have something more than abstraction. Meditation takes us beyond abstraction. When you meditate perfectly, that is to say with no thought or no conscious awareness of self as the doer, as the action, as that which experiences the action, when the mind is not only silent but that part of the mind that could become conscious that the mind is silent dissolves in light, then we see and feel purity. We become it – the purity of eternal light.

In those moments, which are samadhi, the transcendental light permeates your being and washes away impurity. It breaks down the fears, the hatreds, the desires, the greed, and the jealousy, the bigotry, the smallness. All those different selves which are limited, binding, and hurting, are washed away. They cannot stand up to the clear light of reality. They vanish, as phantoms vanish when the sun rises. The shadows dissolve, but unless you take tide against the sea of trouble, unless you energize yourself, reach deeply, and learn to still the mind completely, to become absorbed in that perfection which is existence, the shadows will not go away. If you do nothing, the shadows will become darker, stronger, more rooted in your awareness, harder to get rid of.

Purity is also developed in action, not only in meditation. Purity is developed when we love. The scriptures recommend love and service to the enlightened to develop purity. The concept is simple to understand. Search this world, find that being whom you feel has the greatest light and the greatest radiance, and become their apprentice. Listen not only to what they say but to what they don't say. Meditate on them and become one with the light of the eternal, which they reflect. As the moon reflects the sunlight to the earth, so the liberated soul reflects the light of eternity to this world.

However, when you meditate deeply enough and you go inside a liberated person you will see, not the moon, but the sun itself. You'll see that there is no longer a differentiation between their awareness and that eternity which you seek. Beyond space, beyond time, beyond condition, there is only eternity. There is no separativity. This is your own condition. If you go deeply enough within yourself you will see, not the reflection, but the sun itself – eternity.

Purity develops through caring. You need to care about light and the matters of light – the matters of truth, of religion, of spirituality. As you engage your mind in the scriptures, in the *Bhagavad Gita*, in *The Way of Life*, in the writings of enlightened spiritual persons, your mind will become pure. As you learn to love the company of the holy, of those who seek light, and spend time with them as opposed to people who are still trapped in desires, frustrations, hatreds, and jealousies, so your heart will become pure.

As you learn to accept that the body is transitory, as you watch it grow, develop, and age and decline, with love, but without attachment, the body will develop purity. Feel that your body is like a group of flowers. When someone gives you flowers, you enjoy their beauty, their purity. You delight in it. At the same time you realize that one day, the flowers will wither, they'll fade, and that is natural and proper. When that time comes you discard them, without sadness, without remorse. It is a natural cause of events in this world. You remain, but the flowers go. New flowers come.

In this sense, realize that you are not the body. The body will blossom and then it will fade, and then you will discard it. You will remain, after this body of yours has gone away. This knowledge allows you to love the body without attachment. Thus the body becomes pure, absolutely pure.

Spend time engaging your mind and your being in light. Spend time with spiritual friends. It matters not really what you do together, whether you play monopoly, whether you read each other sections of your journals of spiritual experiences, whether you get together once or twice a week and meditate with your friends in small groups, take walks, go to the movies. Whatever you do, if you do it together, then you're keeping the company of the holy, those who seek light. This will energize your consciousness. Regardless of what you're doing physically, an inner dialogue is taking place between yourself and those who you are with. You are teaching them inwardly what you know; they are sharing with you what they know. Purity is gained through strength.

Avoid the company of the wicked, that is to say, those who would do injury to you or to others. Like a disease, their energy is something that you can catch, and it will fill up your being. Once it is within you, it is hard to rid yourself of it. Your own nature, you must realize, is pure, spotless, pristine. Through association we drag ourselves down or we can raise ourselves up. It is the mind that brings us to illusion. It is also the mind that liberates us. You can use your mind to discriminate and to choose what to do at every moment – something to advance yourself, to bring more purity into your being.

It is as easy to love as it is to hate. It is as easy to be courageous as it is to fear. It is as easy to do that which is right as it is to do that which is wrong. It is as easy to be still as to be active. To aspire in the inner life is not difficult, to become pure is not difficult. You must make choices that will lead you to freedom and liberation, not to enslavement to the wills and actions and desires of others.

Every being generates a field of attention. When you spend time with someone or if you think of someone, you enter into their field of attention. That is why you should try and think of, and spend your time with, those who are holy, with those who seek light. If you think of an enlightened person, you enter into their field of attention. If you think of a celestial being, you enter into their field of attention. If you think of a friend who's aspiring, a spiritual seeker, you enter into their field of attention.

Try and become conscious of what you think during the day. This is part of yoga. Watch your mind. Observe it from a distance. Become conscious of what you're thinking. If you find yourself thinking unpleasant thoughts, then eradicate them from your mind, either by consciously directing your mind towards something holy, towards a holy person or a concept or an idea, by thinking of a spiritual philosophy or thought or image; by making the mind still and stopping all thought; or by using the power of your will simply to eradicate those thoughts. These are your three choices if you wish to develop purity in the mind. When unhappy thoughts, thoughts that would deceive you or hurt you, come into the mind, either displace them by focusing all of your attention on your teacher, on spiritual friends, on God, on enlightenment; or stop thought completely and become empty; or reject thought with willpower, simply throw it away.

One needs to do this all of the time, at every waking moment. As you do this again and again and again, the mind will become pure. These thoughts will come less and less. Higher thoughts will grow spontaneously. You must be vigilant and watchful all of the time, because a negative thought will enter you. At first it will be a vague feeling, it will seem innocuous, but then it will take root in your consciousness and it will grow and develop, and soon it will be almost impossible to eradicate.

Pray for grace. Reach to the eternal. While the eternal has an impersonal aspect, it also has a personal aspect – it has both. Eternity does live and does exist and it does answer our prayers. At the same time it has an impersonal aspect which disregards all of existence. Approach the personal aspect. If you need money and you know that your father won't give you any, you can go to your mother. Even though your father turned you down, your mother may slip you a twenty. In the same sense, the impersonal aspect of existence may ignore you, but then there's the personal aspect. There are intermediaries, the gods and goddesses, the celestial beings that help many spiritual seekers who have prayed to them. Just as you may not be able to reach the president of a company, if you can reach an intermediary, they can go and intercede with the president of the company and help you reach that person, so there are carrier beings, gods, goddesses, who aid many spiritual seekers and have throughout the ages.

There is only one prayer, and that is the prayer for light, the prayer for purity, the prayer for perfection. To pray for material things just to fulfill your desires is silly. You'll only bind yourself further. You must know and trust that if those things are necessary they will come, and if they don't come, they're not necessary. At the same time, right livelihood is essential. You should seek to advance your fortunes in this world, to set up a strong base so that you can practice your spirituality and be of service to others. This is purity too. But at the same time, in and through that, while you do that, you must think of eternity, think of light, think of perfection. As you do this more and more, you will find your consciousness will transform. You'll become happy, free, and complete. Your meditation will deepen, your awareness of what it is to exist will multiply as you find that you are eternality itself.

Purity is something, in other words, that can be consciously developed. It's something that we each have in seed form inside of us, but unless the seed is germinated, nothing will grow. You must observe where you spend your time, with whom, what you think of, what you expose yourself to and what your motives are. Again, expect to have impure moments, impure thoughts, impure ideas. You're quite human, and you will have these things for some time. One day they will go away and there will be nothing but pure thoughts and pure actions. Then there will be happiness.

Ego is impurity. You must become conscious of your ego, and when you enter into the ego, when you find the ego operating, you must ignore it. Push it away, think of light. Don't be selfish. Your selfishness only makes you unhappy. Rather be selfless. Consecrate and dedicate your life to perfection. Then you will see real transformation take place, inside you, real happiness, real freedom.

Set your sights on the highest goal and settle for nothing else. Find that person whom you feel to be most enlightened and learn from them, study them, reach into them. Meditate on the transcendental truth, on silence. Learn from the purity of nature. Spend your free time with those who also seek, who can laugh more openly.

Don't be so concerned with what you do but what your motives are. Constantly examine yourself again and again, and when you find yourself lacking, when you find that your motives are impure, don't condemn yourself – that only increases the hold of impurity. Rather, accept your limitations but know that you're working towards changing them. Know that it's not up to you, that by your own puny, human volition you can never accomplish anything. It is only with the grace of the eternal, with that light of the superconscious working through you, that you have gotten to where you are now and that you will go forward.

Invoke that light, reach for it, cry in the depths of your meditation to eternity. Then be willing to smile, in both success and in adversity. Be willing to laugh freely, at yourself, at your humanness and at your divinity. Develop a pure heart. Don't be concerned whether others understand you or misunderstand you. You have to live with yourself at every moment. Your life will be joyful and complete when you have a pure heart and your motives are unsullied. Your life will be miserable if you have an impure heart. No matter what your outer condition is, unless you have inner peace, there is nothing.

Blend yourself with the transcendental light until you can't tell the difference between yourself and that light. When you find yourself in the human consciousness, accept it, continue to work with it. Don't be offended by your own lack of purity. Rather, feel that like the seed that will grow and develop, so you too are in a formative and early stage. You will not stay as you are now, provided you work towards change and you do the things that I've just suggested. Then completion, perfection, and refinement come into your being. Then the dark oppressive forces of maya cannot hold you. Then the dharma shines through you. Let us meditate for just a couple more minutes, OK?

HUMILITY

Humility is the conscious awareness and acceptance of eternity as your own body. Humility is the time that you spend in love – in love with existence itself. When you don't love existence, you feel that you're separate from existence; you're separate from this world, and you stand back from it. You hide.

Humility is courage in that it's the open acceptance of your own perfection. Humility is the ability to see through darkness and perceive light, not only on the other side of darkness but in darkness itself. Humility means that we're willing to take tremendous chances with our life, with our death and that which lies beyond. Humility in its simple form is an image that is applied in the *I Ching* – a mountain within the earth, the hexagram of modesty or humility. The mountain exists within the earth. We don't see it, but its strength and power are there. Humility is something that exists and has a strength and power but is unseen.

Humility is the most important quality in the spiritual life. There is no quality that is more important because whatever qualities and powers you possess, if you do not have humility, they're all in vain, whereas if you have humility, you're halfway to God-realization. Humility is not enough, but I say it's the most important quality you can possess in your arsenal of spiritual qualities because it is the only one that, when it is lacking, spiritual growth stops.

The absence of humility is ego. Ego stops all spiritual growth. Just as during an eclipse we fail to see the sun because the moon gets in the way, so the light of knowledge, of dharma, of truth, is eclipsed by the ego. Even though just beyond it there may be nothing but light and perfection, unless we can break through the ego or dissolve the ego there is no spiritual progress.

You are happiest when you are humble. You are most miserable when you are very egotistical. The ego sense suggests that, "I am the body. I am the mind. I am temporal. I exist in this world. I was born at a certain time. I'll die at a certain time. The space in between those times is what I call my life. The time after that is my death. Then there's my rebirth." The sense of ego is the sense of separativity: "I am a finite individual. I suffer. I feel joy. I feel pleasure. I feel pain." Ego synthesized is selfhood, the sense of self-importance that you really matter. Nothing could be further from the truth.

Humility means freedom – freedom in its earliest stages – because it provides growth, and growth takes you out of the cycle of change that you're currently in, which is stagnation. Humility leads to absence, to the void and beyond. It's very easy to be humble when no one else is around. There's no reason for us to demonstrate our superiority because no one challenges it. We can sit and be humble. When we interact with others the ego manifests. We have to show that we're superior or that in some way that we know more, we're more spiritually advanced, we love more, we're kinder, or we're not as developed, we're the worst, everyone is better, everyone meditates better than I do. That's ego – the best or the worst.

Humility accepts moderation. Humility feels that there is someone, somewhere who can do anything I can do, better – except for one thing: no one can be better at being me. I have no importance. I will come and go in this world and be forgotten. That's freedom. Yet at the same time I am important, in the sense that I do have a role to play in this cosmic game, that there is something for me to do. I may ease the suffering of another, I may give joy or I may die in the attempt, but I must play my role, be it great or small. That's humility – without self-importance, without self-indulgence.

The ego seeks fame, fortune. Humility doesn't seek at all – it accepts. The ego wants to climb the highest mountain so it can stand on top. Humility is content to be in the valley or to be on top of the mountain or anywhere in between. Humility knows that whatever is the dharma, whatever is truthful and right, will eventually persevere. Humility accepts that God places each one of us in the right place at every single moment, not a moment too soon and not a moment too late.

When Hamlet speaks shortly before his death and he says, "There's a special providence in the fall of a sparrow;" what's to come is to come and what is, is; what will be, will be – there's a deep understanding of his destiny. He recognized that his death was imminent, he sensed it, but that death was proper because God does everything perfectly, eternity does everything perfectly.

There is never a time when you and I have not existed. We have always existed and we will always exist. There is never a time when you and I have not been all that there is, the realization that Atman is Brahman, that the knower is the known, that everything is one, that separativity is an illusion of selfhood. The fact that you see a manifold world with different times and different places and different conditions – this exists only because of a lack of humility, which we call ego. When there's nothing but humility, there's nothing but spiritual oneness. Then there's no separation, no disassociation, no unhappiness. Your life is pure joy, pure ecstasy, when you live in humility.

Meditation is humility. In meditation the mind stops, thought ceases. When thought stops, the world stops. When the world stops, perception stops. When perception stops, the sense of "I" as perceiver falls away. When this occurs, there is nothing but eternity, nothing but humility, nothing but perfection. Absence is humility – the absence of thought, the absence of doubt, the absence of ego. Only the ego can fear. Only the ego can experience hate, lust and jealousy. Humility experiences none of these things. Rather, it merges in the transcendental awareness of perfection.

To develop humility, you have to love humility. This is easy to do because you simply must consider, who are those people whom you really love the most? Who are those people whom you consider to be noble, self-sacrificing? Are they the people who make a great deal of noise in the world? Or are they rather quiet, except when they must act? Then they act with efficiency and purity and then withdraw.

Who would you rather sit next to at a party? Someone who will talk on and on for hours and hours about themselves and how wonderful they are and will only let you get a word in edgewise just so they can keep you enraptured in their conversation about their own wonders? Or would you rather sit next to someone who will ask you questions about yourself, who is genuinely interested in who you are, what you do, what your life is like, what you feel?

Humility is the latter, ego is the former. We prefer humility in others, and if we prefer it in others, we can soon prefer it in our self. If you wish to cultivate humility, then you should associate with those who are humble. Remember, humility doesn't mean hiding in the corner and pretending that you're not strong, pretending that you don't have talents and capacities. Humility, rather, means to be what you are. "Above all else: to thine own self be true, and it must follow, as the night the day, thou canst be false to anyone." Humility means coming to the root of the matter, sitting and honestly looking at yourself and saying, "This is me for better or worse, in sickness and in health, for richer, for poorer, even at death we don't part." (Audience laughs.)

It's with that basic assumption that humility begins. You own a big store; you just bought it. The first thing you do is you go in and take stock. You see what kind of inventory there is. There may be a lot of one product, a lot of bread, a lot of milk – if you bought a supermarket – but there may not be many canned goods or fresh fruits.

Now, taking stock is a very important step. If you try and pretend that there are a lot of vegetables and you deny the fact that there's a great deal of rye bread, then when the customers come there's going to be a terrible problem because you'll say, "Well, I'm sorry, Mrs. Smith, we're out of rye bread," and she'll see that there are 500 loaves of it. On the other hand, if you say, "Oh yes, Mrs. Smith, we have a wonderful, wonderful selection of bell peppers," then she'll go and see none at all.

This is how most people lead their lives – in illusion. They don't take an accurate stock of themselves. They don't see their imperfections, or they create perfections in their own mind that don't exist. They're always trying to be someone else. The idea is that someone else, this distant image, is someone who's better, someone who's happier. The people next door, somehow their life works and mine doesn't. The person who sits next to me in meditation, somehow they meditate better than I do. They're purer. This is the ego, not humility, speaking – the ego feeling sorry for itself, feeling miserable and lonely and discouraged and depressed.

Humility has nothing to do with these feelings. Humility accepts that the very nature of existence, the very nature of a human being, is joy – complete, unadulterated, ecstatic joy. Humility accepts joy rather than sorrow, accepts joy rather than frustration. Humility does not live in the prison of illusion that says that this world is a dark and terrible place. Rather, it says that those perceptions are phantoms, that everything is eternity, everything is God, everything is divine, that there is nothing that isn't perfect, that the only reason we don't see that perfection constantly is because we lack humility because we're seeing life in our terms, through our perception, through our eyes and not through the eye of eternity itself, which is humility.

When you meditate, you should meditate on humility. That is to say, you should feel that you're very, very small and the world is very large. Then you should feel that you are the very large world, and then you should feel that beyond the large world you're nothing. That is to say, we go beyond form and formlessness and there's nothing, nirvana, where the wind doesn't blow – stillness – that that very life essence that we call existence is our body. Real humility means that you have the courage to accept that you are eternality itself, that you're not simply a finite person, but that you are existence.

Real humility also means that you are willing to give someone a bigger slice of pie than you get, when it's your favorite pie – a difficult thing to do. It's easy when it's not your favorite, to say, "Here George, this is a good one! Oh, please, you take the bigger piece." (Audience laughs.) Humility means realizing that it's fun to give everything away, particularly the things that you are most attached to. The outer things are the easiest. It gets difficult when it involves giving away your pride, giving away your sorrow, your hatred, your enmity, your jealousy, and your desires.

Humility can give everything to God. It says, "Everything came from the source, everything returns to the source. I myself came into this world, I know not how. One day I will vanish from this world. I give myself totally over to you, oh Lord, oh infinite reality, and I trust you completely and implicitly because you are my very self." This is humility. Humility is the conscious acceptance of eternality, the realization that freedom is not something that is yet to come, but that freedom is perfect awareness, perfect being.

Humility is really something that develops as life goes on, I think. We see humility, of course, usually in small children, about age two months. (Audience laughs.) Then as soon as the consciousness of "I" develops, the sense that, "I am. Look mommy, look at me. Look how wonderful I am. Look what I can do. Look at me up in the tree, jumping out of the tree. Look mommy, how I can hurt you, how I can make you feel bad." The ego, "I," starts very early in life, and ego is fostered by everyone around you.

Everyone will admire you when you do well. What a horrible thing to do to someone. Whenever anybody does well spiritually, I totally ignore them. It's the greatest compliment I can pay them. They're doing well, why should I ruin it for them? Why should I say, "Oh look how wonderfully you're doing!" Because as soon as I do that, the chance is my friend will become egotistical. It's like passing someone some poison and saying, "Here, have a drink."

You should feel inside yourself that when someone compliments you, listen, don't deny the compliment. If someone says, "You did a wonderful job," say, "Thank you," but don't believe it. Don't put yourself down and feel that you did a bad job, but don't be taken out by what they say.

If someone says to you, "Look what a horrible job you did," don't feel bad. Don't argue, but don't feel bad. You must feel that praise or blame are immaterial. You know what you are; you know your worth. No matter what anyone says about you, no matter what they write in the paper, if they herald you in the headlines today or if they forget you tomorrow, it doesn't affect who and what you are. You're still the same.

Try not to be caught up in what others say about you. Whenever anybody says anything nice to you, you know that's a great test in a sense, or a great obstacle or a great opportunity – and that's when you're doing well and people come up and say, "Oh wonderful! Oh, gee, you're doing so well! How wonderful!" If, when the crowd is admiring you, your radiance and your light, and you can sit there and just know deep down inside that you have no worth, that you're emptiness, or if, when everyone hates you, when they throw stones at you, when suddenly you've become unpopular, if you can think well of yourself – that's humility.

Humility is the ability to love. Without humility you can't love. Love means looking beyond the self to the other mature love. In selfish love: "I love myself, I'm wonderful, I am the greatest, I am the most important, I am miserable." In selfless love we see beyond the finite consciousness and we see that there is someone else to love. If you suffer in love, if you have problems in love, it's because you don't have enough humility. If you really have humility when you love, then there's only one thought: "What can I do for my beloved?" Not: "What can my beloved do for me?" That's ego. Humility is: "What can I do for my beloved? At every moment, at every second, how can I help them? How can I make them feel better, how can I ease their pain? How can I help them in their vision that they see in their life, that they want to manifest? It doesn't matter whether the one I love loves me, whether they ignore me or whether they even abuse me. If I really love them, my love will be unaffected because I see God in them, I see eternity in them, and that's what I love."

To love with humility is to know perfect freedom. We see marriages, relationships, the soap opera of existence. It doesn't work. Why don't basic relationships between human beings work? I mean, we go back to Cain and Abel. It didn't work then, and they were brothers. Why doesn't love work? Because people lack humility. When there's real humility, love always works, it can do nothing but. If you've never really loved and had that love turn out perfectly, it's because you were egotistical, because you still wanted a piece of the action. You wanted to own the property, to wrap it up, to take out a second trust deed.

The idea that you acquire people as some people acquire money or property, is ego. The thought that you can own anyone, that you can control anyone's life – you are not the doer. It is the self that operates in and through all of us. None of us can do. None of us can see. None of us can feel. We're blind, deaf and dumb. It is only that self, which is our life, which is our life force, that makes us who and what we are. The realization of that self is self-realization. To realize that you are not the doer, that the ego is but a cloud that passes between you and the sun, and to see through that to eternity, is our goal and our purpose.

You see, humility is so, so important. Spiritual progress doesn't occur without it. When you're in the ego is when you're alone. You can be in a crowd full of friends and be miserable because you're alienated

– the ego alienates. You can be alone, be humble, feel God and eternity everywhere, and be perfectly happy. Humility is the most important thing.

People who are humble don't talk too much; they listen. If you find that you talk a lot when you're with others, when you don't listen – not only in the silence of not speaking, but listen in your heart deeply to what's going on inside them – it's because you lack humility. You're filled with pride. You think your words are so important, your thoughts are so important – more important, obviously, than someone else's otherwise you'd be listening and learning. That's when you stop growing – when you stop listening. We learn to listen to others, not even to their words, but to their hearts, to their souls, which resonate. Then we listen to God. We listen to eternity. We listen to nirvana, to its silence. That's when real learning takes place. That's meditation.

Examine yourself, examine your life, and decide. Take inventory, take stock of yourself. How egotistical are you? How much humility do you have? You can tell by your level of happiness. Whenever you're unhappy it's because you're locked in ego. Whenever you're truly happy, when you're feeling that deep wellspring of joy moving through you, it's because humility is operating in your life. When you can recognize this, then recognition is liberation. Because when you recognize that the ego is making you miserable, you don't identify with it. You identify with your soul's humility and then the ego dissolves and there's unalloyed joy in your existence.

It's necessary to value the spiritual life. There is nothing else, except darkness, people walking in shadows, shadows walking in shadows and deeper shadows until there's nothing at all, no light. If you're fortunate enough to have found your way, even a little bit, to the light, then indeed you're blessed. But the only way you will advance spiritually, the only way you will increase that, is through humility. Let someone else take your place in line. Let someone else be first. Let someone else achieve realization before you, if that's what's right. Don't stand out; be in a room and remain unnoticed.

Practice humility constantly. Whenever you start to think well of yourself, push those thoughts aside. Whenever you start to think ill of yourself, push those thoughts aside. Have a healthy respect and love for yourself and have lots and lots of self-confidence, but don't be taken out by your own ego. Because if you stand and praise yourself, you stand and praise yourself alone, whereas when you admire others you become one with them, and the world loves you.

Value humility. Try and grow into it more and more. Meditate and then live a life of perfect humility. That is liberation – humility. Whenever you think you're right, you're wrong. You may be right in the physical world, your assumption may be correct, your logic may be impeccable, but you're wrong. Spiritually you're incorrect. Whenever you feel that you don't know anything, that you're an absolute beginner, you're right.

Make friends with humility, it's my advice. Humility is my best friend. I've always valued it above all other spiritual qualities. Real humility is something that no one else will see, unless you have a spiritual friend who has real insight, or a spiritual teacher. No one will know about your humility, if it's real. Who's to see it? The world is filled with egos too busy looking at other egos. Only one who truly discriminates will see and admire your humility and be inspired by it.

Remember, when you're humble it's like wearing a beautiful flower. You wear your humility. It inspires others, it really does. It generates energy and power. Humility has tremendous power – tremendous! Think of Gandhi – that was humility in action; he changed the shape of an entire nation with his humility – and others. Whenever we consider someone great, really great, nobility of the soul, what we're recognizing is the quality of humility. We can have a marvelous baseball player who's batted the highest score ever, but if he's very egotistical about it nobody really likes him. The athletes we remember are not those who ran the fastest, but those who ran swiftly and were humble. They're the ones who stand out.

If you seek eternity, light, and luminosity, seek humility first – first things first. Take inventory. Look at your ego. Realize that it doesn't help you, it only burns like fire, and not the fire of transformation. Be willing every day to work on it again and again through your meditation, by giving more of yourself, giving those things you don't want to give, freely. It's an exciting adventure to give those things that you've always held onto. You'll be rather taken aback by it if you do. And mostly give the negative propensities, the harmful qualities that you house, to existence itself.

Give everything. Give your whole self, your life, both the good and the bad – don't hold back anything, and just give it all to eternity. Accept that you are that – you are that matchless, eternal reality. That's true seeing, true humility.

THE YOGA OF LOVE

There are four principle pathways that lead to enlightenment: the yoga of love, the yoga of service, the yoga of knowledge, and the yoga of mysticism. Each of the yogas is a way to eternity, to eternal realization. In the course of an individual being's evolution we will practice each of these yogas. In one incarnation, in one lifetime, we may just focus on the path of love, in another the path of service, perhaps in another knowledge or mysticism. One path is not superior to another. Each path has something special to offer. It is a way, a bridge between the finite and the infinite, between here and eternity.

The path that is followed by most persons in the beginning of their spiritual search is the path of love. Love is the easiest and most effective way to begin our search for self-realization, for ourselves. Love is the highest of all qualities that we can experience. The more we know about love, the more we experience love, the happier and more complete we are.

We live in a world that is very interested in love. The songs on the radio talk about love. Everyone is always looking for someone to love, someone to be loved by. As a matter of fact, it seems that love is an obsession in our world. Yet it would seem that for all that people go through to experience love or to give love, very, very few people, if any, gain real happiness, or satisfaction, or freedom, or peace from their love. Why is this?

Love is, in its essence, a free, formless strand of luminosity. It is a light that uplifts our awareness, that transforms our consciousness, that kindles in us the flame of self-giving, knowledge and power. Love brings future into the present. It can cause us to take a quantum leap in our spiritual growth. It knits families together, friends, lovers, societies, nations and perhaps one day a world. If we examine the essence of existence very closely, we'll find that the essence of existence is love. There really is nothing that isn't love. God is love. Truth is love. Beauty is love. Everything is a formation or an aggregate of love.

Naturally there are different forms of love, different expressions of love. We can really say that the gradation of love is determined by to whom that love is directed. In the most immature type of love we love ourselves. We're interested primarily in our own satisfaction, in our own happiness, and we don't really care too much about others – self-love, the love of the ego. In more mature and advanced states of love, we love others, the world, God, eternity. In the most advanced state of love we don't love for any reason or any purpose. We don't even direct our love necessarily to an object. We just love for the sake of love.

Love is beginningless and endless ecstasy. It's an unfathomable mystery. It is the study of our lives.

Most people suffer in love because of attachment. Attachment means that we're interested in a net return on our investment. I'm going to invest something and I want to receive something back. Not only do I want what I invested back, but more. This is the capitalist notion of love. This kind of love doesn't work very well. As a matter of fact, it destroys the very nature of love. Love is giving. Love is enjoying. Love does not seek to please itself, but it offers itself and its life to others. When we are engaged in a love of limitation, a love in which we try to get something back, we're never really satisfied. Even if we can get back what we want, or what we thought we wanted, we're not really satisfied because we know deep down inside of us that we really didn't want anything. We just wanted to love and be loved. That was all.

To find out what it is you really want in life you have to be very, very honest. You have to be willing to accept your divergent selves and to always do what is right. To apprehend what is right, it's necessary to meditate, to give to others, to purify your being and your nature, to become humble, pure, free, to accept the hard times and the easy times. The art of spirituality is really learning to be happy – in any condition and in any circumstance. This is the art of love.

The yoga of love is the yoga of acceptance. In the yoga of love, following the pathway of love, we're not trying to put our own interest forward. Love teaches us that that which is most important is self-acceptance. We begin by loving and accepting ourselves. We realize that we have many, many different selves inside of ourselves. There are many different voices that speak through us. We learn that those around us are an extension of ourselves or that we are an extension of them, not only the people, but the plants, the animals, the things, both animate and inanimate. All things have life, form, and existence, and we learn to love all. Beyond what we call existence is nonexistence. Beyond the form is the formless. Beyond matter is spirit and in spirit there is nothing but love. Its very nature is love.

To practice the yoga of love, to follow the pathway to enlightenment, we need to become aware of the spirit's residence in matter. In the yoga of love we come to see that matter and spirit are really one. They're not separate. It's only the ego that separates. Our ego, our sense of identity, says, "I am this, I am not that." The ego lives in duality, it divides everything. It says, "This is good, this is bad; this experience is happy, this experience is unhappy," but the ego is really a false perception of self. It's an idea, a transitory identity that we've picked up, just as when we're out walking in the woods we might pick up a little burr. Now if that burr begins to dig into our skin and it gets deeper and deeper inside of us, it starts to hurt. It begins to cause a wound that will eventually fester, and if it's not properly treated that one little burr could incapacitate us completely. It could make us very ill, perhaps even cause our death.

The ego, while seeming somewhat innocuous, while seeming small, perhaps not worthy of paying too much attention to, is very, very dangerous – dangerous in the sense that if you love light and joy and perfection, if you want to bring a transcendental beauty into your life, you simply can't mess around with it – it's dangerous. All things are not good for those that live. If you eat something that's poisonous, you'll die. While God exists in poison, as He does in all other things, still it's not proper for us as human beings to eat poison because while you may be consuming God, you'll die.

It's necessary to realize that we have a specialized nature, that in this world, and in all worlds, there are things that for us as beings in this world, in this form, are harmonious, and there are things that are not. The ego is not harmonious with happiness and spiritual development. It's something that we have to live with for a while, but in the process of spiritual transformation we refine it. In the fire of love we melt the ego down again and again and again. What is there when the ego is gone? Eternity, love. The ego is not our identity, it's our false conception of identity. Our real identity is eternity. Each one of us is much vaster than we realize. We encompass all of existence, yet a particle of our awareness is focused in this world, in the moment.

The art of love is to embrace both the moment – the people in the world, the experiences – and also to embrace that which lies beyond the moment, eternity; to accept both the finite and the infinite; to realize that we have a human nature, at least in the beginning stages of our evolution, which wants certain things, which desires, which dislikes, which seeks pleasure and wants to avoid pain; and that we have another nature, a deeper nature, our real nature – real in the sense that it lasts forever, while the other nature is transitory and passing. That is our higher nature. Our nature is spirit.

Throughout spiritual history people have tortured themselves and made themselves miserable because they simply couldn't accept the fact that they had two sides, and that they really weren't two, they were one. It was only because they were looking through the ego and through the limited mind and the body consciousness that they thought that they really had a body at all. There is no body. There is only eternity. That's our real body. The stars are our blanket. Time doesn't even exist, except in our own minds.

In spirituality we take a trip on a boat, we cross the ocean and we go to another shore, and in that shore there is nothing but light and perfection. Then we come back and we try and tell others about it – some believe us, some don't. The shore, of course, is not in a physical place, it's within us. The ocean is nirvana. We cross nirvana on the boat of our love to reach the shore of eternity.

It's necessary when you follow the path of love to love those around you first. You need to feel that the people in your world are the right people. Desire tells us that we should have someone else in our life, and you should feel that if someone else is supposed to be in your life, they will be in your life – you can't stop them from coming if it's the will of eternity – and that if someone is in your life currently and they shouldn't be, they will leave, otherwise they should be.

On the path of love we don't feel we necessarily have control. In some of the other yogas we feel that we have control. We determine our own destiny and that's the proper way to feel in those yogas, but in the yoga of love we feel that it's only God who does everything. We can't breathe one breath without God because God is breathing in and through us and God is our beloved. We love God. We love truth. On the path of love we feel that if we love today, it's only because God is loving through us, because there is a special grace present with which we can love. If we find that we're not loving tomorrow, we accept that because we know that that's not the will of God.

In other words, we feel that everything is the will of God, that we are only instruments of Her will and we learn to just love and accept. Our love is not for personal reward. In the yoga of love, while we certainly love those around us, we love our life, our love reaches even deeper and farther. We learn to love that which we don't see with our eyes, hear with our ears or feel with our bodies, that which is beyond the senses – consciousness. Consciousness is existence. It is the very stuff of which life is composed, and when we meditate and still our thoughts, we begin to feel consciousness, we become more conscious of consciousness.

Maya is illusion. It's a Sanskrit word, which means that we're not seeing the totality of existence. Rather, we're looking through a very dark glass and only seeing an obscured vision of existence. Love teaches us how to penetrate the inner worlds, to clean the glass of existence and see reality in its perfect essence.

If you want to follow the path of love, it's a good idea to meditate on the heart chakra every day. The heart chakra is the chakra in the center of the chest. As you know, there are seven major psychic centers in the subtle physical body. The subtle physical body, of course, is the same size and shape as your physical body, and in the center of the chest, not exactly where the physical heart is, there's a spot that we call the heart – anahata. It's a doorway that leads to love, higher love, and light.

When you meditate each day, if you follow the pathway of love, at least for the first five or ten years you should meditate on the heart chakra, at least to start out your meditation. While you meditate there, while you fix your awareness just gently on the center of the chest, you should try to feel love. As you feel more and more love, begin to smile, let go, be free. As thoughts come in and out of your mind, ignore them. Just focus on love. Sit and feel love, gratitude, or joy. If the meditation takes you beyond these emotions, that's fine. Let it take you where it will, but always try to start your meditation, or somewhere in your meditation, by feeling and focusing on love and beauty.

In the yoga of love, one has a teacher. The teacher is a very important element because it is the teacher whom one loves. Now this is a concept that's been somewhat prostituted by many phony teachers who have attracted lots of followers and allowed themselves to be worshiped and put on a pedestal, told people limited truths and then made slaves of them – the cults of personality.

The actual concept is as follows. Right now there are many, many things in your life, many people, experiences and ideas, habits, ways of seeing and so forth. It's very hard to let all of this go, to focus on what is right and what is true. Ultimately you want to focus on God, the unmanifest, that which is beyond this world and all worlds and yet that which is within this world, and meditate on that. This is a very hard thing to do in the beginning. It's like trying to think of the thin air all day. Try to think of the thin air sometime for more than a minute or two, and you'll find your mind will wander. If one has a teacher, an enlightened teacher, one who is absorbed in eternity, who's gone far beyond the plateaus that most human beings have reached and merged their awareness with nirvana, someone who has knowledge and a pure heart – if you come to this person with love, they will show you the ways of love. The ways of love are not always, perhaps, as we think they might be. Sometimes they're quite gentle and fun and filled with laughter and light. Sometimes they're quite abrupt and strict. Love is a many-sided taskmaster.

When you go to the teacher, what develops is a relationship. Once you find someone whom you consider to be the most enlightened person in this world you can find and you start to work with them, you fall in love with them. If you can't do this, if this isn't to your nature, that doesn't say that there's anything wrong with you, it just means that you shouldn't practice the yoga of love. You should practice one of the other yogas. The yoga of love is for those who want an all-consuming relationship with their teacher. They see the teacher as an extension of God, of eternity, which all of us are, all people and all beings are. But for them the teacher becomes a focus, an object of adoration, of complete love, and by focusing so intently on the teacher they are able to drop their focus on the world and their limitations and attachments that hold them back. The teacher is a temporary step, a kind of a surrogate being whom you will fix yourself to for a time. Then when you've become strong enough and developed enough and the teacher has showed you the ways of eternity, or eternity has through the teacher, then the teacher is no longer necessary. The teacher will fall away, or let us say that you'll see that the teacher was eternity all along.

The relationship between the student and teacher is ultimately important. In higher spirituality we don't really study a subject as much as we study a person, particularly in the yoga of love, the path of love. You have to learn their many sides, all their moods. What you're doing is fixating your consciousness on one being. However, this is not an ordinary being. The enlightened teacher is someone who has become absorbed in eternity. While they have a body like others, the essence of their being is light. Their personality is dissolved again and again in the white light of samadhi. They now embrace all of existence. If you look deeply inside them you'll only see eternity, whereas with most human beings, when you look inside, you'll see motivations, subconscious desires, and all kinds of different things.

There are very few enlightened people in this world – fully enlightened, self-realized teachers. They're quite rare and when you find one, you'll know. Your being will tell you. Sometimes, unfortunately, people fall in love not because they really love but because they're in love with the idea of falling in love. Some people think that they have honestly liberated teachers who they work with, but they don't really. They wanted a teacher so badly that they didn't wait. They took who was out there, who came along first, and instead of seeing that the person was perhaps somewhat advanced, or perhaps not advanced at all, they looked into and saw in that person what they wanted to see. But if you really look deeply you'll be able to tell. When you sit in meditation with one who's really liberated there will be light and joy, their personality will have many forms – sometimes it's childlike, sometimes it's strong, but really, all they are is light. There's very little self, just enough to exist in this world, no more.

Now, with such a person, on the path of love, you'll fall in love with this person completely, in rapture. Not necessarily all at once, although even when you first meet them there will be a very strong pull. As you fall in love with them, that is to say, as you feel love towards this being of light, whom we call the teacher, something really exciting happens. The more you think of them and the more you focus on them, the more you become them. There's a spiritual law that whatever we focus our field of attention on, we become. It's very, very difficult to focus our attention on God the unmanifest, just on God as an absolute reality or the formless reality, but when we see God expressing itself through one who is enlightened, then we can love that form. We as human beings find it easier to love other human beings than to love the thin air.

When you see that the teacher works constantly and endlessly for the welfare of others, really wants nothing for themselves, gives beyond exhaustion, when you see that the teacher's power, light, and humor begin to affect you and that you begin to change and that your world dissolves and improves, then you begin to love them more. In other words, the love doesn't come all at once. Real love, while it may start immediately, develops over years, and so the relationship between the student and teacher on the path of love develops for many, many years.

There are some dangers on the path of love. One danger is an over-focus on the teacher, to some extent, or that the love is self-deluding. As I said before, you're not really in love with the teacher, you just wanted one so badly that you decided to fall in love with the one who's there. Some people tend to give away their identity or their independence to a teacher, which is improper. A real teacher will never ask you for your identity or your independence, but the real danger is not so much in abuse. Provided you have an honest teacher, the teacher is going to tell you if you are overdoing it, or the teacher is simply not going to let you give them your identity – they don't want it (Rama laughs). It took them long enough to eliminate their own, let alone to accept yours. Rather, the danger is that the level of your love descends. You see, every day when you love someone you have to bring them a new love. Yesterday's love isn't good enough. It has to be a higher and deeper love. The path of love is not ecstatic love. It isn't that we just love someone or something and that's that. Rather, what we're doing is learning to love in a more deep and a more complete way, all of the time.

The love grows and grows and grows. In time it develops, and as it develops we change. As the teacher sees you changing, the teacher focuses more light, more love, and more attention on you. If the teacher sees that you're not changing, the teacher might hold back for a while. This might be a healthy approach. Or if the teacher sees you're becoming addicted to attention, the teacher will hold back. But in the study of love there are no rules, to be honest. The world may say you're a fool for loving your teacher. They may say that you're wrapped up in idolatry, but if they talked with the 12 disciples of Christ, if they talked with the Buddha's students, with Krishna's students, with the gopis, if they talked with anyone who has ever studied with a person who has attained liberation, they would find that it's always the same. How can you stop your heart when you love?

People in this world do the most foolish things for love. They'll settle down in one town to be with someone they love, they'll give up a career, they'll change the way they dress, dye their hair, give up vast sums of money, they'll do anything for love. And that's for love of a human being who doesn't necessarily fulfill you, who may get tired of you in a couple of years and push you away or whom you'll get tired of. What can we say of a person who gives their all for love of a teacher who leads them to God or for love of God? This is a sensible person because their love brings them something every day – it brings them the light of immortality and eternity. If you follow the path of love you really shouldn't expect to be understood by others. The path of love is its own reward. Your love itself, that experience, is what completes you. There's no place to go, there's nothing to attain, there's nothing to be reached. Love itself is all that you want, and that's certainly what you receive.

The path of love has many opponents – fear, self-doubt, self-pity, anxiety, hate, lust, greed, avarice – all the usual friends. All of these are obstacles to your love. The most successful way to combat them, these dark clouds that pass between the light of you and that which you love, is to feel that love itself will rescue you. That is to say, love will come from afar, from the distant skies, if you cry deeply enough within yourself, and take care of everything.

One who practices the yoga of love is like a child. When the child has a problem, when it can't cope with something, it cries, and when it cries someone comes and helps the child. In the path of love, rather than pulling our willpower together or using our discrimination or working, we just cry inwardly. We sit in meditation and we cry to God, we cry to the light. With our whole heart and our whole soul, we reach and reach and cry and cry, as little children, knowing that God will do everything for us, that we're too insignificant and small to really be able to do anything, except cry – not unhappily with unhappy tears, but an inner cry, a feeling of reaching to God, saying, "Oh God, God, please come to me, please illumine me, please act in me and through me. I don't know what's right and what's wrong. I can't tell anymore. I could be doing what I feel is right and perhaps I'm deceiving myself. Perhaps it's all my ego and my vanity. Please show me what's right or don't even show me. Please just do it, whether it brings me happiness or unhappiness, riches or poverty, sorrow or joy. Please act in and through me. I love only you."

If you have a teacher you would feel, "Oh teacher, I love you more than anything and anyone else in all of existence. When you smile at me the world lights up. If you frown, my world ends. If I create a block between us through my foolishness, my pride, my arrogance, my jealousy, my fear, my self-love, then I suffer. I suffer and suffer and it's only when I remove those obstacles that I'll feel happy again, but I know that you love me no matter what I do because you are all love. You may be strict with me, you may be lenient. I trust you and I know that whatever you do or say is for my own good. I've looked into your heart and seen eternity and I know that eternity, through you, will always guide me and shelter me and protect me. I will do what you wish, I'll do my best for all, but even so I know I'm an insignificant creature and not capable of fulfilling the dharma. Please show me, please guide me. If I make a mistake please correct me, but more than anything please love me, and let me love you. Because as we merge our beings, as we fuse the light that is our reality together, that's my completion. That's when I see that I am you and that you are me. 'I am thine and thou art mine.'" This is how one should feel about the teacher.

One should feel that one's friends, the people who meditate around you, who are in your spiritual center, who seek, are likewise pilgrims on a journey. They're traveling to eternity also. You should love them, respect them, and whenever you see a good quality in them, you should admire it. If you see the friend as strong or self-giving, if they meditate well, then the proper attitude for one who follows the path of love is to respect and admire that quality because whenever you respect and admire a spiritual quality, it starts to grow inside yourself. If you see faults in others, look the other way.

You must feel that everyone is growing and developing, everyone has to go through a trial and error process of finding what is right, and actually, everything is right, even the errors are right. Look the other way. Don't linger on imperfection. Know that if you were in a perfected state of consciousness, you would only see perfection in all things. The child in fourth grade who's just learning algebra is not imperfect. While there may be a child in 12th grade who's much better at the subject, more adept because of their years, the child who's learning is not imperfect. The child is perfect in its current stage of evolution.

When you follow the path of love you should feel that each one is perfect in their own right, and that while you can love others and admire them, you should never, ever, ever judge them. You can discriminate and see what's good and what's bad – there's nothing wrong with that. Lack of judgment doesn't mean that you don't see what is or is not. It simply means that you realize and recognize that everyone is constantly changing, that everyone is made up of consciousness, which assumes new forms constantly, and that the judgment that you pass today will only hinder a person in their spiritual evolution. Because your thoughts have some power, and all you do is say to the person, psychically, 'This is what you are, you're fixed, you can't change,' whereas in reality everyone is a flux. It's good to suspend judgments forever. Rather, let everyone be what they want.

Don't try and hold people to you, don't try and push them away. Let life do everything for you. This is the proper attitude on the path of love. Focus your attention towards your teacher, your spiritual friends and do everything out of love. When you find that you're unhappy, know that it's because you're not loving properly. Don't blame others, don't have self-pity. Rather, just meditate, go deep within, and again find that strand of love, not simply the one that you found before but a higher strand of love, a deeper strand of love that will take you more and more into the core of reality.

Relationships are a proving ground for love. That is to say, the friends and associates that we have give us an opportunity on the path of love to practice love. We cannot say that you are spiritually advanced if you are unkind to those around you. The only way you can really evaluate spiritual advancement is to see how someone treats those who are close to them. Someone may be able to meditate well, but if they can't manifest that meditation in just good common sense by loving and being kind to those who are around them, then I can't say that they're spiritually developed. They may have learned to flex one muscle, but we can't say that their whole body is evenly and properly developed. Real spirituality and love always manifest. That is to say, it always goes to those who are with us and around us.

Practice love in your relationships. The key to this is avoiding expectation. It's expectation that makes most people miserable in love. Remember the return on the investment. When you love someone, you shouldn't feel that they should love you in the same way in return or love you at all. If you do you'll be sorry because no one will probably ever love as you do, they'll love in their own way. You have to give people freedom. If you really want people to love you, you should free them.

You cannot compel someone to love. Love is like the wind. It comes when it does, it stops when it does, it changes direction when it does. Who are you and I to criticize the wind? You should feel that love has its own independent form and formlessness, and when someone loves you accept their love and be grateful for it. If they love another, let them love! Who are you to say what they should or shouldn't do? If they stop loving, you should be grateful for that. Know that life, which does everything perfectly, is now moving you in a new direction. The chess piece of your existence is being moved to a new square on the board of life. A new situation will develop.

If there's no one in your life to love right now, then love yourself. A large part of the path of love is learning to love yourself – not to love yourself in the egotistical sense but just to enjoy being with yourself, hanging out with yourself, doing things by yourself. You have to love yourself even when you don't measure up to your own expectations. You have a certain idea of what you should do and what you should be and what you should become. But from my point of view, it's only a silly idea, one in a continuing series of silly ideas that passes through your mind.

It's good to be inspired. If you have a real inspiration of what you should try to do, do it. But if you don't measure up to your expectations, realize that you should just live life without expectations, that your expectations weren't necessarily correct. You need to accept the fact that you will often do exactly the opposite of what you think is right, what you think is proper and natural, and you need to be able to accept that you're going to do that and still love yourself for doing that. Love yourself when you change, love yourself when you don't change. Love yourself day and night, in season and out. Love yourself when you're modest, love yourself when you're immodest. Try to have a more expanded sense of that which you are. Try to feel that you are eternity. There is no morality in this kind of love. There's only goodness. There's only light. And who can say what's right or wrong? Love is its own truth, and if you live the truth, the gospel of love, then you will be fulfilled and happy.

As your love grows – for spirit, for light, for the God within all – you'll find that your attachment to this world will begin to fall away, which doesn't really mean that you won't think it's a fabulous place, but you'll just be less concerned with it, or you might see it a little more correctly in perspective. One of the great things that happened to the astronauts in the early flights was they got up above the earth and suddenly they realized it wasn't very big. John Glenn and others looked down and they saw this little tiny globe, just one little dot among millions of dots. Down here on earth, in one country, in one state, in one city, in one house, the world seems pretty important, our world, but once you get up there and get a little perspective on existence, it's just another dot.

What you need to see is that your current life and all the things that matter to you, are not really so important. They have their place but it's just a little dot and rather, you need to get some perspective on your existence. When we meditate with love we go very, very high – above thought, above form. We go out into space and we see existence in a truer way. If you love very, very deeply, if you love truth and God, your love will cause you to have a union. You'll merge for a while, for a short time, with that truth. You'll become it. Each time you merge with God in your meditation you'll be freer and purer afterwards. It's as if you're going out into the sun, again and again, and each time you go out you get a little tanner.

The light of eternity purifies, and it is only that real love of the infinite that will motivate you. While pain motivates us to a certain extent to go deeper within, to go higher, pain can only take us a certain distance. If we follow the path of pain, that is to say, avoidance, we'll make a certain amount of spiritual progress until we feel comfortable, but once we feel comfortable and the pain has stopped and we don't think it will start again, we'll stop evolving. Love is far superior as a spiritual device, as a spiritual vehicle, because when we follow the path of love we go higher and higher and higher. Our velocity actually increases as we go on, rather than decreases as with aversion, because our love grows and becomes more strong and more perfect.

Love is the strongest force in the universe. Once we harness ourselves to that force, it carries us to eternity. Yet at the same time, love is visceral and real. Love is physical. It embraces all things, all creatures, and all beings. Love doesn't space you out or take you out of this world, it makes you conscious of your own immortality. But love also teaches you to love your own mortality; to love this body that's only here for a little while, just as we love the flowers that bloom for a short time and pass on; to love the skies and the scenes; to love all things in this world and all things beyond this world. As you do this more and more, you will move rapidly towards liberation.

Love leads us to ourselves – this is the mystery of love. What love does and why it does it? It's hard to say. It's an unknown chemistry. Who was it who started this great process? Who invented love? Who are we who experience love? Why does the wind of love blow hot and blow cold? Why are we spun around by existence? These questions can only be answered in your deep meditation.

It's difficult to stop thought, I admit it. It's hard to meditate in the beginning. Love is the shortcut to higher meditation. Above thought is love, and within and below thought is love. Love is a ladder that we can climb through thought. It's very hard to stop thought. Try with your willpower – it's very difficult. But if instead of trying to stop thought when you meditate you focus your attention on love – meditate on the heart center and just let that love grow and increase, more and more – then suddenly you'll find, guess what? Your thoughts are slacking, you're moving into a higher field of awareness, you're feeling wonderful. Light is everywhere and suddenly there's no thought. This is why love is said to be such an easy way to learn to meditate. You're using the positive power of emotion to take you beyond that which would be more difficult. There are other ways to stop thought, but love is certainly the easiest.

When you love, you should always watch the quality of your love. Become an observer and learn to be a little more detached. If you really love, then you're willing to step outside of your own love sometimes to do that which is right. As I suggested earlier, love has different levels. The highest kind of love is a very pure love. It's a love that just gives and gives and gives. In order for you to constantly improve the quality of your love, it's necessary for you to examine your love on a daily basis, not to go through a long, prolonged harangue with yourself about whether you're being good or bad in your love but rather just to look at it and ask yourself, "Am I loving as deeply as I am capable of loving?" Just ask yourself the question and then meditate. Don't try to love or force love in a certain way but just honestly ask your soul, ask your essence, "Am I loving as deeply as I can love?" Then if you meditate, your soul will answer you, not in words but in action. You see, whenever you really go to truth, truth helps you, but it's necessary for you to motivate yourself in a sense, to open yourself to truth. It's necessary to try to understand that while we all have a great capacity to love, very few of us will ever love in the proper way. But you must believe in your heart that you may be one of those few persons who will love in a true and deep way.

Now, you need to ask yourself, "Well, why is it that some people are able to love more than others? What are they doing that I'm not doing?" Don't try and do what they do, just ask yourself the question. Then go to God, your beloved, and say, "I would like to love more deeply and purely, more completely, and if it is Your will, I will do that, if it is not, I won't and I'll accept that. I'll just love You as best I can and love everyone as best I can." With that attitude, you'll find your love will grow and increase. If you just try to love more and more, you'll only get more frustrated. You'll be trying to do something, perhaps, that you're not ready for, that you're not prepared to do, that it's not time to do yet. When you don't get the result you seek, you'll think there's something wrong with you and you'll get discouraged and give up. Rather, the correct way is just to be, but to be very careful – careful in the sense that you want to be very honest with the way that you love.

Real honesty means that every day you have to go to the source several times, to meditate, and to look into the eye of eternity and say, "Please act in me and through me. Please let my love increase, if it is your will. I feel that's the right thing, but even if it's not the right thing I'm willing to abide by your judgment." Then if you meditate very deeply, of course, you'll see that that which you were talking to is your own self – the finite portion of your being speaking to the infinite portion of your being.

In love we listen. In this world people love to talk and be active. Everyone wants to express their opinion. But in love we listen. We listen to the song of the heart. We listen to what others say. We listen to what our own being is telling us about the nature of existence and the nature of truth. Try to be a good listener. Listen in meditation, not to your thoughts but to your feelings. The true teacher of love is the heart. The heart is very, very wise. It makes mistakes from time to time, but it has a wisdom all of its own. Begin to probe your heart. Certainly you may have been hurt before in love, you may have had some bad experiences, but just because you get one bad apple doesn't mean they're all bad, you know, and you can even learn from the difficult ones. Try to feel that love is a modest and immodest teacher who will bring you through the school of existence, which is the heart. While you may be hurt sometimes by your own attachments, you don't love perfectly without first loving imperfectly. You have to go through all the stages and steps. And it's far, far better to love imperfectly than not to love at all, and then, of course, to learn to love perfectly.

There are different levels of heart. There's the heart of just the emotional feeling – you like someone, you don't like them. Then as we probe deeper in meditation we find that the heart has a new meaning. The heart is a place of great light and there are different gradations of light that pass through the heart, just as there are different currents that pass through the ocean. We begin to sail our little boat of awareness on the currents of the heart, and they change and they shift from day to day and from moment to moment.

It is only if you have the courage to follow your heart that you will succeed on the path of love. You can feel what's right and not do it. You can love but not follow that love. The real test, then, on the path of love, which you'll come back to again and again until you pass it, is are you willing to give up everything for your love, for that which you love? No one will tell you who to love or what to love, but you must have the willingness to follow your love as far as it will take you. Whether it's practical or impractical, whether it brings you to destruction or salvation or damnation, it doesn't matter because these are just words and ideas in the empty minds of people who should know better. All there is – is love, and if you follow that love everywhere, at every moment, in all of its rhapsodic conditions, even when the critics say, "You've got bad taste. Your love is too formless," it doesn't matter. Who cares? Let them criticize away. You are still with your love and that's all that matters – on the path of love.

Naturally there are other points of view and perspectives. As we examine the path of knowledge and the path of self-giving and the path of mysticism, you'll find things that in a sense almost contradict what I've said about the path of love. But it only contradicts if you think about it. Each pathway is unique and special and they even have a seasonal accord. The path of love, of course, is synonymous with the summer, the path of action and self-giving with the fall, the path of knowledge with the winter and the path of mysticism with the spring. Love, in terms of the day, is synonymous with the morning, action with the afternoon, knowledge with the evening and mysticism with the night.

While you may not follow the path of love yourself, it's good to learn as much as you can about it because some day you may be a teacher and as a teacher you may have students who follow a path far different than the one you walked upon in your current life. And you will find the four paths really are not so separate. They weave in and out of each other. We have to have love, of course, as we practice mysticism and jnana yoga and karma yoga. We have to have discrimination when we follow the path of love because otherwise we'll love the wrong thing, in the wrong way. We need laughter and power, which we find in mysticism, to love properly, to not be so hooked into our own love that we begin to feel self-pity or attachment. Of course the logical direction of the path of love, the next path that one follows after completing the path of love or while still on it, the path that is closest to it, is the path of self-giving because mature love has to inevitably lead to self-giving.

Practice love, learn love, and live in love. Don't be afraid to experiment with your life and with your heart, your meditation and your being. Just love. Meditate on love, give love. Find that person whom you consider to be most spiritually advanced and be with them, if you love them. If you don't love them, they're not the right one. Then you should go to one whom you can love. Merge your consciousness with that of a luminous being and then from there to eternity. Love those around you and when you don't come up to what you think you should be, when you don't reach the standards that you've set for yourself and your divergent selves run in the other direction, love that too.

Develop self-acceptance. Love all your different sides. Only then will immortality come to you, the awareness of immortality, because as long as you're running away from part of yourself, you're so busy running away that you can't see immortality. As long as you're too busy trying to become something that you're not, you're so busy doing that that you can't see your own immortality. You see, the secret of love is acceptance, acceptance of our finite self, of our life, our birth, our growth, our decay and our death; acceptance of the world around us, of eternity. The message of love is acceptance – self-acceptance in the smaller sense, of the individual personal self, and self-acceptance in the larger sense, of the self as eternity.

Practice love, self-acceptance, and you'll see you'll have a beautiful life, an absolutely beautiful life. Certainly this is the prettiest of the pathways, the most emotional and the most fun, to be honest, in a way. It's the best to start with and sometimes the nicest to stay with. The path of love. Good luck. May your love guide you through the bardo to eternity.

THE YOGA OF SELFLESS GIVING

Why aren't you happy? Why aren't you satisfied with your life? Deep down inside you know that you're not really happy, satisfied, or free. You're entangled in a mass of emotions, you're bombarded by thoughts and ideas that don't make you happy, you live in a world gone mad, where people use technology to find faster and more efficient ways to kill each other, where in every home there's cruelty and unhappiness, where love is just another four letter word for fulfillment of desire, where beauty is laughed at, purity stained, humility ignored.

Why aren't you happy? Why aren't all of you happy when there's so much to have and so much to be? The reason is very simple. At the root of all problems we find one causal answer – self-giving. The reason you're not happy, the reason the world lacks peace, the reason that we cannot find ourselves, is that we lack happiness – happiness that comes from self-giving.

We have two choices in life. These are the north and south poles of our existence. One choice in life is to fulfill ourselves, the limited self, to do things that make us feel better, to do things that give us pleasure and not pain, to fulfill our desires, to get the things that we want each day, each year, to make ourselves happy. The other alternative is to make others happy, to forget ourselves, to ignore our wants, to not be concerned with whether we're happy or not, but rather to take the time and energy that we would utilize in fulfilling ourselves and use it to make others happy. These are our two choices.

From a logical point of view, it would certainly seem that the former rather than the latter is the best course to follow if one seeks happiness. It would seem that hours and hours spent in service to others would be drudgery, that we would become the slave of another person, that there would be very little fulfillment in always working for others. Whereas when we take the time to do the things that we like to do – to go to places we want to go, to be with whom we would like to be, to succeed at the things that we feel we should succeed at, to avoid the things that we consider painful – it would seem that this would be the proper way to become happy.

Strangely enough, it's not. It's just the opposite. And if you don't believe me, look at the world and look at its people. You will find only a handful of people in this world who are really happy, who have deep and lasting joy. Everyone else experiences a superficial happiness, which is here one hour and gone the next, which is followed by depression, each elation is followed by frustration. There is only a very small group of persons in this world who live in a transcendental awareness and are really happy from the depths of their soul. These are persons who elected, at some point in their existence, to take their existence and give it to God, to give it away, to give it to eternity. They are happy – happy in their self-giving. Whereas those who pursue a worldly life, who try to make money so that they can get the things they want, who try to get others to do what they want, to perform for them, who use and abuse in the name of happiness, their own happiness, are miserable.

Whenever you do something for yourself exclusively you're not happy. Whenever you give to others with no motivation for self-happiness, not even subconsciously, then you become free. Why is this? This is a strange state of affairs, it would seem. How could this be so? Well, it's really not too hard to understand, but first we have to take a look at the nature of consciousness and existence and what it is to be a being, and also a brief survey, perhaps, of nonbeing.

A human being is composed of many different parts. We tend to think of ourselves as being one solidified whole, but that's not true at all. On the surface, when you look at the ground, you may say, "Well, I see the ground." But if you go beneath it you'll find that underneath the surface, the grass, and the immediate dirt, the layers of topsoil, there are layers of granite, bedrock. If you go deep enough into the core of the earth, there's molten lava, mineral deposits, all kinds of things. When we see the surface we might say, "Well, this is all there is."

The human being is composed of many substrata. You are not one self. You are an aggregate. You are a collection of selves or energies that have bonded together. Just as the electrons and protons and neutrons bond together to create an atom, so you are an aggregate of energies. These energies form in a particular configuration and we say that this is your personality, your being; it's what you are. When we alter that aggregate, when it changes, then you change.

Think of yourself as sand. The sand is lying on the beach and it has a particular pattern. Suddenly the wind comes along, the wind of dharma, and blows it around – it takes a whole new shape and a whole new form. Human life is like building sandcastles on the beach. We build a sandcastle, we create what we think is a perfect life, and the tide rolls in, the ocean comes in and sweeps it all away and washes it all clean again. This is death. Then suddenly we find ourselves on the beach again and we're building something new, and then the ocean sweeps it away again and again and again. The ocean is eternal existence, eternal consciousness. And we sit on the beach, building.

You are composed of the physical body; the mind which thinks and analyzes; the heart which loves; the ego, the sense of identity, of I-ness. Then there are many, many different selves beyond these selves, different voices from the past, selves of past lives. And if we look further we see that we actually contain all of existence that everyone who has ever been or will ever be is in some way contained in our consciousness, in our awareness. Our awareness is not limited to what our mind thinks. It extends like the ocean, all-where. Like the sky, it's endless.

The sky contains planets, stars, galaxies, far beyond our imagination. It is the net that catches them all. Our consciousness contains many stars, many galaxies, many worlds. At the moment you may be only aware of what's going on one planet, but as you stretch your awareness, as you see, you become aware of all the divergent worlds, all the divergent existences that have ever been or will ever be. You see that they're all at your disposal, that they're all part of you. As you progress in your self-realization you'll discover that there isn't really anything that you aren't, that you can take on any mood, any action, any personality form, be it of this world or any other world. You have no fixed self. This is only an illusion and this is the illusion that causes you to feel pain and suffering, sorrow and frustration and despair.

At the end of being is nonbeing. At the end of life is death. Beyond the ocean is something else – hard to describe, but also a distant cousin, another part of your being – nirvana, eternal awareness. But let us not concern ourselves with nirvana as yet. Let us come back from our celestial journey throughout the cosmos to this solar system, this planet, the person who's listening to this voice – their problems, their hopes, their joys, their agonies, their victories and defeats, their life and their death and that which lies between – you.

You suffer because you try to fulfill yourself. You think of yourself in a limited way. You think that 'I am this, I am that, I am not this, I am not that.' But who is it who tells us what we are? Where did we get this sense of what we are? True, the sense of self was given to us by the world, by our parents, where we grew up, our friends, the things we read, our experiences, all of these things were given to us. But we're the one who holds them together. We're the one who can let them go. We are time. We are the sense of place and position.

In awareness we lose and find ourselves again and again in the cosmic shuffle of existence. Now you have found yourself here and you have a sense of what you are and what you like and what you don't like. Whenever you strive to fulfill yourself, to do something for yourself, all you do is imprint, more and more strongly, that sense of identification. In other words, the problem that we're facing, the reason that we're not happy, is because we see, feel, and believe consciously and subconsciously that we're separate from God, from eternal awareness. As long as we do that, we can't be happy. If the bird is used to flying and you put it in a cage, it won't be a happy bird. It wants to fly; it's its nature.

If your nature is infinite awareness, if you were the cosmos itself, and suddenly you find yourself trapped in a body, in a mind, living in a place, being subject to birth and death, suddenly there's a lack of happiness, there's a lack of freedom. No matter what you get, you'll never be happy because these are all trinkets. They can amuse you for a little while, but you know and I know that you can only be really happy when you become what you really are. As long as you just try to fulfill the personal self, you make that personal self stronger, you define it more and more, you prevent yourself from doing and being what you really are. It's as if someone is trying to awaken you and every time they try to awaken you, you take a sleeping pill, and then another and then another. You go further and further asleep.

When we just try to fulfill ourselves, even though our inner voice, the truth that we know is within us, tells us to wake up, to live, to become all that we are, still we run from it, we hide from the white light of eternity. We hide in relationships, we hide in material possessions, we hide in ambitions, secret desires, hates, frustrations. We hide in our jealousy, we hide in our self-pity, in our insecurity and more than anything in our vanity and our egotism, in our self-doubt. We define a world, we build a house, then after building the house we enter into it and we never leave it. We forgot that we were the ones who built the house and because we built the house, we can leave the house. We could create a new house, a more beautiful house, or we could leave the house and go someplace else.

Yoga is the process of first becoming aware that you've trapped yourself inside a house that you've built, even though you've forgotten – it was years ago and you've forgotten – that there's even an out-of-doors. You just are in the house, once in a while you can look out of the window. In yoga we first become aware that we're trapped, that we're dreaming and not awake. Then we leave the house, which is a limited house, and we build a more beautiful house and we live in that for a while. And we leave that and we build a more beautiful house, again and again and again, until we have the most beautiful home of them all. Then one day we leave that house and we give up houses altogether and we go someplace else, someplace eternal and infinite. That's nirvana, eternity, full awareness of God. We become God. We don't need houses then. We are the stuff that dreams are made of at that point.

Whenever we just try to please ourselves, all we do is cover up another window in the little house that we're stuck in. Whenever we do something for someone else, we affirm that we are not simply in it for ourselves, that our self is not limited to the one who's with us now, but our self is someone else, is everyone else. Self-giving opens up the doorway to the other world. It is the way of freedom. Naturally, in order to practice the yoga of self-giving we must learn to meditate. Without meditation there's no self-giving, there's no sense of how to give, what to give or that we should even give.

There's a treasure that we want. It's deep down under a lake, but the lake has waves and waves and we have no idea where the treasure is located. First it is necessary to stop the motion of the waves. Once the waves stop and the water becomes smooth and clear, then we can look down into its depths, we can see down into the water and locate the treasure. Now, once we've located the treasure it behooves us to go down into the water and get it out, to bring it up to the surface, and then to share it with our friends, keeping enough just to keep ourselves in this world and to have whatever we need but then giving the rest away.

It's necessary to find the treasure first. When you meditate you stop thought, you smooth the mind. Otherwise it's impossible to know where the treasures of eternity are. As long as the mind is active and filled with thoughts, ideas, desires, jealousies, and all types of emotion, we really can't get a sense of where to go or what to do. We just follow what we see in the world, but that doesn't do it. It isn't enough. We must be in touch with the deeper self. We practice meditation each day, several times a day. At first it may seem difficult but soon you become quite adept at it. As you meditate you find a deeper joy, a more beautiful awareness, entering your life every day. You become conscious that there are realms beyond sight and sound and that the very essence of existence is within us, not within our bodies or minds, but within our awareness. The dream fades a little bit and reality comes a little bit closer.

Now, once we've done that, then we begin to practice self-giving. Self-giving means that we have to understand the nature of giving. As we meditate this becomes more clear to us. When most people give, they give conditionally. They give expecting a return on their investment. They give with a sense of attachment: "Well, I'm going to give so and so this at Christmas because it will make them happy. If I give Susan a new Cuisinart then she'll be happy. If she's happy then she'll be thankful to me. If she's thankful to me, my life will be better because we'll get along better. She'll do something for me." In other words, there's a sense of return on our investment.

Very often people give to others to control them and dominate them. The parent gives the child something – possessions, a new car, money. When the parent does this, while on the one hand they're giving just because they want to give, on the other hand it exercises control. They know that the child depends on them. They know the child wants these things and therefore the child has to do what they want. Otherwise they will withdraw the favors and the presents – manipulation, domination, no happiness. Sickness. Psychic sickness.

In real self-giving we're inspired. We don't think about time, place, condition, or practicality. We sense that we need to make a gesture, an offering. We give someone something; whether they acknowledge us or not is not important. We gain enough joy just from giving to fulfill ourselves. This is basic self-giving. As you meditate each day the selfishness will leave you. You will find that you will be able to give purely and freely. As with loving, it's best to love with attachment than not to love at all. With self-giving it's best to give somewhat selfishly than not to give at all. That's one of the steps that we climb on the ladder on the way to selfless giving and selfless love – this selfish giving and selfish love.

Still it's necessary to go further, to expand our awareness, to become conscious of our own immortality and our mortality. How do we do that? True, we could go out and give people a lot of presents. Would that give us a sense of perfect awareness? No, certainly not. That sense of perfect awareness will only really come when we begin to give in a more spiritual way, when we not only offer a small present but our whole life – when we give that away.

The yoga of selfless-giving is a yoga of choice. The primary choice we make is not what to give, how to give or where to give, because we feel that we could fool ourselves. We could think that we're giving selflessly and actually be giving very selfishly. What we're really trying to do then is to become perfect givers. The idea behind this is quite simple.

Right now we don't see that we are God, that we are infinite awareness. We're not aware of the joy of our own immortality. When we give to someone else, something interesting happens. If we give purely, it opens up a doorway in our heart and it gives us the vision to see that those we give to are God. As we serve others and work for others we become happy, but we also see that the transcendental reality exists within those we give to. As we see this in others, then suddenly we see it within ourselves. Then we see that that one light, that one unified reality that we see in others, is the same reality that is within ourselves, that we are one. We are one with those whom we give to. We are one with all of existence.

Attachment is the largest problem. We become attached to things because we desire them. Desires are neither good nor bad, only thinking makes them so. Some spiritual teachers have advocated running away from all desire. From my point of view that's not necessary. What's necessary is not to run away from desire, nor to run towards it. Running towards desire is as much of an attachment as running away from it, in my estimation. Rather, what is necessary is to discriminate and to determine if a particular desire is proper for us.

We are going out to buy a car and we go from place to place. We look at the Datsuns, Toyotas, BMWs, Chevrolets, Chryslers – we have to find the car that suits us. We might see a car that's very flashy, we want it very much, and we can't afford it. But if we buy it and we get saddled with these very expensive payments, we won't be happy. Perhaps we were supposed to use some of that money for our education, for our families. But no, we had to buy some flashy car. We did the wrong thing and now we'll suffer because of it. We know we didn't do what was right. Whereas there may have been a car that wasn't as expensive but that was quite good, perhaps even a used car that would fulfill our needs for now. It's more than adequate. It'll get us where we need to go.

There's nothing wrong with having a car; the desire to have a car is not necessarily bad. Rather, it's just doing it in the proper way, finding which desire is in harmony with the will of the infinite. If you have a great deal of money and you can afford it, you can get yourself that flashy car. It's not a problem. It might be fun. It's a question of discrimination. There are many possibilities in life, but we have to match the proper possibility with the proper time. As you meditate you will come to know what is right, and as you practice selfless giving you'll gain the strength to do what is right.

The highest and best type of giving is done without attachment. Attachment means that the limited self has determined to hold onto something. Now, this is impossible. You cannot hold onto anything in this world. The very nature of this world is transitory. Everything here comes and goes. Nothing lasts. Not even you in your current form will last. It seems absurd to try and hold onto something, to derive our happiness from it, when we know we're going to be parted from it and therefore become unhappy, but this is what we do. This is attachment.

Unattachment doesn't mean not having things or loving or having emotions or being in the world or having possessions. It simply means that we're unattached. We realize that everything comes forth from God and everything returns to God, that something is in our life as long as it should be and we enjoy it. And then when it's removed from our life we're perfectly happy too, because our real happiness was not coming from possessions or people or experiences but just from pure being. If you're happy just to be, then the world can come and give you everything and that's nice. The world can come and take everything away and that's nice. It really doesn't matter because you're innately happy – that innate happiness comes and develops in self-giving. When we practice selfless giving we open the doorway to that happiness.

Selfless giving isn't drudgery. It doesn't mean that you have to go do unhappy things for hours and hours on end. As a matter of fact, selfless giving won't work then. Selfless giving is not martyrdom, it's not particularly painful. It's good clean fun. In selfless giving we're inspired to do something for someone else, to do something for our country, for our world or for God.

We can tell a person's level of spiritual development simply by watching how much they give, how they give and to whom they give. The sign of an advanced spiritual person, of course, is that they've affixed themselves to a spiritual organization and they practice their selfless giving on a spiritual level. Someone who is not quite as evolved would be giving in a more material way, perhaps to their society through political involvement, something like that. Someone who is not quite as evolved as that might practice their self-giving simply within the bounds of their own family. They try to be a good wife, a good mother, a good husband, a good child, something like that.

We live in a world with many, many billions of persons, beings who are all at different cycles, all in different stages in their progression through their incarnations. But a spiritually advanced person, one who's already been through many lifetimes and has kind of worked those things out, practices their selfless giving in a spiritual realm. They're no better than anyone else. We can't say that the person in graduate school is any better than the first grader. Each one is in the proper place at the proper time, but they certainly conduct themselves in a somewhat different way.

If you're an advanced seeker, meaning that you meditate, that you seek consciously, then it's necessary for you to affix yourself to a spiritual group. Find that person in this world whom you feel you can learn the most from spiritually, go, and apprentice yourself to them. They will show you how to give selflessly. As a matter of fact, when you really want to learn anything, and in particular selfless giving, the best and most important thing to do is simply to observe, to be around, someone who practices selfless giving perfectly. People who give of themselves are inspirations. If we think of Albert Schweitzer, Gandhi, Lincoln, and many, many others, not all of whom were famous, we're inspired. We feel that the people who were the most outstanding in this world are those who have given the most of themselves. Self-sacrifice is the highest of all human qualities.

If you really want to learn the art of selfless giving, though, find a spiritual teacher. Find someone who's crossed beyond the boundaries of life and death and who's entered into the sea of nirvana, into the sea of perfection, that ocean of immortal God-consciousness. The reason I suggest this is, the person who knows more about selfless giving than anyone else is not because they have entered into that ocean but because they have returned from it. You see, it's very, very hard, my friend, to attain liberation. It takes countless lifetimes of work and self-giving and meditation. Once you've attained liberation, it's not necessary to come back into this world. You can just stay one with God in immortal consciousness and ecstasy forever, but some persons choose, even after they've had that experience, rather than stay in that immortal bliss all the time, to come back for others. They don't have to. Christ didn't have to, Buddha didn't have to, and many others did not have to. They reached a plane in their awareness, in their lifetime, when they could have just gone off and meditated by themselves but they came back to teach, they came back to give, they came back to die, to suffer, when it was no longer necessary for them to do so.

It's one thing to give because you need to. It's another to give when you don't have to at all. The greatest souls in this world, in a sense, or I don't know if they're the greatest souls but let us just say that the most giving souls are those who give when they don't have to give, who could just walk away from this world and its suffering and merge with eternal existence and bliss forever – a bliss far beyond your understanding, an ecstasy beyond description, a beauty and light that surpasses all knowledge and all things in this and all other worlds; this is what it is like when you cross that boundary into immortal perfection that we call God realization and nirvana – and to come back from that to ease the pain and suffering and misery of others, to talk to those who will belittle you, who will not understand you, who will not listen to what you have to say, but to do it anyway, to serve out your time in this life. If you are fortunate enough to meet such a being then you will really learn selfless giving, just by being with them, just by watching them. Because you'll see that every second, every moment of their awareness is directed towards others, and also they have the power to change and transform the lives of others.

If you really want to learn selfless giving, it's really necessary to be around such a person, and not simply to be around them but to observe them carefully, to watch what they do, not just on the surface, but within, to try to understand what motivates them. What motivates someone who's become wealthy to go out and work in the ghetto with those who are poor? What motivates one who has perfect health to go and work with the sick? Because if you understand that, then you'll understand the root and cause of all existence, that life itself is self-giving. We're not given this life just for our own purposes or our own amusement and pleasures.

It's fine to be happy. It's a material world; you should have all the things you need. If you need a family, if you need friends, houses, cars, careers, if you need to be famous, whatever you need to be, be it. It doesn't matter. It doesn't matter what you have or what you do. It's your motivation that counts. Because if you have improper motivation and have everything in this world – you may have perfect health, wealth, friends, loved ones – you'll be miserable. As you grow older you'll watch it all erode before your eyes and soon it'll be gone and death will swallow you up, only to come back again and experience the same thing again and again. Death is not a release. Death is just a hyphen between incarnations.

One day after many, many lifetimes of being shuffled around this old world, of seeing the up and down of it, we get wise. We decide that the fun in life is to give, and as we do, we become happier and happier. We go and join a spiritual community. That is to say, we study with a teacher and our friends are the other students, people who, like ourselves, wised up a little bit after enough lifetimes, and learned that the fun of life is giving, and we begin to work for humanity together.

A spiritual teacher always has a journey and we hop onto their journey; we travel with them. Their journey is, for a course of years in this world, to try to bring light to others, so we help them with their work. If you want to become a great silversmith, you have to apprentice yourself to a master silversmith. Gradually over the years you will learn the art. One day you'll be the silversmith, perhaps, and you'll have apprentices or you may not be interested in apprentices. You might just make things.

We come to the spiritual teacher and we help them in their work. We help them reach others, inspire others and we watch them. We watch the little drama that goes on in their lives, on this cosmic stage of existence. We watch them deal with the public. We watch them deal with the students. We watch this magnificent process and we learn. We're witnesses to immortality, and as we watch, our heart opens because we're inspired by the self-giving. We're inspired by the God that we see in others and suddenly we find ourselves changing. We find ourselves giving more and more, sleeping a little less, and working a little harder. We find that our lives become rather amazingly beautiful, that they're deeper and more conscious – things that I can't put into words but that you will feel as you walk along the pathway to enlightenment.

Selfless giving is something that, in my estimation, begins at home. I feel that there are lots and lots of opportunities for you to give of yourself all the time. I don't think you have to travel to India to learn selfless giving. I think that selfless giving is right where you are now, that there's always an opportunity. There's always someone to help, there's always some way in which you can perfect yourself through service to others.

In the beginning we have a sense of giving in small blocks, units. We give part of our time or part of our energy to someone else to help them prosper. But as we advance we become aware that we really want to give perfectly and that even though we're giving somewhat selflessly, there may be subconscious motivations. Part of our selfless giving may actually, subconsciously, be selfish.

We approach God. We sit in meditation and we feel eternity and we say to eternity, "Eternity, I don't know what's right or wrong, good or bad. I may be doing what's right or I may be deceiving myself. Instead, what I'm going to do is give my life to you. Giving my life to you may mean leading a very ordinary life or it may mean leading an extraordinary life. It may mean having a family and a career or it may mean going beyond all that to just work for others. It's hard to say. Rather than making a decision myself I'm going to let you decide for me. I'm going to give my life to you, to do with as you will, because I know that you are my self, you are my very being. When this life ends I will be absorbed back into you. I have come forth from you. You are all good and you know all that there is. Please act in me and through me at every moment and every second. Let me be but an extension of your being. Teach me how to give and love selflessly, at all times."

When you have this attitude, when you pray and meditate with this feeling, then you will give selflessly and then you can view everything – everything in your life is part of your yoga of selfless giving. Your yoga of selfless giving is not confined to just several hours a week when you do something for a spiritual organization or do something for someone else. Rather, your selfless giving involves everything and everyone in your life. Remember, it's attitude that matters most. For example, let us say that what you're trying to do is achieve God realization. You want to achieve self-realization, to become fully conscious, to be like Christ or Buddha or Krishna or Ramakrishna. You want to become a perfected enlightened person.

Now you could want to do this just because it would fulfill you or you could feel no, rather than just do this to fulfill myself, I want this to occur because if it does, look how much more I can do for others.

It is much more likely that you will attain liberation if you want liberation for others than just for yourself, because it's a long journey and along the journey you'll get tired. And when you get tired, if it's just for you yourself, you'll reach a point where you'll say, "Well, I really don't want it that much." It's a sour grapes routine. "Oh, it couldn't be that good, I've come far enough, let me rest, I'm tired." But if, when you're very, very tired and you're about to give up and you think, "Well, yes, I could give up for myself but no, there are others whom I will be able to help and they're waiting for me and if I don't complete my task, if I don't do this perfectly, then what about them? They'll suffer." Then you'll pick yourself up, no matter how tired you are, and go forward again and again and again, until you've reached liberation.

If you've set your sights on liberation, on full knowledge of eternity, then you can feel that everything you do in your life can contribute to that. If you work, when you go to work, you should feel that your work is meditation. You should feel when you get up to go to work each day that you are offering it to eternity, and if you can only do it perfectly it will strengthen you. It's part of your yoga. It's like trying to meditate perfectly. When you're with your friends, feel that you're not just with your friends but rather you have an opportunity to serve these people – sometimes by listening, sometimes by talking, sometimes by not talking to them about spiritual things, not thinking that you're so knowledgeable that you can tell them how to improve their lives, but just by being – by being compassionate and understanding, sometimes by being tough. But if you meditate deeply you'll have a sense of the right way to act in all situations with all people. It'll just come to you naturally from your deeper self, from the depths of your being it will flow forward. Whereas if you don't meditate deeply, how can it happen? The message can't get through. The messenger is blocked. Learn to use everything in your life as part of your selfless giving. There's no situation that you can become involved in that you can't use for part of your selfless giving.

Let us consider eternity. Eternity is selfless giving. Think of a star. A star burns up its very substance to give light to others. You need to be like a star. Eternity sends forth all of the worlds, all of the beings we see, the very fabric of existence. Eternity gives life to all and sustains all, transforms all on the wheel of dharma, the wheel of birth, death and rebirth, until all attain perfection. Eternity does nothing but give, therefore it is infinite.

In the *I Ching*, the Chinese *Book of Changes*, it is explained that everything eventually must turn into its opposite. Whatever you do, sooner or later, its opposite will occur. This is the nature of change. That which is high will become low. That which is distant will become near. Your good luck will become bad luck and so on. However, there is one way to avoid the change and that is through constant giving. When the good energy is moving, when the cycle is going in the right direction, if you keep sharing the good energy with others, more and more all the time, then it need not ever turn into its opposite. It's only when it reaches the high point, the zenith, that the law of change dictates that something must turn into its opposite, into an opposite movement. In your life, if you just keep giving to others, constantly, ceaselessly, and endlessly, if you don't really take thought of yourself and your own welfare and your own awareness but just give and give and give, beyond exhaustion, then your life will always be a constant progression. It need not change into its opposite.

Selfless giving is the art of living, as I suggested at the beginning of this discussion. Most people don't live very well. They live very selfishly and when they suffer, it's because they brought that suffering on themselves. But you have an opportunity to be different. You have enough time, enough knowledge, and enough volition to be different. You may be 16, you may be 65, it doesn't matter. All you have is all the time in the world – no more and no less. If you begin today you can change your life forever. You can change your life into forever, into immortal awareness.

Selfless giving rounds the edges in spiritual practice. Many people can meditate very well but they're still very egotistical. You go and see the spiritual teacher and you watch them meditate and you feel power from them, but then you see that they're really egotistical. They're not delicate, gentle, and kind to those around them. How can this be? How can they go into these higher states of knowledge and still be egotistical? It's because they haven't achieved an integrated realization yet. There are still some rough edges of the self that have to be smoothed out. Selfless giving smooths out the rough edges, unties the hard knots. Meditation is not enough. Meditation and selfless giving must always go together. They work together to create immortality.

Selfless giving is downright fun. When you're going through a difficult time yourself, when life is not pleasing you – you're depressed, you're discouraged – forget about yourself for a while. Go do something for someone else. This is the fastest way to pull yourself out of a negative state of consciousness. You could sit around, feel sorry for yourself, and be miserable, or you can simply pick yourself up and go out and do things for others. Don't expect always to be inspired. Sometimes you have to inspire yourself. You could go outside today and have a glum face and be unhappy and miserable and feel sorry for yourself, or you could put a smile on your face and go out into the world, even though you don't feel like it. That's selfless giving

Selfless giving is not convenient. It doesn't mean that today we're struck by a mood and we're inspired and we're going to go help someone else. Selfless giving, real selfless giving, involves commitment – the commitment to make others happy whether we feel like it or not, without complaining and without indulging. This is the higher art of selfless giving.

It's nice to give when you're inspired. That's the adolescence of giving. We feel good; we're inspired. We don't feel good; we're not inspired. But in real selfless giving, mature selfless giving, we always give. We have a certain standard that we uphold in our consciousness that we never allow ourselves to slip beneath. As a matter of fact, we're raising the standard all of the time. We're giving in a deeper, more pure way, all the time. When you really give selflessly, after a while it becomes automatic. If you are unhappy, if you're discouraged, be that way in your bedroom, by yourself, but whenever you leave your room to come out into the world, in real selfless giving, we push all of that aside and we smile and give love to others.

In other words, what I'm suggesting is that selfless giving is not just our actions, it's not just that we go and spend time with others or work for them, but selfless giving extends itself to our emotional makeup. We could be unhappy and discouraged for ourselves, but if we're trying to be in a high vibratory state so we can really be of service to others, it's necessary to be happy. We can be happy even if we don't feel like it, as part of our selfless giving. We can't allow ourselves to be depressed or discouraged. There are people who depend upon us.

There are things to accomplish. We only have a little bit of time in this world before death swallows us up. We must bring light to as many people as possible. Who has time to indulge in self-pity or in moral recriminations, in guilt, in feeling sorry for ourselves? In advanced self-giving you feel you have no time for this. You just push those emotions out. If you were just being yourself, you could indulge, you have time to be unhappy. I don't have the luxury of time to be unhappy. I have too much to do. I have too much to accomplish. Who has time to be unhappy?

When you're young and you're not feeling well, you may not go to school. You mother will keep you home because you're ill. When you're an adult you have to go even if you don't feel well. You have to work. It's necessary. This is growing up. This is maturity. You may not feel like giving selflessly, but it doesn't matter. You have to do it anyway. This is if you're an advanced spiritual seeker. If you're a beginner, if you're just learning how to meditate and just beginning to gain control of your life, let alone give the whole thing away to eternity, then you can just kind of be yourself and be inspired and be a happy creature. Give when you want to, love when you want to, meditate when you want to. But when you enter into the professional league, when you become of interest to me or other spiritual teachers, that's when you get serious about it. You don't need to be pampered anymore. You just want to learn and give and become godlike and live your life for others. Then come and see me, come and talk to me, when you get to that point. Then I'm interested.

I work with beginners, I work with all sizes, shapes, forms and dimensions, physical and nonphysical. But the ones I'm looking for are the ones who have gotten steady enough not to need all the time and the attention, who aren't in it for the glamour, for the rush of light, but have committed themselves to self-giving and their self-giving is not just their physical work, but the way they handle themselves, the way they conduct their emotional beings. Such a person I'm interested in. Such a person I can bring quickly to self-realization. Others must first work their way up the ladder of consciousness just to reach that point, where not just for a day or a week or a month, but for a whole lifetime, they'll have fun. They'll be themselves, but they'll also maintain a standard of self-giving, of conscious control and awareness. These are the persons who have the most beautiful lives on earth. These are the ones who do so much for others.

Your spiritual journey and your spiritual welfare are really dependent, in my estimation, upon two primary factors: one, your ability to meditate well and two, your ability to give of yourself. You'll find the two go hand in hand. The more you meditate, the more you'll give of yourself, and your self-giving will take an ease and a form and a shape, a beauty and a knowledge, that will make it real self-giving. The more you give of yourself, the better you'll meditate. You must do the two. Some people make a terrible mistake. They just give of themselves and don't meditate and they burn themselves out. They get exhausted and after a while they overdo their selfless giving. They don't have any fun with it anymore and they just go at it doggedly, day after day, thinking they're doing what's right, and they're not at all.

As you meditate and provide time for yourself to meditate, you renew yourself. You come back to that inner wellspring of existence in your meditation and you feel beauty and light. You remember why you're giving of yourself. It's fun again. It keeps you balanced. Then you can go out into the world and practice your selfless giving, but you must meditate. Again, just meditation without selfless giving is not enough. You may go into very high states of consciousness, but the rough edges will be there. No liberation will occur because there may be lots of selfish motives lurking within the self that you don't see. In order to work those out, we practice selfless giving.

The two go hand in hand – whether you're an absolute beginner and you're just trying to meditate for a couple of minutes a day and just think nice thoughts about other people and help them once in a while. Or you're an advanced seeker who meditates with perfection in their whole being several hours a day, who's seeking a spiritual teacher or who has one, who's dedicated their life to the infinite, but not just as a formality or because it's the right thing to do but because they really want to, who not only works for others but does so with a smile and with inspiration, with cleverness, with laughter and humor, and who is not all caught up in themselves. That is to say, the person is not thinking, "Oh how wonderful I am, I just have given my life to God and to others."

There's no subtle vanity or egotism, but they're just a regular person out there doing the best they can for others, using the advanced knowledge they get from meditation and from their spiritual teacher to just try to do a better and better job for humanity, without feeling they're important, with the recognition that this world existed fine before you were here and will exist fine after you are gone. Such a person practices the art of selfless giving. They're free from attachment, happy, progressive. And even on those days when the dark winds blow and we find ourselves turbulent and upset, they go out and act as a professional. They do a good job anyway. They have a high standard. Such persons are true karma yogis. They practice the art of selfless giving as it really should be practiced.

Give more and more of yourselves. Don't hold back. Life is so short and there's so much to do. Align yourself with others who seek what you seek. Meditate deeply. Play with your life, have fun with it, and do what you can for others along the way. Don't expect others to admire you or appreciate you or understand you. Just do what you can, that's the joy. Don't wait for a return on the investment. Just give, give, give. But don't burn yourself out either, because if you burn yourself out, then what good will you be for anyone else? If you burn yourself out in two years of intense selfless giving, what good is that if you could have given of yourself for another 20 years and done much more? While it's good to be interested in the short-term growth, consider the long term. Set yourself up well. Get the things you want. If you want a house, car, friends, these things are not wrong. There's nothing wrong with the material – God exists in the material and in the spiritual. It's really all one, but don't be attached to them. They come and they go.

You're out as a child playing in the world, and you're playing with your friends and you're absorbed. But then your mother calls you. It's time to come home. And then you leave your friends, you say goodbye and you come home. God, the infinite mother, has set you in this world to play and have a nice time. Play nicely with others, be kind to them, help them, love them. But always remember, when mother calls it will be time to go home. And She will call one day.

THE YOGA OF DISCRIMINATION

There are four major paths to self-realization. Of the four, jnana yoga, from the point of view of the beginner, is the most difficult. Jnana yoga is the graduate school of self-discovery. Ordinarily in spiritual practice one begins by practicing bhakti, the path of love. The path of love leads to the path of self-giving. The third pathway in the normal course of evolution is jnana yoga, discrimination, and absorption. Mysticism, the fourth way, is not practiced by all. It's a left-handed path. It doesn't necessarily follow in the sequence of the others. Some persons follow the ways of mysticism, some do not, but normally the three paths are covered in this order: love, selfless giving and discrimination and absorption.

Discrimination means seeing that which is real and knowing that which is unreal. That which is real is that which is eternal, that which lasts forever. That which is unreal, or less real we might say, is that which is transitory, temporal, that which does not last but erodes in time. The yoga of knowledge is a way of reflection. The central question that we ask ourselves again and again is, "Who am I?" To find this out it is necessary to meditate, to still our thoughts, and to go within. We discover, ultimately, that we are the self, we are eternity.

There are a number of different approaches that we can use when we practice the yoga of knowledge. The first is elimination. What we do basically is to examine everything in existence and we come to see that everything that exists is transitory and is temporal. It doesn't last. That which is left over is eternal and that is our real self. We look, for example, at nature and we see that the creations of nature – plants, animals, human beings, planets, universes – all the things in nature are transitory. They may endure for a moment or perhaps billions of years, but ultimately they fall away, they don't last. If we look at absolutely everything in the universe and we eliminate all of those things, then that which is left over is God, is eternity, is the Self.

Another way the reflection of knowledge works is to see that there is nothing that is not God. That is to say, when we talk about self-realization, realizing the Self and coming to know that which is, we're talking from the point of view of limitation of the mind. The mind perceives everything in a limited way. The mind is bound up with the ego. The ego has limited perception. Real knowledge or wisdom is to see that you are that – you are eternity. To talk about realizing the Self in a way is discontinuous because there is nothing but the Self, there is nothing but realization. There is really no one to realize the Self. The illusion of self-hood, of an ego, of a separate identity, is false. There is nothing but eternity – eternity has always been and eternity will always be. To realize the Self involves an action. It implies that there is something to realize, that there is time, that there is a temporal world, and that Self is not yet realized, but will be realized by the actor through action. This is not the case. There is nothing that is not the Self. The Self does not have to be realized. The Self eternally is. There is nothing but the Self. This is the knowledge that comes through discrimination.

On the pathway of knowledge we view life as in a dream. We feel that all of this world is a dream. Just as when we go to bed at night and we fall asleep and we dream, and in the dream we can have experiences that seem to have a great deal of substance, they're solid and visceral, but upon waking from a dream – even the most horrible nightmare which filled us with fear, the most beautiful dream that filled us with the greatest joy – all of these dreams fade away. In a dream we can be very thirsty and we can have a drink of water and in the dream our thirst will be satisfied, but upon waking from the dream both the thirst and the satisfaction fall away. Everything and nothing falls away. When we wake from the ignorance of this world, the dream of existence – the dream of perception, seeing our self as a separate body, as an ego, as an identity, as a person – this falls away. All of the experiences that we have ever had fall away. The ideas of life and death, of rebirth, of reincarnation, karma, God, truth, knowledge – all these things fall away. While we're in the dream these are useful notions. But at the end of the dream, on the other side of the rainbow, there's only light, undifferentiated reality. In that undifferentiated reality of the Self there is lasting joy, eternal bliss. All the phantoms of existence fall away.

To realize the Self the mind must become very strong. On the path of knowledge we develop the mind through constant discrimination. Discrimination means inner reflection. We have to look within the Self and fathom it. We have to constantly ask ourselves, "Who am I?" We have to remind ourselves that we are not the transitory body, we are not the person who is having experiences, and we are not affected by action or inaction. We must constantly remind ourselves that we are eternity, we are infinite, we are beyond birth, we are beyond death. Birth and death are illusions; they are part of the dream. On waking from the dream we see that birth and death, the sense of self, the sense of others, all these things fall away. In the white light of eternity, there is only eternity.

The path of knowledge is said to be difficult in that it is the path of samadhi. For most persons there are three states of existence: the waking consciousness, when we're awake and walking around in the dream; the dreaming consciousness, when we're asleep but active in our dreams; and the deep sleep consciousness in which there are no dreams. But for one who practices the yoga of knowledge there is a fourth state. This is the state of samadhi. Samadhi is absorption in God. In the state of samadhi one has only the sense that one is perfect being. There is no awareness of separativity. There's no sense of time, place or condition. Samadhi is the actual awareness of what you really are. There are two types of samadhi: salvikalpa and nirvikalpa samadhi.

In salvikalpa samadhi we are aware that we are God. That is to say, there's no thought in the mind, there's no sense of being a physical being, there's no recollection of a past, there's no concern for a future, there's no sense of the senses or the objects of the senses. We are pure, undifferentiated consciousness, but still there is a subtle sense of "I am."

Now that your awareness has become God, now that you can feel yourself stretching through all of the universes and encompassing them, now that you know that you are the knower, that you bring forth all things and transform them and sustain them, now that you are in that mystical awareness of pure being, absolute reality, still there is a sense of being "that." There is some self-consciousness, not the self-consciousness of the human nature and the ego, where one feels and believes that one is an individual personality structure, that one has birth and one has death, that you are the doer. This has fallen away. There's no longer a sense of feeling, "I am this, I am not that, I do this, I accomplish this." The "I" is gone or we can say the "I" has been transformed into an eternal "I," into an ever present "I." The finite forms have fallen away and we have become God.

Nirvikalpa samadhi, on the other hand, is beyond description. It is the entrance into nirvana. Anything I say to you, anything that we discuss, anything that I describe, is presented from the point of view of the relative world. That is to say, I am addressing to some extent your mind. Your mind works through concepts and ideas. You respond through feelings, emotions. You recollect, you think about the future.

Anything I could possibly describe to you has to be couched in these terms, the terms of this world. That which is beyond these terms, that which is beyond description, that which is beyond understanding, is nirvana. Nirvana is a word that we use to describe that which is indescribable, the endless ocean of existence. In nirvikalpa samadhi we merge in that endless ocean of existence to such an extent that we dissolve completely and there's no "we" to even be conscious that we have dissolved. There's no sense of having ever been anything, there's no sense of being nothing, there's no sense at all.

This is precisely the point that stops most people from attaining self-realization. Because while they're able to meditate and follow the advice of their spiritual teacher and reach a point of great knowledge, while they're able to enter into salvikalpa samadhi and have that extraordinary illumination experience where you just sense and feel your oneness with God, not as an abstraction, but as a reality, the self is threatened by the idea of dissolution, by the idea of no longer existing. But you must know that this is an illusion. Anything that you can think is an illusion. Anything that you can feel is an illusion. Anything that you can see, even your highest understanding of truth, of dharma, is an illusion – an illusion in the sense that it's a limited thought. A limited thought is a limited thought.

You must understand that anything you understand is not a true understanding. Anything that you feel is not a true feeling. Anything that you know is not a true knowing. Anything that you believe is not a true believing. While all of the things that you believe, know, see, and feel do exist in their own right, in the relative existence, still, they're finite and limited. They're ways of looking at existence, but existence is infinite – infinite meaning that it's beyond all ways of looking.

While I can stand on the earth, look at the universe, and think all the thoughts I want to about it, that will not alter the universe. The stars will shine. They were shining before I came upon this world, they will shine after I have left this world. But not really. Not truly! If we really reflect and discriminate, we'll find that all things are created by our perception, that all states exist within the mind, that there is no place to go and there is no one to be. There is nothing to become. There's nothing to gain and there's nothing to lose. Everything is created within the mind. The whole objective universe is created, is ordered, by our perception and by our sense of self. We feel that life is one way, the stars are one way, time works one way. But when we erase perception, when we erase that which perceives perception, then the universe dissolves, and we see that it was never really real to begin with. You are a small dot on the blackboard. We take an eraser and erase it. What then? Absorption.

The dream appears to be real. It does really seem that we are here in this world. It does seem that we have bodies. It does seem that there is time and progression. It does really seem that there is birth, death, and rebirth. But this is not so. In deep meditation, in samadhi, there is no body, there is no mind. All of the things that we call life, all of the combinations of experiences, fall away. What is there? No one can say, because there's no one there to say. Once we remove the self who perceives, once we in effect erase ourselves, then there's no eraser. There never was anyone to erase. We've awakened from the dream and the dream has faded.

All concepts, all knowing, all truths, all religious systems, all beliefs fall away in the white light of eternity. The knowledge is so complete, the bliss is so ecstatic, the perfection of existence is so bright and fathomless, endless – that all of our lives, all of the lives that have ever been or will ever be are but a candle held to the sun. When we hold a candle flame up to the sun we don't see it; in the light of the sun it is gone. All of the ecstasies that have ever been or will ever be of all the lives that we have ever had or all have ever had, if placed together are just a candle to the sun – we can't see them. When we merge with the sun, when we become the sun, then it is limitless and infinite. Eternal Brahman, the Self, the one without a second.

The ego holds us to this world. What is the ego? The ego is a sense of self. The ego is the feeling that you are. But you are not, nor have you ever been, nor will you ever be. You cannot be born and you cannot die because you don't even exist in the sense that you think of existence. This is just a dream. You have dreamed that you were born. You dream of pleasure and pain, you dream of death, but upon waking from the dream, all this will vanish, all this will go away. Nothing but eternity shall remain and there was really never anything but eternity at all.

When we go to the cinema and we look at the screen we see images projected on the screen. At times we could feel that the images are real. We could feel, if we didn't know, that what we see on the screen is actually taking place, that those are real people up there.

However, if we go up and reach for those images and try and hold onto them, we'll see that they're not real, they're only images. All that exists is the screen. Consciousness is the screen. That is what you really are: immortal consciousness. The images on the screen are your perceptions, your feelings, the illusion that life is solid, that there is a material universe. There is no material universe; there is no reality.

All that exists are images. Where do these images come from and where do they return? What is it that projects these images? How is it that we are the screen? How is it that we have forgotten our eternal nature, that we are the Self and that nothing but the Self exists? These questions and all questions like them can only be answered in absorption, because there are no answers. Answers can suit the relative mind. In the dream we can be thirsty and get a glass of water and within the dream we can drink the water and our thirst will go away. But upon awaking from the dream, there's no glass, there's no water, there's no thirst. All of this was a dream that passes away. All of these questions about the Self, about eternity, when asked from the relative point of view, fall away in the white light of eternity, in nirvana, because then we have awakened from the dream.

To practice jnana yoga, to practice the yoga of knowledge and discrimination, it's necessary to have a highly developed mind, not highly developed in the sense that we necessarily have a vast academic background, but rather the mind, the intellect, must be very, very strong. One who practices the yoga of discrimination has practiced the other yogas for many, many lifetimes. One does not practice the yoga of discrimination and knowledge in a first birth or even for many subsequent births. It is only through repeated incarnations, through repeated spiritual practices, that the intellect becomes strong and refined, that we can undertake to discover who and what we really are.

Meditation is an essential part of the practice of discrimination – meditation and reflection. When we meditate and make the mind calm and quiet, the ego dissolves. When there's no thought, there's no ego. Ego gives rise to thought. Thought gives rise to desire. Desire gives rise to attachment. Attachment gives rise to the concept of the limited self. The concept of the limited self gives rise to unhappiness, frustration, birth, death, and rebirth. It is only when you realize that you are not the body and that you are not the mind, that you are not that which is perceived nor that which perceives, that you will be free from the snares of illusion.

Jnana yoga is a very demanding practice. It's demanding in the sense that it's necessary for you to become conscious of the fact that you're not human. We like to feel that we're human beings. We like to feel that we love and care. We like to feel that we have parents, that we have children, that there are those who love us, that there are those who need us. We like to feel that people say good things about us, that after our death others may remember us with fond memories. We like to feel that we serve some purpose in this world, that we aid others, that we help others. This is all an illusion. This is not so.

Sometimes as we practice jnana yoga we come across great obstacles. In our discrimination we feel that life has no meaning and no purpose, which is absolutely true – life has no meaning and no purpose. We then feel that life is purposeless, that there's no reason to try, that life is empty. This is another illusion. The illusion of happiness is one illusion to be avoided. The illusion of unhappiness is another illusion to be avoided. The illusion of purpose is to be avoided. The illusion of lack of purpose is to be avoided.

It would appear that there is time in this world. It would appear that we have gone through experiences that we're having an experience now, just as you're listening to me, and that we will have experiences in the future. But this is not so. This only appears to be so because we're caught up in the illusion of selfhood. But when the movie stops and the lights come up, we see that the screen was only a screen and that the movie was just a projection of images. Good and bad, love and hate, life and death, importance and unimportance, all these are mere relative concepts or ideas that fall away with the attainment of knowledge.

It might seem that this knowledge is cold, that it's devoid of emotion, that it's empty. This is another illusion. It might seem that this knowledge is useful, that it will help us in life, that it will help us go beyond death. This is another illusion. It might seem – this is another illusion. It – this is another illusion. The idea that this is an illusion – this is another illusion. Anything that you can say, think, feel, believe, trust, count on or feel is untrue is an illusion. The fact that you supposed that you were thinking these things is an illusion. The fact that there are these things is an illusion. Nothing is as it seems. This is an illusion. There are no illusions. This is a gross illusion.

Illusion, however, doesn't mean that something is not real. Everything is real and nothing is real. Illusion simply means that something is less real than something else. This life and this world simply and certainly exist. Dreams exist. Who is to say that the reality within the dream is not real? The dream is real, but it does not last. This is an illusion. The reality is real and it does last. This is an illusion. No matter which way you turn there's nothing but illusion. How do we find a way out? By realizing that there's no place to go, that there's no way out, that there's no way in. All that exists is the Self. The Self is infinite, the Self is eternal. You are that Self. There is nothing else. Beyond words, thoughts, ideas, forms and belief systems, there is nothing but the Self.

If this is so, if silence only conveys the Self, if all words and thoughts are illusions in the sense that they spring forth from the ego – the ego being a partiality, a dream, a movie shown on a screen, a flickering image – why do we discuss this? What is there to say and who is saying it? Why should we say anything when to say something is to enter into the world of illusion? It is because people exist in varying degrees of dream.

Each one is aware to a certain extent, and it's necessary to enter into the dreams of others, just as I am entering into your dream right now, to make them aware that they're dreaming. If I enter into your dream and say, "Wake up, this is a dream," if you listen to me and you awaken, then the dream will vanish. But when the dream vanishes, where will you and I be? We'll be right where we always were and always will be – everywhere and nowhere, eternally perfect, infinite consciousness, infinite awareness.

To strengthen yourself for the practice of the knowledge of discrimination, which is really not as bad as it sounds (Rama laughs), it's necessary to learn to concentrate. Each day when you meditate you should devote the first few minutes of your meditation to concentrating. You can do this as kind of a warm-up procedure for meditation. When you start your meditation each day, focus your attention on a yantra, focus on the dot at the center of the yantra and just for a few minutes concentrate on it. This will develop the power of the intellect. If you don't have a yantra then use a candle flame.

Focus your attention on a candle flame, on the center of the flame. Look deeply into it. When you focus on the dot in the center of the yantra, when you focus on the candle flame, you should not move your attention. You should feel that nothing else exists. When thoughts come in and out of your mind, ignore them. Only concentrate and focus fully on that which you have centered your attention upon. If your attention is fully centered upon something, there can be no thought, there can be no experience. If we're looking through a telescope and all we see is what is at the other side, that is to say that which greets our eyes through the telescope, then we're not aware of what's behind us, what's on either side of us, what's above us or below us. All we're aware of is what's at the end of the telescope, what the telescope is showing us.

When you practice concentration, there should be nothing in your awareness but the object of concentration. You should only do this for a few minutes, for three or four minutes, at the beginning of each meditation session. If you do this you'll strengthen the intellect, you'll clear the mind. In order to enter into samadhi, in order to see truth, to see that which is real, it's necessary to be able to stop all thought completely. While you can meditate for many, many years and have some thought in the mind, to really enter into samadhi, into the deeper stratum of existence, you must be able to control thought perfectly, without any sense of controlling thought. Or we could say that there is nothing but self-realization, there is nothing but perfected consciousness, and all you have to do is become aware of that and become absorbed in that. Concentrating for a few minutes each day will strengthen the intellect. Then when the day comes when you're ready to cross the threshold of eternity, you will find that your concentrative power will help you terrifically.

When you enter into samadhi and you seek to make that magical walk between salvikalpa and nirvikalpa samadhi, to merge with nirvana, at that time, as I suggested before, you must do something that might appear to be very, very difficult. It's necessary at that time to focus your awareness not on being or nonbeing, not on truth or ignorance, but to focus it without focusing it. This is the difficult part. That is to say you must realize that you are not the doer, that you are not the action. As you're sitting there and you have that subtle sense, after you've stopped all your thoughts, of self – that subtle self, which is God, that which you've always sought and finally become, you must now annihilate without annihilating. You've attached yourself to an image, still. That image is no thought, that image is God, that image is merging with the perfect reality, that image is nirvana.

Finally all of the things you've worked for all of those years and all of those lifetimes, you finally become it. And now that you've become it, this is the final illusion. Now that you've reached everything you've always wanted, you must slay this illusion without slaying it and becoming caught up in the illusion of slaying an illusion. This is the difficult part.

But if you practice your concentration, you'll find that that time, all those moments spent in concentration for all those years of meditation, all your spiritual practice, all the things you learned from your teacher, all the experiences life has given you will come forward and stand behind you and will give you a terrific strength. And with that terrific strength you will cut aside all illusions. What then? Then there won't be emptiness. Emptiness is just another idea, another illusion. Then there won't be fullness, there won't be perfection, there won't be rebirth, nor will there be the lack of it. There won't be death nor will there be life nor will there be anything other. Then we cannot say anything. That you must experience.

But as I suggested before, let us just say it is a bliss beyond all understanding. It is final liberation. From there - there is no return because there is no one to return. You cannot say, "I have gone into nirvana," because no one can go into nirvana. In order to enter into nirvana you can't be nor can you not be. You cannot say, "I have gone out of nirvana," because the self which could not enter into nirvana cannot possibly leave nirvana. You find yourself in this world, you find yourself out of this world, and there's no one to find the self. There's no self to find.

The yoga of knowledge is very demanding, in the sense that you must lead a perfect life in order to practice it, but a perfect life is not necessarily what you might think. As a matter of fact a perfect life involves little or no thought whatsoever. A perfect life is to observe, to realize that you have no control over the events in your life, that there are no events in your life, that there is no life. Yet at the same time if you find yourself sitting in the theater watching a good movie, enjoy it! You can enjoy the dreams of selfhood, as long as you remember they're dreams. You can enjoy the beauties of this world, as long as you remember that this world doesn't exist. You can enjoy the ideas of salvation, as long as you realize that there's no one to be saved and nothing to save.

In my estimation, self-realization is nothing that can be willed nor is it particularly desirable. This may sound strange coming from a spiritual teacher, one who has been absorbed countless times into nirvana, in countless lives. But you see, as you pass through bhakti yoga, as you pass through love, you're elated, you're fulfilled, and you're joyous. As you pass through karma yoga, you're even more joyous because self-giving is the perfect expression of love. Jnana yoga is not devoid of love. As a matter of fact it's filled with love because the very reason that we practice jnana yoga is out of love. But what happens is we disappear. When we practice bhakti yoga and karma yoga – love and self-giving – there's a sense of improvement. We're practicing these things so our lives can become better. We sense that we're getting happier, reality is more beautiful, we eliminate our attachments that make us unhappy, we just enjoy pure being. But there's still a sense of, "We're enjoying being." We merge with God, there's a sense of merging with God. There's this continuous self which is enjoying itself more and more in more delightful and divine ways.

But in jnana yoga we take that very thing that was starting to have such a wonderful time and watch it go away. We watch ourselves become very, very thin, so thin that we disappear. And the curious thing about it is that there's nothing we can do about it. When you start to go into samadhi, you just find yourself dissolving. It's as if you're a patient who's in a hospital and every day you grow weaker and weaker, and you get so weak that you're not even quite sure what's happening to you. Every day your friends and relatives come and visit you and as you lie there in the hospital bed you look up at them. They smile down at you and you smile at them, but every day you're falling away, you're dissolving. There's less and less of you, and after a time you don't even recognize them anymore. They come and you see these persons standing over you, but you don't really remember who they are.

Then one day they come to look at you and perhaps they still see you, but from your point of view they're not there. There's no longer an awareness of the objective world. You don't see it, because you've gone away. Where have you gone? Who knows? Who can say? They come to visit you and there's no one there. Perhaps they imagine someone is there, but if they really look, there's no one there. The patient has gone away. In the middle of the night the patient left. No one is there. But really, if no one is there, no one is there to watch. The patient is gone, the friends and the relatives are gone, the room is gone, the hospital is gone, the world is gone. Everything has fallen away.

What's left over? What's left when the patient has gone, the friends and relatives are gone, the hospital has gone, the world has gone, the sky and the stars are gone, life and death are gone? What's left? Only that which has ever been, which is and will ever be, that which is God, that which is our true self. And it is only when you become that true self-consciously, when all these illusions have fallen away, of time, place and condition, that you will be perfectly free and perfectly happy. Jnana yoga brings peace, perfect understanding. Not only merging and becoming God but going beyond all descriptions. It is the final haven of the spiritual seeker.

Remember, your own attachments will trip you up. In the beginning of your spiritual practice, if you're new to meditation, then you're just trying to get over your unhappy attachments, your attachments to people, places, conditions, money, and all this sort of stuff. You become attached to things, you desire things, and then when your desires are not fulfilled, you're unhappy. When your desires are fulfilled you're happy for a little while until new desires come and make you unhappy again or until you realize that actually getting what you want is not quite what you thought. But then, one day, all of it falls away and there's nothing but perfect eternity, perfect being. It is that which each of us really seeks.

There's something within you that seeks perfection, that seeks absorption, and until that occurs for you you'll never rest and you'll never really know peace. While the yoga of love and the yoga of self-giving will lead you along the path and will teach you how to eliminate your unhappy feelings, your unhappy attachments – you'll learn how to overcome your bitterness and your hates and your jealousies and your angers and frustrations and all those things will go away and be replaced by selfless love and selfless giving, humility, purity, integrity – you'll have a beautiful wonderful life. But still, it's a life. Still, even though it has great joy, that great joy is nothing in comparison with the ecstasy of pure undifferentiated being, with true liberation from all ignorance, from the samsara, from notions of birth, death, and rebirth. Only that final liberation, or let us say realization that you have always been liberated, that you've never been anything else but undifferentiated consciousness, will cause you perfect freedom, will bring you what you really want and really seek.

Then, it's necessary for you to climb the ladder, to practice the yoga of love, which will purify your nature, and to practice the yoga of self-giving. The yoga of self-giving will round the rough edges of the ego, will put love into action and cause you to mature spiritually. While the yoga of love wakes you up spiritually, the yoga of self-giving gives you spiritual maturity. But then it is in the yoga of knowledge that you will actually become the sun itself, that you will reach that final harbor, that infinite destination. Which does not suggest that you will die when that happens, since there is no death. It does not suggest anything, in that it is nothing and everything and beyond all things.

The yoga of discrimination is only practiced once you have started to go into samadhi. Until that time, in my opinion, one does not practice the yoga of discrimination. In India and other places there are people who fool themselves. They think they're practicing the yoga of discrimination. They walk around all day saying, "Who am I? Who am I?" and they go through these analytical processes. But it is impossible to know who you are until you enter into samadhi. It is only in samadhi that you'll begin to get an inkling of who you are, and finally, it is only in absorption in nirvana that this perfect truth will become clear.

I wouldn't really worry too much about practicing the yoga of discrimination at this point in your evolution. When it comes, when the time comes, then you'll be instructed in this particular yoga by an enlightened soul, an enlightened spiritual teacher – one who has practiced this yoga with success to the point where they can be said neither to exist nor not to exist.

The way you'll really learn the yoga of discrimination is simply by spending time with someone who has perfected themselves in this yoga. You can sit with them in silence and learn everything there is to learn. Because what they really have to teach you about the yoga of discrimination can never be put in words, since the entire yoga exists beyond words, beyond thoughts, beyond conditions. All they can do is frustrate your mind by telling you that you exist and don't exist, that you are and are not and things of this nature, which won't really make a lot of sense to your mind. All it can do is cause you hopefully to rise beyond the mind. But until you can meditate in perfect stillness, until you begin to really enter into salvikalpa samadhi where you can stop all thoughts and become absorbed in eternity, until you've reached that point where you've perfected your lower nature and cleansed your emotional being, jnana yoga will wait.

Once you've done all those things and you have eliminated all of your negative karmas and tendencies, and now instead all you do are good things, all you think are good thoughts, all you do is give endlessly and ceaselessly to others, then when you've done that, when you're getting all A's, then we have to take all the A's away – because even though these good karmas are very good, they're still karmas, they're still limitations. Even though the good thoughts are good thoughts, they're still thoughts. Even though the good actions are good actions, they're still actions and there's still a sense of acting and thinking. Now that you've finally made it to the top we've got to take the top away, because while the top may seem wonderful, while getting A's may be wonderful, still, there's a sense of self and that sense of self will trap you. That sense of self is an illusion, it's another dream, and that dream must fall away. And when that dream falls away and that full wakefulness, that perfected being of existence, then eternity alone will abide and remain. Then there are no words, there are no descriptions. Only then will you really be what you truly are.

We climb the ladder in a way of speaking. We move from stage to stage, from yoga to yoga, from one journey to another. Yet you will find, in my estimation in daily life, that jnana yoga is actually quite practical. Jnana yoga is discrimination and in life you have to discriminate. You see, we talk about the four paths – I talk about jnana yoga and bhakti and karma and mysticism as if they're all separate. To be honest, though, they're all one. There is only one path, there is only one truth, and there is only one reality. Of course, I'm speaking from the point of view of jnana yoga.

Now, there's nothing to do! There's no place to go. There's no one at home to answer the telephone. What telephone? If the telephone rings and there's no one home, is there a telephone ringing? Of course not. All heavens and hells exist in the mind. What mind? There is no mind. There is no heaven, there is no hell. How discouraging to find out after working for lifetimes for salvation that there is no salvation because there's no one to be saved.

The danger, as I suggested, is depression. A sense of, "Why bother?" Since there's no one to be saved, what's the use?" But remember, that's only another illusion too. The illusion of meaninglessness, of purposelessness. What is - is so good, so perfect, so simple, so exacting, that it's beyond both meaning and lack of meaning.

But as I said, jnana yoga is practical. It can help you get through the day. Use discrimination to temper love. While it's good to love, we can be fooled in love or we can be fooled by our own love. Who are we to be fooled, anyway? What are we? Do we exist? Do we not exist? How can you be fooled if you don't exist? Well, let's be practical for a second. When you love without discrimination, then you love blindly. If you love blindly, you don't see. If you don't see, you smack into things and get hurt. How can you get hurt if you don't exist? How can you feel hurt? What hurt? There's no one to be hurt. There's no one to hurt. It's only with this realization that there is no pain. There is only eternity, eternal perfection.

But meanwhile, back in the relative world, if you discriminate, if you use the power of discrimination, then you will see that there is a hidden truth in all things and that you can perceive that truth. Just as all things are not good for us – it's not good for us to eat arsenic, all things are not meant for human beings, while it is good, perhaps, to eat a salad – so all experiences are not good for us. We have to discriminate and determine which experiences are good for us.

If you practice a little jnana yoga in your daily life, it will help you tremendously in this sense. You can learn that which is right and useful and that which should be avoided at your current stage of evolution. The way to do this is very easy, absolutely easy. All you have to do is ask yourself one question and if you ask yourself this question whenever you're trying to decide what to do, you'll always do exactly what is right. You'll discriminate and cut your way through illusion and you'll always do that which is right. The question is very, very simple. The question is, "Where is truth? Is there truth in what I am doing now?" That's all you have to ask yourself.

If you meditate each day and if you practice your concentration exercises, you will immediately know if what you're doing is the truth. Don't try and understand this with your mind. The thoughts will come, the thoughts will go, and you'll think a thousand things and have a million philosophies, good ideas, and wonderful ideas which will change from second to second. But there will be no absolute knowing, no certainty in these thoughts and philosophies and ideas. But if you, with your heart, ask yourself that simple question, "Is there truth in what I am about to do?" then you will automatically know. If there is no truth in it, you'll know, and you won't do that. If there is truth, you'll know. But you must honestly ask yourself, "Is there truth in what I am about to do?"

Always think of the truth, believe in the truth, follow the truth, and finally annihilate the truth with your discrimination. Follow the truth as far as it will go, but then there comes a time when you must go beyond truth. We have a car, we love our car. We're going to take the car down to the beach and then we're going to go into the water. We take the car as far as it will go, but once we get there we have to leave it behind. That doesn't mean that there will be nothing. There's the ocean. We'll swim. It'll be wonderful. Perhaps someday we'll meet the car again. Who knows? Who is asking the question? The question is eternal. Is there being or is there nonbeing? Is there reality? Is there life after maya? No! Yes!

There's only silence and the waves – the sound of the waves in eternity. And then one day they go away and you're the perfection of consciousness, the perfection of God and being. You stretch endlessly. You shine perfectly in your own light – no fear, no worry, no darkness, nothing can interfere with your perfection. You've always been this and you will always be this. That is all that exists. Anything else is but a dream, and dreams have an existence but they pass. Come to know that your true self is unchanging, has always been and will always be, and if you become aware of that all pain will leave you, all suffering, all frustration. Even that which you call joy is a frustration when viewed with the absolute ecstasy that is existence, the absolute perfection that is immortal consciousness.

Try to feel deep within yourself that which is real and always follow that which is real. And when you find yourself going into samadhi, some day when that happens, at that point seek a teacher. Find a liberated soul and ask them to teach you the yoga of knowledge, the yoga of discrimination, because then it will be necessary for you to push aside even your samadhi, even your ecstasy and realize that samadhi is transitory and that nirvana is just another word. Then you'll be in graduate school.

The yoga of knowledge is the yoga of perfection. It is the end and the beginning of all things. It is neither favorable nor unfavorable because there's no one there to favor it. There is nothing and there has never been anything but the Self. Know this. You are the Self. You are eternity. There is nothing else. There is no world, there is no time, there is no place, there is no condition. There is only the Self. You are the Self. There is nothing and there can be nothing else. Thou art that and beyond. Beyond words, beyond condition, beyond immortality and mortality. Be absorbed in that truth.

THE YOGA OF MYSTICISM AND POWER

There are four principal pathways that lead to self-realization. Mysticism is the hidden way. The mystic practices the art of intentionality. Intentionality is the awareness of being in all of its profundity and a gentle humor, a not-so-serious view of our existence, a pure love of life in both its finiteness and its infiniteness.

The path of love seeks to unite us with immortality through love of God. The path of selfless giving seeks to unite us with immortality, with nirvana, through action. Love is passive; self-giving is active. Jnana yoga, the path of discrimination, seeks to unite us with eternity through knowledge. By pushing away all illusions of the self and coming to know who and what we are, we become conscious of our own infiniteness.

Mysticism uses power – the utilization of power to unite us with our eternal self. When we practice mysticism, we deal with two sides of ourselves: that which is seen and that which is unseen. The part of our being that we see is the island of the first attention. The part of our self that we're not conscious of is the ocean of our second attention.

Imagine that you're standing on an island right now. This is the island of your awareness. You can explore the island; it has many parts, many sides. This is what you see and feel in your day-to-day life. But around the island, surrounding it, is something else – an ocean. Within the ocean there are different creatures; some are friendly, some are not. Out in the farther reaches of the ocean, the farther shores are found, other realities, other eternities. But in order to go to those other shores, to reach them, we have to leave our own island and journey through the ocean.

Mysticism is the study of our own island, the island of our first attention, of our awareness in this world. It's the study of the ocean, its currents, its winds, the life forms that exist in it, methods of travel. It's also the study, in its more advanced stages, of those other islands, other continents, other worlds, and of the nature of being itself. It's a very structured study.

When we start to learn about mysticism, we begin by assessing our being. Step one is to consider your island. Your island is probably not in the best of shape – part of it may be overgrown; the palm trees are not healthy; the paths need to be cut; there's a jungle that has to be pruned back and made orderly. This is not something that you do once, but as long as you're alive you have to do this. You have to keep up with it, just as you have to keep up with your yard. If you have a yard around your house, you may cut it every other week. If you let it go, soon there'll be a jungle. In mysticism we turn our attention to our life and we bring order into our life by constantly cutting it back – through analysis and awareness and the skillful utilization of power.

During the Arab oil embargo, those of us here in the United States became much more interested in being fuel-efficient. With the price of oil and gas soaring, particularly in the colder regions of our country, people began to become aware that they were losing a tremendous amount of energy, that they were wasting energy.

Pictures were taken with infrared film of homes in the colder regions. Infrared film is a heat-sensitive film and it records where heat is being lost in a home. A photograph would be taken of a home and the photo would reveal by coloration where heat was being lost – around the windows or the doors, through the chimney or wherever. With this knowledge, the owner of the home could then insulate those areas and conserve heat, conserve energy.

In the same way, in the early stages of the path of mysticism, it's necessary to learn where you're losing energy and plug up the holes in your being. It's also necessary to become aware of where you gain energy and to try and increase the energy that you are taking in and decrease the loss of energy. We start to do this in our physical life, in the island of our first attention, in our day-to-day awareness – let's not be concerned with traveling across the great oceans or exploring other islands until our own island is together.

The first step, really, is to understand where power comes from and increase it within ourselves, because without power we can't do anything, we can't be anything. Everything we do and are, according to the laws of mysticism, is dependent upon our personal power – the energy at our command. You might want to go places and have wonderful times but if you're so weak that you can't get up off the bed, then there's no journey. It's necessary to have energy and power, and of course to direct that energy and power properly.

If you're in a very cold place, if the house is freezing cold, you're not really worried about where you're losing heat. The first step is just to get the fireplace going so that there's some basic heat there. Even if you're losing it, you can stand near the fire and become warm enough to survive. Then you can turn your attention to where you're losing the heat, become even warmer, and then perhaps even increase the fire. Step one is to understand where power comes from.

Power comes from eternity, it comes from the void, from the unseen realms. Each one of us has infinite power within us, but it's necessary to access that power and bring it into your life. There may be a great deal of oil under the ground, but unless you can bring it up above the ground you won't be able to refine it and use it to heat your home. The first step is to understand where power comes from. Power ultimately comes from eternity, from life itself. There are different strands of power, though, just as there's power in the sun and power in the wind, power in coal and oil and things like that.

In mysticism we begin to learn about the different types of power and how we can access them. The primary way to develop power is through making your mind quiet, shutting off your internal dialogue. Thoughts drain you. They block your power. As your mind chatters away incessantly during the day and night, you block the source of power. Within you there's an infinite ocean of power. The sun is always burning within you, but it's in a state of perpetual eclipse because you are blocking it with your thoughts. In mysticism, you have to learn how to stop thought completely. Once you stop thought, the power, light, and energy of eternity will pulse through you. That's step one.

To start with, it's necessary to bring order into your life. The program for the new student of mysticism is to practice gazing exercises. Gazing exercises, which are very similar to meditation, involve the controlled use of will and thought to silence the mind. If you were to practice gazing two or three times a day, what you would do is sit down to meditate, open your eyes, or keep them partially open, and focus on something. You might want to focus on a candle flame, a brightly colored stone, a cloud, a star. Whatever you focus on will have an effect upon you. In mysticism we're dealing with the elementals; we're drawing a great deal of power from nature.

Everything in nature has a certain power, a certain radiance, or aura. In mysticism, we become conscious of the radiance and aura of things and we bring those radiances and auras into ourselves. Whatever you focus on will affect you, so you must be very careful about what you choose to gaze upon. Gazing is not, in other words, an arbitrary exercise where you're just, for a short period of time, looking at something and no great effect will occur. A great effect will occur when you practice gazing.

In the initial stages what you need to do is to gaze on something that is relatively stable. I would suggest a candle flame; a flower; perhaps in the evening, if you're outside, a star; or a yantra – the yantras are the ancient mystical symbols.

Sit up nice and straight and for 10 or 15 or 20 minutes simply gaze at the candle flame, let's say, or at the dot in the center of the yantra. When you gaze, don't exert your concentrative powers so intensely that you get a headache. Just sit back. Sit up straight, though, and focus without focusing too hard, sort of like daydreaming. What you want to do is become aware of the object that you're gazing at. Try and feel it, but don't become totally immersed in it or wrapped up in it either. It's not a hard concentration; it's exactly as the word implies, "gazing," looking at something without a hard focus.

As you do this, you should disassociate yourself from all thought. You should ignore any thoughts that enter into the mind in the early stages and eventually, you should stop thought completely. This will really happen of its own accord as the power of your gazing develops.

The idea involves the spheres of attention. You have a certain sphere of attention. Whatever you direct your attention towards, you become. Right now your attention is directed towards your life's actions, your thoughts, your emotions, the interactions you have with others, philosophical ideas, visceral physical experiences.

It's necessary for us to unhook ourselves because right now we are definitely hooked. We're hooked on sensory experiences and ways of seeing things and what we need to do for a while is simply unhook our attention and free it. In other words, we've been looking at something for so long that we've forgotten anything exists. We're so busy looking straight ahead of us that we've forgotten that there are things on either side of us or behind us or above or below or within. By gazing, we're learning to unhook our attention from the way that we now view and see life.

As you sit and gaze for 10 or 15 or 20 minutes at an object and ignore thought and gradually overcome thought or go beyond it – step up to a higher level where there is no thought – you will unhook from seeing life through your eyes; through the senses; through the sensory apparatus; through your intellect, which reasons and analyzes; and also through your emotions which feel. These are three very fine methods of perception – sensory perceptions: seeing, touching, tasting, feeling, smelling and hearing; or analysis: thinking about something, analyzing its qualities, comparing and contrasting; or emotions, feeling: feeling love, joy, fear, apprehension, oneness. These are the three primary methods of perception.

You're going to develop a fourth method of perception, which is the second level of attention. This is intuition. With intuition we "know" things. We can know what something looks like without having to look at it physically. Actually, we can see what it looks like completely. We can feel something without having to go through an emotional process. Intuition is shorthand; it's a faster method of apprehending the true nature of something. We're going to learn to develop the field of attention called intuition, the second field of attention, to a very fine and exacting point. To do this, though, it's also necessary to bring order into the primary level of attention, the island of the first attention.

Early in mysticism it's necessary for you to work very intently, for the first five or six years that you practice the study, at bringing order into your life. You need to bring order into your physical life on the basic level. Your house has to be clean and orderly, everything in place. Anything that you don't need in your life, you eliminate. You go through your closets and eliminate any clothes you really don't wear and give them to someone else or just throw them away. You go through your paperwork, and you're always caught up with it. Your desk is never a mess. Everything is in order. Your career is in order: it's the right one, you're happy with it, you're working hard at it. You're getting enough physical exercise, your body is in good shape, and you're watching your diet. You're not sleeping too much, nor are you sleeping too little. Your relationships with others are good, clean, efficient, happy, and progressive. Your relationship with yourself is good. You don't sit around and feel sorry for yourself; you don't wish for things that you can't be or become. You're taking charge and control of your life. This is simply on the physical level.

On the mental level it's necessary to sharpen your mental faculties, to become precise in your understanding, to not be lazy mentally, to not sit around and watch television but develop your mind. You need to become aware of the transference of power. While in the primary exercises in mysticism and practicing our gazing we develop our awareness of the second field of attention, we also have to see where we're losing power. But more of that in a second – let's drop back for a moment here to the gazing exercises and developing more personal power.

Personal power comes in many forms. We have it within us. As you learn to stop your thoughts, as you practice gazing each day for 15 minutes, then maybe half an hour or 40 minutes twice or three times a day, you'll shut the mind off. As you shut the mind off you'll find more and more power entering your life. You'll simply have more energy.

Power can also be accessed through the elementals. Everything has a power – fog, wind, fire, water. These are all conductors of power and in more advanced mysticism you'll learn how to bring power through these elements, from these elements into your being. There's also power in the etheric, in the ocean that surrounds the island. You can learn how to conduct that power.

When you gaze, don't try and do anything in particular. Just have fun with it. Sit there, twice a day or three times a day and focus your attention on the object of gazing – look at it and get lost in it. But be very diligent. When you start to think, push your thoughts away or if your thoughts are occurring, be very unattached to them. As you do this, you'll gradually unhook your awareness from the sensory. While you're gazing at something – and this is a sensory experience, that is to say, your eyes are focusing on one point, and you can blink and relax your eyes or shut them once in a while, you don't have to be too rigid about it – but while you're gazing, let your other attention wander wherever it will.

You will find that after gazing you'll be in a very relaxed, tranquil state of mind and that suddenly, as you practice gazing for some time, this form of meditation, you'll find that you'll begin to feel less physical. As you walk around through the day, as you interact with people, as you talk to them, there won't be as much of a sense of being a personality but rather of being a whole person.

You will feel that your island is getting larger. Your island is getting larger and larger all the time, or you might say that before we used to think we were the island – all our feelings were those which occurred on the island – but suddenly we find out that our awareness is actually stretching out beyond the island into the ocean that surrounds the island, and we're feeling ourselves as being part of the ocean too.

Once you're practicing gazing every day, this form of mediation, you'll begin to see your power increasing. Then you have to turn your attention to your life and start going through it, going through your physical life, and bringing order into it. You need to do this again and again as long as you live. The house of the mystic, as I suggested, is perfectly clean. Everything is in complete order, but it's not a nihilistic order, it's not an unhappy order. It's a balance that we have to achieve. You'll find that as you go around through your life ordering things, while you create outer order, you'll also create inner order. This order will free you from the physical and its confines.

Your home is a very important place. In mysticism we feel that our home is everywhere. Our home is the earth, our homes are the stars in the skies and the ether and that which lies beyond. We draw a great deal of power from our home, particularly the room we live in and sleep in. That's why your home is a very special place. It should be exactly as you want it to be. The room in which you sleep is very, very important because that's where you do your dreaming, and it's an energy base.

It's a good idea to have your meditation table in your bedroom, to set aside a special corner where you meditate and practice your gazing exercises and other exercises every day. Try and keep this area very clean. Perhaps put a rug down and have a little table that you put your candle on, some flowers, whatever it may be that you're gazing on, but it should be a very sacred place. You'll develop a very strong field of energy there. This energy will permeate your whole room; this energy will help you at night when you sleep, in your dreaming. As you're outside the house during the day, your inner being will constantly come back to your room and your home, in which you're developing a very strong vortex of energy, and will draw energy from it. It's your base of operations. After you've been out in the world all day and you've been kind of worn down by the world energy, when you come home, as soon as you walk inside your house you'll feel that vortex of energy and it will renew you. Your home is where you're developing a field of energy and awareness.

Everything in your home should be as you'd like it to be. It should be a beautiful place, filled with light and color. You should live in a neighborhood where the energy is clean and good. If you don't like where you live, you should change it – it's very important for the mystic because the mystic draws power from where they live. You should never be concerned about spending money on where you live – it's a very, very important thing. Better to drive an older car and spend a little more money on your rent because it's where you spend a great deal of your time and you should feel very good about it. You should feel you're living in a place with good energy, basically.

You have to assess the power of the area where you live. That's why for those who live in Los Angeles – there are many fine areas – but I recommend Pacific Palisades. It's a very good area. It's a place of power. Certain areas of the earth have more power than others, and if you're drawing power from the earth, if you live in a place of power, the energy is with you. It's easier to meditate. It's easier to walk between the crack that separates the worlds, into eternity.

There are places on this earth where there are holes, you might say, in space. These are places where it's easier to pass into the other worlds. We call them places of power and if you can locate your home in a place of power, it'll just make it easier. If you're trying to fly a kite it's much easier when there's wind. If you're very advanced in mysticism, you don't need wind – you can bring the wind up yourself. If you're even more advanced, you can fly your kite without any wind. But in the beginning it sure is a heck of a lot easier if there's some wind around. If you like to fly a kite, you should live in a windy area. If you're interested in practicing mysticism, you have to pay a great deal of attention to where you live. It's always best to live by water, if you can, within a mile or two of the ocean or a lake or a river. The energy or the power within water is a very stable energy and whether you're conscious of it or not, your being will be drawing power from the water. Water is a marvelous conductor of energy.

Speaking of water, it's very important to take showers or baths two or three times a day, if you're practicing mysticism, because water is a terrific neutralizer. During the day we pick up all kinds of different energies that come through the ether and through other human beings, and if you take a shower two or three times a day it cleanses you, not only physically but psychically. It neutralizes any bad energy that you pick up. Try and locate your home near the water if you can. Try and have a lot to do with water. It's a beautiful element.

Keep your house perfectly clean, beautiful, have nice art objects around, flowers, plants. It's very important to have a lot of nice plants in your house. The energy of plants is very conducive to spiritual development. Plants give out a radiance of life. Not only do they give us the oxygen that we need to live in this world, but they also provide us with a luminosity – they have a very high strand of luminosity.

What I'm suggesting is that you're affected by everything in your environment, more than you realize. While you may not see the effects physically, they affect you psychically, they affect your spiritual development, and in mysticism we pay attention to everything. Even the most minute things affect us and we pay attention to them.

You have to draw up a plan for your life. You need to find a place that's a place of power to live in. You need to find a home that feels right – we do it all on intuition. Power will draw you to it if you really want it. You need to have your house in great order. You need to work at a career that feels progressive and good, and you can't be afraid to change midstream if your career doesn't feel proper. You need to associate with people who have higher levels of power. Granted, at work, or just in the world, we're going to associate with all types of people – and that won't necessarily hurt us; it can actually help us if we handle it properly. But in your free time you should associate with persons who are also seeking power because you'll draw higher power from them, and they'll draw higher power from you. If you're just dealing in your free time with people who have no interest in these studies, then they'll pull your power and you'll find yourself being drained.

It's necessary to assess whether the people you spend your time with in your personal life are elevating your consciousness or slowing you down. It's easy to do this. After you've been with someone – not during – see how you feel. Sometimes you can be with someone and feel very elated and excited, but you can be inwardly drained by them. Inwardly they'll take your power and you won't realize it. When two rivers first come together, there's a great deal of commotion, there are a lot of waves. When you initially meet another person or when you have contact with other people, as the two waves of energy – the wave of energy that's in your consciousness and the wave of energy that's in their consciousness – come together, sometimes there's a lot of turbulence. You might sit with someone and feel that things are going well – there's a lot of exciting energy, you see a lot of light – but that isn't necessarily the case, that's only the surface. One of the rivers could be very polluted, and while on the surface there's a lot of action, the pollution in one river could be absorbed into the other river and pollute them both. It's necessary to pay very strict attention to how others affect you.

As I suggested, at work and in the world we have to deal with all kinds of people, and that's fine. We shouldn't be afraid to go out in the world. As a matter of fact, for the mystic, it's a field day. It's wonderful to work and live in the world. It gives you an opportunity to learn about power, to watch it in action, to gain power from others and to help others. A mystic loves the world, loves nature, and loves people. But at the same time, it's very necessary in your own time, when your life does not cause you to be with others, to spend time alone so that you can feel your own energy field and develop it, and to spend time with others who generate higher energy.

After you've been with someone, after they've gone away and you're no longer in their physical presence, about 20 minutes later, see how you feel. This is how we evaluate. Are you in a higher energy state than before you were with that person, or are you in a lower energy state? If you're in a lower energy state and this happens on a regular basis, then you need to eliminate that person from your life. Or if you can't eliminate them – if they're a relative or something like that and you feel you have strong bonds with them, a strong connection – then minimize your contact with them, and when you're with them put up a shield. Just simply become aware that they're draining you psychically.

Now, they may not realize it. They may not mean to hurt you at all, but they still may. You could spend some time with someone who's carrying a fatal disease, and you could contract the disease. They could be the nicest person in the world, and they didn't mean to hurt you. But nevertheless, if the microbes get in your system and you catch the disease, you'll be ill and perhaps die. Simply because others don't mean to hurt us doesn't mean we shouldn't avoid them. If they're sick we should stay away from them unless we're strong enough to cure them rather than pick up their illness. That's not going to help them or us. After you've been with someone, evaluate, and see how you feel.

Now, everybody's moods go up and down. One day you'll be higher, the next day you'll be lower. Simply because you've been with a friend and after being with them you feel a little drained, that's just part of loving and giving. You have to be willing to be with people and once in a while be drained by them a little bit. Once in a while you'll elevate them. That's not what I'm speaking of. Sometimes we have developed associations with persons that are just not right, and we don't break away from them because we're attached. Therefore you really get your power drained. This, of course, happens to women constantly. As you know, one of the primary reasons that women don't attain enlightenment is because they're manipulated and dominated by men – have been for thousands of years. The subtle bodies of women are very fragile, and as men constantly throw sexual energy at them it damages the subtle body, it drains their energy and their power.

You have to learn a new lifestyle, is what I'm suggesting, if you practice mysticism. It's a very tight lifestyle. It's fun and it's exciting. It's very realistic. You have to look around and find out what's going on, not just on the surface, but within. When you see that people are harming you, you have to be willing to push them aside. You have to generate enough of an energy field yourself, through your gazing and other practices, so that when you're out in the world you won't be drained by the world.

Everything is an opportunity for the mystic. Everything is something to be learned. You should never be afraid of experience, but on your own time you have to minimize your contact with things that will drain your power. Start to look at your life, examine it – this is something you do as long as you're here in this world – and see, "Where am I losing power?"

You could have had a relationship that was very, very good for years. You might have been married and it was wonderful, but now it's changed. The relationship no longer adds to either of you, but you're draining each other. Well, the sensible thing to do is break it off. While a certain amount of pain may be connected with that, believe me, it's much better than the pain of dragging it on for years.

Start over. Spend time with people who are more like yourself. We change. Just because you get along with someone for a short period of your life doesn't mean you have to spend your whole life with them. You have to be smart. You only have a certain amount of time in this world. You must always feel that death is around the corner. Never be afraid of it, but recognize its importance. It can come at any time. Don't assume because you're 20 or 30 that you'll live to be 70. We never know if we'll see the end of the day or night. You should live every minute as if it's your last moment. Live your life fully. Don't procrastinate and put off change. Do it now. If you live that way every moment, then you'll have an impeccable life.

Examine your career, whether you're at school, at work or you stay at home most of the time. Determine if you're using your time most efficiently. At the office, do you waste time talking with others when you could be working? Are you always associating with the same people in the office? Have you gotten into an energy drain with them?

Don't talk too much. Mystics don't talk too much. They're silent. Talk and enjoy conversation with your friends. Conversation is a wonderful way to share energy, alleviate tension, and just bring love into our lives. But only talk if you have something to say. If you don't have something to say, if you can't contribute, it's better to listen. Don't listen to those who have nothing to say. Better to be by yourself a little bit.

Now, here you have to be careful. Some people will tend to be indrawn and hear these words, and say, "Well, gosh, since the people in my office are not seeking mystically or spiritually, I'll just sit by myself all the time." All you'll do is make yourself a target. Inaccessibility is very important for one who practices mysticism. You want to pass through the world and not draw attention to yourself. Whenever you draw attention to yourself, people will focus their awareness upon you and they'll send you energy, and the energy that you'll receive is not necessarily good. If you sit in the office and you're too obviously different and you never talk with anybody and you're in your own little world, everybody is going to regard you more than had you blended a little bit. This is not a very healthy thing to do. They'll start to send you bad vibrations and bad energy, and you don't need it. You're very sensitive in the early stages of your development to these different energies.

Blend with the world. Have enough conversation with people so that you blend, but no more. Don't overdo it. Yet don't be afraid to stand aloof, to be by yourself. If we look at those who have been great in the world – Einstein, Buddha, Christ, Thoreau, Emerson, Lincoln – these were all people who went their own way. They didn't follow the party line, but they did so with decorum, they did so with good manners. Always exercise good manners. Be inaccessible. Observe the way you dress, the way you wear your hair – all these things matter. You're picking up points, either pluses or minuses.

Blend with the world. We don't want people to see who or what we really are because they can't fathom it. Most people are so caught up in the dream of this life that they see nothing else. They're caught up in their own fears, frustrations, and illusions. Don't rock their boat. If you do, they may get angry. Pass through the world quietly and become aware of eternality. This is the way of the mystic.

With those of like mind who understand, you can share your understanding. But don't try and convert others or explain what you do to others. Rather, just appear very evenly in the world. Don't stand out. When you stand out, it's just your ego. Be humble, blend, converse with others, be friendly, but be inaccessible. Don't talk to people about your life and your beliefs; keep it to yourself. Talk in a level which people can understand. Talk about baseball or the weather, a little bit about this or that, but don't become too involved unless there's somebody you have very deep communication with. Naturally, if you meet someone whose heart is open, who's interested in higher perceptions, then you can share more with them. But be very careful. Human beings lose most of their power in their relationships with others.

It's very advisable for women to be conscious of how they dress – just don't attract a lot of attention to your sexuality. You've grown up in a society that tells you to display yourself. It's terrible. How can you even have an integrated personality when you're always something on display, an object, a commodity, when you're trying to show yourself off hoping somebody will come along and buy you? It's ridiculous. There's no integrity in that. Dress any way you want to, but be aware – be aware that you're always being watched, that human beings are very conscious and that you pick up energy from people all the time. Blend. Don't stand out either way. Don't be too conservative; don't be too liberal. Simply blend. It's much healthier this way.

We're going to pay attention, then, in our early study, first of all to gazing and meditating. Meditate several times a day to develop power. Then we turn our attention to our lifestyle. We begin by selecting a nice place to live and keeping it impeccably clean. We keep the house in order; we keep our friendships in order; we pay attention to where we go to school, where we work. We're friendly with people – friendly enough but not overly friendly. We don't talk too much; we listen and we learn from life. We spend our free time with persons like ourselves whom we have fun with, who are advancing themselves to higher and higher rungs of consciousness.

We're always aware that there's danger in the world, all of the time – danger of physical violence from others who are not particularly stable, danger from the unseen, from the astral, from negative forces. We're not afraid of danger but we're aware of it. Never underestimate your opponent. The day you do is the day you lose the battle. Respect your opponent, but always know that you can win, if you're clever, if you have enough power, and if you learn the art of patience and waiting.

The mystic is extremely patient. Sometimes it's necessary to wait through a whole lifetime just for one event to occur. You have to be conscious of time and use time to your advantage, but at the same time you have to be very patient and know that eternity does everything properly. You have to have terrific faith in life. Then you can begin, as you bring your life into more and more order, to develop the second attention.

Now, the second attention will develop when you find a teacher. It's necessary to find a benefactor or teacher, one who lives, or who is, the second attention. Such a person has a very strong energy field. They won't look necessarily different physically than anyone else. As a matter of fact, they probably won't stand out at all. That's part of their inaccessibility. But this is someone who has practiced mysticism for many, many years or lifetimes and they have a very strong second field of attention. They live in it constantly. They're no longer aware of just the sensory, mental or emotional interpretations of existence but they live in the ocean all of the time. Occasionally they come on land just to make sure things are going well on their island, but most of the time they're out there in the ocean, traveling, becoming, whereas you are always clinging to your island and it's enough once in a while just to put your foot in the water and maybe go for a short swim. For them, it's unusual to come back on land. They come back on land just long enough to make sure that things are well attended, the gardens are growing well, the pathways are properly cut, and then they're off again.

You need to find a teacher of mysticism, one who generates that power and energy. The way you learn about the second attention is by spending time with them. While you're gazing in meditative exercises and tightening up your life and learning about dreaming, inaccessibility and all of the different things like that – those things will help you develop a certain amount of power – you can't really expect to begin to move into this second level of attention until you have a teacher. The way you move into the second level of attention is that the teacher takes you there. If I'm out in the ocean and you're on land, I can extend a hand and bring you out into the ocean. I can teach you how to swim, teach you how to dive, teach you how to travel through the water. If you just try and go in the water on your own, you'll drown. But with some instruction, you can learn to be a very good swimmer.

The teacher teaches you about the second level of attention. Now, the second level of attention, you have to understand, has nothing to do with this world yet it has everything to do with this world. It has nothing to do with this world in the sense that you can't think about it or discuss it. It's an act of power. I deal with the second level of attention, for example, when I take my students out to the deserts or up into the mountains or to the ocean, and we go to a place of power. A place of power is a multi-dimensional field of existence where it's easier for us to walk through the doorway to the other worlds. I personally can walk through the doorway anywhere, as any teacher of mysticism can – the doorway is everywhere, there's nothing but a doorway – but for those who are new, it's much easier, and even for me it's much more fun, to go to a place of power.

Now, when you go to a place of power with your teacher, the teacher will have you walk with them, or perhaps talk or perhaps be silent. But what the teacher is doing is broadcasting a power, an energy to you. The teacher is actually opening up your second level of attention and exercising it. You'll find, as you go on these journeys with your teacher, your second level of attention will begin to develop. Suddenly you'll develop powers and abilities that you won't even know how or where they came from – they came from the teacher. The teacher developed them for you. It's a transference principle, but it won't work unless you're leading a very tight life, unless you're meditating every day, unless you have great dedication to the study.

The biggest obstacles to developing the second level of attention are the ideas in your mind, your dependence upon senses and your attachment to your emotions. Once we eliminate this, it's very easy. You have an idea, a description of the world. You see life in a certain way. This description has been fixed from the moment of your birth. Your parents, society, books, language, advertising, everything has helped to contribute to your description of the world, the way you see life. The way you see life is not really the way it is. Life is a flux, it's fluid, but you're ordering it in a particular way. You're focusing your attention on certain things, ignoring other things.

The first thing you have to do is learn to let go. The way we cause a person to let go, of course, when they're practicing all the things that we've discussed, is by bombarding them with pure energy. We just take tremendous energy and force and bring it through a person. We turn up the heat – about 50 degrees. As teachers and benefactors we have enough power, which we draw from the elementals and from eternity, generating through us to bring a person right out of their mind and right out of their body awareness into the second attention. In other words, the teacher is actually lifting you out of the first attention. On your own it might take you a hundred years to get out of the first attention. The teacher can bring you out of the first attention in a few minutes, really. But once you've been brought out of the first attention and into the second attention, your first attention will rebel. If we bring you into a cosmic level of awareness, then afterwards you're going to run away from it and want to hide. You're going to want to cling to the physical structure of your being. It's necessary, also, to teach a person how to integrate their experiences in the second level of attention with the first.

Let's say we go out to the desert together, and when we're out in the desert you see the world dissolve, the stars spin around, you move through different multi-dimensional planes. Now what are you going to do with all of that when you come back home, when you have to go to work the next day? Well, you can do quite a lot with it, as a matter of fact. You can see that the desert is everywhere, that the multi-dimensional planes are everywhere, and that you can sit in your office and work and type, have business meetings and do whatever you need to and at the same time be aware of eternity, look inside people, see everything that's happening within them, both subconsciously and consciously.

Eternity is everywhere. That takes a while to do, naturally. The very structure of your being, which you're familiar with, your idea of the world, will feel threatened. Suddenly, when we show you things that are not supposed to be according to your description of the world, you'll say, "Well, this is all impossible. This is frightening. I can't deal with this. I'm going to hide out in that which is familiar." But your description of the world is limited – it limits you, it makes you unhappy, it frustrates you. You have to decide whether you want to stay with it or go beyond it.

Your senses are a problem. You're so used to seeing life with your eyes and your feeling – physical feeling, tasting, and so on – that you don't realize that there are other ways to cognize information. We have to teach you to go beyond the senses. The senses and the intellect are fine in their place, but you don't want them to dominate you. The same is true of the emotions. You associate love with certain pastimes and activities – hate, fear – you have all these associations and we just have to dissolve them all. What we do in advanced mysticism is, we take the dust of your being and reorder it.

You have a certain structure, just like an atom has a structure. It has protons and neutrons and then around it, it has bands of electrons. There's a certain structure that makes an atom of hydrogen or an atom of helium. What we do in mysticism is we take the structure of your being and we reorder it. We dissolve the bonds that hold the personality and the self together and we allow them to reform. We take a handful of sand, which is your being, and we put it carefully and gently down on the ground. And the wind comes. The wind blows the patterns around again and again. The wind is dharma. The wind is the power of eternity. We as perceivers simply learn the art, not of ordering ourselves consciously, because the conscious mind can't possibly order the depth of our being, but of opening ourselves up to the wind of eternity and allowing eternity to order us. This is the art of the mystic.

The art of the mystic is to unhook themselves first from the way they perceive life, which is limited. You do this by exposing yourself to other ways of seeing and feeling. If you're stuck in one dimension, let's pass you through ten other dimensions and in doing so you'll try and get stuck on each one. As soon as we take one way of seeing life away from you, you'll want to grab on to another. That's OK. Each way of seeing that we offer you will be less defined than the previous one, until finally you have a very fluid way of seeing life. You'll have a very simple description of existence which will allow you to live in this world and get through the day just fine. But it's so fluid that you can drop it at any moment and zip off into eternity.

Imagine that you have ten layers of clothing on. You can't possibly go swimming. Every time you want to go swimming, you have to take off all ten layers before you can just get down to your bathing suit and hop in the water. It's a very cumbersome process – so cumbersome that you might not even want to bother. What we do in mysticism is gradually take off one layer at a time and keep it off, until we've got you in your bathing suit all the time so you can just hop in the water and swim. Then we have you swimming most of the time and just coming back on land once in a while. Then we start exploring, as I said, the other islands, the other realities, and then finally that which is the cause of all realities, that which makes everything that is. We enter into eternity itself, which there's no way to describe. Those are the most advanced levels of mysticism.

In mysticism we take ourselves and we hurl ourselves into the light of eternity, and that light changes us and transmutes us. It refines us again and again until we become the light of eternity itself. We do this by using power, energy, and consciousness. We turn our attention to our physical life and order it. We practice gazing. We find a teacher who can teach us these arts, the arts of power.

In mysticism there's a great deal of laughter and happiness because some of the things we have to learn about in mysticism have to do with what is not only on the surface of the ocean, but what is below it. The surface may be happy and have pretty sailboats on it, but underneath there may be some sharks – "Jaws" is lingering there. There are entities, negative forces; there are people who use power badly, bad occultists who may try and attack you and steal your power; all kinds of stuff goes on. It's a tough neighborhood sometimes. In mysticism you have to learn to be fearless, courageous, and powerful and deal with these things. It's really not a problem.

The danger of the practice of mysticism is obsession. This is why it's a difficult path, and I don't recommend it for most people. I would only recommend this path if it is your nature. A lot of people who undertake the practice become obsessed with power. They forget that power is simply a device or a vehicle to take us to eternity – to just make us laugh and make us happy and cause us to merge with our real self. But along the way people become so caught up with power and powers as they develop them that they forget. They were on a journey, a journey to eternity, but on the way they forgot that they were on the journey. They got so caught up in their experiences or something that happened to them, that they stopped traveling. People become obsessed with power – obsession is the primary danger.

We break off obsession by laughing at ourselves, by learning to be funny, by just seeing the joy in life and by having a terrific, terrific love for this world. In mysticism, we're really not in a hurry to get out of this world because we feel that there is nothing but this world. Rather, we seek to see eternity in this world. We know that one day we'll go beyond this world. Just as we were not in it, at one point we'll leave it. But while we're here we love the earth, we love the waters, the hills, the mountains, the streams. We're very connected with nature in the study of mysticism. That terrific love of this life and this world and that which makes this world keeps us balanced. It keeps us from getting too caught up with power; it keeps us from being obsessed.

Our ability to laugh offsets the terror of the infinite. When you look at the infinite, when you deal with that vast ocean, it can frighten you. You're on your little island, you just look around you, and it's almost too much at some times. But when you laugh, it brings the world into order. The humor is important – being able to laugh at yourself. The vortexes of energy that you pass through in mysticism are so strong and powerful – as you watch yourself change from second to second, dissolving and reforming – that you have to develop a good sense of humor to deal with the absurdity of human beings and of this world. The laughter is very important in mysticism, more than in any of the other yogas. The sense of love for this world, and for the people who inhabit it, is very important. Balance is the key question in mysticism – the careful balance of power, of light and of love.

I think personally that mysticism is the happiest of the ways. Mysticism is the path of the warrior. It's the way of adventure. I've practiced mysticism and, of course, all the paths in a number of different lifetimes, and I teach them all in this life. I like mysticism because of its pure joy, because it gives people tremendous life transformation. It's the fastest of the paths when a person can tolerate it. It's the slowest of the paths for most people because they don't do well with it, they become obsessed with it.

All of the four yogas have their place – they're really all one; they're different aspects of the same thing. We divide them to make it easier to understand them. We learn them in modular blocks. As I suggested in our tape on the path of love, I teach all four of the yogas in succession throughout the year. Actually, even during a season, I hop back and forth, but I teach the yoga of love in the summer, karma yoga in the fall, jnana yoga in the winter and mysticism in the spring.

I deal with all of them all of the time because I don't separate them – to me it's self-realization.

You should learn them all – that's my advice. Focus on one, but learn them all because you'll be using them at different points in your development. But I think you'll find that at least the principles of mysticism will help you terrifically as you deal with society and the world and life. You won't want to run away from life or the world because it's the challenge that makes us stronger. It's the ability to go into your office and do well, to succeed with people; to be happy, but to be cautious and not lose energy; to become conscious, not simply of this world, but of all the worlds and play among them; to be compounded and absorbed again and again in that eternal light.

Become perfectly free – this is the world of mysticism and power. Of all the four yogas, it's the most useful for a person who lives in the world. But they're all useful, they're all perfect, they're all pathways that lead to eternity and immortality.

Enjoy them all. Good luck!

SPIRITUAL ABSORPTION AND NIRVANA

SPIRITUAL ABSORPTION

The purpose of life is to be absorbed in spirit. Spirit is an undefinable reality that exists within us, around us and beyond us. Spirit is the essence of all existence. When we see life or the world, time, matter and experience, we feel that life is solid, that it's visceral, that it has meaning. In the world of matter we're born, we grow, develop, decay, decline, and die. In this world that's all there is – growth, maturation, decay, and death. We are all on the wheel of time. Time gives us birth, time gives us death, and time gives us rebirth.

There is a way beyond time, beyond birth, beyond death and rebirth. The way is not to avoid birth, death, and rebirth. The way is not to avoid pleasure and pain, hope and sorrow, sadness and frustration. The way is not to accept nor is it to reject. The way is to become without becoming, to act without reason, without hope, without disbelief, without antagonism. The way is to be absorbed, to be absorbed in eternity itself. Not just to think of God or see God or feel God or even to be God, but to be absorbed, to enter into that endless ocean we call nirvana, to be absorbed, to return to the source, to become immortality itself.

Absorption always exists, always has existed, and always will exist. Absorption is not so much a state of mind or being as it is a clear perception of reality. Reality comes in many forms: people, places, histories, pasts, presents, futures, civilizations, planets, universes, lokas, deities. Absorption does not negate any of these things. Spiritual absorption is not an ending nor is it exactly a beginning. It's simply the integration of that which is and that which is not. You are and at the same time you are not. You are this moment, but you're not the next. You are this week, but you're not next week. You are this life, this moment, yet you're trapped in time.

You think of the future. You live for the future, planning, thinking, evaluating, always hoping that if everything is properly aligned it will all work out. But you must understand, in this world, in this loka, in this physical dimension, on this earth, in this world of time and change, nothing lasts. Everything here is transitory. Your life will end; this world will end. Nothing lasts. The nature of this world is dissolution and transformation. To feel that you can accomplish something that will last is wrong. Nothing lasts. Nor is that wrong, it's not supposed to. This world is eternity as all worlds are eternity. Eternity takes many shapes and forms but ultimately eternity is formless, meaning it can adapt any form and yet at the same time its essence remains beyond form.

The truth of all ages is this: be absorbed. Don't think that spiritual realization, peace, joy, comfort, happiness will come to you because these things, like all things, are transitory illusions. If happiness comes today, tomorrow unhappiness will follow it. If peace comes today, the next day disruption will come. Just when your system is all worked out, something will upset it. That is the nature of this world - that is correct. To be upset about that is foolish.

One must accept the transitory nature of all things and what's more, absolutely delight in them. God does everything perfectly, eternity does everything perfectly. Nirvana is perfect, all things are perfect, except that human beings, and other beings, sometimes feel that things are not perfect. We try and make something into something that it is not and then we suffer. We suffer because we become attached to friends, to places, to things, to ideas and ideals. There's nothing wrong with friends, places, things, ideas, or ideals. All exist suspended invisibly by eternity itself, but for us, in our confusion, to mistake them for something they are not is only to enter into the world of disappointment.

To think that our car will last forever, no matter how much we love it, is foolish. It will only cause us suffering when it changes its current form. To think that people we love will stay the same is foolish because people change. To think that our own ideas are important is foolish. Ideas are not important. People are not important. Places are not important. Time is not important. Nothing and everything has little or no importance. All that matters is eternity. Eternity is God; God is the world, the places, the people, the times, the events. God is existence and nonexistence. It cannot be reasoned, but it can be easily understood.

Be absorbed. Absorb yourself in eternity. Don't worry about this world. Don't worry about your bank account, don't worry about your friends or your family, don't worry about your job, don't worry about your health, don't worry about worry, don't worry at all. Be absorbed. When you think of the future, when you plan, when you think of the past, when you regret, you lose yourself in the finite, you lock yourself into a cage from which there is no escape. The cage is the human web of consciousness. Be absorbed.

To try and leave this world, to try and enter onto the wheel of karma, to spin on it and then to leave is impossible. That which exists must always exist. That which is born must die. You can't escape from rebirth, you can't escape from pain and suffering and sorrow. There is no way out because you exist. And if you exist, you must accept the conditions of existence: birth, growth, maturation, decay, and death. To leave this world is impossible in a sense, because this world is all worlds. Wherever you go you take yourself with you. Wherever you go, if you exist, you take birth, growth, maturation, decay, and death with you. These conditions exist in all worlds.

Be absorbed. When you are absorbed there is no world, there is no time, there is no place, there is no condition. It's not that these things don't exist. When you are fully absorbed in spirit, when you attain liberation, self-realization, satori, when you merge with nirvana, it's not that the worlds, the times, the places, the loves, and the cares don't exist – we just don't see them. In this world we see the world, in the dream we see the dream, but when the dream fades, when we awaken from the dream, the dream soon is gone, we forget. The worst nightmare fades, the worst pain goes away. The most horrible suffering recedes. Even the greatest joys vanish. For this world, my friend, is but a dream. This life is but a dream. All of this that we see and even that which is unseen is but a dream of God's, a dream of nirvana, of endless light.

To be absorbed is to awaken from the dream of life and death and rebirth. To be absorbed is not to go against the flow nor to go with it, nor to become the flow. It is to be absorbed. To be absorbed in nirvana is perfect perfection, beyond words, beyond reason, beyond remorse. Be absorbed at every moment. Be absorbed in meditation, be absorbed at work, be absorbed with your friends, your families, your loves, your cares, your frustrations. Do not attempt to leave this world because there is no world. There is no leaving, there is no coming, there is no self. These are but ideas in the mind of God.

Be absorbed. Be absorbed in perfect perfection, in perfect immortality. Rest assured that eternity does all things perfectly and that you yourself are eternity. If I hold a candle to the sun the flame vanishes. The flame still exists, but it is not perceived. When you are absorbed in spirit, when you think of God, of spiritual teachers, of the highest precepts of existence, constantly, then you will not see the suffering or sorrow of this or any world. You will not see frustration. You will not see death.

This is not a narcotic. This is not a simple forgetting. Rather it is a right perception of the nature of existence. Existence is seamless and perfect. Be absorbed in nirvana. Let go of this world. Don't focus on it so much. In this world we see nothing but news. We hear nothing but views. We listen but we don't hear. We see but we don't view. We have forgotten the secret of secrets – immortality is all that exists. Be absorbed and cut this world away. Cut all worlds away. Throw away desire and hope, love and hate. Be absorbed beyond all. Think only of that which is the ultimate good. It is not the condition of your life or of your body or of your mind that matters but the condition of your spirit, and your spirit is perfect. Be absorbed.

Be absorbed only in immortality. Don't try and be something that you are not. Don't try and be anything that you are. Don't try at all. Be absorbed. Most people feel that one day they will attain, one day they will give, one day they will be – these are idle dreams and fantasies. These things never come to be because we are not. We are not separate individuals in the flow of existence. We are not even existence, which is but a dream. Be absorbed.

Be absorbed in God and light. Settle for nothing else. Tomorrow does not exist. Yesterday does not exist. Be absorbed in this moment and in this moment see eternity. Stop procrastinating, stop feeling that tomorrow, tomorrow, tomorrow you will have an opportunity to realize God, to be what you've always wanted to be. This is but another illusion. Now, let go. Let go of your body, let go of the world, let go of your loves and your hates and your desires. Let go of your ego, let go of your bondage, your frustration, your happiness, your dreams, your cares because there is no perfection in them. There is no peace in them; they are all transitory. You are immortal consciousness caught up in a transitory world.

Be absorbed. Focus not on this one simple world, but on all of eternity. Turn your attention elsewhere and be absorbed. Be absorbed in God consciousness, in perfect perfection. There is nothing else except idle dreams and fantasies.

Be absorbed. Know that within you is truth and light, but truth and light is not exactly as you might think. Be absorbed. Allow immortality, allow eternity, and allow mortality. Put up with your silly self, put up with your frustrations and your illusions. You are quite human and you are supposed to be. You are quite immortal and you are supposed to be. You are really neither. All is a play of existence, world upon world, scene upon scene. The play goes on forever. We wake up in one lifetime and we play a role. We wake up in another lifetime and we play another role. We wake up forgetting, gradually remembering and then we fall asleep again, and we dream another dream of immortality.

Be absorbed. Accept the illusions of life without criticizing them. Meditate in stillness. Still your mind each morning and each evening when you meditate. Still your heart during the day. Don't give yourself to others. Give yourself only to the God in others, to the immortal perfection in others. Don't think of people, think of truth and love. If you see truth and love in people, then think of truth and love in people, but don't think of people because they are transitory, they do not last. They are but shadows. Love light. Light is your real friend. Light will never ever fail you. All people, places, and conditions of this world will come and go, but light will always be with you. Stay with light and love light.

Be unafraid of all. There is nothing to fear. Death is but a mere tickle. Life is the same. Immortality is all that exists. Listen to these words and be absorbed. Meditate with your eyes closed. Release yourself, give your life away to God, to eternity. Don't try and live it for yourself anymore, you've tried that and it only ends in limitation and frustration.

Be absorbed. Allow life to be you. Enjoy the moment, enjoy this world. Enjoy everything and enjoy nothing – nothing being immortal consciousness, nothing being eternal awareness. Be absorbed. Love unconditionally all, but save your deepest love for eternity. Think of God at every moment because every moment is God. Think of truth at every moment, for every moment is truth. There are no eternal rewards. There is only eternity itself, matchless, perfect and shining, your real nature.

Be absorbed. Lose your mind, your heart, your being in the ecstasy of existence. The fathomless ecstasy of nirvana, beyond feeling, beyond non-feeling, beyond self and non-self is nirvana, the shining void, endless, perfect, has always existed, and will always exist – the fabric of reality itself sewn into different forms and patterns, yet beyond all forms and patterns. All worlds spring forth from nirvana, all worlds return unto it. The self itself is but a projection of nirvana; we are all projections of nirvana. There is nothing but nirvana, nirvana being immortal consciousness. Be absorbed.

Be absorbed in that which you are and that which you are not. Don't fight, don't struggle. Be absorbed instead, because if you fight and struggle you will either win or lose and be satisfied with neither. Be absorbed. It is the way between life and death, the way between success and failure. It is only in absorption that true peace will come, that true rest will come, that real spiritual liberation occurs – not an egotistical serving of others, not an egotistical loving of others, not an egotistical knowing – be absorbed in immortality itself. There is nothing and no one else but your dear friend, eternity, who has always loved you, who will always love you.

Enjoy the transitory but know that it is transitory, a mere reflection of the eternal. Enjoy the beauty of the children's pageant, but realize that the children go away. The curtain closes, the auditorium empties, and you are alone, alone with your own immortal reality. Watch your self-form appear and disappear in the maya. Know that the maya, the illusion, is God too.

Don't condemn. Be absorbed. Don't judge. Be absorbed. Don't judge your judgment. Be absorbed. Be absorbed in eternal perfect awareness. Be absorbed.

There is weather in the world. There is weather in immortality. Weather takes many forms. Where does it come from and to where does it return? This is your concern, not the weather. There are vibratory patterns in the subtle physical world. There are winds of dharma, just as there are winds in the skies of this world, and in all worlds the wind of Shiva blows, the transforming energy of existence moves all the worlds and all the conditions of maya. Be not concerned with weather, be not concerned with transformation. Rather, know that which is transformation, that which is the cause of all that transforms, that which is behind the surface. Be absorbed in that, your real nature.

This transitory body, this transitory personality, are not yours. They are but donations from eternity. Enjoy them while they last, but be absorbed. Remember, you are the master of all conditions of this and all other worlds. You are the mistress of immortality. Stop trying, stop giving, stop loving. Do not deceive yourself, it is not you who try or give or who love. Be absorbed. These ideas, no matter how wonderful and good, only bind you. Release them all and be absorbed. Become a slave of immortality. Do the bidding of God. Fight if you must against God, but know that God ultimately always wins. Your higher self always wins.

Be absorbed. Be a mistress of eternity. Eternity is your lover. It comes and awakens you. It challenges you. It asks things of you. Do what it will. Be a loving mistress, be passive, watch the passing of generations, the births, the deaths, the transmutations, and be unaffected. Feel love, feel sorrow, feel joy, live fully, but feel none of these things as you feel them. Watch with the eye of the sage, with the eye of intuition and see beyond this physical plane, beyond all planes. Enjoy your transitory nature; be absorbed. Look deep within, look far beyond, but remember it is not you who are seeing through your eyes, not as you know yourself to be. Fathom that, plumb that, feel that.

Be absorbed. No more promises, no more good intentions, no more resolutions, only absorption. Give this world up and yet love it and serve it fully. Give up your family, your friends and yourself, but stay with them all. Be absorbed. Forget success and failure, yet try to be successful and don't mind failure.

Be absorbed. Learn the lessons of immortality, be they difficult or be they easy, with an even mind. This evenness of temperament will come through your meditation; through directing yourself to a realized spiritual teacher who is absorbed and who will channel the light of the dharma to you; by meditating on the dharma, on the gods and goddesses, on the self, on the personal or impersonal aspects of God, on nirvana. Be absorbed. Spend every waking moment and every sleeping moment enjoying the play of immortality.

Be yourself. Try not to be someone else. Be that which is, allow yourself the freedom to express yourself in whatever way you need to. It's not what you do that matters, it's not what you say. There is nothing that is not holy or spiritual; be absorbed. Be beyond definition and categorization. Allow immortality to work through you. Be but a mere instrument, and that instrument should be so absorbed in the perfect perfection of existence that it knows not even that it is absorbed.

NIRVANA

Nirvana is an endless expanse of unused consciousness and awareness. Nirvana is something that we eternally are. Nirvana is reality. Nirvana is not a time, a place, or a dimension, although it includes times and dimensions and places. Nirvana is beyond the ocean, beyond the sky, beyond eternity itself.

We are alive, we believe, we think, act, conceive, rebel, oppress, liberate. We are alive. We do things without knowing why, inventing answers that satisfy our minds, projecting reasons into the sun and the sky. Long before we came into this world, long before this world, nirvana existed, empty of thought waves, permanent, eternal, everlasting, brighter than ten billion suns, without shape or form yet giving all things shape and form. When this world has gone away, when all the people we know, all the beings who have ever been have said their last, done their last, nirvana will remain.

Nirvana is an end to pain and suffering. This is a world filled with pain and suffering. The absence of nirvana is suffering. A spiritually liberated person like myself, or someone else who has crossed the ocean of life and death and come to rest in nirvana, is the opiate to life. Human beings seek us out because when they're in our presence they no longer feel the pain of separativity. They seek us out and for a few brief moments or hours or days or years, the pain of life decreases.

But then something lures them back to the pain. They seek rebirth, they seek salvation in this world or in some other world. They forget the perfection of awareness, nirvana, the causeless cause. Why do we seek suffering so? Krishna and Arjuna come to mind: Krishna, the liberated soul, he who has become nirvana; Arjuna, the seeker, who wants, yet does not want, liberation. Liberation means extinction of all that you know and all that you love – to the ignorant. To the wise, liberation rather is going beyond this world, beyond time, beyond place, beyond space-dimension, beyond maya, becoming the suffusion of eternal light.

But only the illumined know nirvana. Nirvana does not cause anyone or anything to cease in this world or any other world. Nirvana, rather, is perspective. It's a release from bondage, not simply the bondage of the body or of time or of this world, but the bondage of vision, perspective; thinking that we're someone or something trapped in a body, in time, in place; thinking that we're important, that we matter or feeling that we don't matter.

Nirvana doesn't cause this world to go away because this world has never really existed in the way that we think that it does. Our absorption in nirvana does not alter cause or effect. Rather, what happens is we become absorbed in nirvana. That is to say, the "we" that we always knew is replaced by another we, which is nirvana, in which case this world dissolves, life dissolves, death dissolves, all peoples, places, dimensions, times, causations, pains, loves, all these things dissolve – insubstantial, transitory, like a cloud that moves through the sky and appears to be quite solid, and is, for a time. Soon the winds of time move through it, causing its whiteness to separate and soon it dissolves before our eyes, it vanishes into the sky, it's gone.

All these worlds which seem so substantial to us – our careers, our families, our friends, our concerns, even our silence in meditation – vanish, as does the cloud in nirvana, nirvana being not an end or a beginning. Beginnings and ends are ways of seeing things that we, women and men in this world, create. Nirvana just is.

Why are we so afraid of dissolution of the personality? Why do we seek to be eternal, to suffer forever? Answerless questions. Nirvana is absorption. Suffering is being. Being and nonbeing are really the same, different words to express the same idea. There is no such thing as nonbeing, in the sense that most people mean it. Nonbeing can only be a projection of one who has being. Without one who has being there's no projection of nonbeing. If I don't exist, how could I have a concept of nonbeing, of forward and backward in time? These things really don't exist, except that I give them life, but if I, who am the cause of all things, the creator of all heavens and hells, vanish like the cloud, dissolved in eternity, formless, then all of these things cease to exist. It is I who give them form, it is I who give them formlessness, but if there's no I, then there's no heaven, no hell, no eternity.

A spiritual seeker seeks an end to suffering. The spiritual seeker spends lifetimes looking for an illumined person, one who has become absorbed in nirvana, what Shankara calls liberation while living, that is to say, while still in the body one has attained to liberation. When you come to such a person, when you sit and meditate with them, you experience a minor liberation, a touch of nirvana, just to be in the presence of such a holy person, and we remember – we remember dissolution.

One can only suffer if one is still one. If one is no longer one there is no suffering, no sorrow. But in the mind of one who suffers, suffering matters. Suffering is something to seek because suffering perpetuates being, and the thought of nonbeing, which is created by being, is awesome, frightening, terrible. You may climb to the very highest mountaintop, but then to leave the mountaintop and to go into the thin air itself – it seems impossible. To travel across the deserts, to the ocean, then to swim out into the ocean and disappear, to disappear from your own sight, not simply to lose awareness, nor to become awareness, but to lose sight – nirvana, the ultimate reality. All gods and goddesses, beings and places, astral worlds, physical worlds, the samadhis, all come forth from nirvana.

Nirvana is not separate from life. To think that nirvana is juxtaposed to life, that it's antithetical to life, is really a lack of vision. Nirvana is not empty, meaningless, or foreign in any way. There is nothing but nirvana. But we could say that there are two types of nirvana, from the point of view of the relative mind. There is nirvana in its absolute form. Then there is nirvana as seen from the point of view of form. In the first case, nirvana is not something to be experienced, since there is no longer an experiencer, there is only nirvana, perfect, seamless reality. The second is nirvana in form, nirvana in self-awareness, self-awareness as a being perceiving nirvana. You look, you see the hills, the mountains, the people, you see nirvana, you are part of nirvana seeing other parts of nirvana – two forms.

The spiritual seeker seeking liberation from pain and suffering, which is this world, the transitory, comes to the enlightened person and says, "Please show me the truth. Reveal to me what is right. Show me the dharma, the absolute truth, the way. I want to suffer no more. I seek perfection." And the teacher, who is nirvana in veiled form, through personality, reveals the way, gradually teaches the student the steps to erase one's self. The student follows the steps, learns to meditate, learns to become pure, humble, self-effacing, self-giving, but one thing still remains: nirvana, in its absolute formlessness.

The student will follow all the lessons, if the student is an excellent student, one out of tens of thousands of millions, and will come all the way to the verge of nirvana, to the verge of dissolution. At that moment something will rise up within that student, within each person, and will stop, just short of dissolution. That part of them which is still being will fight for life like the patient on the table who's fighting for their life.

But nirvana has nothing to do with patients or tables or teachers or students. Nirvana is neither concerned nor unconcerned. Nirvana is limitless perfection, everything that you are, all loves, all places, and all peoples. All forms are nirvana, in veiled form. Nirvana is veiled by maya. Maya is illusion, the illusion of separativity, seeing nirvana from this world in separate forms, as opposed to the perfect formlessness of nirvana. To go beyond the categorical mind completely, to go beyond the self, to exhaust all one's karmas, to become nirvana, only then is one beyond the wheel of birth and death because one is not. There can be no death for one who no longer exists, for one who is no longer one. There can be no rebirth. Vanished without a trace. Absorption. Neither death nor birth nor rebirth.

Everyone suffers in this world. All of you who are listening to me, suffer. Even when you are happy you suffer. You suffer even in happiness in the respect that you are not in the effulgence of liberation. The body torments you, the mind torments you, the world, the ignorance, the cruelty torments you, but simply the mere fact that you are not liberated torments you more than all these things.

There is great beauty in this world; there is love, compassion, joy, gratitude, friendship, strength. There is much beauty in this world and in other worlds, but all of these beauties come and go, they're transitory. They should be enjoyed, they should not be shunned. But all of the beauties of all the worlds that have ever been and will ever be, all of the ecstasies that have ever been and will ever be, all of the joys, the loves, when stretched from end to end throughout eternity, will not even be noticed in nirvana.

A candle held to the sun is not seen, so great is the light of the sun. The light of nirvana is greater than a hundred billion suns. The ecstasy is beyond expression, the silence beyond contemplation. The way is free and clear, yet few will reach it and of those who reach it, how many will return? None. That which comes out of nirvana is not the same as that which went in. We walk into the room, the door shuts behind us. Were somebody to open the door and look into the room, they would see no one there. Gone, vanished without a trace. If someone walks out of the room, who's that? Nirvana in veiled form.

Karma binds us to this world, to any world, to anything, to the idea of being someone; selfhood we call it. Karma means essence, substance. Desire creates the illusion of selfhood. We are free-flowing consciousness, we are the thin air, but a desire passes through the air as a cloud does and so the self is born. Something identifies with that desire. Something says, "I am here and I am experiencing this desire. It is my desire." That desire leads us astray, it leads us to something, it offers us a promise, it says, "I want this," or the desire becomes its opposite, aversion, "I don't want that." Likes, dislikes, the pairs of opposites are formed. Soon we construct a world of desires and aversions. We want pleasure, we don't want pain. We want life, we don't want death. We want joy, we don't want sorrow. But life is merely a dream. This world is not substantial, desires are not substantial, all places, persons, and conditions are not substantial. Right now you're in a dream, but you've forgotten that you're in a dream. You think that you're awake, you think that you know – you don't.

Nirvana is waking from the dream of life. The dream, no matter how beautiful, is still a dream and compared with the reality of existence, it is nothing. Nirvana is ecstasy and beyond, an end to suffering, joy and love beyond expression. Nirvana is neither empty nor full. It's not an end to your being, rather it is your eternal being. Seek ye nirvana, seek the skies. This world is transitory. It is not our real home. Our real home is nirvana. Remember, break through your amnesia and remember. Remember in meditation. Sit in silence, stop all thought and recollection will take place. The mind will become calm, shining, perfect. No longer will the mind be the mind, nor the body the body, nor this world this world. All that will exist is eternity.

The void is a projection of nirvana. The physical world exists. Above the physical world are the subtle physical worlds, the astral worlds we call them. Above the astral worlds, the void. The void is the sky in which the planets hang. The ether is the astral. The void supports both the physical and the astral. It's emptiness in the sense that it's background. The void is the active projection of nirvana. It creates the worlds, holds the worlds in suspension and dissolves the worlds. Nirvana is that cause beyond the void because the void itself is transitory. Nirvana is not that which is transitory.

The way to seek nirvana? To begin with, love is usually the best. When we start our journey, we need to learn love. Love is unity, unity and multiplicity. As you meditate you will learn about love. You will learn to love your body, even though it doesn't last; to love your mind, whether it's filled with pure or impure thoughts; to love this very beautiful world, which we are visiting; to love the beings in this world, the spiritual seekers, those who have no conscious interest in spirit yet are naturally spiritual, that is to say their inner being is attuned to eternity while their conscious being may ignore it; those who are vile, who hate others; those who suffer; those who are condemned – to love them all. We learn to love the nonphysical beings, the gods, goddesses, beings, forms, forces. Each one is a projection of ourselves, each one is our self. As our love grows, division ceases. We no longer see the world, people, beings, places, existences, lokas, as separate, but as our own being.

Then we go to the ocean. We leave everyone and everything behind. We take a walk to the beach by ourselves, and we sit on the sand and we look out at the ocean, and we contemplate that which has nothing to do with life as we know it, that which has nothing to do with love, joy – the other world, beyond this shore – we contemplate that void and we become one with it. We learn to love it, its shining, immutable reality. And we see ourselves in it. We see that we are not a person, we are not a body, we are not a mind. We are eternity, we are the shining void, we are the worlds, subtle, physical, the beings. And that's where most people stop. If they get that far, they stop there because again, the fear. The fear of dissolution, the fear of perfection haunts us, but a day will come when you, like I have, will find that, without knowing why or how, you will walk beyond that point and dissolve, swept away by a wind that you couldn't control, try though you could. Then you'll dissolve. There are no words to express it, what it's like.

You may reappear and you'll find yourself in the world again, half man or woman, half nirvana, just enough form to act in this world. Then you'll become the opiate of the masses. They will seek you out to be near you, to feel that infiniteness and you yourself will lead a strange, strange life. Strange in the sense that you will no longer be exactly human, you will be nirvana. Yet you will find that you still exist, you still have a body, what Shankara calls liberation while in the body. And you must wait out your time and go through this life, nirvana serving others, nirvana accessible through the form, to itself, in and through itself.

Then one day the body will pass away. It won't be any different, since you didn't have a body. Others saw you as having a body. There was no body. Nobody at all. Nirvana. Beyond eternity, beyond time.

DEATH AND REINCARNATION

Death is like the ocean. We stand on the shore of life looking out into something that we cannot see the end of. Death appears to be endless. We see its vague beginnings as a person leaves this world, as their consciousness leaves the body at the time of death. They enter into the ocean; they go beyond the horizon. We see them not. We know not where they have gone. Strain our eyes though we may, we cannot see beyond the horizon of this life. Death is a hidden country. It is a land beyond sight, beyond sound, beyond the conditions, laws, and limitations of this world.

Today I would like to share with you a few thoughts on the subject of your death and the experience of death and rebirth. The horizon is not endless, nor is the ocean endless. On the other side of the ocean there is land, on this side of the ocean there is land. The ocean is that body of flux in between the land. While first appearing to be endless, when we journey in our boat into the ocean of existence we find that while the ocean is vast, it is not endless, death is not endless, nor is life. Life and death are two states of awareness. Really there is no life and there is no death. The idea that there is life, the idea that there is death, these are apprehensions that our mind presents to us.

What I mean by that is that the sense of life and death that we have is not necessarily correct. You may feel that you know what life is and surely you do. You know that which you've experienced, but there may be parts of life that you have not yet seen. We can say that you know life to an extent. You probably know even less about death. Yet most people have very fixed ideas about what life and death is. They're quite sure that they know. I would suggest that most people know almost nothing about life and death. They're like small children who at the age of four or five feel they now know all there is to know about our world, its societies, structures, political systems, customs, laws and so on. The way you come to know, the way out of life and death, is through love. Love is the bridge that unites life and death – always remember this.

Death is not the end, nor is it a beginning. It is an endless beginning or a beginningless end. Death is a field of awareness. It consummates life. When we live, we feel that we exist. We're on the light side of the moon. We feel that the dark side is somehow different. When we die and we walk through that invisible door to the other side, we forget about life. We lose our awareness of this world, the memories fade. We still exist, but just as on this side, on the light side of the moon – life, we've forgotten about death – so when we enter into death, most beings forget about life.

Life and death are part of a cycle that we call the samsara. The idea is quite simple. There is God, eternity, eternal awareness, a life force, an essence, an energy, a power – that is existence. We are all part of that. It is us, we are that. This endless existence has always existed and will always exist. There has never been a time that it did not exist and without time it exists also, in time and beyond time. It creates time. It can do anything in no time.

In a facet of the consciousness of the infinite God there is something that we call time. Time is a sense of separativity, a feeling that you as a perceiver – one who has experiences, memories, dreams, foreshadowings, beliefs; one who feels pleasure, pain, joy, sorrow, love, hate, jealousy, enlightenment and so on – that you as a perceiver experience eternity separately. That is to say, you are standing back from the horizon looking at the horizon. We call this life.

Life is the ability to perceive. In order to perceive we must have a sense of separativity. That is to say, we feel that we are standing back from something so that we can see it. When we lose the ability to perceive, we call this death. When we can no longer distinguish our self from anyone or anything else, we call this death. Death is an endless awareness, whereas life is a finite awareness. Death is something that can be experienced on a physical level, it's also something that can be experienced on a psychic level.

For most people death is conceived of as a physical experience. When they die they lose awareness of separativity. They merge with eternity. Look for them everywhere, though we may, we can't find them. Before we knew where they were. They occupied a body in time and in space.

I remember that after my mother died, when I was quite young, I tried to find her. One day, perhaps just several months after she had left the body, I was driving in my car and suddenly I thought I'd go visit her. My mother lived in another town in Connecticut. I lived in southern Connecticut and she lived in eastern Connecticut at the time, and so suddenly I thought I'd go visit her as I often did, every several weeks. I had forgotten for a moment that she was no longer alive, strange though it may seem. Suddenly I was about to turn my car – it was just an inspiration – I was driving along and thought, "Gee it will be nice to go see Mom," and suddenly I was about to turn my car to go and see her – I was driving on the highway at the time – when I realized or recalled of course that she had died, just several months before.

And I was surprised that it had slipped my mind. How could I not remember having gone to a funeral, all the things that occur when one we love dies, and it seemed strange to me. But yet she had always been there, and then she was gone. And I realized that she was no longer on earth. In other words, what I'm suggesting, and this is, I think, a common phenomenon for many of us, is that when a person first dies, someone we've been very, very close to, we intellectually accept that they have died, that they are no longer with us, but something inside of us doesn't necessarily accept that right away. It takes a while, and I think it's only until much later, when we're alone, that suddenly it dawns upon us what's really happened, that someone we've been very close to is gone. And I remember thinking, as I was driving on the Merritt Parkway in Connecticut, that my mother was no longer in this world, that I could search anyplace I wanted to and not find her, that that presence, which I had called "Dorothy," was not to be found. It had returned to the source.

Death, then, is a change in location. It is not an ending of an energy, rather it's an absorption of a field of energy, which we call a person. That life essence that you feel inside yourself or inside any living thing leaves this plane, this material world, and goes elsewhere.

Death is nothing to fear. If you remember back as far as you can, you will remember death, that is to say, the absence of a physical, spatial-temporal location. If you remember that there was a time before this life when you were not in this life, if you remember back then, you will remember no pain, no fear, no horror and that's what it will be like when you die. You should never fear death. Death is not unpleasant. Death is not frightening. It's a completion. We return to the source. We merge back into God.

Reincarnation is the process of awakening. Each one of us has an essence that does not change from lifetime to lifetime. Imagine that you are asleep and that you're having a series of dreams. In each dream you find yourself in a different location. You're a different person in each dream; you have the sense of a different personality. One dream ends and another dream begins. Yet that which is perceiving, the perceiver, the person who is experiencing the dream, the main character through whose eyes the dream is taking place, is always the same. The personality may be different. You might be having one dream in which you are a woman. In another dream you're a child, in another dream you're an adult male, but yet that actual essence, the perceiver that is inside all of those people in the dream, the protagonists, and the central characters in a dream, that essence is the same.

Life is a dream, a dream of many existences. You have a central essence that is unchanging. There was a time when that essence was not aware of its own separativity. At one time you were part of a celestial light of pure knowledge, radiance, and perfection. You existed timelessly, endlessly, as God. Then the eons of eternity moved and that ultimate intelligence, which is your real self, created a dream which we call this world, created many, many dreams without the sense of having created them, which we call the different planes of reality, the physical worlds, the nonphysical worlds. It dreamed itself into those worlds in countless forms and caused those forms to evolve, all projections of itself, parts of itself. It then caused those forms to forget, to forget that they were part of an essential whole. Gradually it awakens them, the severed connection is rejoined, the separate parts remember that they are in essence one. This is the process of reincarnation. Reincarnation is remembering, remembering who and what you really are, that you are a timeless, endless existence.

Reincarnation in this world, as in other worlds, follows a process of linear development. That's one way to look at it. There are many theories about reincarnation. Some people feel that when you reincarnate, that life essence first comes to this world and it goes through a series of incarnations and different levels of creation so that for many lifetimes you incarnate in the mineral kingdom, then the plant kingdom, the animal kingdom, the human kingdom, and that eventually a time comes when you leave the human incarnations. You no longer incarnate here and then you move into subtle incarnations, that is to say, incarnations without a physical body, in the other worlds, the nonphysical worlds, and that eventually after countless subtle incarnations you return to the primeval essence of God. This is a cycle that takes place periodically. The infinite reality that we call God projects itself forth in a cycle of evolution, creating countless worlds, sustaining them, dissolving them eventually back into itself. This happens periodically. This is one theory of reincarnation.

I personally think that this is a very limited way to look at reincarnation. It certainly is accurate in a way, but if we expand our awareness we can see reincarnation very differently. Reincarnation is all about time. The idea is that there's a fixed reality called the moment. You live in the moment right now. If there's a fixed reality called the moment, meaning the now, then we can divide time and we can say that not only is there the now, but there's also the future, that which will occur after the now, and of course there's the past, that which will occur or has occurred before the now.

Why do we perceive this way? It's because our attention has fixated on this thing that we call the now. It is possible for you to unhook your awareness from this moment and project it into any moment so that you could experience this moment as the now, or you could experience any moment as the now. You could move into the future, you could move into the past – all time is eternally present – and experience any moment as the now. You can experience simultaneous moments as the now. That is to say, you could be aware of being at this moment in this moment, in this world, in this time. You could also exist in several futures and in several pasts all at once, or you can experience time in a very, very different way and that is not to divide time into the idea of past, present or future, not to have a sense that you've had past lives or that you'll have future lives, but rather just to see that there is no time. This understanding will free you from incarnation because there can only be incarnation and reincarnation, birth and death, if there's time.

I'm looking at a blackboard and I've drawn lots of diagrams on it with different colored pieces of chalk. All of the things that I look at exist, but if I take an eraser and erase them, then there's nothing. Time creates the world. Time creates space. That is to say, we define space through time, but when we erase time, there's no space, there's no condition. A person who has attained, or experiences, or is what we call enlightened, or enlightenment, lives in a world without time. That's how I exist; for me there is no time.

Now, we wear different hats at different times. That is to say, when we go into work it's necessary to dress a certain way and act a certain way. When we're at home with our friends we relax, put our feet up, and dress a different way. If I'm out jogging I dress a different way. It's not necessary for us to be fixed. We're flexible, we can change and adopt different roles. It is with time. In the physical work-a-day world it's necessary to deal with time. You need to have a sense that, "Well, gosh, I have to get up at 7:00 a.m. and meditate for an hour, and I have to go to work and it takes me 45 minutes on the freeway, then I have to do a certain amount of things today, today being the 9th of September. I have to accomplish a certain amount of things. I have to make plans for what's going to be happening next quarter in our business – projections, tax filings. At the same time I have to be concerned with my sister's birthday, which will be coming up."

In this world as we exist as human beings it's necessary to deal with time, and this does not in any way contradict timelessness. It's a different hat that we wear. Yet while you are operating in time, as you are attending your own funeral, as it were, you can be aware of the timeless. That is to say, you can be in the moment and beyond it at the same moment – they are the same moment. This is the enlightened perspective on time. It's as much of a fixation to say that there's no time exclusively as it is to feel that there is time exclusively. Both are ideas, both are ways of seeing life, but in enlightenment we flow in and out of all ways and at the same time remain beyond them.

Then, it's quite accurate to feel that there is reincarnation, to feel that the soul or essence of a being, what they call in Sanskrit the atman, does exist. That it takes thousands of incarnations, that in each incarnation the soul grows, evolves, and develops, that the essence actually releases more energy in each incarnation.

Think of reincarnation as school. The child goes to school and in each grade the child learns, grows, and develops. One day the child graduates from school, goes, and does something else. In each lifetime we grow and develop, we become aware. Death is going to sleep. Life is awakening from the dream.

In each human lifetime, looking at the incarnations that you have had on this planet in the physical world, we evolve, we make progress. It's like climbing up a ladder. But we forget. You may have had a very advanced incarnation. That is to say, in your last lifetime, or perhaps four or five lifetimes ago, you had a very spiritual incarnation – perhaps you were a monk or a spiritual aspirant, someone who devoted their life to the enlightenment process. Then for the last few lifetimes you may not have reached that level. While the essence of all your lifetimes is contained within you, just as within the DNA is the racial history of our species, so within the subtle physical aggregate that we call the soul there's a kind of a history, you might say, of all of our lifetimes. The impressions are there. We don't always reach that point of evolution. It does come back eventually, but what I'm suggesting is that in the process of reincarnation, while it is true that in each lifetime we are making progress, we are growing and evolving, it's not necessarily a straight line. Every incarnation is not, I suppose, what you might call "higher" than the preceding one. There is an overall course of advancement. We can see a difference.

Each lifetime is a set of experiences. We can divide the human incarnations into three basic sections. In the early human incarnations a human being is not aware of much more than the physical. They're not really interested in spirit, they live for sensory gratification, and that's the way they should be, just aware of the physical. In other words, the outer being, the physical being, the physical mind, is not very well connected with the soul essence, which is pure knowledge. A human being will have hundreds or thousands of lifetimes like this. One can say these are like the animal incarnations and the same soul that is in a human body can have had animal incarnations.

Then the soul enters into a more human phase. In these incarnations the intellect becomes more operative. Reason is developed. A person is more in touch with elements of the soul essence and there's some basic spiritual development. A person becomes interested in religion, things like that, philosophy.

In the third segment of the incarnations, spirit becomes dominant, an interest in spirit. After thousands of incarnations in this world a person begins to meditate and seek their soul essence, to find their identity. That becomes the most important thing in their world. They no longer are satisfied by the things of this world. Up until that point, like the child playing with a series of toys, they've been very happy to play with this world – with power, politics, material possessions, love relationships, all of these things have been wonderful toys that have provided hours and hours, lifetimes literally, of amusement. But then a time comes when we put away the toys of childhood and we graduate to something else, and that is the spiritual quest for enlightenment. We begin our journey, and this journey takes thousands of incarnations. In each lifetime we learn something new about spirit and its essence. After hundreds of thousands of incarnations, one finally attains enlightenment. Enlightenment doesn't occur in one lifetime. It really occurs gradually over a series of lifetimes. Once you have attained enlightenment, then a number of options are open to you, which we'll talk about in a couple of minutes.

But let's consider the off-world incarnations for a minute. What I've just described to you is a kind of standard way of looking at incarnations. However, this physical world that we're in right now is not the only world. There are other planets in the physical world, in the physical universe, but also there are other universes that are not physical. We call them lokas. These are other planes of existence, other dreams that God has, that are very, very different than the dream we find ourselves in now. I myself come from a different loka. That is to say, some souls have their origin, they begin the series of their incarnations, in this loka, the physical world. The physical world not only meaning this particular earth, but all places that are like this earth, that are subject to the physical laws, that have matter and energy and so on. But then, some souls begin their cycles in nonphysical worlds. One is not better than another. You could have been born in Australia and you could spend all your life in Australia, or you could travel and migrate to America.

Some souls will, in a certain cycle of the creation, spend all of their incarnations in one loka. Some will change lokas from lifetime to lifetime. In one lifetime you may be born into one loka, in another lifetime another. Normally a person will spend a series of incarnations in a particular loka. You may come into the physical loka, meaning the world, the earth or other worlds like this, for ten thousand or a hundred thousand incarnations. Then you may shift to a nonphysical loka for maybe another hundred thousand incarnations. Now this may seem like a lot of time. I mean, it's enough just to get through the day sometimes, let alone a year, let alone a lifetime, let alone a hundred thousand incarnations. But if you remember that you are timeless, that you are eternal, that you have always been and you will always be, then a thousand lifetimes or even a million really isn't all that long. You get a different time sense, in other words, after a while, as you get a broader perspective on existence. Yet you haven't always been in this current form. Now let me try and explain this.

You date your birth, your inception in this world, as your beginning. In my case I was born on February 9, 1950, in this lifetime. Before that time I didn't exist, from the point of view of this world. But when I started to breathe in this world, you could say, at the time of birth, that's when I came into existence. Then someday I will leave this world, I will no longer be here. And we say that that's the time of death.

That is one human lifetime. The events that occur within that lifetime, the days, the weeks and months and years, encapsulate our experiences, our feelings, our hopes, our loves, our frustrations, all those different things.

Now from the point of view of reincarnation, we could talk about our existence in a slightly larger form. We could date our existence back to the first incarnation that we had, and just as we have a birthday, the day we were born in this world, so there was a time when we actually took our first incarnation. Our first incarnation may not have occurred on this earth. It may have occurred billions and zillions of years ago someplace else. But there was a first one. Now the question arises, of course, immediately, well what was before that first incarnation?

Before that first incarnation, you were the essence. You were not divisible, you were one with God. Then when you first manifested, when you first moved out of that infinite light and part of that light filled up a form, be it a physical or a subtle physical form that was your first incarnation. There will eventually be a time when the sleeper awakes from the dream and you will not take incarnation anymore, but that probably won't be for a long, long time. And when you do, it isn't that you won't be, let's just say you'll be God again. Difficult to explain, but I think you can grasp what I'm pointing in the direction of.

Then, your first incarnation may have been in this loka or in another loka. Most people in this world, on this earth, are originally from the physical loka or from some of the lokas beneath the physical. There are some people in this world who came from other lokas, and one birth is not better than another, one loka is not better than another. All are aspects of God, but an understanding of the lokas you pass through can sometimes help you understand why you deal with life the way you do. Some people are very oriented to the physical, and that's because their primary loka of origin has been the physical loka. Others came from lokas of spirit, of light, so they gravitate more to light than they do to earth. They may love the earth, but their natural inclination is more towards light. Others may gravitate more towards energy because they came from lokas where energy is very manifest in a very strong way. There are a number of different lokas. It's like having different dreams.

But ultimately what matters is where you are now. This is the essential point that you should concern yourself with. Where you've been is an interesting historical fact, but where you are at the moment is our primary concern.

Enlightenment is the awareness of eternity. Not to be aware of eternity as an objective reality, but to be eternity's awareness, to be aware eternally, to be eternity and aware. Awareness eternal, eternal awareness. Reincarnation is a process by which that awareness becomes aware of itself. That's reincarnation.

Karma is action. Karma is a Sanskrit word that suggests that there is a cause and effect relationship in space and time. If you save a dollar every day, then at the end of the year you will have put away $365. That's karma. Karma occurs within a particular lifetime. For every action, there's an equal and opposite reaction. The idea of karma is that if you do something to someone or something, it comes back to you.

Most karma is not physical. Any physical karma that occurs actually is a reflection of subtle karma. Most people have a very simplistic idea of karma. That is to say, they think that karma means that because, let's say, you hit someone, someone's going to hit you someday, or you brought someone a present and someday you'll get a present. That isn't what karma means, really. Karma has to do with awareness. The idea is that you generate a certain field of energy, and that field of energy creates awareness, your awareness, and depending upon the type of energy you generate, that will condition the energy field, which you call life, that you experience, and that there's a causal effect from one lifetime to another between these energy fields that you call life, and that your perception of life is regulated by what you did to some extent in your prior existences.

If you took a French class and it was introductory French and you studied it very well and you did a really good job, then you'll find that when you take a more advanced French course it will be easier. If you didn't do a good job it will be very difficult. Karma suggests that in each lifetime we have a certain number of experiences, but that we develop our awareness in a certain way, and that that awareness will be with us in our next life and that awareness will cause our happiness or unhappiness.

If you didn't learn a language well and suddenly you went to a foreign country, you might have an unhappy time because you couldn't communicate. If you learned the language well it might be just the opposite. If in your past lifetimes you have not become as aware as you could be, then in this lifetime you may be groping with a lot of inner problems. You may be plagued with doubts, frustrations, fears, jealousies, or hang-ups. Whereas if you worked these things out in your past lives, then in this lifetime you'll be able to deal with them more easily. Karma, in other words, is our mental state. And while our mental state, to some degree, is affected by the world that we're in – by our parents, societal conditions and so on – the actual deeper field of awareness, which comes out more specifically when we begin to meditate but exists to begin with, that general field of awareness that we call personality, that which is behind the ego, is a progression of our past lives – that's karma.

A person who hates, a person who injures others, they experience karma. Some people call that bad karma. Their karma doesn't mean that physical things will happen to them that they've caused to happen to others, but it means that they will suffer. Because by experiencing a lot of hate, by causing others to suffer, they'll put themselves into a mental state that's very low. And in that lower mental state, which they will also have at their next birth, they will experience anguish and frustration. A person who dedicates their lives to the welfare of others, who gives constantly and works unselfishly for the well-being of others while remaining humble and happy, advances their awareness so that they will experience more happiness in this life and in other lives.

What I'm suggesting is that if you have good karma, that doesn't mean that you'll be born into a wealthy family in your next lifetime. Rather, what it means is that you'll have inner wealth. Your awareness of spirit will be greater and therefore you'll be happier. You can be born into a very wealthy family and be unhappy. You could be mentally deranged, you could be tormented by guilt and jealousies, you could be unhappy. You could be born into a poor family, but if your mind was vast and broad and your spirit conscious, you could be happy. Karma is not a physical reward. It's not a reward at all. Nor is bad karma a punishment. They're operable results from things that have been done in prior births or within this lifetime.

Reincarnation is awareness. You are trying to become aware of the timeless center of existence. In order to access and bring out the knowledge from your past lives, be they past lives in this loka or in other lokas, it's necessary to meditate. A certain amount of this information will come out spontaneously, without having to try, but to really bring out the deeper essence of your being, the knowledge and powers from your past experiences, it's necessary to meditate.

When you meditate you open the doorway to eternal awareness. When your mind is in an operative state, when you're always filled with thoughts, your thoughts and the images of thoughts and ideas that pass through your mind are like a screen that stands between your conscious self and your deeper self – the aggregate of forms, all the different selves within you. When you stop thought the curtain parts and the knowledge and powers – all the different selves from your past lives, all the different things that you are – gradually emerge and rejoin you. You become one with them. The personality from this life dissolves and all the personalities from the other lives emerge, one at a time, and then they all merge, all the personalities merge, into one being. All of your old friends return.

When you meditate for a specific period of time, you stop thought – and this process occurs automatically, you won't necessarily be conscious of it, you'll just be different. But it's important to try and meditate not only at specific fixed times, but all of the time. This will happen automatically. If you meditate each day, for an hour or two a day, you open that doorway. You'll find that also then, as time goes on, you'll spontaneously meditate, there'll just be less thought in your mind. There will be enough thought to think whatever you need to think, but the rest of the time the mind will be still, and as it's still you'll become aware, not so much of the specific memories from your past lives, because really they're neither here nor there, but you'll just become aware of awareness itself. All those various selves will emerge.

That's why it's so difficult to explain to a person about the nature of God or truth, reality, because these perceptions are so deep, there are no words. When you meditate you will recall what truth is, what life is all about. You can recall death, dying and being reborn; you can see the dreamer in the dream – all these things that I've only lightly touched upon in our conversation today.

Feel that death is not the end, nor is death a beginning. Death is simply a different dream that we have for a while. There are intermediate states that lie between birth and rebirth, which we shall be discussing on the Tibetan Rebirth tape, but what is of real importance, in my estimation, is right now. If you can gain a sense that you exist in this moment and live that moment fully, and at the same time begin to perceive that you are an aggregate, you are not one personality but that you are a collection of selves that have existed timelessly, and that you even have future selves, which you can perceive, and that beyond all those finite selves is one infinite, perfect reality that human beings call God.

If you can perceive that you are all of those things both within this moment, other moments, other lokas and yet beyond all of that in nirvana, then you will be at the core of life, then you will be able to play in this world and enjoy time, enjoy your life, enjoy your death, enjoy your rebirth. You will also be able to, in this life, in this moment, see eternity, which is beyond all lives and beyond all moments. It's not necessary to wait for death to understand existence. Death does not bring any more of an understanding of existence than life does. Awareness does. Awareness is. Awareness is eternal understanding in life, death and beyond.

Try not to think so much. Try not to work out the systems of life, death, and rebirth. Eventually you will understand them. They're quite technical, but all those technicalities don't really matter. You may not understand how the car works that you drive, how the fuel injection system works. You don't really need to – all you need to do is know how to drive it. At this point in your evolution, don't be concerned about the technicalities of the rebirth process. They become interesting in very, very advanced states of spiritual consciousness and they can be used for special forms or ways of attaining enlightenment, which we will discuss in the Tibetan Rebirth tape.

But for now, just become aware of both time and timelessness. As you meditate, allow those different selves to speak through you. You don't have to think about them or focus on them. Don't worry about having a recall from your past life experiences. You're not trying to remember specific data or what a certain day was like or a certain world was like. You've had those experiences. Live in the now, look at this world, look at the people here. Because if you're too absorbed in your past experiences you'll miss now.

It is nice if you can bring through the power and knowledge of the past lives into this life, which doesn't necessitate the exacting knowledge of who or what you were or what you did. The knowledge just comes. That will come through meditation and self-giving. In your passive meditation, as you sit and still the mind, and in your active meditation in which you work for the welfare of others, these things will return to you. It happens automatically. You don't even have to try. If you just meditate and work for others, it will happen.

But once in a while, take a walk on the water. Walk out on top of the water, beyond the horizon into eternity, and then you'll understand there is no death, there is no life, there is no time. There's only eternity. Perfect, matchless, shining, fun, brilliant, effulgent, humorous, exciting, awesome – totally awesome.

SAMADHI AND THE SUPERCONSCIOUS STATES

According to Brahmananda, one of the advanced students of Sri Ramakrishna, the spiritual life can be divided into two phases. The first section or phase is separated from the second section or phase by a person's entrance into samadhi. The second phase of self-discovery begins with the entrance into samadhi.

I'd like to consider with you for a few minutes what the nature of samadhi is, examine the concept behind the samadhis, and try to gain an understanding of not only why an individual seeks to go into samadhi and how that occurs, but also what the result of this process is.

There are four basic states of awareness that a human being experiences. The first is the waking state of consciousness. The waking state of consciousness is that awareness – or that field of awareness, that aggregate of awarenesses – that you experience when you're awake and your mind is active. The waking state of consciousness includes your moods, emotions, thoughts, feelings, and perceptions. From your greatest happiness to your lowest depression, from your strongest belief in yourself and in God to complete self-doubt, from lust and hatred to pure and noble self-giving, your prayer and meditation, all of the things you experience while you're awake are part of the waking state of consciousness.

The second state of consciousness is the dream state. When you go to sleep and enter into the world of dream, you walk through a doorway into another type or level of existence. This is the dream state. All of the experiences that you have in the dream state – whether you are experiencing yourself as you are in this lifetime, that is to say in the dream you conceive of yourself as the same person you are now with the same name, the same identity who's in a dream having experiences, or if you dream yourself as something else; sometimes in a dream you may find that you're another person who's having the experiences within the dream – regardless of what experience you have in the dream, whether it's a frightening dream, a happy dream, a revealing dream, a dream in which you have meditative or spiritual experiences, all of the experiences and awarenesses that you have in the dream state belong to the second primary level of consciousness.

The third level of consciousness is the deep sleep state. When you are neither awake nor in the dreaming state, you are said to be in the deep sleep state. That is to say, your body is asleep but you are not dreaming. In the deep sleep state, there is no sense of "I." The ego is not operative. The ego is the identity, the "I," the sense that, "I am, I exist, I am a certain way, I am not another way." This is the ego sense, the sense of "I." Naturally, in the waking state there's a sense of "I." It is you who are listening to this tape; it is you who are having the experiences that are occurring right now; it is you who reflect on the things that have occurred in your past; it is you who project or consider the future. You are the experiencer, you are the doer, you are the recipient of actions. That's the sense of "I" that you have in the waking state.

In the dreaming state, it's the same thing. You may dream yourself as yourself, or as I suggested before, you may dream yourself as another person or another being. But still, whoever is experiencing the dream has a sense of "I." I am the experiencer of the dream, I am the person or the being who is in this dream who's passing through whatever world or reality you're in in the dream state. But in the deep sleep state, there is no "I" consciousness. One merges into a third level of awareness, which is egoless.

Almost all human beings spend their lives and lifetimes revolving between these three states of awareness. Even most higher spiritual experiences, that is to say, experiences that a person has in meditation or through prayer or just spontaneously, we would classify as having occurred in the waking state or in the dreaming state. Because while you are having a spiritual experience of some type – suddenly you're feeling ecstasy; suddenly you feel yourself merging with the light of God; your awareness has quadrupled; you're seeing into alternate realities; you're feeling a deep peace, joy, power, whatever it may be – there's still a sense of you are the one who's having the experience. Without that sense of "you," there's no one to relate the experience, to remember the experience. That's why we classify your higher spiritual experiences in the waking state. Of course you can have them in the dream world too.

The dream world is a real world, as real as the waking world. It's a different plane of awareness. We call it the astral world in which you can create, just as someone can make a movie and can create a world in that movie with scenery and lighting and actors and actresses, scripts and so on. Each night when you go to sleep you do the same thing, and actually you do the exact same thing when you're awake. There is really very little difference between waking and dreaming. But more on that another time.

In a person's cycle of incarnations, after you've had many, many lifetimes and you've moved into the third cycle of incarnations, the higher spiritual incarnations, a person will have a continuous flow of spiritual experiences. They've dedicated their lives to self-discovery. They're meditating each day and going deeper within themselves. They're learning to find a deeper purpose and meaning to life. But a time comes when a person begins to experience the fourth state of awareness, the fourth bardo of consciousness, the fourth level of ecstasy.

The fourth level of ecstasy is samadhi. The first level of ecstasy is the waking state, the second level of ecstasy is the dreaming state, the third level of ecstasy is the deep sleep state, the fourth level of ecstasy is samadhi and the superconscious states. Samadhi is not simply meditation. Samadhi is absorption, absorption in eternity. There is no difference between samadhi and the superconscious states. Various spiritual teachers and enlightened persons have discussed and classified the samadhis. Some say that there are four samadhis, some say that there are five. Some say that there's something beyond samadhi called nirvana.

Now, to begin with, you must understand that when we discuss the samadhis and the superconscious states, it's really impossible to pin down what they're like because when we're discussing them we're looking at them from the point of view of this world. That is to say, you are listening to what I say and as you listen to what I say, you are analyzing, feeling, weighing, trying to come to grips with it, as you should be. The perspective that you have in your examination of the samadhis at the moment is that of a perceiver. You, the ego, the "I" consciousness, are turning your fields of attention in the direction of the samadhis. But it's impossible to really understand the samadhis through the ego sense. However, the ego sense, your sense of "I," needs a description, which is why, of course, I'm making this tape, because the mind has to have some idea of what lies beyond itself so that it can go beyond itself.

You've gone someplace on a wonderful vacation. You went to Hawaii, maybe you went to Maui or Kauai, and you saw the volcanoes, the rain forests, you felt the tropical winds blowing in at night as you sat on the balcony of the hotel. You listened to the surf crashing. You've had a beautiful experience. Now you've come back to try and share that experience with your friends because you felt it was worthwhile. But your friends are deaf and your friends are blind. They've never seen, they've never heard. How are you going to try and describe the beautiful experiences that you had in Hawaii? They've been blind all their lives, so it's not as if they've ever seen a palm tree, it's not as if they've ever seen the stars at night. You can't do it through Braille because even if you could, they have no sense of what you're talking about. They can't hear, so how can you describe what the surf sounds like or the trade winds, the tropical winds as they blow at night, the sounds of the birds, the night birds calling? This is what it is like to try and describe samadhi and the superconscious states to someone who has not experienced them. It is like trying to describe this world to one who has no senses.

But still, it's necessary to paint a picture. The picture is important because it gives us at least an intellectual appreciation of why we're engaged in the process of self-discovery. An old parable is told sometimes in trying to explain this point. Three friends were out climbing a mountain, and one, the one who was in the lead, reached a very high ledge above the other two. He looked down to the others and said, "God, this is the most beautiful thing I've ever seen," and then he went over the ledge and he was gone. The other two didn't know what to do at first, so one of them, the next one in line, climbed up and peered over the ledge and said, "Oh my God! This is the most beautiful thing I've ever seen," and then disappeared. The third person had to decide if they wanted to see what was over the ledge. They had to climb up themselves and see, or they could just go back down the mountain without knowing. Of course, no one knows what that third person did, but we can assume that he came back down, since we have the story.

You can observe a person go into the superconscious states; you can watch them dissolve. They can't explain to you what it's really like, but if you sit and meditate with someone who's in samadhi, who goes into the superconscious states, a field of energy is generated around their being that is so strong that you will experience to some extent what it's like. You'll get a feeling for it. Or, if you can meditate well, you can meditate on someone who is enlightened, who goes into these states of awareness – even if you are quite a distance away – and access that consciousness and light. But before we get into how you go into samadhi, let's take a look at the different samadhis.

As I suggested earlier, Patanjali and some others have said that there are a number of different samadhis, and there's no exact agreement on how many there are because there's no way to describe them. Where one begins and another ends is very difficult. Some say there are three, some say there are four, some say there are five.

I have a very simple system for explaining the samadhis. I feel that there are two samadhis, only two. One samadhi is salvikalpa samadhi, the other is nirvikalpa samadhi. Salvikalpa samadhi would include all of the lesser samadhis because I don't think they're really all that different. Nirvikalpa samadhi, however, is qualitatively different. I find this much easier, but choose whichever system you prefer. All of them are imperfect ways of describing that which is indescribable.

Now, salvikalpa samadhi means the following. When you enter into salvikalpa samadhi, any of the lesser samadhis, not that they're very lesser (Rama chuckles softly), you merge with eternity, you become God. In most advanced states of meditation, a person meditates on God or truth, light, joy, nirvana, the Buddha, the Christ, whatever it may be. As they meditate, they have experiences, but there's always the sense of being the enjoyer: "I am enjoying eternity. I am experiencing the ecstasy of existence. It's all-pervasive and there's an awful lot of it. There's a reservoir. It's filled with wonderful, clear, pure water, and I'm sitting here drinking it. Some days I drink more, some days I drink less." That's meditation. Advanced meditation is drinking a lot of this pure water, which is more than most people do, who don't drink at all or don't even know that there's pure water to drink or run away from it or shoot those who drink it and oppress them.

Salvikalpa samadhi means not simply sitting around drinking lots and lots and lots of this water, which has a purifying effect on one's life and one's being and gives you strength and clarity; that is advanced meditation and it occurs after many, many years and lifetimes of practice. Salvikalpa samadhi, in other words, doesn't just mean having a really high meditation where the room fills with light, everything is bright and shiny, and you feel one with the dharma and the flow. That's not salvikalpa samadhi, that's a high meditation.

Salvikalpa samadhi means that you lose your individual awareness as a person. You no longer have a name, an address; you're no longer in this world at all. There's no sense of the earth, time, space, past history, future possibilities. All of that goes away. All of that is completely erased. You dissolve, but in your dissolution you become something. You become God. You become eternity. There is a sense – not in the human sense, not in the way of thinking, "I'm God" or "I'm eternity," if you're thinking these thoughts you're not in salvikalpa samadhi – that you are the all-pervasive existence, that existence has an awareness which cannot be described in words. That is salvikalpa samadhi.

In other words, you are no longer drinking the water. You jumped in the water and dissolved in it, and now you have the sense – not as you did as a human being, not through thought or understanding – that there is an awareness that permeates all of eternity, and that is what you are. Thou art That. That thou art. That sense of timeless perfection, which you are, again, not from a human point of view – that's salvikalpa samadhi. You have become God, in other words. You have become eternity and you're conscious of that, again, not in the way that most people are conscious.

Remember, this doesn't mean that today you sat down and had a wonderful meditation and you just felt ecstasy everywhere, you felt the pure joy of perfection, light was everywhere, there was nothing but light. That's not it. As long as you're still having these types of perceptions you're having very wonderful and very advanced meditations and that's quite fine, but you haven't come near the samadhis yet. In the samadhis there is dissolution and undifferentiated reality. There's no sense of light. There's no sense of joy. There's no sense of God. There's no sense of perfection. There's no sense of bliss. There's no sense of peace. All these are experiences that are had by an individual, but you are no longer individual. Your individuality melts and merges with eternity.

Some people fool themselves and they think that they're going into samadhi. But one thing I can tell you about samadhi is it's not pleasant. It's not happy. It's nothing to look forward to. It just is. Nor is it unpleasant. Nor is it something not to look forward to. But people seem to think that samadhi, in the spiritual life, is the pot of gold at the end of the rainbow, and it's not – because there's no rainbow and there's no gold and there's no you when you're in samadhi. There's no way to describe it.

Some people think that, "Well gosh, in samadhi there's no emotion, there's no joy, there's no light." And that's true. But nor is there a lack of emotion, a lack of joy or a lack of light. There's simply no way to describe it. All I can say is that in salvikalpa samadhi, that essence that you are is aware of being an essence. That's salvikalpa samadhi. That's a very advanced spiritual state. If you are capable of going into salvikalpa samadhi in this life, if you attain that, then I would say that you were enlightened, partially enlightened. Partially enlightened.

Nirvikalpa samadhi is beyond that. The only way I can describe it for you at all in words and images is simply to say that nirvikalpa samadhi is an end to everything and a beginning to everything. Nirvikalpa samadhi means that there will be no "I" sense at all, even of "I am God." You will not even have the conscious awareness of being undifferentiated reality. It's beyond the knower and the known; it's beyond the subject and the object. There's no way you can describe it. Anything that you can say about it can't possibly be it because if you're saying something about it, you're still in the mode of a perceiver. It's only when the perceiver goes away completely that nirvikalpa samadhi exists.

Nirvikalpa samadhi means the seedless state. That is to say, nothing grows from it. If you have a seedless orange, you can't grow an orange tree from it. Nothing comes forth from it, there are no karmas. Whereas in salvikalpa samadhi, something comes forth from it because there's still a sense of perception. Perception generates karma, but in nirvikalpa samadhi, there's absolutely nothing, nothing whatsoever.

Nirvikalpa samadhi is nirvana. I see that the terms are interchangeable. Nirvana is basically a Buddhist term which means the extinction of the self, which does not necessarily mean death as we have come to know it. Some people think that nirvana means an end to all things, an end to all life, sort of perpetual oblivion. But perpetual oblivion is just another idea. Perpetual oblivion is another thing that someone could experience. That has nothing to do with nirvana or nirvikalpa samadhi – I use the two terms interchangeably.

The only way that you can possibly come to have any understanding, in my estimation, of salvikalpa or nirvikalpa samadhi, is to meditate in person with someone who's enlightened. A partially enlightened person – we would say a saint – is someone who experiences salvikalpa samadhi. A fully enlightened person, someone we would say is self-realized, is someone who enters into nirvikalpa samadhi. When you enter into nirvikalpa samadhi, you never come back.

In order to enter into nirvikalpa samadhi, you have to walk into the ocean, and you're made of powder, and when you walk into the ocean, you dissolve. There can be no possibility of coming back because there's no you to return. This is where it gets a little tricky to understand. Because that doesn't mean that if you're sitting in meditation and you go into nirvikalpa samadhi, that an hour from now you won't be out mowing the lawn or driving your car. But it won't be the same you. Each time you go into nirvikalpa samadhi, you dissolve the glue that binds the aggregates of the self together, and a new being forms.

The same is true to a lesser extent of salvikalpa samadhi. This is why they're useful. The reason we seek to enter into salvikalpa samadhi and nirvikalpa samadhi is because they make us what we really are. Each one of us really is eternity, but we're caught up in a human form, we're locked into an idea of ourselves and reality which is developed over countless lifetimes. In order to become enlightened, to achieve perfect perfection, to go away from all the misery and suffering of human life, it's necessary to go into samadhi.

Again, samadhi is the culmination of lifetimes of spiritual practice and meditation. It's nothing that you will experience after four or five years of meditation. After many, many years of meditation you will begin to experience salvikalpa samadhi, if you've had many years of meditation in other lifetimes. If this is your first lifetime meditating, then it is extremely unlikely that you will experience samadhi, in this lifetime. You'll experience very, very advanced states of awareness, blissful beyond description, ecstasy that's unfathomable, knowledge that's impossible to describe. Don't feel that if you're not entering the samadhis that you're missing anything, exactly. It's not that way. Just to move into the advanced states of meditation takes many lifetimes and many years, and if you never went further than that, that would be more than enough. I mean, you'll experience ecstasy.

The samadhis are beyond that. They are beyond. The samadhis are like the highest peaks in the Himalayas. You may have climbed many, many mountains and enjoyed all the mountains and had wonderful experiences and feel your life is complete. The samadhis don't make your life complete. They're beyond life and they're beyond completion. The way you learn about them is by sitting and meditating with someone who's in those states. That's how you learn to go into samadhi.

It is possible to go into samadhi on your own. Let's say this is an incarnation in which you're meditating; you've meditated in other lives but you have not experienced the samadhis. In other words, this is the first life that you're going to enter into salvikalpa samadhi. If you enter into salvikalpa samadhi, if it is the first life that you're doing so, it is unlikely that you will also enter into nirvikalpa samadhi. It might take you another hundred or a thousand lifetimes of passing through salvikalpa samadhi. It is possible to do it in that same life, but that isn't what usually happens. Usually there are many lifetimes of entering into salvikalpa samadhi before the final entrance into nirvikalpa samadhi, into nirvana.

There are many lifetimes of being a saint before you become a perfected being, or before you've perfected your being. Actually, I don't think there are any perfected beings. I think everyone's a perfected being no matter where you are or what you are. We're all perfected beings – perfect at being what we are now, which is all there is.

But that perfected consciousness, that lack of awareness of all that is transitory, is samadhi. It's of great advantage to someone because the reason that you suffer, the reason that you are deluded in maya, in illusion, that you have all kinds of problems, is largely because of what they call the samskaras. The samskaras are the past life tendencies. These tendencies are not so much habits in the sense of, "Well, for the last 50 past lives I've always gotten up on the left-hand side of the bed. Now, in this life, I do the same thing because I'm drawn to do that." Habits of the personality are something that develop within an individual lifetime. The habits that you now have are habits that really developed within this life. Phobias, fears, and all these sort of things, in most cases, occur in this life. Once in a while there is a carryover. Once in a while a person might have a fear of drowning or tidal waves or something like that because in a past life they had an experience where they drowned or went through a tidal wave.

But this is pretty rare, to be honest with you, because there is very little memory, even subconsciously, of the past lives. A lot of people today are interested in past life therapy. They think that it's kind of an extended Freudian analysis, that if they can simply look back, not only to their childhood but to their past lives and see what they did, they'll come to understand why they do things now. This is quite popular and I don't think it's exactly true because there is not that much of a causal effect between individual actions in one lifetime and another. There is an effect and a connection between states of awareness. In a past life you had a certain awareness, and that awareness will give rise to an awareness in your next lifetime. That is true.

The samskaras, then, are not the things we did in an individual lifetime, but it was the way that we thought, the tendencies, the way the aggregates are formed. A human being is not made up of one self. You have many, many selves. The old motto "Know thyself," in my estimation, should be changed to "Know thy selves," because you're made up of many, many beings.

The Buddhists sometimes talk about the anatman, meaning that a person does not have a soul. In the Hindu tradition and the Christian tradition we talk about a soul, or an atman, a self, the same self that incarnates from lifetime to lifetime. Now, in most forms of Buddhism, the Buddhists don't feel that there is not a self. What they're disagreeing with is that the self is not fixed.

Buddha indicated that the self, that part of you that incarnates from lifetime to lifetime, was causal. That is to say, there was a connecting link in each lifetime. It wasn't as if there was a being that was there in one lifetime and then in the next lifetime there was no connection. In his own case, when he discussed his past lives, he was certainly implying that there was an essence that incarnated from lifetime to lifetime. But what he was trying to suggest was that most people have a concept of the soul that is almost like a personality. And what he said was, rather than that, the soul is composed of aggregates. It's like saying that there are seven or eight basic colors and we can put those colors together in varying combinations.

Perhaps there are seven musical notes and we can put those notes in varying combinations and produce different melodies. In each lifetime the notes re-form in a slightly different pattern, but that pattern is an outgrowth of the pattern that was in a previous life. Imagine that in the first few incarnations, the aggregates, the essences that make a person – almost like the atomic structure in a nonphysical sense – are very loose. There isn't much to it. It's like a very simple atom, like an atom of hydrogen as opposed to some of the more complex atoms that have more protons, neutrons, electrons, and valances. As incarnations go by, the atom gets more complex. That is, your being, the part of you that reincarnates from lifetime to lifetime, the aggregate, grows thicker and denser. While this is good and it stores up knowledge and power, at the same time there's a problem with it because it means that a person becomes more fixated.

The more lives you have, the harder it is to change, yet the stronger you are. It's a kind of funny dichotomy. That's good in development. It's important that one become more and more fixed. But then you reach a point in higher spiritual development where what you want to do is erase everything that you've been. It's as if all your past is written on the blackboard, and if we could erase it, your past would no longer exist. What we're going to do is erase what's written on the blackboard. The way you do that – the only way you do that – is in samadhi. When you go into samadhi, either salvikalpa or nirvikalpa, what happens is you erase, you loosen, the aggregates. You simplify them. The way that you're able to go into salvikalpa samadhi is through spiritual refinement. After many years of meditative practice and many lifetimes of meditative practice, you gradually loosen the ties that hold you.

Imagine that you are a balloon, the big balloons that people ride in, with a little basket underneath. You're sitting, waiting to take off, but you have all these sandbags. They're so, so heavy, there's no way the balloon can take off, try though it might. Gradually you unload the sandbags one after another after another. Each time you meditate, this is what you're doing – you're unloading the sandbags that hold you down to the ground. Let's say that the sandbags come in different sizes. The first ones weigh 100 pounds, then there's some that weigh 50 pounds, 20 pounds, ten pounds, five pounds, two pounds and so on.

Let's say that the initial ones weigh the most. Once you get rid of those, then you start to float up a little bit in the air. Then in order to go higher, you drop some of the ones that maybe just weigh 20 pounds or 15 pounds. Then in order to go higher, you drop some of the ones that weigh ten pounds, then five pounds and so on, until all you have left is the balloon and the basket itself. Then you drop away the basket and hold onto the balloon. Then if you go high enough, the balloon disappears and you with it. Gone, vanished without a trace. No one can say where, which doesn't mean that there isn't a where, it's just not visible to the human eye.

In meditation, when you meditate now and in other lives, what you do is you get rid of the gross obstacles that hold you down, the biggest ones. Once you've gotten rid of those, then you can begin to meditate more freely and you'll experience more light and perfection in your life. Then you have to start to work on the 20 pounders, which you do in advanced meditation. Once you work through those, then you've just got some very, very light ones and then you have the basket. When you drop the basket, the thing that you ride in, the personality form, that's salvikalpa samadhi. And then there's just the balloon and you're soaring at an incredible rate, and then when the balloon dissolves completely, when it's gone, that's nirvikalpa samadhi.

The things you're dropping are idea forms and aggregates from your past lives – ways of seeing, believing, feeling, ways of looking. In other words, states of consciousness that you've fixated on. The samskaras, then, are the ways that we have evolved through series of lifetimes to deal with the world and existence. These were good and fine ways to deal with existence, but then we reach a point where those ways are no longer applicable to who we are and what we are. In other words, it was necessary for us to learn a certain art, a certain way of dealing with life and the world and reality that has caused us to reach where we are now. But those very tendencies and methods, which therefore helped us and aided us in our self-discovery, can ultimately become a hindrance, and so we have to pass beyond them.

Samadhi is useful from the point of view of this world, from a functional point of view. I don't think it has to be useful; it is a refulgent reality itself. But in terms of the linear evolution of a being, when you start to go into samadhi, you cast off all the things that you've learned, all the selves that you've been so that you can become what you truly and really are. That, you might say, is the purpose of entering into samadhi, aside from the pure experience itself, the experienceless experience.

The superconscious states, which are what we experience in samadhi and then beyond them, which is nirvana, which is indescribable, are the essence of reality. You might say that it's like a house. A person builds a house, they build a home, and they build different rooms in the home – bedroom, kitchen, living room. Each room has something special about it, has something special to offer, a special beauty, a different feeling, a different ambience, a different atmosphere. But that which is the space within all the rooms – the backdrop, the pure essence from which all those rooms have come forth and to which they will all return – is the superconscious.

The superconscious and the void are interchangeable terms, as are full enlightenment and self-realization, in my estimation. Enlightenment – we could just say enlightenment itself, which would imply full enlightenment – and self-realization or God realization are interchangeable terms. These all mean the same thing. It means that a person has integrated their consciousness with existence until there's no longer a separation.

The void is the superconscious states. The void is the backdrop in which all of the worlds exist. All of the different realities and lokas – both physical worlds, in other words, and the nonphysical worlds, form and formlessness – exist in something. The house was built in a certain space and dimensional plane. The house comes into that dimensional plane and occupies it for a while. One day the house will dissolve, but the space will still be there. The void or the superconscious states are the space in which existence is. Existence and nonexistence are like houses or rooms in houses. They come and go, but the void is the backdrop, the superconscious states. Nirvana is beyond that, down the street and to the left.

As you reach into the superconscious, you find the meaning of life, the purpose of existence; all the things that you've ever looked for are in the superconscious. They're also in the physical, in the finite. They're also in the waking state, in the dreaming state and the deep sleep state, but they come into their absolute fullness, all the knots of existence are untied, everything is clear and becomes what it truly is, in the superconscious.

The way that you enter into the superconscious is, as I've suggested, that for many, many lifetimes one just evolves through the basic incarnations. Then you move into a set of incarnations in which you're seeking spiritually, praying, meditating, things like that. Then there'll come an incarnation where you will find and study with an enlightened teacher. The enlightened, self-realized, or God-realized teacher, interchangeable terms, is someone who teaches you how to enter into the superconscious. The way they do that is really not so much by teaching you how to enter into the superconscious, that's part of it, but the first part of the training really is to teach someone how to let go of all the weights. The weights are the attachments.

It's very difficult to describe or explain this, but a self-realized teacher such as myself or someone else who does the same things, has the power or the power operates through them, to bring a person into the superconscious. Let us say, for example, that Susan wouldn't have been able to go into the superconscious states for 50 more incarnations at her current rate of evolution. But if Susan comes to see an enlightened teacher, a fully enlightened teacher, if Susan is receptive, meditates, and has somewhat of a developed consciousness to begin with, the enlightened teacher can project Susan, can lift Susan, temporarily into the superconscious.

If you're at a football game and you're a child and everyone's standing up and you can't see, your father or brother can lift you up, and even though you're not tall enough to see and it might have been many years before you'd grow that tall to see over the others, your brother or father can lift you up or put you on their shoulders so that you can see. Then you'll understand.

What the enlightened teacher does is to lift the student up so that they can see. Then the student has to go through all the various stages and steps of letting go of all those weights. No one can do it for the student. The teacher can point the way, but the student has to do it themselves. The ability of the teacher to project the student into the alternate realities, into the superconscious states, is dependent upon the student's receptivity.

If I'm conducting a public meditation and 500 people come, and I'm meditating on all of them and trying to do my best for all of them, there may be five or 10 people who have meditated a great deal in past lives or in this life who are very, very receptive. It's very easy for me – because they have already let go of a lot of the weights – to move them into the superconscious. For some people who are just enshrouded in maya and they have nothing but weights, it's harder. You can give them a glimpse, but they won't see as much. What you do as a teacher with your students is you give them constant glimpses. You move them into the alternate realities constantly. Each time they advance, each time they let go of another weight, another attachment, another way of seeing things, you can take them a little further and show them the next step. It's really a two-party process.

It is possible to do this yourself without a teacher, but it is extremely difficult because there is no one to lift you up and show you the next step. But it can be done. Another thing that the teacher does in this process is help you dissolve some of those samskaras. If you'll remember that when you enter into salvikalpa or nirvikalpa samadhi, it just dissolves these weights. Each time you go in, it dissolves more weights.

Enlightenment doesn't occur all at once. There isn't one day when suddenly you achieve full enlightenment. Enlightenment has occurred over a period of time. In Zen we talk about satori and experiencing satori. Satori is salvikalpa or nirvikalpa samadhi. The idea is that after many years of meditation, one day you have a flash of intuition, you see life in its true essence, you go into salvikalpa samadhi. Just one experience in salvikalpa samadhi will change your life. You'll never be the same. The old self will dissolve and you'll experience a rebirth. In this life, you'll be reborn and transformed.

Once, though, is not enough, as Jacqueline Susann told us. You may change and develop one new self, you may have one rebirth, but it's necessary to have that experience repeatedly, to dissolve yourself again and again in the white light of eternity. Each time you do that a more refined self will return, until finally the self is just a thin film, just enough self to exist in this world and transact with the world and no more, so that you are conscious of your eternality in a waking state. In other words, as time goes on, as you go in and out of samadhi repeatedly over a period of years or lifetimes, you reach a point where there's not much difference between the superconscious state and the waking state. After a while they start to merge.

In my own case, I had achieved enlightenment, or enlightenment occurred, in past lives. When this happens, at a certain age you'll just start to go into samadhi. Certainly you'll be drawn to spirituality beforehand. I spent 11 years meditating and being part of a spiritual community and working for the welfare of others constantly, which I was drawn to do without knowing why. I went into salvikalpa samadhi several times over those years, but I never really knew what it was, per se. They were just those enlightenment experiences that come and go.

But then after 11 years, suddenly I started to go into samadhi every day, starting really in 1980. I had no choice. It was not something I could choose. I couldn't say, "Well, today I'm going to go into samadhi." It would just happen repeatedly. I'd sit down to meditate and I'd go into samadhi. In the evening I'd just be sitting at home and I'd go into samadhi.

It would never occur – it never does – at an inappropriate time. Eternity takes care of everything. If I needed to do something to function in the physical world, if I had to drive a car or talk to someone, it wouldn't occur. But it would occur again and again and I just watched myself dissolve and re-form again and again. I was a new person constantly, sometimes many times a day. As this happened over a period of years, there was less distance between the enlightenment that was within myself from past lives, we might say – this is a way, of course, of trying to describe something that's really impossible to describe – and that which I was in a waking state, so that now I'm always in a perpetual state of enlightenment. But for me the process hasn't ended as of the making of this tape on the tenth of September, 1982. Still, many of the powers that I developed from past lives, and just the integration of that enlightenment, is continuing so that each day there's less difference for me between the waking state and samadhi. There really is almost no difference now, but any differences are gradually being wiped out.

You see, when you start to go into samadhi, in my estimation anyway, it's not something you choose. The entrance into samadhi is something that only happens to a few people out of millions. Those people are not any better than anyone else, that was just the dharma or destiny. It does happen to everyone who meditates, eventually. But most people in this particular world are not very advanced spiritually, or their advancement is buried very deeply. In other worlds, samadhi is a common experience. Nirvikalpa samadhi, of course, is not common at all. Salvikalpa samadhi is common in the other worlds, the other planes of reality. Nonphysical beings go into salvikalpa samadhi all the time. They exist in it, many of them. But nirvikalpa samadhi, full enlightenment, is rare, because then the world dissolves and eternity dissolves. Life dissolves. Death dissolves. God dissolves.

When this starts to happen to you, which it will one day, you won't be able to start it or stop it. It's kind of like a terminal disease. Your old self is dying completely and it happens in stages. To reach that point though, to get the process going, it's necessary to find an enlightened teacher because when you work with an enlightened teacher, it's kind of like a mini-samadhi. Coming back to the analogy that I was using before, it's like being held up by your older brother so that you can see above the crowd. Well, it's like that, but it's a little more. It may take Susan 50 more lifetimes before she starts to go into samadhi, just meditating every day, but if she meditates with an enlightened teacher, she may do it in this lifetime.

Now, the only reason that Susan would have an enlightened teacher is owing to past births. In past lifetimes she's done pretty well spiritually. That's why eternity would direct her to an enlightened teacher, and she'd recognize an enlightened teacher in this lifetime and work with him. Because when you meditate with someone who is in the samadhis, who's absorbed in nirvana, particularly if you can meditate with them physically, to start with, once or twice a week to be in a room where they are, to be in that field of energy, there's a parameter of energy that's projected around them for a certain distance, almost a radiation. And if you sit in that and meditate, if you can make your mind quiet and absorb that, it's as if you yourself were going into the superconscious. It brings you into the superconscious just to sit in that light. It doesn't really matter whether the teacher is formally meditating or not because the teacher is always projecting that light, it's always coming through them, if it's a truly enlightened person. If it's a truly enlightened person, they're not making a big deal out of themselves. They just accept it. They're just an instrument of eternity and that's that.

But nevertheless, there's an operable result. If you can access that energy, it is to your advantage if you seek enlightenment. The more you can meditate with them the better for you, because just to be around that energy causes tremendous transformation. It helps loosen the glue of the self that is binding you to this world and this life, to the attachments and all that stuff. But some people think if they just sit with an enlightened teacher, that's all that's necessary, which is nonsense. It will make it possible for you to make your changes. It will make it easier, you can do them more quickly, but still you have to work out your own liberation. That is to say, you have to go through all the experiences. You have to learn and grow and develop.

When the time is right, when a person is really ready to begin the higher study, the graduate school of self-discovery, they will find an enlightened teacher and work with that teacher. As they work with the teacher, as they spend time with them, as they're around the teacher, they'll make very fast spiritual progress.

Then they learn to develop an inner connection with the teacher. That is to say, after spending a couple of years doing that, let's say four or five years, a person is then able to inwardly contact that state of awareness. You may be a thousand miles from the teacher but you've grown so close in your hearts, there's so much love between the two of you, that you can be with them inwardly, regardless of where you are. It's just about as strong. In other words, you'll be able to access that energy that flows through them, and then, of course, one day you learn to not have to go through the teacher as a source but to deal directly with eternity without going through a form. That happens when you become enlightened, and then you'll reflect the light of eternity to others, or just shine.

Samadhi and the superconscious is all there really is. It is the fourth level of ecstasy. It's that which you seek, that which you'll become. It's inevitable. It's your destiny. It's just a question of when. But if you wish to make time stand still, as it were, then you should follow your heart.

Be not concerned with the things of this world because they are transitory. Find that teacher who you can love the most, go, and be with them. Listen to what they say, but listen to more than what they say because they just try as best they can to explain to the blind and deaf things that can't be explained.

There can be all kinds of misunderstandings if you pay too much attention to their words because remember, they're just ad-libbing most of the time. They're just trying to wing it and say, "Hey, folks, there's no way to really explain this. I'll explain it one day one way and I'll explain it another day another way and if you compare both days, you may say, 'Well, gosh, he or she, they're contradicting themselves.'" Not really, there was no way to explain it accurately on any day, so you just do the best you can, depending upon the receptivity of the audience, what's at hand, the culture you're in and so forth.

But don't really worry about what they say so much. Listen to what they don't say, and not only to the teacher, but to eternity itself. The teacher's just a direct form for you for now, kind of a surrogate who helps you just become aware of what you really are. The teacher isn't really even there much anymore. They're just dissolution in manifest form.

Samadhi and the superconscious – not really much you can say about it, except you can definitely direct a person towards it, point the way, give encouragement, correct things that will not lead to enlightenment. And of course, if one is enlightened, you can just be a channel of that light of samadhi, that perfect bliss, that fourth level of ecstasy, so that others can come into that light and, like a moth to the flame, be burned up.

THE CARETAKER PERSONALITY

In the process of meditation, we find that we are not one continuous personality, we are not a body, that what our real being is, is light. We are one continuous consciousness and this consciousness is a consciousness of light. This is our nature, our substance and our essence.

When you meditate very deeply and go inside yourself or experience yourself, that is all there is – one continuous, all-pervasive, perfect, all-blissful consciousness. When we have our eyes open, when we're in the world, we don't see that continuous consciousness in quite the same way that we do when we're in meditation. Rather, we see it in manifestation. All the peoples, places, beings, and forms that you experience in this or any other world are supported by that continuous consciousness that is the soul of reality. Just as a great fleet of ships floats upon the ocean, supported by it, so all of life floats upon an essence, a fathomless essence.

All things arise from this essence, are sustained by it, float in it for a while and then one day they dissolve back into it. This essence is not physical, although it sustains the physical. It is not even spirit in the conventional sense of the term spirit. When most people say spirit, they're referring to what is termed the subtle physical or astral, the etheric planes of being. It is invisible and yet manifests itself in and through the visible. This is its mystery, the mystery of eternity.

In meditation, in self-discovery, we seek to make our mind quiet so that we can perceive this essence, this eternal reality which is existence. When you do this, a happiness and joy that is beyond description fills every atom of your being because there is such goodness, such completion in the source of life, in the essence, which Lao Tzu referred to as the tao, which some refer to as God, some nirvana. There is such completion and perfection there that all else seems immaterial, in the sense that we have gone into the very nature, into the very heart of existence, and there we are complete.

Whereas when we're in the world of women and men we see all around us division, partiality, cars running down the freeways, people talking, wars, birth, maturation, decay, and death. Plants, forests, cities, slums, stars, all of the things that we are conversant with in the physical world, follow a cycle and this cycle is nature.

Nature is the outer reflection of the timeless perfection of existence, this ultimate intelligence, which has no parent, which has always been and will always be, which is beyond time, place, and condition. Each day when you meditate, each day when you give more of yourself to others, you open a doorway to that which is always there but which you do not always perceive – your essence, that which completes you. When you get caught up in the storms of your passions and emotions, you forget. Already you have forgotten, since you came into this life, that which you came from. If you look really deeply inside yourself, not inside your body per se, but inside that which is your awareness, you will see – as you open up the cover of the book of your life and delve deeply into the chapters and pages – this all-luminous perfection.

As you become more conscious of this all-luminous perfection, as it's something that you still yourself in each day, you will find that it will have a great effect upon your life. You will find that you no longer exist in the planes of being, of awareness, that most human beings do. At first this may seem frightening or awesome because you observe, after your adventures in meditative consciousness, that your personality is dissolving or it might be more correct to say that your personality is only a shell, it's only a very thin cover.

Everything that you thought yourself to be, what you assumed you were – your memories, emotions, thoughts, feelings and concerns – is only a thin, thin shell, the outer perimeter of your being. But inside your being is infinite awareness, endless, fathomless perfection. Just as a snake sheds its skin, so as you meditate and you experience that which you really are, you shed your personality. The person you grew up with and have come to know over the years begins to change. You outgrow the limited personality structure and you seek to live without a personality, that is to say, just to be in that essence all the time.

Still, in this world, it's necessary to get through the day, unless you plan to go off to a high mountaintop and you have all the supplies you need and you never have to deal with anyone and can sit perpetually absorbed in that state of meditation. If, like most of us, you live and work in the world, it's necessary to find a way to deal with traffic jams, tax forms, people who love you, people who make demands upon your time and energy, a high-tech society where computers are the language of the day, where children no longer study

Greek or Latin but instead now study Pascal, BASIC, COBOL, Fortran. It's necessary to learn to deal with your turbulent emotions. You can sit absorbed in meditation and be nothing but that perfect ecstasy and light beyond any description, but then, after meditation, an emotional maelstrom may sweep around you and through you, pulling you into it. Fears come through you as do doubts, ideas, great inspirations, passions, loves, hates, sorrows, wonderful feelings of love and self-giving. They sweep through you.

A moment ago you were absorbed in meditation. There was no question. There was no answer. There was only a still perfection so complete that you actually forgot about this life and this world. It went away for you. You reached the purpose of fulfillment of human life. You merged with the Self, that which you really are and we all are. You became one with God. You've gone up to the top of the mountain and not simply talked with God, but merged. But now, here you are again, in the world, after this incredible transcendental experience where you were absolute knowledge and absolute light and absolute perfection, and your phone is ringing and someone wants to talk to you and the bills are waiting to be paid and the world is running away in its own ways. The newspaper is telling you of fresh disasters. Your body is growing old. You're tired.

The energy fields from all the other human beings who are so caught up in a storm of turbulent emotions sweep through the world every day. They touch you and affect you even if you're not physically with others – their energies, those energies that make this world a world of constant transition. You're sensitive to them. How do you deal with it all? Ideally you would maintain that perfect tranquility and joy, that radiance which can assume any form or any emotion, in and through all of your activities. But some days that's tough to do.

The caretaker personality is a way that has been evolved whereby you can deal with the world, your families, friends, your own emotions, while you exist in the world. When it's not necessary for you to use the personality form, you can put it on the shelf and let it rest and you can just be absorbed in the all-blissful light. You can be in complete awareness, in other words, using every part of your mind, every part of your being, absorbed in its ultimate purpose.

But when you have to step into the world, you need to wear something. At home you may lie in bed with nothing on or at best go around the house in a little robe, but when you go out into the world you have to put on a uniform. If you're in the business world you may be wearing one uniform. If you're playing sports it may be another uniform. If you're going out with your friends it may be a casual uniform. If you're a nurse it's a white uniform. In other words, we wear different types of clothing. We try and wear clothing that's suitable to an occasion. If you're going mountain climbing, you're not going to wear a three-piece designer suit. If you've been invited to have lunch with the president, you're not going to go in your jogging shorts, unless, of course, you're Woody Allen.

The caretaker personality is a way of choosing what you wear, not simply in terms of clothing but in terms of personality. As you meditate and go more deeply within yourself, you come to see that you don't have one personality, you have many, many personalities. "Know thyself" is a splendid idea because it is that absolute self that we come to know, that timeless reality. But at the same time it's also apropos to know thy selves, because you have many, many selves. There are many, many personality forms that operate through you, and as you peel back the layers of your outer being you come to see that many selves are what you are, and that these selves all speak, they all have different voices; they talk through you. Of course, beyond these many selves is that one immutable, perfect light.

All of your selves float, suspended, as a fleet of great ships floats in the ocean. For a while our attention is focused on one ship. We're onboard one ship, experiencing what's there, then we find ourselves in another ship, then another. The different selves that float in a suspension of consciousness, this aggregate of different realities, which is what you are really made up of, speak from time to time. These are inner selves. We have inner selves, but we also have outer personality forms.

What I would like to do is present a few caretaker personalities that you can adopt to work in the world and to have fun and to be joyous with. These are uniforms that you wear, clothing that you put on and that you also take off. Wear that caretaker personality which is apropos, which is appropriate, for what you are doing. Don't be afraid to be creative and change these caretaker personalities. Modify them as you will and you'll find that they tend to modify themselves in time.

I'm suggesting that you be an architect of your own being, that just as you can choose your clothes, so in advanced yoga and meditation, you learn to choose your personalities. This occurs when you have the realization that the personality is not really your real self, but just like your clothing, a transitory experience.

If you had become convinced one day when you were walking around that your clothing was your skin, you might always wear the same clothing; you didn't realize that there was anything underneath. Similarly, most individuals don't realize that there's something beyond their personalities that actually the personality is something that is not the complete self but it's something transitory that comes and goes, whereas the real self is that which is eternal, unchanging and perfect.

In the early stages of meditation, let's say the first seven to ten years that you're intently practicing meditation every day, those years in which you're sweeping your island and cleaning it up, bringing discipline into your life, eliminating and controlling unhappy thoughts, unhappy emotions, learning to go deeper and deeper into that still and perfect reality of being, Brahman, the one without a second – there are two basic caretaker personalities that are very, very helpful for dealing with the world and with yourself.

The first caretaker personality is the child, the second is the warrior. Each has its own conditions, each its own strengths. One is appropriate in one situation, the other in another situation. You can alternate them by day or by minute as is necessary, and you'll find it easier and easier to alternate them as the flow of consciousness becomes freer in your being from your meditation. If the water is frozen into ice then the ships can't move. Our fleet, if the ocean is frozen, is locked tight. When the sun comes, when the light comes and the ice thaws, it's very easy to move the ships around, there's nothing to it at all. They just glide back and forth or we don't even have to direct them. The wind will blow them where they're supposed to be, you might say.

The first caretaker personality is the child. The caretaker personality of the child is innocence. Just think of the idyllic, if you will, qualities of the child – excitement, love, trust, humility, purity, joy. I'm speaking of a very young child, a very good child, about age four – the child who looks with wonder and awe at all of the world, who sees magic in everything, who is not preoccupied with her or himself, who becomes absorbed totally in the moment. If a child wants a cookie, that's all that matters in the whole world, but as soon as the child has a cookie the child is off on another adventure. The child doesn't give up or get frustrated because things don't work out the way she or he had planned, because a child doesn't plan.

The child lives in the moment. If the child meets with a frustration and cries and is upset, within a moment the child can be running off to play someplace else, having forgotten, not being hung up. The child doesn't sit around and live in the world of memory but lives in the moment; all that matters is the moment. This is the child who grows, who learns the language in a year, who adopts concepts. As most people get older they tend to lose the elasticity of their consciousness, they don't shine as brightly. Their subtle being becomes worn and tired. The child has a perfect subtle physical being. The child is luminous, radiant. The child doesn't know that it can't do certain things; it isn't filled with fears. These are just some images of the caretaker personality of the child.

You can use this caretaker personality – in other words you can enter into this mode of consciousness, you can choose to do so – when you're with friends whom you can trust; who love you and whom you love; when you're with yourself; when there's no one else around; in other words, when it's safe. The child should not be around people who would abuse it because a child has no natural defenses. Its own innocence will not necessarily protect it.

Some people make a great mistake. We saw a lot of this in the 1960s when a lot of people tried to become like children again. They were using various chemicals – LSD, psilocybin, mescaline and things like that. These chemicals did to a degree loosen up the ice of consciousness. However, they did so in a very volatile way. It was like taking a sledgehammer, going out, and smashing the ice, and it only broke through in certain places and then it would freeze again as soon as the effect of the drug wore off, and even during the experience it was not clear. In other words, psychedelic drugs gave, and give, people a certain glimpse of that which lies beyond, but it's like going to the fun house and looking in one of those mirrors that change your shape. You don't see an accurate reflection. You may be very tall or very small or very fat as you look in one of those fun house mirrors. The view that drugs give, while it is a reflection to some extent of the nature of reality, is bent out of shape and it doesn't last. Also, those drugs do have a detrimental effect on the subtle physical being.

The problem with the people from the 60's was that most of them adopted the caretaker personality of the child. They found while they used these various drugs and opened their being up, they were able to make some tremendous changes in the structure of their being. This is originally why people like Timothy Leary and Richard Alpert were very fascinated by the potential of these drugs. They found when they used them that a person who in a sense might be fixated, who couldn't change – an alcoholic who for 30 years had been an alcoholic and there seemed no real possibility of change, who'd tried everything – might take one of these drugs and the effect was so strong that that person would actually change, they would become a different person, perhaps a person who didn't drink. They were initially very excited as serious psychologists about the possibilities that these new chemicals offered, and as they used these chemicals they found they had glimpses of eternity with them. These glimpses of eternity caused them to seek further, to learn about meditation, other forms of self-discovery.

However, the problem with these chemicals is that the reflection is not clear, it's bent; and that the effect, the change, does not always last. In some cases it did, but it was a rougher change – the transition wasn't smooth. Also, these chemicals very often would have a negative effect. People who used them too much would become very spaced-out. It undid the glue of their awareness, but the glue didn't necessarily re-bond properly. The personality structure would partially dissolve or two might meld together, or in some cases the glue just wouldn't rejoin properly and the person would be in a very confused state of mind, perhaps for the rest of their life. These chemicals do offer certain opportunities for total and intensive change, but they have to be used very precisely in a very specific way. Even then, all they can do is give someone an initial boost and get them out of where they are. If the person is stuck, they can provide a quick change, but then the person would have to leave the chemicals behind and adopt a means that worked better, such as meditation.

Of course, what I recommend to most people who have not used those chemicals is to not bother to use them, to use meditation directly to disassociate yourself from the fixated personality and to learn to adopt the caretaker personalities. While meditation may take a little bit longer, it works. The psychedelic drugs that people use to do this only last a short time. You come down, in other words, whereas when you meditate, as time goes on, you gently acclimate yourself to living in a more fluid state of being and the power becomes greater and greater as the years go by. You become more and more fluid, whereas with the psychedelic drugs you reach a plateau and stop. With meditation you'll never stop, and you don't have to worry about the interfering possibilities, the negative side effects, in other words.

Persons who have used these chemicals should feel that that's what life gave them at the time. If you used LSD or mescaline or psilocybin to change the personality structure, then don't feel that you did anything wrong. Life gave you those chemicals to use, to see something. Now, you may not have used them properly. You may have gotten caught up in just tripping out and having sense experiences and not using them properly – properly meaning not in any specific way. This seemed to be the great controversy between Leary and Kesey at the time, with Leary saying that, well, there's a certain way to use these chemicals, a ritual way, for self-discovery, and Kesey taking a more Taoist point of view – don't think about it too much, just do it, there is no right and there is no wrong. Both are interesting points of view, but ultimately both irrelevant. Lost in time. Washed away by eternity.

If you've used these drugs to alter the personality structure, just feel that that was right at the time, but that it is no longer right. Even marijuana and hashish alter the personality structure, but in my estimation it doesn't do it very well. I think it's better not to use any drugs whatsoever and to deal with meditation, which is millions and millions of times more powerful and does it absolutely perfectly.

These folks in the 60's used these various chemicals and some do today, and of course they have been used for thousands of years. People who use these chemicals usually adopt the personality of the child afterwards. They were the "flower children." The flower children, without knowing perhaps what they were doing consciously by using these chemicals, were bringing out the first caretaker personality. However the flower children modality doesn't really work in this world. The flower child has trouble dealing with the rapid transit system, with the complexities of a high-tech society.

You can use the caretaker personality of the child at home, with friends, on a walk by yourself. Be a child. Look at life through the eyes of a child. Christ advised that unless you enter the kingdom of heaven as a child, you don't get in. That was his point. You have to have that way of looking at things. It's a very safe, very pure way. If you live in a monastery you can perhaps – unless you're running it – stay in that pure caretaker personality all the time. We've seen an image of it, of course, in The Brothers Karamazov by Dostoyevsky, in Alyosha. This is the caretaker personality of the child. When we think of many saints – innocent, pure, St. Francis – that's the caretaker personality of the child. A very good one to use. I recommend it highly, some times.

But when you deal with the world more directly, I suggest the caretaker personality of the warrior. The warrior is calm and efficient. The warrior uses discipline. The warrior is happy. The weapon of the warrior is laughter. The warrior learns to be impeccable, to use her or his life as a way of attaining liberation. The warrior also is always at the beck and call of others. The warrior can be of service – think of King Arthur and his knights with their code of chivalry, certain standards. While the commoners in the land may have fallen down to the lower depths, you rise above that, and even while others may not be interested in nobility of the soul, courage, valor, self-giving, sacrifice, dedication, kindness to others and protecting those who are weak, the warrior does these things.

In a trashed-out world, the warrior shines in armor – the samurai in the true sense of the term. The warrior never feels sorry for him or herself. If the warrior has to be upset, the warrior does so alone, and when the warrior goes out with others the warrior smiles. The warrior doesn't have time for self-indulgence, for self-pity. The warrior will feel a certain amount of remorse for a comrade who has been lost but then goes forward again. The warrior doesn't look back, although the warrior carries the sword of discrimination and certainly learns from experience.

The warrior is never at rest. While the warrior takes breaks – a little R&R – the warrior is always practicing and training. Even though there may not be a battle for another year, the warrior always stays in training. The warrior loves the art of being a warrior and experiences deep kinship and comradeship on a very mature level with other warriors. They embrace, they live freely. The warrior has true humility, if the warrior is a spiritual warrior, and the courage and cunning to succeed in even the most difficult of situations. If you adopt this caretaker personality when you're in the world, then you'll find it very easy to effectively deal with the world.

I often recommend two of the books of Carlos Castaneda, *Journey to Ixtlan* and *Tales of Power*, because don Juan and don Genaro, who are Carlos's spiritual teachers, teach Carlos the way of the warrior. As you read those two books you'll get a deeper sense, not so much by Carlos's experiences but by what they say as reflected in the writings of Carlos, what this warrior is all about.

You can think of an image of the warrior and you can adopt this mode. Just put yourself into that place, into that consciousness, when you go out and deal with the world. And you can think of the child who just reaches to God in innocence, who is absorbed in joy at seeing a flower, at being with someone, who grows ever so quickly when you are in safe surroundings. Remember that the warrior, the real warrior, is always humble, as is the child. That's their true condition: humility.

These two basic caretaker personalities can be used when you deal with your being. You can use them with your internal emotions. If doubt, fear, or anger enters into you, be like the child. Be too innocent and pure to even notice, or be like the warrior, fight against them, or simply shove them away. The child focuses on beauty, or you could say the child sees beauty in all things. The warrior knows what's what. The warrior knows that there's both good and bad, but the child may not know that there's good and bad because perhaps there isn't for the child.

The warrior applauds good and fights against bad, against evil. The child walks through this world the innocent, seeing light and joy in everything. The warrior is always looking over his shoulder to see if there's someone behind him. He's always considering who may be around the next block. The warrior doesn't think negatively; the warrior thinks of light. The warrior is always looking for someone to be of service to, someone to help. The warrior has courage. The child has flexibility.

Use these two caretaker personalities in the first years of your meditative practice. Adopt them. Use them as images for what you should be. Modify them as you will. You'll find that they'll help you terrifically in your spiritual growth and development. Throw away the personality form that you have now. Stop trying to think of yourself as being a certain kind of person. You change constantly. The only reason you fixate is because your mind tells you that you're a certain kind of person. The reason the child grows more quickly than you do is that the child isn't fixated. She doesn't think, "I am this, I am not this, I like chocolate, I don't like vanilla." The child is too busy trying everything.

As you advance further in your self-discovery you will find that there are other caretaker personalities you can adopt. These are perhaps a little more subtle and I don't really recommend that you emulate them until many, many, many, many years of meditation have passed, when you're truly grounded in the spirit of existence, when you live in a meditative consciousness all the time, when you've eliminated all hate and aggression and all fear and all selfishness from yourself. When these things have all gone away, when you live only for the welfare of others – not just as an idea, but you're of service to others 24 hours a day – when you've swept the island of your being completely, then there are some other forms you can use.

One is the witness. Feel that you are a witness to eternity. You can't do anything, you can't act, all you can do is observe and witness. You're like a piece of paper on which someone writes down the history of the world. Feel, in other words, in this caretaker personality, that you are not active, that you are very, very passive. As you watch your life go by you, as you watch people, places and things, don't feel that you can act. Oh, you'll observe yourself acting, but realize that the infinite is acting through you, that you're only an instrument of eternity. Simply witness all that you see. Don't try to form or shape anything. Just let the river of life flow through you. Be a witness to eternality and immortality. Don't have a sense of self as actor, as doer; feel rather that God is the doer, that God does everything in you and through you. At best all you can do is witness and observe the play of reality, the play of life as it moves through your being.

Another advanced caretaker personality that you can use is the seer, the visionary. Feel that you are a visionary, that your main purpose in life is just to see. Constantly look more deeply into all things. Never let your vision rest. Constantly look through eternity, always trying to see that which is at the end of eternity. Be concerned with conditions, the nature of change, why change occurs. Look at the causative conditions of all things. Feel that you are a seer, in other words. You are vision and that's your sole purpose in life and in existence.

Another caretaker personality is the dream. Feel that you are a dream, that you don't really exist at all. As you walk through life, everyone and everything you see is part of that dream. Enjoy the dream and remember that what you really are is not simply the dream, but the dreamer. Somewhere you are asleep dreaming yourself into this dream. Remember that you are at once that which is in the dream, and at the same time you are the dreamer. If you can wake up within your dream, which you should try to do with this caretaker personality, then you can make the dream into whatever you like. If suddenly you realize, in other words, during a dream, while you're in the dream, while you're one of the beings that's in the dream, that it is a dream, then you should be able to manipulate that dream. You should be able to say, "Well, here I am in this dream. And since all things are possible in the dream, I can create whatever I like."

Another caretaker personality is the sage. You should only employ this personality after you've been going into samadhi for some time. Feel that you are an embodiment of wisdom and humility. There is nothing that you want for yourself. The sage seeks only to serve others. If there is no one to serve, then be absorbed in meditation or in preparing your being to be of more service to others. Feel that you are wisdom and light.

Another caretaker personality that you can utilize is the image of sacrifice. Feel that you are a living sacrifice, that is to say, you are only in this world to give to others beyond exhaustion, that your very purpose is to ferment life, to give life, and that your own personal health, safety and welfare is of little or no importance. You'll maintain yourself just enough to keep yourself going so you can be supportive. In other words, your life is the life of constant self-sacrifice.

There are many, many more advanced caretaker personalities. When the time comes they'll come to you. Try to be conscious, though, of your being. Realize that you have the power, you might say, to be whatever you'd like to be, but that you need to fashion yourself in a certain image of perfection. There are many images of perfection and you need to catch on to one. They're elusive at first, like the fish swimming through the water – you can reach to grab it and it's gone. Realize that you are not the body or the mind, that your real essence is that immutable light which is beyond change, yet you have a surface being that's in a constant state of revolution.

Don't feel that you have to be stuck with the personality you've got now because as you meditate you'll watch it dissolve and go away. But you do need a personal form to deal with the world. I suggest that you adopt, on an alternating basis, the caretaker personality of the child and the warrior and then, after many, many years of meditation, that you try some of the other more advanced caretaker personality forms.

Whenever you have the opportunity, however, push all the forms away and be the formless. When you have the chance, let all those different selves wash away, whether it's the caretaker personality of the teacher or the student, the warrior, the child, the sage, self-sacrifice, the witness, whatever it may be. There are many, many of them. Let them all fall away and just be that eternal essence that you are. Sit in meditation and be absorbed. Be absorbed beyond time, place or condition. Let the radiant light of existence be you. Be absorbed in eternity, beyond time, place, suffering. Be absorbed in life. And then use the caretaker personalities as an artist uses colors to paint beautiful pictures.

Paint the beautiful picture of your life. In the beginning, your paintings may not look too good – they don't when you're learning, you know. But as time goes on you'll become a master artist, a Rembrandt, a van Gogh, a Matisse, and you'll make perfect paintings. Each one different, each one unique, each one a reflection of God, which is all that we really are anyway. We're just a passing image, a reflection, not even a substance.

THE TIBETAN REBIRTH PROCESS

With the advent of the books of W. Y. Evans-Wentz and Alexandra David-Neel, the peoples of Europe and the United States began to catch their first glimpse of the spirit of the land of Tibet. Up until that time Tibetan yoga was relatively unknown in the West, and as W. Y. Evans-Wentz and Alexandra David-Neel began to publish accounts of their journeys to those snowy regions, a small but steadily growing flame of interest was propagated among persons who seek spiritual answers and insights into the workings of the cosmos. Both Wentz and Neel went to Tibet, associated with Tibetan lamas and themselves were initiated into basic forms of Tibetan yoga, and I certainly recommend their books highly for colorful insights into these processes.

However, neither Wentz nor Neel either claimed to be or was enlightened. Both were seekers on the path and what they tried to do was present the ancient wisdom of the Tibetan Buddhists, primarily through the translation of the ancient Tibetan documents. These translations were made by monks they had associated with, and many people have come to read these documents, particularly the well-known *Tibetan Book of the Dead*, and assumed that their readings of these documents has given them an entrance into the mystery of Tibetan yoga. It is my position, however, that most uninitiated persons who have read these documents have probably been more confused by them than enlightened by them. What I would like to attempt to do in the next hour is to talk with you about Tibetan yoga, as it was practiced hundreds of years ago.

Tibetan yoga is founded on several principle ideas. The first idea, of course, is that all human beings are part and parcel of consciousness, that consciousness is existence itself, and that consciousness has a field of attention through which it becomes aware of different participles of reality or eventually it becomes fully conscious of all of existence, which is, as you know, what we call enlightenment; that there are specific ways that this enlightenment takes place, in other words, enlightenment isn't an accident, it's rather a science; that there are other universes other than our universe, universes not so much in the physical world as universes of mind, of spirit; that all of the universes operate through specific types of laws and once you've learned and mastered these laws you can operate in and through these different universes; and that you are capable of uniting yourself with the void, with eternity.

The Tibetan Book of the Dead has to do with the rebirth process. The Book of the Dead discusses the various bardos. The bardos are the intermediate planes of existence that occur between death and rebirth. The Tibetan Book of the Dead is often used, or certainly was used in recent times, after the advent of death. When a person would die, a monk would come, or a family member, and for several days they would read from The Book of the Dead with the feeling that the spirit of the deceased would be able to hear the reading. The Book of the Dead is really a TripTik, it's a AAA Guide, a road map, through the nonphysical dimensions. The belief of course that surrounds it, or that underlies it, is that all creatures and beings in the phenomenal universe are on a giant wheel, the wheel of birth and death, and that at the end of each lifetime you die and you will be reborn in another world.

The Tibetans believe that there are six primary bardos or worlds into which you can attain rebirth. In each of these bardos or worlds, or lokas, there are countless sub-worlds. The earthly plane is an intermediate world, it's kind of in the middle of the six. The six are seen as a circle. Very often if you look at a Tibetan thangka, or Tibetan art, you'll notice that there's a symbol of the wheel of life. It's a big circle and it's divided into six quadrants. Usually at the top of the circle will be the world of the Buddhas, of the enlightened ones. At the bottom of the circle there will be the hell worlds. There will be other worlds, four other worlds; usually there's a world for the angels and saints, a world that reflects the consciousness of the animals and several others. Each of these worlds is a state of mind, a state of existence.

It is the belief of the Tibetan Buddhists that your next birth will be determined by the composite of your thoughts and actions in this particular lifetime and the chain of causal actions from your past lifetimes. It's as if you're going to be going to college and you'd studied French for a while in high school. When you got to college they gave you a placement test and depending upon how you did on the placement test, they would assign you to a particular level basic, intermediate, or advanced in French. Your awareness at the end of any given lifetime will determine what world you reincarnate in, what plane of existence, what state of consciousness. That which you have dwelt most upon in this lifetime will be that which you return to. This is the fundamental belief. The thing that you have thought about most is what you'll be drawn back to.

The Tibetan Book of the Dead has been construed as a book that can allow you to attain a higher birth or to go beyond the wheel of birth and death completely and to enter into nirvana, which is not necessarily the extinction of existence, it's simply beyond description. It is away from the samsara, the world of cause and effect, birth and death, pain and suffering. It is beyond all that. A person who practices Tibetan yoga is seeking a higher rebirth, either a higher rebirth simply because they want to enjoy a better state of existence; a higher rebirth so that they can eventually go beyond the wheel of birth and death to a state of permanence and absorption in God, in nirvana; or a higher rebirth so that with that higher rebirth they'll be in a better position to do more for others, to become a bodhisattva, one who serves others and helps them to attain enlightenment.

The Tibetan Book of the Dead, as I suggested, is read over the body of one who has recently died in the hope that the instructions contained within the book will enable the wandering spirit, as it passes through the bardo, through these intermediate planes of existence, to gain a higher birth. This is really a great misunderstanding of the purposes of The Book of the Dead. While certainly there is a time shortly after the onset of death where one can, if one knows how, go beyond the wheel of birth and death to nirvana, the principal use of The Book of the Dead is not to counsel you in what to do shortly after you die and leave the body. Rather, it is to show you how to obtain a higher birth or full enlightenment and absorption in nirvana in your current lifetime, not in some future lifetime, or to bring your future lifetimes into your current lifetime.

At the time of death, at the moment of death and shortly thereafter, there is a moment when you are set face to face with the clear light of reality. In other words, you will see, shortly after your death, this incredible light, and this light is so bright in its appearance that it frightens most persons. When you see this light, while initially you may be attracted to it, suddenly you'll be seized with fear and you'll try to run away from that light. If you had been able to accept and embrace that light without running towards it or away from it, in other words, if you could be neither attracted nor repulsed by that light, then you would pass on to spiritual liberation.

It's kind of like asking you to keep your composure in the middle of a nuclear test, when you're at ground zero, and as you watch your being - being atomized and vaporized to just be calm, relaxed, and happy. If you still have any fears at that time, they will come out. At the moment of death when you're set face to face with the clear light of reality, with the essence of existence, if you still have any attachments to this world, people, desires, they will all come out. All these things will arise. They will all stand before you and it's necessary for you to be neither attracted nor repulsed by any of them. If you are, which most people are, you will then drop to a lower level.

Imagine that suddenly at the time of death you're on the roof of a building and there you're going to have a kind of examination. Everyone you've ever known, loved, hated, been indifferent towards, every fear that you've ever had, whether it's of things in the darkness that you can't see or losing control, people who love you suddenly hating you, poverty, whatever it might be, all of the things that you've always desired and been attracted to, in other words, all of your thought forms, will suddenly, while you're on the roof of this building, parade before you and show themselves to you. If you run away from your fears, suddenly you'll find that you'll fall through the roof of the building and end up on the top floor, the next floor below the roof. If you are suddenly enticed and attracted by any of these things, the same thing will happen. Whereas if you're indifferent, if rather than even noticing these things, which are but shadows of your thought forms, if instead you allow yourself to be absorbed by that clear light of reality, that infinitely bright light, if you don't run away from the light and towards the things that you desired or away from the things that you feared, if you can be neutral at that point, then you'll be absorbed in that light and become it and you'll disappear as a snowflake does when it falls into water. You'll be absorbed in nirvana and you will no longer be reborn. It's a tricky moment.

If you're like most persons, however, you'll fall through the roof down to the next floor, and there will be another light, a different color light, a very bright and beautiful light, a greener blue light, but again it will be very strong. Again you'll be set face to face with your fears and desires. This process will go on again and again, you'll drop from floor to floor. Each time you're either attracted or repulsed, you'll drop. If you can maintain on any floor, that is to say, as you are set face to face with these various visions, the wrathful and beatific visions, when you can accept them as your own self, if you can do that on any of those levels, then you will be reborn on those levels these are the higher worlds, the higher lokas. You could say that each time you're set face to face with the various lights of the different levels and bardos of existence, if you can accept them, then you'll attain rebirth on that world. You won't have to go any lower on the scale of consciousness. If, however, you become confused and deluded, if your spirit wanders aimlessly, if you can't meditate and become perfectly still and allow eternity to just move through you, then you'll sink all the way down and be reborn.

Now even if at that point things still haven't gone well, you'll have another opportunity. You'll experience what they call "the judgment." That is to say, at one point in your progress, before you reincarnate after your last death, you will suddenly evaluate yourself. The judgment is reflected in the Christian theology in Saint Peter waiting at the gate with the Book of Life examining both the good things you've done and the bad things that you've done and coming to some kind of a judgment. If you've done a lot of bad things I guess they send you to hell, and a lot of good things you'll get to go to heaven. Well, the judgment is just a reflection of human consciousness. At one point you will review your life, or all of your lives, your spirit will, and you'll try to come to some kind of an evaluation of who and what you are. If at that time when you go through that trial, in the sense of a courtroom trial, when you judge yourself, if you can at that point be neither attracted nor repulsed by the judgment, your own self-judgment, if you can feel that it really has nothing to do with you, even though you watch a part of yourself going through this recollection process, this measuring, "Am I good or am I bad," then at that point you can be liberated and attain a higher birth.

In other words, as one passes through the bardo in between lifetimes, there will be a number of opportunities for you to select, based upon the evolution of your consciousness this is your placement exam, what world, what level of existence you will reincarnate in in your next life. This is the Tibetan belief. However, if you do terribly in the placement exam, there's still an opportunity to get a relatively decent birth, which has to do with the selection of the family into which you will reincarnate, which again is a process that I shall not describe here, which, if you are interested, is outlined in a kind of a convoluted form in The Tibetan Book of the Dead.

The Book of the Dead, if you've never read it, is an extremely difficult book to read. It has highly symbolic language, very repetitive. The Book of the Dead as we see it today is actually a corrupt form of The Book of the Dead, which was never written down originally but memorized and handed down from guru to student for many, many thousands of years. The Book of the Dead was finally written down to preserve it when the lineage was lost, when the enlightened teacher did not produce an enlightened student to pass on the true knowledge of the rebirth process. It was written down so that others, as they came by the way, might understand part of this doctrine and be able to use it to their advantage.

But the idea that simply hearing the words of The Book of the Dead will cause you to be liberated upon dying is absurd. This is the corruption of its intent and meaning. The Book of the Dead constantly suggests that at the time of death what you should do is meditate upon the guru, the teacher. In other words, The Book of the Dead was not written for the general public. It is a book of the secret doctrine of Tibet, which simply means that the doctrine is secret, not to hide it from others, but that when a person hears the secret doctrine, unless their consciousness is advanced enough, they won't understand what it means. It'll go in one chakra and out the other, because while you may hear what the words mean, in the Webster's dictionary sense of the words, the words actually suggest states of being, which you will only perceive if your consciousness is wide open.

The Book of the Dead was intended as an advanced spiritual guidebook for persons who had reached the end of their evolutionary cycle and who were ready to make the jump to light speed; who had practiced spiritual disciplines in hundreds and thousands of lifetimes and now they were learning the very, very fine points of the rebirth process; who had spent their lives studying, their current life, with an enlightened teacher who would teach them these fine points.

The Book of the Dead at that time was not a book of the dead. They were the secret oral teachings that were transmitted from enlightened teacher to student. They were only written down when it was feared that the way would be lost, and so as a kind of gift to mankind they were written down with the thought that those who read them might never understand them. They might take them on the wrong level, in other words, but there might be someone out there who did or it might help reawaken one who had traversed these higher ranges in a previous lifetime. And when that person reincarnated, even though there might not be an enlightened teacher for them, if there was not one on the planet at the time, if they were drawn to The Book of the Dead, reading it over, it would bring back or help jar their past life realizations and awarenesses. This was the intent of the author.

It's as if you were walking around in the world with amnesia and suddenly you came upon a book, somehow you were just psychically drawn to it, and it was a book that talked about things that you used to know. As you read them over they would perhaps trigger or jar your memory and help you leave that amnesia and remember what you once knew so well.

It is possible at the time of death to use yoga to attain a higher birth or to go beyond the cycle of birth or death, but it's really like a final examination. If you haven't done any work all semester in school and suddenly the final exam's the next day and you try and study all the material in one day, you won't do well in the final exam, you won't pass. If you've done a very, very good job, if you've learned everything there is to learn, when the final exam comes you don't really have to study at all. You might just brush up on one or two things, but you'll go in and do a fine job on the exam. At the time of death, simply hearing The Book of the Dead isn't really going to make a difference. If you've worked on your consciousness all of your life, if you've learned to meditate perfectly, if you've learned to overcome your fears and your attachments, then at the time of death automatically your being will walk through the bardo when you're set face to face with the clear light of reality. In other words, when you see God at the time of death, rather than freaking out and running away and ending up in a lower bardo, having seen this again and again in your own meditation every day, it will come as no surprise, or shock and you'll just be absorbed.

You see, the real trick is not even to seek liberation, from the technical point of view, at the moment of death, because that's just another attraction. It's rather just to meditate and be absorbed by the clear light of reality, and if it is the will of the infinite that you should reincarnate in any world, you're more than happy to accept that. Be neither attracted nor repulsed, not even by liberation.

The real purpose of Tibetan yoga is not to counsel you at the time of your physical death. Rather, it is to suggest that the bardo is present now. The Book of the Dead is really not simply a map of the various dimensional states that you will pass through death and rebirth. Rather, it is a map of consciousness that exists now, and the idea is that you can reincarnate and have a higher birth without having to physically die. This is what we call the short path, which is what I taught in my Tibetan incarnations.

The short path means as follows: it might take you ten thousand incarnations in this world to attain enlightenment. Gradually, from one incarnation to another, you will grow, evolve, and develop. In each lifetime you learn a little bit and develop. Each day, if you go out into the sunshine for a few minutes, you'll get a little sun, a little radiation. Gradually you'll get a tan, but if you can go out into the tropics, in one day, you can get a tan that might have taken you years to develop just a little bit at a time. Needless to say, there's a danger of burning – it has to be done just right.

The short path, then, is a way of going through thousands of incarnations in one lifetime. You see the thing is, when you have to physically die to radically change states of awareness it's a real hassle, because when you die, after you go through the bardo, the little in-between zone between your death and your rebirth, it's very confusing. Once you reenter this world you have to go through childhood again and adolescence, and it may take you many, many years before you regain the evolution that you had in your last life, or you may go through some lifetimes when you don't even come back to where you were before.

Some people ask sometimes, "Well, why should I be in such a hurry to attain enlightenment? What's the difference? Why not take a hundred thousand lifetimes since I have all the time in the world anyway. Why do it in twenty lifetimes?" There is no right or wrong in this matter. You have to just select what you feel is best. The obvious advantage to having fewer lifetimes, from the point of the perceiver, is that as you advance more quickly you suffer less. Some people are under the illusion that, "Well, if I go through all my lifetimes really quickly, then I'll just stop living. In other words, after I finish the cycle of lifetimes and I attain liberation, then I'll be destroyed. I'll be absorbed in nirvana and I won't be anymore and I don't want that to happen. I like life and I like living so why not stretch out the incarnations as long as I can?" It's not like that. At the time of liberation you don't cease to be. You don't even necessarily stop reincarnating. If you want to reincarnate you can reincarnate as long as you can and come back and aid others, or if you just want to be absorbed in eternity that can occur anyway. You have choice, in other words, if you want choice.

Rather, the advantage is that as you even approach enlightenment, you live in a state of bliss instead of pain and suffering as most human beings do, and also, the more advanced you are, the more you can do for others. The primary motivation is either to get away from pain and suffering and frustration – and compared to the bliss of eternity even the so-called happiest moments that most people ever experience are suffering – to go beyond suffering to joy and bliss and light and/or to be motivated by the fact that there are other people in the world who suffer. If it will take you eight years to become a teacher and instead you could do it in four, if you become a teacher in four years, if you can learn the same amount, then you can get out in the field sooner and help people instead of just logging an additional four years to learn the same things.

The short path is available for those who want it, to pass quickly to enlightenment, and I teach the short path and the long path in this lifetime, but my emphasis, of course, is the short path because I've had that emphasis in other lifetimes, to bring or cycle a person through hundreds of lifetimes in one incarnation, which certainly doesn't mean that you can bring everyone you work with to enlightenment, far from it, but you can get them a lot closer. It depends on how the individual accesses the teaching and training process. The short path is for your serious student. The long path is for your happy student.

In Tibetan yoga, what we call the Tibetan rebirth process, what we're doing is really not teaching you how to get a better incarnation after this life ends, but rather how, within this life, to cycle through thousands of lifetimes without physically dying and losing all that time and awareness in the confusion of the rebirth process, and hopefully to attain enlightenment in this lifetime or if not, to get so close that in your next lifetime or shortly thereafter you will attain enlightenment, as opposed to 5,000 lifetimes from now. Why go through 5,000 more lives of birth, childhood, adolescence, adulthood, old age; 5,000 lifetimes of pain, suffering, transitory joys? Certainly there's much beauty in it. But since you've done it before, why keep seeing the same movie again and again? Why not make the jump? That's the voice of the short path.

The way that you follow the short path of Tibetan rebirth is to first and foremost declare to eternity what you want. You have to feel that the most important thing is to merge with eternity. That has to be your top priority. Then it's necessary to find a teacher who teaches the short path, to find a bodhisattva, a liberated, enlightened person who lives in this world, who accepts students and who will accept you as a student. That teacher will then show you, map out for you, a course of study, which you will follow both inwardly and outwardly, and what I'd like to share with you now is not so much what that course of study is about, because that varies from individual to individual and if it's your dharma to find out what that course of study is, that will happen, if it's not, it will not, but rather to deal with some general principles that are applicable to everyone, some of the things you'd learn in that process, in other words. The specifics you will only learn from your individual teacher and only after you've studied for many years with that teacher and the teacher is certain that you are ready for them, the advanced steps, in other words.

After you've studied for five or ten years with a teacher and done very well, exceedingly well, in all of your groundwork, your purity, humility, integrity, self-giving and so on, when you've really shaped yourself up, in other words, taken the teacher's advice and so on, changed over and over again, then the teacher will see that you are ready. The teacher doesn't hold back from you, but you can't teach someone the advanced moves until they've learned the basic ones.

Once you've mastered the basics, then your teacher, the enlightened teacher, if you have one, will one day show you some of the more advanced steps that will really help you go through all of those lifetimes so quickly, and of course a part of that is simply to be around or with an enlightened teacher because the field of energy that is generated by the living presence of such a teacher is so strong that being in it and meditating with that teacher, becoming absorbed in the light that comes through that teacher, escalates you through your lifetimes very, very quickly. But be that as it may, let's consider for a few moments how consciousness works – that is to say, that the bardo is not something that you will have to wait for death to go through, but it's here right now, and what that is all about and how it works.

There is no time. Time is a fixation in your mind. This is the first principle of the Tibetan rebirth process. If you believe that there is time then you will be bound by it. If you are bound by time then you will feel that your body must occupy a causal space for a specific period of time. That is to say, since you're here now in this lifetime you must experience what's in this lifetime. How can you experience what was in another thousand lifetimes if time really exists? Time would bind you to the relative conditions of this world. You must see that there is no time.

Time is an arbitrary invention on the part of the human race to try and clock and catalogue experiences. And it's proper, it's good to have time, it's good to have calendars, it's good to have a watch so you know what time it is, but when you move into the higher meditative states you see that that's all just a way of looking at existence. It's a useful template, but in actuality there is no time, which is why it's possible for us to go through a thousand lifetimes in one lifetime. We can only do that if there's no time. Time changes as you move through the different planes.

At the time of death, physical death, the aggregates that are your collected self – in other words, all the strands and fibers that join together, that create your personality – dissolve. They go back into a variety of sheathes, they're reabsorbed, they go back where they've come from. In order to bring you through the same number of experiences inwardly that you would have passed through in thousands of lifetimes, it's necessary for us to dissolve your old self. Listen carefully, oh nobly born, you need to be set face to face with the clear light of reality now, because there is no tomorrow and there is no past, there is no future. All that exists is the clear light of reality. You are a drop of consciousness floating on that clear light of reality, blissfully asleep. Blissfully awaken and dissolve in the clear light of reality. Hear these words and be liberated from the bardo of suffering.

It is necessary for your old self to die and after the time of death to be reborn into a higher self in this life. Then that higher self must die and you must be reborn again into a higher self. You must go through a thousand selves in this lifetime or however many it takes or however many you can, and experience inwardly, not necessarily outwardly, everything that you would have experienced in each of those lifetimes. You must enter into a different time cycle. There are three roads that lead to Los Angeles. Each of them has a different speed limit. You can be traveling in all three cars simultaneously. One car is doing 35 miles an hour, one 50, one 75. They will all not reach the destination at the same time. One will get there sooner. You can be in all three cars at once and each one will reach the destination at a different time.

It is necessary to learn to dissolve your old self, that's the first step. To dissolve your old self you must first want to. You have to sense the need for a higher rebirth. You're willing to let your old personality wash away in the clear light of eternity. You don't have to choose a new self. You see the trick of the reentry process, that is to say – let's say you can meditate very, very well and go into salvikalpa samadhi. If you go into samadhi, at that time your old self will actually dissolve. Samadhi, that type of meditation, is such a powerful state of existence, your old self dissolves; it's gone. Now, getting rid of your old self is the easy part, in my estimation. Again, that's a great art just to be able to go into salvikalpa. But that's the easy part. The tricky part is the reentry process.

You sit down and you meditate and let's say you go into salvikalpa samadhi. You're absorbed in eternity. Bam! The old self goes away and you don't exist for a while. It's exactly the same as death. In other words, what I'm saying is that you can die in this lifetime without your body having to die and experience everything you would experience at death. I do that hundreds of times a day now. The tricky part is not that, but that suddenly there'll be a new self born. It will be you. Oh, your memories and everything will still be swimming around, you're not going to lose all that. I mean you're not going to walk out into the world unable to function or anything, but the actual structure, the weave of your energies that hold you together, that make you what you are, will be loosened for a while in samadhi. Then they will reform. The trick is to let them reform by themselves. The mistake that most people make when they have a high spiritual experience is they are attracted back to their old lifestyle, their old habits, and their old ways.

If I could give you kind of a mini-perspective on this, imagine that you go on a vacation. Let's say that you want to make some big changes in your life. And it's really hard to break through those old habits and routines, but you go on a vacation for two weeks, you go to another place. There you see life in a different way. You have different experiences, everything is new and shining. And you make a lot of good decisions about, "Well, when I get back I'm going to change my job and change my relationships and move to a new place, and I'm not going to get angry at people anymore and I'm not going to feel sorry for myself, and I really see now that I've kind of stepped out of the world that I've been living in, how I can really change and really put it together. While I was there, gosh, I was so caught up in everything, it was just enough to get through the day. But now I've gone over to Hawaii and I've climbed on the top of Haleakala, I'm up on top of the volcano and I just have a feeling of being above my life and the world. I've flown up in an airplane and looked down and my world, which seemed so important, my God, when I look down through the window of the jet, there are millions of people down there. Each one has a life as complex as mine. My life is not that important and I can see how I want to change it."

But the problem is when you go back in, with all your new resolves, you are attracted back to your old habits. These are the samskaras, the tendencies from your past lives or from this life. Great, sure you were all inspired to change that job, to move, but suddenly you get back and there's a huge bunch of bills waiting for you. Suddenly you get depressed, suddenly you feel, "Oh gosh!" You start to doubt, "Maybe I shouldn't change, maybe I should wait another month before I try for that new job." In other words, your old habits and routines pull you back, your old desires. Because the reason that you didn't change, the reason you were a fixed self, was that you made yourself that way by what you wanted.

You see, the change in spiritual discovery doesn't simply mean we're going to become nicer or it doesn't mean you have to give up the things in your life – your car, your house, your family, that has nothing to do with it. To change means that you have to dissolve. You as you've come to know yourself will go away. You have to let go of yourself and let yourself dissolve and reform in the white light of eternity. The trick, then, is not going away on vacation. I mean that's a good trick to begin with. To get into samadhi is not easy. But the trick is coming back. That's the art that the spiritual teacher teaches you. First the spiritual teacher teaches you how to go up, then how to come back, how to reenter and not be dragged back into your old self but to enter into a new one.

Now, you do not actually have to wait until you can individually go into samadhi to do this. That's the advantage of the enlightened teacher. The reason that they say you should have an enlightened teacher is, of course, not just because the teacher can point things out, but the teacher has a power. When you meditate with an enlightened person, even though you are not capable of going into samadhi yourself, if you're a good meditator and if you've taken the teacher's advice and swept the island of your being and put yourself together and made yourself lucid and pliable and eager and inspired and happy and balanced, when you've gone through the basic years of self-discovery and not just walked through them but done well with them, then when you meditate with a teacher, if you have a self-realized teacher, the teacher's meditation can be so powerful that it actually dissolves your self. Then for a period of about a week – it depends how powerful the teacher is, but usually for about a week maximum – the glue that holds together your personal form will become loose and then it is possible for you to reenter.

Instead of taking another hundred incarnations of spiritual practice to be able to go into samadhi by yourself, if you can be accepted by and work with an enlightened teacher, and if you're really gung ho, the teacher can give you that experience in this life. The advantage to having that experience in this life is not just that the experience of samadhi is enjoyable, but it allows you to make that big step, and the teacher doesn't do that with you once but again and again and again. The teacher can just lift up the curtain of immortality so you can peek under and get a view, but then you have to put yourself back together.

Now, the way you reenter, which is the tricky part, is by not trying. If you try too hard to rebuild yourself it won't work because any image you can project or think of will be limited. Rather than following an image you project, you let God work through you, to select for you. Rather, in other words, than having to do, you just have to stay out of the way. The river knows exactly how to flow. Your job is simply, during that period of time, to neither be attracted nor repulsed by any ideas, not to seek your old ways nor to shun them, but just to allow eternity to reorder your being.

And this will be tricky. Let me give you an example. I recently took about 350 of my students out to the desert and when I was out there I meditated on them very intensely, and I brought them all through the bardo – in other words, I melted the glue that held them together and put them into a very fluid, pure state of awareness whereby they could make a tremendous transition, what I call an epiphany. Now, about a week has gone by since our journey and now the glue has reformed. During this week, each of them had an opportunity to make a tremendous transition. However, at the same time during the week they would be confronted by all of their attachments, all the things they want or they thought they wanted, that their old self wanted or their old selves from past lives wanted. And also all the things they feared would appear before them and if they ran towards the things that they had wanted previously, then they would want them again and they would lock into that personality that wants things like that. If they ran away from their fears then they would become the person who is afraid of those things. You see, all a person is, as we define person aside from an aggregate of memories, is a formation of attractions and repulsions.

What makes one person different than another – aside from physical shape and coloration and so on – in terms of personality and structure? Imagine that a person is a circle. Everybody is the same circle. My circle is no different than your circle, but what makes us different then? What creates character? What creates it, in terms of consciousness, are the areas within the circle. You can segment the circle, right? You can draw lots of lines through it and cut it into little pieces. There will be many areas within the circle and you can color each one a different way. Those colorations, the things that make you what you are, are your desires, your ideas of yourself, the way the ego works and sees itself and the things that you are afraid of, the things that you are repulsed by.

If you were to look at yourself in terms of a circle you would be filled with all kinds of lines and shadings. If you were to look at me as a circle you would see that there are no lines drawn within the circle, and that the circle sometimes isn't even there. Sometimes the outer circumference of the circle dissolves and occasionally it reforms. This is, if you are familiar with Zen and the "Searching for the Ox" pictures, the shorter set of pictures, where in each of the succeeding pictures the ox gets whiter and then finally self-alone, the ox is gone and the person who seeks the ox is gone. It's the same principle that is espoused in Zen, but just through a different symbology than in Tibetan form.

The way to a successful rebirth, then, is by not doing, not trying, which doesn't mean that you're not active in the world and at your job and working. It means internally, not what you're doing physically. Physically we drive our cars and go places and so on, but while that show is going on there's an inner show going on. Your mind is talking, thoughts and emotions are passing through you and the trick is not to hook on to any of them while you're in this very fragile intermediate state, and just not be afraid of the light.

Now, some of my students after their last journey have been kind of very disassociated all week. In other words, their consciousness finally reached the point they've always wanted it to. We worked all trimester with a lot of meditations to bring them up to a certain point and then with our trip to the desert and an evening meditation before that, each of them was given an opportunity to move into this higher state. The glue was melted, but some of them, then, during the next week felt very disassociated. They weren't themselves anymore and that was absolutely correct – they weren't themselves anymore. They weren't any self and some of them thought, "Well, my God, here I am in this negative state and I just don't seem to have a center." You see, they became afraid; that's one of the fears again that you have to deal with, not only in this process but when you physically die. Again you're trying to find, "Oh God, I'm out there on my own, I'm alone, I need a fireplace, a family, comfort, a roof, identity. Identity! I have to have identity! My God, I'm drifting alone in the void! I'm dissolving! What'll I do?" You see, that sort of feeling.

Now, there's nothing to be afraid of; the void is nothing but light, your real self. It's not empty, but your mind will create and project these various fears with which you try and hold yourself back from enlightenment and absorption. The trick is not to be afraid, but when your worst fears appear before you, just to smile at them, and you'll find there's never anything to be afraid of, that dissolution and creation are only ideas. Rather, you just embrace your fears and smile at them and say, "Hi! Oh, you're my worst fear? Well, come on in, sit down, let's have a bite to eat." You'll find that that fear will dissolve and that there was never anything to be afraid of, there was only light and perfection and God.

And you don't chase the things that you always wanted. If you're supposed to have something in your life, it will come, or just trust that you'll always do what's right, but don't be attracted. Just watch your desires pass by you. You see, Tibetan yoga is the art of perceiving. It's the art of just sitting and watching the world go by, being active in it, working, doing whatever is right and normal for your life situation, but just watching the world go by in inner terms. That is to say, sitting at a point of distance inside yourself and pleasantly observing everything happening, enjoying what comes to you, not being afraid to enjoy, not feeling the need to run after. But at the same time being detached, just living in that pure light of God which is bliss itself.

Tibetan yoga, the rebirth process, the short path. Not meaning that at the time of death it should be practiced – it can be – but rather practicing in life, seeing that life is death and that death is life, that there's really no difference; to learn not to be afraid of anything because there's nothing to be afraid of. Everything is your self. All your worst fears – the Tibetans, of course, symbolize all the fears with these awful five-headed, fire-breathing, snake form monsters or something (Rama laughs). They like to personify things or they personify the beatific states of awareness, the formless ecstasies and beautiful goddesses and angels and stuff like that. They don't have to have a form, that's just their symbolic way of trying to represent them and what they're saying is, don't be afraid of anything. The worst thing you can imagine is still part of yourself, since you're one with God and all is God. It's only your fears and your foolish attractions that prevent you from seeing the perfection that exists in all things.

Embrace without embracing, love without loving, fear without fearing. Don't mind what you go through in life, just don't get hung up in it, and the only way you can do this, of course, is by meditating. You can hear the ideas but not practice. You must meditate to get that power and that distance, that absorption, to be capable of making the jump to light speed, of going into the higher consciousness and watching the old self dissolve and enjoying it, just as you throw your old clothes away and then go out and buy some new clothes. But not the same kind – something nicer, more refined, more beautiful. And by changing your outfits again and again and again, until finally you wear the most beautiful clothes or nothing at all, and then you merge with eternity.

The Tibetan rebirth process.

LIVING AND WORKING IN THE WORLD

The greatest challenge awaiting you is living and working in the world. Traditionally, seekers of the infinite light have renounced society and gone into places of solitude to meditate, pray, fast, practice various spiritual arts and to gain a sense of community, a fellowship with others who speak a kindred language.

If we look back at the history of spirituality, we see that the great, enlightened souls were often very reclusive. They lived on top of the high Himalayas, in caves and forests. Very few of them really entered into the world, or if they did live in somewhat of a societal setting, they had their students build monasteries, convents, ashrams – places where the students and the teacher could live together and associate with each other without having to deal with the world.

The reason they did this is certainly self-evident. Most people in this world are not interested in light and spiritual development at this stage in their evolution. They're still playing their war games, their oppression games. They're still trying to limit others in the name of their own happiness. As a matter of fact, after you have practiced meditation and spirituality for some time, you begin to get a sense that you're on the wrong planet. There's a feeling that you don't belong here because when you look at the world, you look with eyes of love and joy and beauty. And when you enter into the nine-to-five world, the competitive business world, the world of freeways, nations, wars, political systems, families, ethnic groups, power groups – the world, as you know, is not a particularly attractive place, the world that men and women have created.

This earth itself is nothing but beauty. But human beings have been a disease, from a certain point of view, a kind of a bacteria that has infected the earth, that has destroyed the forests, the rivers, polluted the oceans, that is currently destroying the ozone layer. Human beings have not taken very good care of the resource that sustains them. They don't seem to realize that if they destroy it, they destroy themselves. A most unusual species.

Yet taken individually, human beings are incredibly beautiful. If we look at any person, they have sensitivities, inner light. While they may be in a certain stage in their evolution where they're a little confused, just as a third grader does not know everything, we can't necessarily find fault with them for that. They're doing the best they can with what they have. Indeed, what we should have is an attitude of tolerance, not of perdition. We should feel that all of humanity is our family – and I always think it's a good idea to put as much distance between yourself and your family as possible (Rama laughs), unless, of course, you have an exceptionally enlightened family.

In today's world it's really impossible to get away from humanity. We live in a media jungle, what McLuhan called a global community. All of us are joined together by media – television, satellites, newspapers, magazines. Even if you live out in the far reaches – there are no longer far reaches – because in an instant, through the marvelous aid of electronics, you can be in touch with any part of the world. As a matter of fact, it's pretty hard to avoid it.

The problem is that a great deal of the information that comes down the pike is not very good. The consciousness of most human beings has a certain focus. And while all people are good and many people think noble thoughts, by and large we live in a world that is interested in sensations. The news that greets us is in many ways very similar to the sights that greeted those who went to the Roman Coliseum to watch the games. There's an urge within the human species for blood, for violence. People derive a strange pleasure from hearing about the misfortunes of others. This is the way the world is. To think badly of the world or of humanity for being this way is like condemning, again, all the second and third graders in the world. Tolerance is necessary.

Living in a world of darkness. In other words, the dark ages have always been present, in a sense, from the spiritual point of view. Many spiritual communities have flocked off to the woods; they still do today. They live in seclusion and this is an interesting way to live. I think it's as valid a way to live as any other. It just depends what your purposes are. I myself have always been a lover of society and nature at the same time – because I see God in the flowers and in the city streets as well. I don't see that there's essentially a difference. Sometimes it's fun to be in one and sometimes it's fun to be in the other.

It is my belief that you really can't escape the vibratory energies of this world. That is to say, even a few hundred years ago the population of our planet was much smaller than it is today. Each person who lives on this earth creates a vibratory energy and when the planet was not as populated, the energies were not as volatile. But as the population continues to escalate, the weave of the energies gets stronger and stronger and it has an effect on everyone who lives here. Even if you live on top of an isolated mountain, it can't be isolated in terms of energy. As you meditate and you develop more sensitivity, or let's say you just become more aware of the sensitivity that all human beings have potentially, you are affected strongly by these energies.

As far as I'm concerned, in terms of spiritual evolution, while it used to be that you could go live in the convent or the monastery and get away from it all – and in a sense you could, you could just put physical distance between yourself and the population masses, the unenlightened masses who were interested in their own pleasures and pastimes, which might not have been your pastimes – that's really not possible today because even if you just go a few miles away, the energies are so volatile in the world that you really can't get away from them.

Oh, there are some places where there'll be less – Hawaii, a few other places, parts of Switzerland – where you can, to some extent, get away from it all. But even so, I don't even think it's necessarily good to try. Because if you're interested in helping humanity, which is the hallmark of real spirituality, at least in my estimation, it's pretty tough to help people when you've separated yourself from them. In other words, you can help a lot of squirrels out in the forest, but aside from an occasional ranger or park visitor there aren't too many people you can be of service to.

Secondly, there's a real problem with separating yourself from humanity. While you will assert, and I will certainly agree, that humanity is not at a very high state in their evolutionary development – they're currently inventing bigger and better bombs to blow themselves up with – the same silly stuff that's been going on for thousands of years still goes on, the same repression. While we've developed an interesting technology, human beings really, in my estimation, have not evolved very far. We don't have a much greater sense of humanity than the ancient Greeks did or the ancient Chinese. Still, when you start to separate yourself from humanity, a funny thing happens. When you feel that you are a spiritual seeker and you want to step back from the world, in many cases an egotism or an egotistical attitude begins to develop, and you see this, unfortunately, in many spiritual groups. It's the "holier than thou" attitude.

The most important quality in self-discovery, in the so-called spiritual life, is humility. If you have all spiritual qualities and do not have humility, then all is lost from a spiritual perspective. If you have humility and nothing else, then don't worry, all other spiritual qualities will follow humility. Persons who isolate themselves from the world, unless they're truly humble, usually begin to develop this subtle sense of superiority which is very detrimental to their spiritual growth and development. The idea is that, "I can see more than humanity. I'm more advanced spiritually, therefore I'm better. I'm removing myself from the dirty world with its wicked people because I am superior, I am chosen." This is not a very healthy attitude for people who claim to be interested in love. From my point of view as one who, again, teaches not so much the basics in spiritual discovery but the advanced aspects, the graduate school of spirituality, while I recognize that very often there is a common need in people in early spirituality to do this, it's quite detrimental to persons who are interested in full enlightenment, God realization, liberation.

Sometimes it is necessary to put something down very heavily, even more than you might suppose. For example, many women who have been abused by men for thousands of years need to separate themselves for a while from men in order to form their own identities. In other words, their identities have been lost by living in a male-controlled world, where the males dictate what the image of a woman is. Naturally, you're going to have to have some kind of reaction for a while to balance the scales. Women are going to, if they're interested in enlightenment, have to stand back from men for a while and associate more with each other to develop a proper image. While some may view this as extreme or going overboard, it's necessary. It's a necessary reaction for a time. But then, after that new identity has been developed, there has to be a relocation in the world, a coming together. But for a while, sometimes, there needs to be separativity.

Someone who's an alcoholic, for a while, might have to put down alcohol. In other words, it might be OK for someone to drink who can handle it properly – who uses but does not abuse. For that person, for a while, when they first break away, there may be a need in their being to just say to all who come within hearing distance that alcohol is the worst, that people who use it are foolish and so on. Now eventually, if that person really beats the problem, one day they will become more moderate and they will be able to accept that others may like it, but they simply don't. But it's foolish to think that people can go to that state right away.

In spiritual development, many people, after being inculcated in the world for a long period of time, have just gotten so locked up in worldly values and ideas that they really believe that what matters is owning a bigger car or having a happy family. They really think that their mortgage payments are important. They believe in a better facial tissue and that the right toothpaste can make your life perfect – the consumer mentality. For these persons it's a good idea to step back from the world for a while because they've forgotten that they're in the middle of eternity and that God is the source of all. And that while all things are good, one should not become so entangled in the world that you don't see the world – not seeing the forest for the trees, in other words. If you've gotten so wrapped up in your relationships with other human beings, in your career, in your thoughts about yourself and your own introspection, if you're too wrapped up in your own spiritual development and how well you're doing or how poorly you're doing and your self-image and what others think of you, then you've lost it.

You've forgotten something very important, my friend, and that's that you're only a visitor here. You will not be here long. You are here for 60, maybe 80 years, tops. That's not very long, I assure you, when you measure that against eternity. Best to consider eternity and not to worry too much about the fact that somebody bumped into your car and you got a dent in it. Give value to the world – you are here, treat it well – be kind to those around you, but don't get too attached to this place. This is just a motel that you're staying in; it's not your home. You're just passing through.

For some people, when they begin to break out of the maya, there's a need to reject the world and its strange value systems. In early states of spiritual development we have to recognize that some people will need to walk away from the world, to be by themselves more, to leave their families, their friends and perhaps seek out some solitude in nature, to draw into the self, to weave a cocoon. But then they shouldn't stay in the cocoon. The butterfly should emerge from the cocoon after going through the metamorphosis and share its beauty with everyone and just fly, just enjoy the gift of flight.

In advanced spiritual practice, then, it is no longer necessary to run away from society or the world. As a matter of fact, it's detrimental because one wants to be neither attracted nor repulsed. If you're interested in being of service to the people of the world, it's a good idea to be around them. And third, there's a great danger in separating yourself from the world and from the people of the world and developing the subtle egotism which will defeat all of your other spiritual practices.

If you become so sensitive that you can't bear the vibrations of the city street, then you have not been practicing your yoga and meditation correctly. While there will be a residual drain, naturally, when you enter an area where the energy is a little bit lower than your own cycle, spiritual practice should make you strong enough that you can go out and live and work in the world and deal with it, and then come back to your home, to be with your other friends who speak the same language you do, to go to your spiritual meditation meetings and so forth and recharge your batteries and then go on out for another adventure. Living and working in the world.

How do you deal with it? How do you deal with society with all of its incongruities? How do you deal with sitting in your office after you've just come back from the desert, where you've been meditating? You watch the room dissolve and fill up with light. You're floating in another world, the sea of consciousness, and the guy at the desk next to you is too busy looking at the legs of the secretary, when maybe he should be thinking about his wife – or he's busy looking at you.

How do you deal with a boss who tells you to produce more and more and to use pressure techniques to sell, when you're interested in God and liberation? Where is that beautiful pine forest grove for meditation as you're sitting on the 405 Freeway at 5:00 o'clock, and the traffic is definitely not moving? What do you do with the violence, when someone pulls a gun on you in the street, when someone breaks into your home and rips everything off? How do you deal with the incongruities of existence, of a world of people who are cruel to each other, sometimes without even realizing that they're cruel? How do you deal with it? Very, very skillfully. Living and working in the world. It is necessary to be part of an organic fellowship. This is the advice of the *I Ching*, that ancient, venerable Chinese book of wisdom, to which I subscribe so heavily. The *I Ching* counsels us – the sages who wrote the *I Ching* a long, long time ago – that the wisdom of the self-taught is heavy and ponderous. While you may make a certain amount of spiritual progress on your own, it's lacking in something. It's heavy, it's ponderous.

Something occurs in learning with others that's marvelous. The edges of our egotism are slowly worn down. If you take a piece of glass and flip it into the ocean, after it's been out in the ocean for a while its sharp edges will be worn away. When I was a child we called this harmless glass. We'd be down at the beach and we'd see these little pieces of glass washed up and you couldn't cut yourself with them. It's necessary for the ego to be worn down. It's very easy to sit by yourself and think that you have no ego, but in your interactions with others you will begin to see where you really are. I always feel that you can judge the level of a person's spiritual advancement by how they treat those around them in everyday situations. That's the sign if you're really living your spiritual practices.

It's very good then to be a member of an organic fellowship of beings, a member of a spiritual community. But in my estimation that community does not have to separate itself from the world. That is to say, I think that you can maintain your own dwelling, your own apartment or house, condominium, tent, and live in a city or a town or a village or whatever in which many other people who are a member, perhaps, of the group that you're involved with, that is to say, the persons you meditate with – all of you live in the same area but not all in the same house.

The problems with ashrams are many. They have their strong points. When you live in one building with a lot of other spiritual seekers, very often you will find it very difficult to be yourself. There will be a certain party line that everyone follows. In other words, there will be peer group pressure. Two-thirds of the people will act a certain way and they will expect that everyone else will act the same way. You may find yourself trying to speak like, or adopt the attitudes of those who are around you when they're not really suitable for you.

Spirituality is individual. The most important thing in spiritual practice is to be yourself. Your self or your selves will change constantly. It's very important in spiritual practice not to try to be like others. You can emulate the good qualities you see in others. If you see someone who has humility or purity or beauty, just your perception of that and love of that and admiration of that will cause that quality to start to grow, will foster its development in your own being. But be yourself, that's the most important part.

In my estimation, in the current world, what is advisable is to band together with others who practice self-discovery, but to not necessarily live with them. Oh, you might share a house with a few people, those persons in the spiritual group who see as you do – because there may be people in the spiritual group who see very differently. Sometimes it's fun to change that group every six months or every year, or you may enjoy living by yourself. Sometimes it's fun to live by yourself for a while and then live with a group or live with one person. Two people are good together. Three, as the I Ching tells us, is a difficult number. Beyond four it gets kind of crowded. I personally like one, two, and four. Three is interesting, but usually one will feel left out. Two will be closer. And again, I think beyond four the energy web gets too confused, but do as suits you.

I think it's good to spend a lot of money on where you live, as much as you can afford, probably a little more, because that is your place of power. While you're going out into the world each day and picking up the energy and vibrations of the world, where you live should be very, very beautiful. I wouldn't worry about saving money for the future. The future will take care of itself, which doesn't mean that you shouldn't save, if that's your propensity. But I think that the best investment in yourself is yourself. Anyone who has ever made a great deal of money will tell you that their best investment was always in their own being, in their education, in their lifestyle. Because you are the product. If you don't take good care of the product, then the product is not going to do well. If you're not happy, you're not going to succeed.

Rather than worrying about how much money you're spending on where you live, I'd consider ways to make a little more money, to upgrade your lifestyle because in the world, with all its strangeness and convoluted vibrations, you need a safe place, a safe house, where you can come and that's your retreat. In other words, your retreat doesn't have to be out in the forest, it can be right in the middle of the world.

I think it's nice to pick a community that's beautiful, physically. Physical beauty is very important. If you're living in the middle of the ghetto it's pretty tough to deal with. You can do it, but it's harder. Why give yourself a hard time? The ghetto shouldn't exist. The world should be a garden; every home should be beautiful. If people were enlightened, it would be this way, but they're not. Why should you live in a place that just reflects the bad consciousness of humanity? No, move to a beautiful place, a community that you feel is balanced.

It's always good, if you can, to live near the ocean or at least a body of water – the vibratory energy is much better. If you find such a place, live there, and live in a very nice place, the next step is to fix your house up beautifully. The house should be beautiful. Some people, in spiritual practice, are very austere. It comes from their past lives, I think. They live in these very primitive settings. They might even rent a nice house and then they'll just have a mattress in their room, a complete lack of beauty.

While I enjoy simplicity, still there's nothing wrong with having some furniture in your room and some pretty pictures and nice curtains. If making your room a world of light and beauty upsets you, then I have to tell you, you're very attached. Spirituality doesn't come by getting rid of your furniture. Spiritual refinement, however, is making your home a beautiful place because it will renew you, as beauty renews us, and its higher psychic energy will add to your spiritual advancement.

My suggestion then, for the person who lives in the modern world, is to join a spiritual community that you feel happy to be in. A spiritual community will usually have a head, one individual who is the most spiritually advanced in the group, who will try and aid others to help the community run smoothly, but yet will let everyone live their own lives.

I think it's a great mistake to join a spiritual community and give them all your money and sign over your property, you know, sort of the cult mentality. I understand that for some people it can be a big spiritual step forward, a great self-giving, but I think that in the modern world it's good to maintain your own identity. I don't think it's necessary to live that way. That won't give you enlightenment. Enlightenment will come through service to others, but in order to serve others well you need a base. Those spiritual teachers who say, "Follow me, give everything to me," I don't know, they must have pretty large size bank accounts (Rama laughs). While I'm sure there are rationalizations and justifications for it in their minds, and we'll let them go their way and feel that they're doing their best, from my limited point of view, if you're interested in enlightenment, that's not necessary. Independence, a little Emersonian independence, is healthy.

Once you've found a nice place to live, settled in, either by yourself or with some others in your spiritual group – because you meditate together or you're all vegetarians, you speak the same language – it's fun to live together, you renew each other. If you're living in a community, of course, with others, who are doing the same thing, it's fun. You'll go downtown and you'll see some other people who are glowing on the sidewalk as they walk by. You build a web of energy in the community, in other words. A lot of you live together, but not all in the same residence, each maintaining your own domicile or small groups doing that.

Then it's necessary, of course, to work out the relationships, which never exactly work out, between those of you who live together. If you live by yourself you don't need to worry about this particular part of the tape. However, if you live with others, it's necessary to care for them deeply yet be extremely unattached. Living with others is a great experience. It teaches you a lot about yourself and it gives you the opportunity to grow through service to others. But you have to always be very tolerant and realize that nobody's perfect, that everybody goes up and down and will, constantly. You're always going up and down in your cycle, whatever your level of evolution is, as is everyone else, and that will not change.

Living with people is just like keeping up with anything else in life. It's like keeping your house clean. You may clean the house on Saturday, but next Saturday you have to clean it again. With people, every single day you have to bring something, which is love, to your relationships with them. Yet you have to give each other enough room.

People who are engaged in spiritual practices and advanced meditation are very different than other people. Their changes are much more volatile. Their emotions go up and down like the winds because, if they're on the short path, they're going through hundreds of lifetimes in one life. When you first move in together you may get along just fine. Five months later, or even three months later, it's all changed. Because you've changed. Don't feel the necessity to make it work when it doesn't work. Feel free to separate, to re-form with new groups, to move to a new place. While this may be taxing on your landlord, don't worry about it, be unattached. At most you'll lose your security deposit.

In other words, realize that the people you live with are never going to suit you. They're not supposed to, nor are you supposed to suit them. What you're trying to do is help each other, have fun with each other and leave each other alone. Don't feel that you're supposed to bring each other to spiritual liberation or salvation, but rather to ask each other each day, "How was your day at work?" Be kind, but don't be the master spiritual guide. Let everybody be themselves. Let everybody make their own mistakes and learn from them.

Naturally, if someone is having a hard time, try to cheer them up. If you see something they don't, gently point it out, but there's a way to do these things. I recommend that all of my students read a very marvelous book called *How to Win Friends and Influence People* by Dale Carnegie, to read it several times. Mr. Carnegie was a master at human relations. There is a way to get your point across so that it will be very productive and help people, and there's a way to not do that.

Give some thought to your household. It's very, very important because if things are not going well in your household, it's very hard to deal with the world. If things are going well in the household, then you can go out into the world and feel good. But if you are upset at home and then you have to go into an upsetting world, two minuses create a real problem.

Set up a social contract with the people who you live with. That is to say, decide what's happening. Who's doing the dishes and so on. Make sure that everybody keeps the house spotlessly clean. If somebody doesn't, then you should talk to them. If it doesn't work out, rather than berate them every day and become enemies, move. Live alone or just live with one person, which I think is ideal, actually, in most cases. It's easier to deal with just one person and their changes.

Experiment with your life, but be up front about it all. Don't just sit there and get angry because somebody leaves their dirty shoes in the wrong place. The last thing you need is to worry about things like that, and also expect that it's going to take a great deal of responsibility on your part and don't wait for other people to be responsible. You go ahead and be responsible and you make sure everything gets done right. Don't be afraid of working four hours longer than anyone else. It doesn't have to be equal. Who said it should be? Each one of you is independent, and you're making spiritual progress by doing the best that you can, not by waiting around for others to act.

Be kind and be generous, but don't be foolish. Help others, but if they become leeches, if all they do is want is economic help and support past what is necessary, then just let them go their own way. You have to be unattached because sometimes you think you're helping people and you're hurting them. Sometimes you can help and give somebody a new start and a helping hand, but there are people who just, unfortunately, sponge off of others and when you let them do that, either emotionally or financially or in any way, you're not helping them. It's better to let them go out and make it on their own.

Advanced spirituality is not for people who have difficulty with living their life. It's for people who are getting their careers together, their lives together, their physical consciousness together, who are mobile, who have succeeded, in other words, in the world. It's not for people who just want to run away from responsibility and society and their families. Rather, it's for people who have already succeeded or are quickly learning how to succeed at the game of life.

What I teach is not for people who still have basic personality problems. It's for people who have mastered life, who are successful and now want to become successful at something else. While we do a certain amount of remedial work with people and try and help you restructure your life and give you some new input on jobs and community and things like that, the point is you're already supposed to be very successful or, if not, moving quickly in that direction. The last thing we want to worry about is the physical. What you're here to learn about is the other side of your being. You should have your job together, your career, your education, your lifestyle, all of these things should be improving constantly. You should be getting better at it and not having major problems again and again.

Economics is a very important consideration of living and working in the world, for several reasons. First of all, it's been my experience that money is a marvelous thing. Money enables you to aid others. You can have all the great intentions in the world but if you don't have the money to go behind the intention, you can do very little for people in the modern world. I think money is great. I also don't think it means very much. It's just paper, but if you use it properly you can do a lot with it.

A lot of spiritual seekers, for some reason, suddenly want to reject money and the world. They think that being spiritual entails being poor, and I think that demonstrates a definite lack of power. While I know that many people who practice spirituality have an aversion to money because perhaps in their past lives they made mistakes with money, it dragged them down – remember, be neither attracted nor repulsed. Money is neither good nor bad. Oh, we've seen how it's been abused in this world, maybe now we can see how it can be used.

I think money is great if you use it and channel it to aid others properly. And I don't think that you should be afraid of making money. As a matter of fact, I think that you should think of all the ways that you can make money, and you should make as much money as you can. Because if you really love humanity, then you want to do something for humanity. If you want to do something for humanity, honestly, just between you and I, I can tell you next year or next month how many people I will be able to be of service to based strictly upon budget.

In other words, I have a given number of years to live in this world as an enlightened person. During that period of time I will come in contact with a certain amount of people. If I can double that amount of people, then many people would have better lives. I'm a resource, but the resource is strictly limited by finances. We try and use what we have as cleverly as we can, but at the same time, it's strictly economic.

I've been teaching meditation in this life, as of this tape, for about 14 years. I've been doing this out in the world and I've run monasteries in other lifetimes and ashrams and all kinds of things, Zen centers. One thing that I've learned is that economics is important, that the fear of money is as great an attachment as the love of it. I think you should be very impartial. But if you do love others, if you are interested in the welfare of others, then I think it's perfectly healthy to feel that you should make as much money as you can. Because what you can do is live as nicely as you want, have everything you feel you need and take anything else and give it to a spiritual cause, to your spiritual organization, whereby you can see that money create miracles in people's lives, as it has in yours.

Keep everything you need, have everything you should have. If you want a Ferrari, get a Ferrari. But once you have what you want, or even on the way, ask yourself, "How much do I not need?" And use that for the welfare of others. That's self-giving.

I know of nothing that hurts a person spiritually more than being poor. If you're always trying to think about how you're going to pay the bills, if you're living in a place that has a lower vibration because you can't afford a better one, if you're worried about money, it's living hell. You may not have experienced this, but if you have, you understand what I'm saying, and you can't meditate or make good spiritual progress if you're all wrapped emotionally because of a lack of money.

What I would suggest is to make as much money as you can in a career that you like. Now if you have picked out some career that you just simply love and adore and it doesn't pay much, that's fine, go follow your career. But it seems to me that if you're going to put in eight hours or seven hours a day, and if they'll pay you $15.00 for one skill and $5.00 for another, you might as well make the $15.00. Because remember, when they're paying you, it can't be too good. In other words, every profession offers you something, but at the same time you're not doing it for free – the idea being that if you could just do as you wanted and had all the money you needed, then you wouldn't be doing your job. You'd be doing something else. They're paying you for your time. They're buying your life, they're buying your days, they're buying most of your waking life or at least half of it – five days out of the week and sometimes more. They're paying you for something that will never come again. I think they should pay you well because you should feel that your time is very valuable.

When you work, you should do a superlative job. When you work, you should do it with excellence because whenever you work with excellence, that adds to your consciousness. Whenever you don't, that detracts from it. Even if it's a simple filing job, typing, computer programming, being a doctor, lawyer, student, whatever it may be, you should succeed. Success is a sign of a good spiritual consciousness. You don't have to be success oriented, you should just do it. You should do everything perfectly and keep working at it. Because if you feel that your work is part of your yoga and you do that eight hours a day, all the energy you put into it will advance your consciousness, your meditation, and everything else. In other words, there's nothing holier than work. Nothing's better for you than working. I work from the moment I wake up until I go to sleep. I wouldn't know what else to do.

Selfless service gives you tremendous spiritual advancement, and working at the local plant, computer programming, whatever it may be, is as spiritual as teaching people how to meditate. It doesn't matter what you do, it's why. If you're working every day to define your consciousness, to maintain yourself in the world so you can practice spirituality and so that you can make extra money to help your spiritual group grow, to touch more lives, to bring more light into people's lives who want that light, not into people's lives who don't, then your work is the holiest thing that you do.

You should feel that there are many, many people who are just waiting in the world, as you, perhaps, once were, for someone to touch their lives. There are many people who aren't interested in spirituality but some are, and you could make the difference in their life. If you don't think so, you're wrong. I see lives change and transform constantly, and it's people who help out economically who make that happen, as well as those who work in other ways. But in this world, money is power. In the inner world, light is all. In the outer world, economics allows light to travel.

As you may know, I have a favorite profession and that's computer science. I feel that the computer world is a fine place for spiritual seekers to be because the mindset that it takes to use computer technology is the Zen mind. It's very similar. In other words, as you meditate your mind changes in specific ways and those ways are perfect for people who program computers and work in the computer field. It's very similar. Also, computers – you know, we're just seeing their advent in the world – but the introduction of computer technology is very much like the introduction of writing. There was a time when almost all of the planet was illiterate and then writing came along. Very few people could write, and the change in our society that writing brought about, which was incredible, is smaller than the change that the computer revolution will bring about. Technology, like money, is a very good thing, in my opinion. We've seen the abuse of technology, but the use of technology we have still to see. We've seen it in medicine and a few other places: contact lenses, birth control, electric typewriters, hair dryers.

A lot of so-called spiritual people are scared of technology. I really don't understand it. They're under the assumption that somehow technology is associated with the establishment and the establishment is bad. This is a very pedestrian way to see the world. Technology is fantastic. What fun! I'm not quite sure where computers got such a bad name among certain circles. I don't know, people have the idea that they're these big, dark, gray metal machines that bring about impersonality and the lack of emotion, and I certainly don't understand. There are few more challenging or fun experiences than to do a computer program because you use your total mind. It's very jnana yoga, it's marvelous. Within not many years, in the primary grades, every child will be learning programming. In other words, if you're not interested in computers, you are part of a species that is about to become extinct. Pretty soon languages like COBOL and Fortran and Pascal will be spoken as fluently as English and French and Japanese and German. In other words, with the spiritual vision that I have, I see that the change is so radical and so good from this technology, that those who run away from it are like the Stone Age tribes who ran away from fire. Those tribes who had fire succeeded. It's foolish not to accept God in any form.

I think that computer programming, for a person who lives and works in the world, is ideal – or many other professions, medicine, law, whatever you prefer – but it helps you develop your mind, is what I'm suggesting, in a way that's very similar to the way that we develop the mind in meditation – clear and precise logic. At the same time you get to work on your own and not necessarily interact with too many people. It's a fascinating field for many reasons.

I have a program for people, which I suggest sometimes, who want to change their jobs. It's amazing – again, this may not apply to you – but I meet a lot of "spiritual types" who don't really have it very together in the world. They're very nice people. They meditate nicely, but they have trouble succeeding in the world. They just don't have a skill or they don't like their job. I have a little program I suggest to people. You may have a better program. I just find this one works for a lot of people, and that's that if you don't have a skill, learn to type. Everyone should learn to type. Get yourself a used electric typewriter and a little book and sit down and teach yourself. Once you've learned to type, which you can do in about two or three weeks using one of these little self-taught courses or taking a little typing course at a night school or something, then get a job typing. Start with a temporary agency, then learn word processing. Take a word processing course at a community college. Word processing is absolutely fun. I have a word processor and it's just a fancy typewriter, but you work with a screen and they're really neat. It's like playing an electronic game. They're very practical; they enable you to text edit and do all kinds of things. Also, you'll make a little more money, about twice as much.

Then investigate the world of computers, if that's your interest. Take some courses. Begin to find out what it's all about. Now, you may be at a point where the last thing you need to do is get involved with computers. I'm not suggesting that everyone should go do that. But what I'm saying is, if your life is in a state of change, and you're at the point where you are considering a career for many, many years, I think from a spiritual point of view it's a very interesting career to examine. Or whatever suits you. You follow your own heart in the matter. That's always the best. But I see something spiritually, is what I'm trying to say, about this particular field. It also allows you to make a tremendous amount of money with which you can buy space around yourself.

You see, in the world, as the society and the population gets denser and denser and it gets darker out there, which it's definitely doing – we're moving into a lower cycle now, there's a new dark age coming in – money buys you space. It buys you protection in a world gone mad. You need to find something that will give you enough money to make you independent. If you have an old car and it breaks down on the freeway in the middle of the night, you never know who's going to come along – you don't want that sort of thing to happen. We live in the world of violence. There's an astounding crime rate and you need to be able to buy a little space around yourself so you can lead a more refined life and keep yourself in good shape so you can then do more for others. You work it out in any way that you think is best.

When you work, when you're out in the world, when you're not in the little, beautiful environment that you've created for yourself in your home, when you're going to the movies, which I suggest is the best form of spiritual recreation I know, you need to adopt a certain attitude when you're out there, when you're dealing with people. Again, for work, rather than for me to spend two or three hours explaining how to deal with people at work, I think Mr. Carnegie has said it as well as I could in his book, *How to Win Friends and Influence People*, and I would suggest that you read it, not just once, but a few times or maybe once a year.

You know, it's interesting, there are many men in business, heads of Fortune 500 corporations, who attribute a great deal of their success to that little, tiny book. They read it about four times a year; it's kind of their Bible. Now, I don't think it has to be your Bible, particularly, but the points I would bring across about how to deal with people at work, how to be inaccessible and so on, all these different things, he brings across in his own way. How to deal with the business world is what his book is all about and I think it's rather good. Let him say it instead, perhaps.

What I would suggest is that it's necessary when you deal with the world or with your university or whatever it is, to adopt a certain attitude. And that's to be very unattached, to work very hard for those around you, but to keep your distance. Don't feel that you have to fit in, it's not necessary. If your work is good and if you're pleasant, that's enough.

Some people who are spiritual seekers, when they work in the office, they make themselves targets. They make themselves very accessible because they withdraw so much or they dress so differently that they become a center of attention and all you do is pick up bad energy, alienate yourself and then you have to deal again perhaps with the possibility of that egotism that I suggested. You think that you're better than the people there and actually you're not. No human being is better than another human being. All are equal.

So, blend. That's the key word. Blend. Be pleasant, be nice, do your best for all. If people don't speak the same language you do inwardly, respect them, but don't feel that you have to necessarily become close to them. Be close to those who you naturally feel drawn to, in other words, but don't feel obligated to go to the office party. Or, if you do, go to the office party but then after an hour, politely leave. Follow your intuition, in other words. If you follow the crowd, you end up where the crowd goes. If you wish to enter into the world of light and life, you have to walk to the beat of a different drummer.

The only other item I would mention is violence. It's necessary for you to be very security conscious. A lot of spiritual seekers for some reason seem to think that because they meditate if they walk down the street at night that they will not be vulnerable to attacks like other people are, and this is foolishness. The protective force that you're given as a spiritual seeker is to have the insight to see where you shouldn't be and where you shouldn't go and how you shouldn't act. Be very conscious of danger. It's everywhere, which doesn't mean that one should be paranoid. One should be alert and aware. If you come out of a meditation and you leave your house, while you may have been in a lovely consciousness, don't assume that the rest of the world is. As soon as you hit the street, in other words, switch into a different mode. You need to be able to shift levels of consciousness like you can shift gears on your car. Immediately adopt the caretaker personality of the warrior, which I discuss in the "Caretaker Personality" tape, when dealing with the world.

Be alert. When you're walking down the street always know who's around you, who's behind you. Carry mace. There are a lot of crazy people out there. Don't make yourself a target. Be inaccessible. Don't stand out in a crowd. Be very, very security conscious. You will see a continual erosion in terms of violence in our society for many, many years still. It's going to get worse. I think a self-defense course is marvelous, for men and women particularly, a basic course where you learn what to do in an emergency situation. I think that there's nothing wrong with keeping a gun in your home or apartment. I think you should always be conscious when you pull into your house if there's someone behind you. Look in your rear view mirror.

We had an unfortunate event occur recently. It didn't turn out too badly, but one of the women in the meditation center was on her lunch break and she was sitting in her car. She was reading a book by Paramahansa Yogananda at the time, *Metaphysical Meditations*. She works in a nice neighborhood; she didn't expect a problem. Suddenly there was a gentleman at the car window who put a gun to her head and asked for her money and her purse. He was absolutely a gentleman because he then walked away instead of raping her or killing her, as may have occurred. What she should have done was taken a little money and gone to a restaurant, a nice restaurant, a café, and read there. She was trying to save a few dollars. How silly. Even if she wasn't hungry, she could have sat in a nice café, ordered a piece of pie and ignored it if she didn't want to eat it, but sat there and read.

In other words, you have to think about where you're putting your body. You've got to feel every situation out constantly, with your meditative awareness. I've been planning to go to a movie, let's say. I'm planning to go see a new movie on Friday night. But if ten minutes before going I get the feeling that the people there are not going to be the people I want to be with, if I feel that intuitively, I should be able to switch to another movie. Never be a slave to convenience. You have to be alert and aware constantly. You have to be constantly vigilant when dealing in the world because it's a world of life and death; it is a jungle. While we are happy souls, happy birds flying through the sky, still, when we land, we have to deal with the fact that there are tigers down there, and it behooves you to be very wise when dealing with the world.

Again, you don't want to go to extremes. You don't want to be afraid of the world, that's foolish. We're warriors. The best warrior is the one who never fights because they don't have to, they avoided the fight. Use your meditative awareness to look around you. Be conscious. Don't be so caught up in yourself that you don't see who's next to you or who's behind you. Be sensitive. You should be looking out. Don't always be introspective and looking in. Look at this marvelous world – that's when you'll see the beauty, you see. When you turn your field of attention to the world, not only will you see potential problems but you'll see potential opportunities.

What I'm suggesting is a tone for living and working in the world. I've given you some reasons why I think it's good to live in the world, as opposed to withdraw from it, which doesn't mean that withdrawal might not be fun sometimes for a few years. I might do it myself, sometime. But I think it's very healthy to live in society. While Thoreau went and lived at Walden Pond for two and a half years, after two and a half years at the pond he went back to the world. It was a neat phase, he learned a lot and then he went back to apply what he had learned to society.

What I'm suggesting is that it's very healthy to live in a

spiritual community; to maintain your own residence, a little democracy in action here; to participate in society but not get caught up in it; to live in and work in the world; to not be afraid of money; to live in a nice place, in a healthy environment; to bring your physical life together, your career together; to realize that those who you live and work with are imperfect, as are you; to not become a spiritual elitist; to have fun with life; to go to movies, nice restaurants; to enjoy this world; to not separate yourself from it because where is God, if not in the world and the people of this world? Living and working in the world can be great fun.

But also reserve time for solitude. I don't think you have to go backpacking for two weeks in the mountains. If you're on the fast path, on the short path, you can spend one day, one afternoon hiking in the woods. That day is eternity and you can get all the spiritual release and renewal you need. You can go to the beach at sunset for half an hour, meditate, and release all of that built-up energy.

Meditate, associate in your free time with your spiritual friends and make friends wherever you go – at the dry cleaners, the laundromat, wherever it is – there are nice people and you can smile and not necessarily talk to people about spirituality. They don't want to hear about yoga and meditation but you can say "Hi" and just be a nice person.

Be very wary and remember that there are many people who might appear to be nice who are not. Use the discrimination and the spiritual vision you're gaining from your meditative study to see beyond the surface and look deeply within people, to not become a victim but to be a victor, to adopt that mentality, to be a road warrior in a world gone mad, to do all these things simultaneously. It's a great challenge. It's great fun, and you can do a lot more for people.

This is one approach, one way.

PLEASURE, PAIN, AND THE SENSES

Our journey today concerns illusion, the nature of illusion and the way out of illusion. Illusion is a state of mind. It's a way of seeing things that is not exactly correct. Everything that we see with our eyes, feel with our bodies, taste, touch, hear, everything that we think, everything that we feel with our emotions, all things that we are drawn to because we consider them to be pleasurable, all things that we seek to avoid because we consider them to be painful, these are all a product of illusion.

Illusion comes in many different forms. Illusion means to not see things exactly as they really are. If you're depressed you can walk through a field of flowers and see nothing to make you happy. If you're joyful, if you're elated, you can walk through a dark and desolate area and feel nothing but joy. While perception on the physical level certainly colors our experiences, perception on the mental level or on the emotional level has even a greater effect upon our awareness. But let's begin at the beginning. Let's begin with pleasure, pain and the senses.

In order to get a clear picture of reality, of what we are and what we are not, it's necessary for us to look beyond the body. Most people use their physical body as the ultimate point of reference, as the polestar in determining their life's awareness. We conceive of ourselves as being a body, occupying a certain amount of physical space, being so many centimeters tall, weighing a certain amount, being a particular color, having green or blue eyes – we think of ourselves as being physical, in other words.

Now, my point all along has been that you're not really physical, that you are, if anything, a breeze. You are a wind, a wind of luminous awareness that is sweeping through a dream, a landscape that constantly changes that's made up of a variety of different colors, and that as the breeze of your awareness blows through the valley of your dreams, through the different colors, it gives life to them. Death is the transmutation of this awareness, when the breeze blows in a new way or ceases to blow at all and becomes something that we really can't feel. You might say it goes someplace else.

Life is the beginning of the wind. What was before the wind? What remains after the wind? Only eternity and eternality, that which has always been and that which will always be – nirvana, the void, completion, ecstasy beyond imagination, God.

Here we deal with the wind. And when the wind blows, even in the outer world, in the physical world, it's always a good sign. Because there's energy or prana in the wind; the force of life itself is the wind.

In the realm of the senses there is little or no wind. That which you call a body, that which appears to be dense and physical, packed full of atoms and molecules, DNA and RNA, protoplasm, that which you call a body I say is not physical. I say that it is only physical because you think it is physical. Simply because you can touch it and taste it and see it, simply because you can put your ear to someone's chest and hear their heart beating, this to me proves absolutely nothing. This to me is a dream of limited awareness, as all of life is a dream.

The senses are dreams, five different dreams that run together. The senses are the dreams of limited awareness. You are, if anything, spirit, what I call the wind. The wind blows and frees us all from the trap of maya or illusion. You consider yourself to be physical. When you think of yourself you think of your body. I would suggest that your body is only another image in the dream, a dream that is given life by the wind.

Pleasure, pain and the senses. When we have a sensory experience we label it. For example, when you eat something that you like, when you have an orgasm, when you see something beautiful, when you hear a melody that you like or the voice of someone you love, when you smell the fragrance of flowers or a scent that you particularly enjoy, these are the dreams of the senses. The senses are a modality, a method of perception. The senses are a reflection of a body's awareness. Just as you consider that the experience that you have of certain senses or through the senses is pleasurable, so you have also determined that there are a variety of sensations that you experience through the senses or as the senses that you consider to be painful. When someone hits you or you're ill and your body aches – this is pain. When there's an acrid smell, something very unpleasant; when you see something that you don't like, that's ugly; when you hear discordant sounds; when you taste something that's not to your liking – this is pain.

The difference between pleasure and pain is choice. What one person considers to be pleasurable, another may consider to be painful and vice versa. The yogi or yogini, one who seeks to yolk or unite their consciousness with God, that is to say with infinite awareness, comes to see and realize that there is really no difference between pleasure and pain, that all are sensations and that one should neither seek pleasure nor shun pain. Because as soon as you seek pleasure or you try to avoid pain, you trap yourself in the pairs of opposites.

Pretend for a moment that you're outside. You're walking around having a wonderful experience. Life is lovely. Now let's say you come up to a building and you go inside the building and it's a very curious building. There's a central corridor, a hallway that runs down the building, which bisects it, and there are doors on both the left- and right-hand side. If you open a door on the left-hand side, perhaps the first doorway you come to once you've entered the building, you'll go into a room that smells absolutely beautiful. If you close that door and instead go to the room directly opposite on the right-hand side of the corridor, there's a room that smells with awful stinks.

The next door up on the left is a world of beautiful things you can feel. You can go in and feel silks and satins, just beautiful sensations. In the next room, on the right-hand side opposite that room, are painful experiences. If you walk in someone hits you, someone strikes you, there is cactus that you can stick yourself on.

The third room on the left: when you walk in you see nothing but beautiful lights, scenes are projected in front of your eyes, landscapes that are wonderful. In the room opposite on the right-hand side: terrible scenes, awful things, painful lights, darkness.

The next room on the left: wonderful things that you can taste. The room opposite on the right: unpleasant, awful things to taste.

The room on the left: all the wonderful music and sound that has ever been. The room across from it on the right: awful, terrible, shrieking sounds, unpleasant.

Ten rooms, and for each person the rooms are a little different and you cannot have the rooms on the left without the rooms on the right. One could enter into such a building and become so engaged in the ten rooms that you forgot there was an outside, that there was something beyond the ten rooms. Let us say that the experiences were so powerful and so intense in these rooms that you forgot all about the fact that there was something beyond them. As a matter of fact, all of life only appeared to you to consist of what was in those ten rooms.

The rooms on the left-hand side you liked. Those are pleasurable experiences through the five senses. The rooms on the right-hand side of the corridor are what you call painful experiences of the five senses. These ten rooms comprise one aspect of your life.

One who practices yoga is able to walk through the corridor of the senses and remain unaffected. This doesn't mean that feeling does not emanate through the senses, but simply that there's no one there. Someone calls you on the phone. They talk for hours endlessly. You're tired of them talking but you can't stop them from talking. You go out into the world, there are the sounds of rapid transit buses, jet aircraft, people all around you. You go walking through a shopping mall, being bombarded by sensory messages telling you to buy this, experience this, feel this, advertising directing you to pleasure – this product will be more pleasurable, it will end an unpleasant experience. The realm of the senses.

One who practices yoga and meditation does not seek to run away from the senses because the senses, as long as they are there, will continue to dream. They will continue to bring forth a variety of different types of information in and through your being. Rather, the way is to not be there. The reason that you're occupied with the senses, which ultimately lead to frustration, is that you have focused your attention upon them. The art of the perceiver is to focus your attention on the infinite, not on the finite – or on the finite as infinite, or on nothingness, or on all things, or to not focus at all, or to not be there to focus. These are the options in the operable world having to do with the basic levels of attention

If you must have happiness, you must also have unhappiness. If you must have love, you must also have hate. If you must have good, you must also have evil. If you must have day, you must also have night. These are the pairs of opposites. But there really are no opposites. There really are no senses. There really is no good or bad, day or night, love or hate. You can't win and you can't lose, except that you're having a dream in which you believe you can. There are two alternatives. One is to alter the dream, to dream a different dream. The other is to put an end to the dreamer, to awaken from the dream of life.

The senses are wrapped up with desire. Consider who and what you are for a moment. You are consciousness, consciousness trapped in a body. The body is the body of illusion. The cells are the windows through which you look at existence. Or to put it another way, the senses are the windows through which you look at existence as you sit in the prison of the body. Your awareness was flying through the sky and it became trapped in the physical plane. And now you sit in a dark room and there are five screens, like TV monitors. Each of them gives you a level of perception, but there are only distant, faint images on the screens.

The pairs of opposites create desire. That is to say, that which causes you unhappiness in life is desire. Desire is neither good nor bad, only thinking makes it so. Ultimately there is nothing good or bad, only thinking makes it so. What you call pleasant and pleasurable, someone else will feel is unpleasant. What you feel is unpleasant they will feel is pleasurable. Everything is definition. However, you can write the dictionary. You can define or redefine everything. You look at a flower that you love and you say it's beautiful. You look at another flower that you think is not very nice. Now, you've already locked yourself into a terrible situation. If someone sends you the flowers that you like, you'll be happy because you will experience a sensation that you enjoy. Or you will be happy because you desired, you wanted a particular sensory experience, which was the perception of the flowers that you liked.

However, if someone sends you the flowers that you don't like, then you won't be happy. You desire to receive a certain type of flower, but the ones that you considered not to be beautiful arrived. Therefore you will be unhappy because your desire was not fulfilled. Or perhaps no one will send you flowers at all and you'll become despondent because you will receive nothing. There's no way out of the world of desire. It's like being in a giant maze, and you go round and round in the maze trying to find a way out, but all you find are more convoluted corridors and passageways.

The senses give you a limited amount of freedom and that freedom is initially attractive. The senses open you up to a particular vision of yourself. And who's to say if what you see and feel with the senses is correct or not? However, there is another level of perception, another way of seeing things, which you're also familiar with, called emotion.

Emotion is feeling and it operates through the pairs of opposites as do the senses. But emotion is not so much a physical feeling, although it can be triggered by a sensory experience. You could have a pleasant experience – someone could touch you – and you enjoyed that and that would trigger an emotional response. Your heart would love. Someone could strike you, could hit you, a sensation that you don't like, and that could trigger a response of fear. The emotions, in most cases, cannot really be triggered by the senses. Emotions are the prisms, the crystals, the glasses through which we view the senses.

On our chain of evolution we have the objects of sense experience, that is to say, a flower. We have the senses, which perceive or transmit the five screens, the TV screens, which show us five different ways to perceive the flower: the way it looks; if we touch it with our bodies, the way it feels; the way it smells; if we were to taste it, the way it tastes; the way it looks, the coloration, the form. We apply the five screens to the object of perception, the sense object, and we see it in five ways. All of that information then is passed through the emotion or the emotional level of being. That then is passed into the intellect, to the mind, which cognizes the experience, which considers it, which evaluates it, which measures it against past experience and memory, which looks at it from the point of view of desire. Does the shoe fit or is it a bad fit? Is it what you desired or is it not what you desired?

The intellect or mind analyzes, separates. Behind the mind is a luminous field of consciousness in which the mind floats, that viscous sea of eternal awareness in which operates the intuitive mind, which some call the over-mind. This part perceives the essence of an object without the use of the senses. It intuits it. The senses provide you five screens to examine an object. Those screens are filtered by emotion and by the intellect. Remembrance and desire, attraction and aversion, operate through the intellect. But at the same time you could sit next to your friend the flower, close your eyes and experience its essence, having shut off the five screens: seeing, tasting, feeling, smelling, touching. Shut off the five screens and you will find, when you still your mind, when you enter into a meditative state, that you can experience the flower, not necessarily as flower, but as essence, as being.

Suppose the five screens that you have – your five little television monitors, which then go through the filtration process of the emotions in the mind, which you thought showed you very clearly what was there – suddenly are inadequate. Oh, while they did show you accurately certain information, they didn't show you everything. For example, here in Malibu where I'm making this tape today, for the last four and a half months when we looked out from our home over the ocean, all we could see was the horizon, no land. Then about three days ago, suddenly the air changed and it became very clear, and we looked out at the horizon and we saw a huge land mass, one of the Santa Barbara Channel Islands – a huge island that was there. It was like Brigadoon; it had never been there for the five months we lived here. There was no island and suddenly there was a huge island.

The senses paint a certain picture for us of the world. They reveal to us the way something looks. It is not that the senses are necessarily inaccurate, nor is it necessarily that they're accurate, but let us say that they don't necessarily show us everything. Intuition, then, the intuitive approach to understanding, is another way, a more direct and immediate way, that is not subject to as much error and as many problems as sense perceptions are, to view existence.

Now, classically, in the history of spirituality, there have been many attempts to reach the intuitive level, in other words, the ability to cognize or experience something without experiencing it as most human beings do. People have attempted to still their senses through mortification, through austerity, fasting, disciplining themselves. People have attempted to go beyond the senses through the use of drugs or intoxicants, or to expand their sensory perception and see it in a new way. Some people have sought to shun the world. The idea is to not look at that which is beautiful because it's a trap, a beautiful trap. Because as soon as you become enraptured by the beauty of the world as you see it through the senses, then you're snared into the pairs of opposites.

You were walking by the house and having a good time outside and everything was fine – good old undifferentiated reality; you were a wind blowing through an empty, cloudless sky, no point of reference, everything was perfect. Suddenly, something in you was attracted to one of those five rooms on the left-hand side of the corridor, which you called beauty, and you were pulled down in there. But once you get inside the house, the door closes behind you, you can't get out, and you wander aimlessly from room to room. As much pleasure as you will experience, so you will experience just as much pain; as much joy, so just as much sorrow. This is what we call human life. As long as you are human, that is to say, as long as you fit the definition of human, as one who exists within a body as a body, who is in the realm of the senses, then all of the toils, frustrations, good times and bad times that we've come to call life must be for you. But there is another way and that way is not necessarily in the rejection of the senses, nor in the rejection of beauty, nor in the aversion of that which you call ugliness or pain. Rather, it's simply a question of focus.

Think of the senses and desires like fly paper. You've all seen the cartoons in which there's a character who gets stuck on a piece of fly paper and they push it off with one hand and finally free it from the other hand, and now it's stuck on their other hand and then they get it stuck on both hands. Very sticky stuff, difficult to get rid of. Desire and sense perceptions are like that. Sometimes the more you try and get away from them, the more caught up in them you become. The very desire to escape sense experience, to escape pain or pleasure, can trap you as much as pleasure and pain in their simpler forms. Everything is an illusion, even the idea of going beyond pleasure and pain is an illusion. It's a description, modified through the intellect and the senses.

The way out is to become still. The more you struggle, the more you'll get stuck. To just continue to act is to get stuck also. Rather, what I'm suggesting is to become so still that you dissolve and disappear and that the entire situation is gone. Because the only reason the situation exists, the only reason the senses exist, the mind exists, personal history, memory, emotion, pleasure, pain and the senses exist, is because you give them meaning. If we allow you to dissolve, if we dissolve ourselves in the white light of eternity, then we will find that what seemed to be so real – being in the house of the senses – was only a dream. We were in a terrible, terrible nightmare and it was all so real. Within the context of the nightmare we could have tried to get away, but we may never have gotten away because the nightmare may have been endless. If we can but wake up from the nightmare, it all goes away. We're waking up from the illusion of selfhood, which is engendered by the belief that you are an individual perceiver.

What I'm suggesting is that nothing is solid, that nothing looks the way it is, that everything is light. Not even light as a perception, but light as a word to describe that which is beyond cognitive perception. When you meditate, when you stop thought, you'll go beyond the realm of the senses. You will not experience a modification of what you did before. What you are erasing are not your senses or the objects of sense experience or the emotions which color them. You don't have to, in other words, get rid of your loves and your emotions. Nor do you have to eliminate your memories of times gone by or even your expectations of the future.

Yes, true, you can modify the software of existence. You can remove expectation, you can limit desire, you can restrain the senses – these are all various forms of yoga, various pathways. But what I'm suggesting is that all of them only take you into more modifications, in my estimation. They're all partialities. The only way to truly transcend, to wake up, is to no longer be as you now are.

We don't want to change the fabric of life – who are we to do that? Rather, what we want to do is to meld with eternity, to become part of that eternal light, beyond light. Substance beyond feeling. Essence beyond believing. There and there alone is existence. And when you live in that nonexistence each day, which we call God realization, satori, nirvana – words, words, words – when you live in that essence, then as you exist in this world, as you meet pleasurable or painful experiences, as your emotions filter around you, as your desires soar through you, you're unaffected. You're unaffected by the transitory movements of existence and you can look at a beautiful rose and see its beauty. As a matter of fact, you can redefine definition, look at anything, and see beauty because everything is beauty if you decide that it is. If everything is beauty, there is no ugliness.

You don't have to feel that pain is particularly unpleasant. Everybody is so afraid of pain these days. They'll do anything not to experience a little pain. To seek pain is not good, it's just an attachment. To run away from pain is not good. That is to say, when pain comes to you in life and there's not a whole lot you can do about it, you shouldn't be afraid of it. Oh, you will be, it will hurt as long as you're still there, but if you're not there, who's there to hurt? No one and nothing.

What I'm suggesting is that there's an ultimate good that we call love. Not the love that is the opposite of hate, but the love that is compassion, that transcending perfection which is existence, which is the crystal beauty of life and death and beyond, which is the light of existence that weaves the fabric of the dream that you're now in and all the dreams that have ever been or will ever be. And that that is love and if you turn your attention to that love, then the relative information that comes through the senses and the mind and the body and the memory and the experience and the intellect which discriminates, that all of these things, which would make you happy or unhappy, which would bind you to the conception of being a limited spirit in a body or just a body, don't even exist. All of the joys and pleasures that have ever been, all of the pains and frustrations that will ever be, all of the experiences that have ever been had, when put end to end will not even be seen in the bliss of eternity of nirvana.

Rather than get all caught up in trying to battle yourself, which seems to me to be self-defeating – why try and destroy what you are? – rather than hate yourself because you don't make the kind of spiritual progress you think you should, as I see so many people do and be miserable, or love yourself and get caught up in your ego when you think that you've made some kind of marvelous spiritual progress and trap yourself in that, rather than get caught up in any of this sticky fly paper that everybody calls life, what the heck, why not instead focus your awareness on eternal things? Because in this life you will have to go through the dream of this life. You will have to experience birth, growth, maturation, decay, and death. There's no way around it, but that's not necessarily an unpleasant dream, my friend. As a matter of fact, you'll hardly notice it.

When you go to the dentist's office, if you focus on the experience, on the pain, and oh, how awful it is, and you're filled with fear – a terrible, unpleasant experience – it can ruin your whole day. Or you could go to the dentist's office and meditate so deeply that you wouldn't even notice there was an office. Well, what is pain then?

Don't run towards pleasure. Don't run away from pain. Both will trap you. Be indifferent to both. That is to say, enjoy both. Don't make a big deal, in other words, out of your life, your experiences, your memories, your desires, your pleasure and pain, your life or your death. If I take a candle, to bend the well-worn phrase, if I take a candle with the flame and look at it in a dark room, my God, that candle flame is so bright! In the darkness that candle flame will illumine everything, it will be all that exists, I can look at it, and it will be the brightest of flames. If I bring that flame into a cave where there are people who have never seen light, it will blind them. They will think that they have seen the ultimate radiance, those people who have lived in that cave in darkness for so long that they have forgotten what life and light is.

But then if I take that flame and I go outside in the bright day and I hold it up to the sun, you know, I won't even see that flame – that flame that a few moments ago was the brightest light that has ever been to those that had never seen light – now, as I hold it to the sun, it will not even exist. And if I take that sun, which is so bright that you can only look at it for a few seconds without losing your sight, and I hold it up to a supernova, an exploding sun, I can't even see it. And if I take that supernova and I hold it up to the white light of eternity itself, which is that which creates, sustains and transforms existence, which we call God, nirvana, eternity, I can't even see that supernova. And if I dissolve my own perceptions in the body of the self that perceives, then there's no one to see, the dream has ended, we have left the realm of the senses and we're awake in the world. We're traveling the bardo of consciousness and experience in the plane of time, in the realm of the senses, the substance is matter, and the time is eternity.

Refocus your field of attention. Look instead at eternity. Don't be caught up in your happiness or your unhappiness, your career, your life, your job. Enjoy all things. Don't run away from them. Don't be afraid of your desire. What I'm suggesting is that by living a certain type of life you won't necessarily attain self-realization. There is no certain type of life that you have to lead. It really doesn't, as a matter of fact, much matter. What does matter, however, is that you refocus your field of attention to God. When your awareness is focused on God, then you can be with anyone in any situation – single, married, celibate, active, in pain, in pleasure – it doesn't matter, because who's there to notice? And even if there is someone still there to notice, notice what? When your consciousness is wrapped up in the immortal light of perfection, when all you care about, see, and feel is God, what difference does it make? You can be in your office, you can be out jogging, you can be driving in your car, you can be lying in the hospital dying, what's the difference?

Because you don't see the things that others see with their eyes. While they all see ten images from the five screens filtered by the intellect, passed through the emotions and the reflections and the aversions and the attractions, which we call desire, with the limited conception of the body as life and death, as the non-body, the extinction of the body – these things don't really exist for you. Rather, you're looking at light and beauty. You are light and beauty, fathomless light and beauty, all of the time. That is the real nature of existence, and those who say that you're not a realist and you don't really see life "as it is" are shadows, reflections of the one light, which is eternity.

My simple, patented method for dealing with existence, its trials and tribulations, its good days and bad days and wonderful nights, is to not try so hard. I always see everyone, all my students and everybody in spiritual practice, oh God! They're trying so hard to be so good and so perfect, and that's wonderful and that's admirable and nothing will be lost, they'll amass a lot of good karma and then they'll have to spend many lives working out all that good karma. (Rama chuckles.) Rather, what I would suggest is that you just love God and stop worrying about trying to get ahead in the spiritual league, and that if that love is complete, as it grows and that rapture increases, as you turn your awareness more and more to God – which doesn't mean that you don't look at the world because God exists here too, you know – but as you do that more and more, then this world will matter less and less and soon you won't even see this world. It'll be our candle in the sun and the supernova and the white light of eternity. There'll be nothing but light, nothing but perfection, nothing but beauty, immortal essence.

And then you'll look at your friend the flower and your friend the flower will be more beautiful than ever, and your friends the people and your friends the experiences and your friends the emotions and your friend the body, they will not be any less important. Rather, all of them will be expressions of that divine essence, which is perfect light, because eternity is everywhere and nowhere. It's not simply in the sky, it's here on earth too. In all the moments you've ever had and experienced in this life, there's been eternity.

What I suggest, then, is to become aware, to open up your heart and feel eternity, not to pay too much attention to the newspaper, just to pay enough attention so you know what's going on, but no more. To just bask in the light of eternity and let everything follow its proper course and don't be too impressed by your successes or your failures, by what life brings to you or what life takes away. Don't get trapped in that house with the ten rooms. Rather, be an essence, a wind, a breeze that's flowing through the sky – that's eternity!

And if you ever need a sense of identity, if it gets a little undifferentiated out there for you, then only assume one identity: love, the love that binds all things together, the love that is liberation.

Liberation doesn't mean going off to some university and getting a degree and being issued a certificate of liberation. It means no ego. Dissolved. Dissolution. Gone. No forwarding address. Nirvana. Or it means being here in the world playing.

That's what's expressed in the "Searching for the Ox" pictures in Zen. If you've ever looked at that sequence of pictures, which we'll talk about perhaps some time, you see then there's self alone. The last picture is really not a picture of leaving this world. While the experience of satori is had, while you become absorbed in that light, then there is playing in the world, the final picture. As you find yourself moving back and forth from the superconscious where you're compounded and absorbed in light, you'll find yourself again playing in the world with just enough essence and substance to play. Realization doesn't lead us to death or to the dissolution of the self. Oh, the self dissolves again and again in that white light of eternity, but it brings us back to this world, to play in it. But we're different when we come back.

Before self-realization we're trying so hard, the struggling being. Then we melt in that white light of eternity; we can't see ourselves – the candle in the sun. The sun, even, is gone. Then we find ourselves here again, but we've been transformed by that experience. Then all we can do is play in the world, just play.

Pleasure, pain and the senses. Just another passing experience as you sit on your raft with Huck Finn cruising down the Mississippi. Once in a while we stop the raft, we get off, and we go out and have an adventure. Then we get back on that river of dharma, that old Mississippi. We go a little further down, with Huck and Jim and the King and the Duke and all the other cast of characters that are there in our lives. We're all on a river, on a raft called consciousness.

Don't be afraid to stop and get off and have a few adventures. But remember, when it gets thick out there, head back to the raft like Huck and get on the raft and head further down river.

HOW TO ACHIEVE SPIRITUAL BALANCE

The way to achieve spiritual balance is without trying. Spiritual balance is something that all of us innately are. There are many different types of balance. Normally when we think of balance we have a preconceived notion of what balance is. That notion comes to some extent from our experience as physical beings in the physical world. For example, when we think of balance we think of a basic ratio and proportion, an equation, that permits life to exist – as in an ecosystem where balance is achieved through a symbiotic process in which one organism aids another organism in its survival.

Ultimately everything is always in a state of balance. We sometimes prefer though one form of balance to another. For example, you may feel that emotional balance is a state that you call happiness. Happiness is achieved for you in a specific way. Happiness may mean making enough money. Happiness may mean having people love you; feeling physically fit; sensing that the work you do is of value not only to yourself but to others; sexual fulfillment; infinite awareness or infinite consciousness; spiritual evolution and a sense that you are making progress, that you're not just walking through the doorway of life again and again without anything occurring but there is a sense of movement or growth; prestige. Some of these are qualities that might fit into your equation of spiritual balance. Emotional balance and personal balance.

However, from my point of view spiritual balance is not so easy to achieve in an ultimate sense. There's relative spiritual balance, the spiritual balance that you can achieve just by having a harmonious life. But life itself is transitory. It doesn't really last. Each one of us is a reflection of an eternal process which is really something that cannot be fathomed or understood with the mind, although we can penetrate its mysteries and enter into and become one with its essence. Spiritual balance is a process that occurs over many, many lifetimes or incarnations. We could say that the process of reincarnation is a process of balance. In each lifetime there are certain formations within the cells that need to be worked on. Imagine that we have a piece of wood, and the piece of wood has a shape and a beauty all of its own. Perhaps it's a limb from a tree and has a lot of nuances, formations, bark, different parts of it, each part having a special beauty. But suppose what we want to do is transform it, change it, reshape it. Let's just say that that's its destiny. Why? Who knows? None of us know why destiny is. We only know that we are destiny.

The piece of wood begins to transform in our hands. We take a bit of sandpaper and we decide to work on the roughest corner first, the most jagged edge, and we begin to sand it down. Then after a while we put the piece of wood down, and we're tired and we go off and do something else. We come back and pick it up another day and work, perhaps on a different edge. Gradually, day after day we sand away until finally the bark is completely removed, all the rough edges are smooth.

Now, had we taken a photograph at the beginning of this process, and now at this stage of the process, we would see two really dissimilar forms. The form now that is in our hands really doesn't resemble the initial tree. It's smooth, and shaped somewhat differently and the bark is all gone – the spiritual transformation process. Now suppose we decide to take that piece of wood and we continue to sand it. Each day we sand further and further, until one day there's nothing left. Spiritual balance.

Spiritual balance occurs through love. Love is the ultimate equation. There are different types of love, however, and not all of them are particularly harmonious. When most people love, there is a great deal of ego involved in their love. When you love, there's a sense of trying to possess someone, to hold on to them. And even more than that, there's just an intolerable identification with what I suppose we could call humanness. There's a sense of being a fixed person or personality, in a fixed body, in a fixed continuum of space and time. And you as such have assigned a value to yourself, almost a numerical value and you are trying to affix or in some way interact with another mind body emotional complex in space and time. This is love. Extremely limited.

When you enter into the spiritual process, you change. Your rough edges are sanded away, your outer covering falls away. And you find that you're not exactly a person any more. After many years of meditation and spiritual practice, you will discover rather, that you are a field of light, that you have no definite form or shape or color. While you can remember a past history of yourself to some extent – you can remember what you did when you were in fourth grade, or you were 15 or you were 20 – while there are certain recurrent memories, there is little or no association with that which you are now and those memories. Just as the butterfly as it flits from flower to flower may dimly remember its days as a caterpillar, still there appears to be no relation except through the function of memory between that which the butterfly is and that which the butterfly was as a caterpillar.

All time is eternally present. The timeless lies just around the corner. We experience the timeless in time. Spiritual balance cannot really occur in the world of time without an understanding of timelessness, because it is timelessness that gives meaning to time. Time has no value without eternity. You have an hour to accomplish something. You have to use that hour completely. If you don't use the hour completely, then there'll be nothing left over. What gives the hour value is the sense that it is an hour, it's a defined, measured unit of time. What creates the unit is consciousness in a body. A sense that there is division and time. But ultimately what really allows that division is timelessness. A vast ocean stretches out endlessly, never beginning and never ending. We're standing on the shore, and we see to the horizon, we quantify. There's a sense of dimension. But dimensionality can only come and gain form from that which is dimensionless. This world only exists in your mind because it is within a void. By void I mean an endless ocean of nonexistence and existence that does not have a definite form, shape, or color. The background to that which you see is that which does not appear to be, or which is not. The vacuum of existence in which all things exist, from which things rise forth, which sustains and preserves, and to which things return, the ultimate spiritual balancing act is to have one foot in eternity and one foot in time and to not know which foot is which.

Spiritual balance comes about, to some extent, according to the foot that's in this world, through self-effort. Self-effort is extremely important, yet self-effort is not something that can be commanded, or even in my belief, ultimately inspired. When I begin to instruct a new student who seeks enlightenment, I look at that person's potential. I measure not what I see, but what I don't see. I gain an intuitive sense and understanding of the level of aspiration of the individual – how much they want, how much they want God, how far in this life do they wish to be sanded down. Do they wish to go all the way down to that level of commonality, of voidness? Is this their final lifetime in which they seek completion? Or is this just another day when I'll get out my sandpaper and sand away for a while and then after a few rough edges are completed, I'll put the paper down and walk away. I can only do as much as I am allowed to do by an individual who is eternity. Ultimately, it is not I, but you who decide how far you will advance in any given lifetime. I am powerless to act, unless called upon to act by the inner being of an individual. It is necessary to sit alone, to be in a place where there are no others, there are no other people in your physical proximity, no other vibratory energies, to sit alone and meditate and as you meditate to feel eternity, your thoughts will run rampant back and forth through your brain, your emotions will be like storms, like squalls that come in across the ocean. One storm comes in and the blue sky of two minutes ago dissolves in darkness. Webs of rain fall down from the sky, the sea churns, then, in ten minutes the squall is gone, the air is clean. Twenty minutes later another squall comes by. They come again and again, in from the ocean. Emotions are turbulence. Sometimes turbulence is fun, sometimes turbulence is exhilarating, to go down to the beach when the squalls come in, to stand in the wind and let the rain pound against your body. Sometimes it's good to stay inside, be absorbed, and let everything pass without noticing it. Different approaches. States of mind and states of existence. All the same, ultimately, yet for you as an individual in time, quite different.

The question of being has to arise at some point. What are we being, how are we being, who are we being? The question is only answered in meditation. When you sit quietly with no thought in your mind, when you push the squalls of emotion aside, when the thought storms go out to sea, a light will come. This light is existence in its pure form. You will recognize it, it is yourself. For lifetimes you have searched trying to find meaning and purpose, only to find that the only meaning and purpose is light itself. Meaning and purpose are meaningless and purposeless ideas when you are in that light, the transcendental light of existence. It is its own answer. It requires nothing, it costs nothing, it is the final completion. Float in that light for eternity because there is no time. In that light there is only eternity. We come from that light, we are that light, each one of us is a body of light. We forget though. We think that we're physical, we think that we're in time, in motion, when we are really a flux.

How is it that we came to believe this? How is it that we lose sight and everything appears to be so physical, so dense, so solid, when ultimately everything is the light, the energy. When you take a photograph, let's say you have a Polaroid camera. Now, what do you do when you take a photograph – well, we get someone, let's say we get someone who's walking and we snap a picture of them. We have just frozen reality, just as we freeze a river. We take our Polaroid picture and watch it develop and what we see is frozen time. Time was in motion. It was fluid – someone was walking. We took their picture and stopped the action. The action didn't start or stop with the picture, although the picture was certainly part of the action. The action continued smooth and formless. But our picture shows a stopped action – if you believe in pictures. The trick is to look at the picture and see the action continuing as the picture is an extension of the action.

But frozen time is a simile, a kind of a rough metaphor for the way you see life. When you look at a table, or a tree or a person or yourself in the mirror, when you think of an idea, when you probe existence you are fixed time. You are a photograph. Something inside you has taken a photograph and stopped the action. In meditation, we reverse the process. The photograph dissolves and everything becomes fluid and natural again.

We seek eternity, not knowing why. That which is our essence wants to return to its original formlessness. Perhaps so it can incarnate again in a new way. Perhaps just to rest in the lap of eternity forever.

Spiritual balance is not something that is really achieved through self-effort. Spiritual balance occurs largely through being yourself. To be yourself is a most difficult process for most persons because they really have no idea who or what they are. To determine who and what you are you have to gain a sense of who and what you are not. By subtracting who and what you are not from everything else in existence and nonexistence and beyond both, you will definitely discover who and what you are.

When I speak of spiritual balance, I am suggesting a state that is not individualized or particularized in any way, shape or form. Even to say it is a state implies boundaries. Whereas I would suggest that spiritual balance is a flux, it is a way of being, being continuous being. The river is flowing. We walk down to its banks and we look at it. The water in the river is our life, it flows. We can place our hand in the river, our feet into the river, we can get into the river itself and float with it. Further down, we can get out of the river and come back on the land again. This is meditation. Spiritual balance is a river. It flows through us. Unhappiness is a form of spiritual balance. Frustration is a form of spiritual balance. Anger and depression, denial, doubt, guilt, self-pity, hate, all forms of spiritual balance.

There are different balances. And it is best not to seek any of them. One does not really pass through the bardo of existence without experiencing a little bit of everything. It's kind of like going to a restaurant where they have a very, very vast menu. And you just have to try everything. In one lifetime you'll try self-pity. In another hate, in another frustration, in another anger. Because you just have to try everything on the menu.

Dessert of course is different, the superconscious. To meld your consciousness with eternity – to be devoid of self-pity, anger, hate, frustration, even joy, love, and wonder – to go beyond everything and nothing. Spiritual balance. For the beginner, it's difficult to reconcile the idea that hate can be a form of spiritual balance when it would seem that what we're trying to do is to love, to be of service to others, to develop humility, purity and integrity, and I would agree, it's difficult to understand, and I don't think one should even try.

There are many conclusions that you can reach in your search for spiritual balance. And I think it's good to reach as many as you like, as long as you remember that they're only conclusions, they're abstractions, they're leaves blowing by you in the wind.

Humility and purity are my favorite fulcrums for balance. I have lots of students in this life and in other lives, in this time and in other times, who work with me. I bring them to balance. My favorite fulcrums are humility and purity. It amazes me how people underestimate the power of the force. They think that they can stop meditating and start meditating. They believe that they can avoid spiritual transformation. I assure you no one has that power. Eternity is the only power. It dictates all. You simply write it down in your stenographer's pad of existence.

Spiritual balance really has a lot to do with being funny, I think. People tend to get so serious about something that they can't control. I try to be funny. It seems to come kind of naturally. Self-giving is the best mantra I know. A lot of people ask me sometimes, they say, "Gosh, Rama, what's the best mantra?" They all want the secret code word. It's like when I was a kid and we had the Captain Video Decoder Rings to get the secret message that they'd flash on television. Everybody thinks that if they can get the right word or holy phrase down, the right meditation technique, that it will make all the difference. While that may make you feel better, it isn't necessarily true. Or, I would suggest, the best mantra is self-giving, because as you repeat it again and again, you change. It's the only one I know of that really works.

If you're trying too hard, you'll burn yourself out. I see this so often. People come into the spiritual life, they have high aspirations, hopes, and all of those things are really justified – everything you've ever wanted and much more will happen, I assure you, as you meditate and progress spiritually. You can't imagine, at this stage, the ecstasy, the final consummation as you merge with eternity. It's quite alright!

But some people try so hard to be good. And I admire that. I'd rather see that than the opposite. But they try so hard that they don't have any fun! They think that they're going to do this all in a day, a week, or a month, or a year – maybe even a lifetime! It takes a while, you know, and there's really no rush. Let life dictate the speed. What you should just do is have fun, meditate, and enjoy it. Be with your spiritual friends, your teacher, or whomever life puts you with, and enjoy it. Enjoy everything that comes to you, enjoy everything that goes away. Try and hold on to nothing, because whenever you hold on to something, you hold yourself down. Be free with your time, your money, and your love. Be extremely conservative in everything you do. Danger is everywhere in the physical world, and in order to preserve the balance of your life, you must be conscious of that. Don't waste your time, and don't waste your money and don't waste your love, don't be foolish. The balance is right between your eyes. The balance is the step into nirvana. The dissolution of the frame of reference that you have which you call yourself into eternity. The balance is not something that can be taught, although it can be shown. Today I'm showing you about spiritual balance. Not so much in a structured lecture, I've forgotten how to do that, I think, at least today. Rather, today, we're just sitting here, watching eternity go by, in strands of tape, frozen eternity melting and thawing into your being. The river of life flowing. Not exactly sure of where we are, but confident of where we're not.

When you meditate, try to feel your heart. The heart is the love. Don't worry about physical location. Bring together your higher emotions. We have darker emotions and lighter emotions. The lighter emotions make us happy. As you sit and meditate, as you're trying to figure out "what to do," bring together your higher emotions and sit there and just bask in love. Think about something that makes you happy. Feel some joy.

Then, ignore your thoughts. Then, stop your thoughts. Push them all aside. Then, drop that which was pushing them aside. Then, un-then. Dissolve then. With that thin layer of perception that remains, the blanket that covers existence, become so motionless and so still that your own motionless and stillness no longer is or is not. Blend. No questions about balance and identity – please.

Humility – I keep coming back to it. I suppose it's the one thing that everybody forgets about. It is really the thing that liberates you. You see, humility means a lack of self-consciousness. Self-consciousness is ego. Ego is that which destroys spiritual balance, or, we could say, ego is the fulcrum of spiritual imbalance. Humility is its opposite. Humility and ego, you dance between the two in life. Humility means waiting. Waiting and waiting. You're called into God's office, and God has you wait. After an hour or two you begin to get impatient. You read all the magazines that are there, the old, outdated *Newsweek*'s and *Life*'s and *Time*'s, there's nothing left to do and you begin to get angry. "Why is God keeping me waiting? I've been waiting for so long, what, does God think I have nothing better to do than sit around and wait for Her? Huh!"

Humility means learning how to use your time to sit and look out the window forever, to go beyond time and to not be so concerned with you. You trap yourself in your own self-importance. You think you're important. Perhaps to yourself you are. Perhaps to a few others you are. But God will keep you waiting as long as you think you're important. Finally, one day, when you give up being important, She'll show up and talk to you for a while. Until then you'll have to wait. Sorry.

The spiritual transformation process takes a while. And when you come to a spiritual teacher, you should come knowing that you are going to be shown how to change every single imperfection in your being. To do this, you have to be ready to go through every part of yourself and reorder it. There is no success in this process. And if you feel you want to succeed and do better than others, then you're definitely going to have a hard time. It doesn't mean you'll fail, but it's going to be tough for you. If you feel that you're going to enter into the spiritual community and climb up the level of the organization and become president and that that means success, then you're going to have a very tough time. If you are able to come into a spiritual organization with an enlightened teacher, and just see the teacher occasionally, and meditate, if you never did anything special or had a special conversation with the teacher outwardly, but you were just delighted to be there and to learn and listen and grow, then you would be a good student. You would have the humility and you would grow. But those persons who want attention only add straw to the fire of their ego, making it burn brighter. You should come with willingness. You should want to serve eternity. When you want to serve eternity, if that is your real motive, a happy motive, or if you've come just to become absorbed in existence itself, then you are ready to study and grow. But if you think you're going to make a place for yourself, in other words, if you are going to receive goods, commodities and things that will help you to establish yourself in some kind of position of power, then you should go out and go into a business, you'll do very well there. And several lifetimes from now, when you've steadied yourself down, and you want to learn about selflessness, you want to find out how to be humble and pure and you're content to wait and be patient and let eternity do it in its own way, then at that time, come back to me. Come back to the inner life. Then you'll be ready. As long as you'd like to play in the world, that's spiritual balance. You can play and play and have all the fun you want and all the sorrow you want. You can think you're right, and perhaps in your own way you are. And you will work out your karma on your own.

But when the time comes, when you can no longer fight the light, then you will come to us. You will not be able to stay away, for I am eternity talking to you, and as eternity I can tell you, there's nothing to avoid, there's nothing to seek, there's nothing to find, except your own eternal light, your own eternal formlessness. And there will be no real lasting happiness or completion, until you give up, until you stop fighting God. Fight as long as you like, it's your privilege. As long as you wish to remain separate, you can. But when the time has come to come home, to fuse yourself back with that which you really are, to remember, and overcome your amnesia, then you will return. Spiritual balance is returning. It's remembering what we are. It's blending back with the source. Beyond all cognition, beyond all emotions and feelings, to that absolute oneness of immortal existence. that's self-realization, that's spiritual balance. And it coexists in everything and with everything, in any form and any world. There is nothing that it is not. The dream of life fades and wakefulness occurs.

THE SUBTLE PHYSICAL BODY

There are four primary states of consciousness: the waking state, the dream state, the deep sleep state, and the superconscious. The waking state is a dream, a dream of wakefulness. The dreaming state is a dream of phantasms, multiple realities, world upon world, vortex upon vortex, characters shuffling and reshuffling their identities again and again, multiple experiences on multiple planes. The deep sleep state is the dream of stillness and silence, of rest, in which there is no dreaming, no wakefulness, no thought patterns. And of course the fourth state, which I refer to frequently as the fourth level of ecstasy, is samadhi and the superconscious states, nirvana and so on.

The physical body relates to the physical consciousness. We're aware of the physical body when we're in the first state of consciousness, the waking state. When we enter into the dreaming state, we become aware of the subtle physical body. It's a different type of body. The subtle physical body is the body of dreaming. In the deep sleep state, we are not aware that there is a body. The awareness of the physical and the subtle physical go away. In the superconscious, we are beyond all definitions and limitations.

The subtle body surrounds and protects the physical body. Many people are familiar with the subtle physical through the aura. The human aura, which is not that difficult to see if you meditate and you've developed a little bit of sensitivity, surrounds the physical body. The aura changes color from time to time, depending upon the intensity of the kundalini energy that is passing through it.

A great deal of attention has been placed on the coloration of auras and the significance of the colors and things like that. There really is no significance at all to the colors of the aura, except that they are what they are. One might have a blue aura, a green aura, or a gold aura, but they're simply the reflections of the infinite colors of the soul. While certain levels of consciousness tend to correspond to certain colors, one is not better than another. In the same way that a child in first grade is not in any way superior or inferior to someone who's in their last year of college or graduate school, so the various planes of consciousness are equal. Superiority and inferiority only occur in the mind of one who is in a dualistic consciousness.

The subtle physical body is made up of ether. The physical body, according to the ancient yogis, was made up of fire, water, and air. These elements, these three elements, would constitute the physical condition. Think of them as symbols. There's not too much that I can say or explain about them. It's something that you just have to feel inside yourself.

Think of fire as heat – one aspect of the kundalini or of the infinite awareness, one way of seeing life, the fire of the sun that generates life. The fire of the sun is in the solar plexus, in the navel chakra, and in the root center, the base chakra at the bottom of the spine. Think of those two chakras in your being as fire.

The heart chakra and the throat chakra you can think of as water, if you will. The lower three chakras could be fire, and the chakra, the energy center, in the center of the chest and also in the throat would correspond to the element of water – just to try to give you a sense of the tonality of these things of which I speak, for which there are few if any words. Air would be connected with the third eye, between the eyebrows and slightly above, the agni chakra, and the crown chakra would also be connected with air.

Now, there are some slight variations. For example, the throat chakra is really a mixture of the air and the water. You might say that's where the element changes, so there's a mixture. The chakra at the very base of the spine is pure fire. The second chakra up, around the area of the spleen, is fire. The navel center, though, is a combination. It's a transition point, so it's an area of both fire and water. That is to say, these two elements come together there, in the subtle physical body. Then the heart center would be pure water. And the throat center would be a junction point. It would be water moving into air. The third eye would be air, and the crown center would be air. However, the crown center would be a junction point between the air and the ether.

The subtle physical body is a body of light. It is a much truer body, it is closer to what we are really like than our physical bodies are. The subtle physical body is composed of strands or luminous fibers of energy that interconnect different planes and times. The times are what we would refer to as the past, the present and the future. And the planes of consciousness are the seven principal planes of awareness, of existence. They're all interconnected through the chakras or gateways that are in the subtle physical body along the spine.

From the base of the spine to the crown of the head there's an astral tube, which is called the shushumna. It has two lesser tubes on both sides, the ida and the pingala. The kundalini energy, which is the basic life principle or life energy that works through the subtle physical body, moves normally up and down the ida and the pingala.

It does not move too much through the shushumna. The shushumna, you might say, is not accessible to the kundalini in most human beings.

As you go through the various stages of the enlightenment and self-realization process, the kundalini, of its own accord, will flow up the shushumna, through the various chakras, the seven chakras, eventually reaching the crown of the head. When the kundalini reaches the crown of the head, one enters into one of the samadhis, the advanced states of consciousness. Each time the kundalini moves through a different junction, a different chakra, it opens a doorway to another world, or it makes that opening possible.

Now, this is a schematic diagram. I can show you a schematic diagram for a television set or a radio, a wiring diagram. It's just a bunch of lines drawn on a piece of paper, and those lines will have very little to do with what the actual TV or radio is like. The radio or TV is composed of transistors or chips, tubes, electronic parts, each of which, if you hold it in your hand, has a life of its own. When they work together in various combinations they create circuits, structures, all of which produce an image which you see on a television, perhaps in a computer, something to store or process data and so on. It interprets a radio signal or a frequency.

Try not to spend too much time delving into the nature of the chakras in the subtle physical body in its schematic terms. Many, many books have been written, some of which are authentic, describing the different chakras, colors they're associated with, mantras they're associated with, strands of kundalini energy. And I've observed that people spend so much time studying these things that they miss what's important. These are only ways of trying to describe something in the physical, which is not in the physical. It's a blueprint.

Let's just look at enough of the blueprint to help us in our self-realization process, to help us have more fun and become more conscious, but let's not get fixated or stuck with it. Because you can learn all of these little terms and Sanskrit words, and know nothing about God-realization and be totally bound and shackled by frustration and your desires and depression. Whereas if you experience light, you're liberated. You're complete. You're free. You are your true self, which is not who you think you are.

You think that you are a person. You're under the illusions of selfhood, that you're a body, that you're a mind, that you have a structure – not so much in terms of how you think of yourself, but just the way you feel inside. Inside there's this sense of this person who's thinking. But that's not really how you are. You're a limitless expanse of light with no mind whatsoever as you know mind to be. Unless of course, you move into the plane of consciousness where there's mind, in which case you have mind. What I'm suggesting is that you exist on different levels.

On different planes you're different. And in the process of meditation and self-discovery, we draw ourselves from plane to plane, planes of awareness, different dimensions you might say. In each plane, we see that we are something else. We have a different identity. We assume a different role. Then there's something that transcends all of the planes, all of the seven planes, which is the superconscious. There are seven floors in the building, and we can go onto various floors and talk about them. It's strange, each time we get off the elevator on a different floor we're different. We have a different body, we have different memories, different feelings, different abilities. But then we can go beyond all seven floors into the sky, into the universe, into eternity. That's the superconscious.

The chakras, then, in the subtle physical body, are the gateways, are the guardians of the doorways of the different planes of consciousness. The planes of consciousness are realities, eternities, worlds, all of which are part of what we call the samsara, the illusion of existence. There are different dreams and you can walk into these different dreams. Right now as you listen to me you're in a specific dream. The dream you're in has a certain tonal awareness, a feeling. Then there's something beyond and beyond and beyond until you move into the undifferentiated reality of nirvana, at which point all descriptions fall away.

The subtle physical body is a body of light. Just as the physical body is composed of thousands and billions of cells – there are nerves and bones and tissues and chemicals and DNA and RNA and all kinds of exciting things, and they all work together – so the subtle physical body is equally, if not more, complex. It's composed of countless strands and fibers of light. And these strands and fibers of light coexist along with the physical body.

This etheric body, the subtle physical body, is similar. Its shape and size can change, and we can have more than one subtle physical body. You can create the etheric double, you can project another subtle physical body. You can have two at once, if you're an advanced yogi. You can gain the power to do this or create multiples, hundreds, thousands of them. But most people have one. It can change shape and form. Just as when water is poured into a glass, it will take the form of the glass, if it's poured in a plate, it will flatten out. Water assumes the shape of the vessel that it's poured into. Consciousness assumes different shapes and forms.

Your subtle physical body follows the form of your physical, more or less. However when you dream at night, when you're asleep, your subtle physical body will very often change form and travel through a succession of different planes of awareness that we call the astral. There you make your own movies. You write scripts, hire a cast, lighting, orchestration. Sometimes you'll put yourself in the picture, sometimes you'll just stand back and direct. These are dreams – experiences in other worlds where you can go and for a time you can create your own reality. It's like the places I used to go when I was a kid where we could go and we could make our own ice cream sundaes. You'd go into this place and pay the guy two or three dollars and they'd have 50 different kinds of ice cream and toppings, and you name it – you could just go and create your own sundae and you'd sit there and eat it and then you'd walk out. That's dreaming.

In dreaming, we go into a world where the forms of reality are variable, and the part of us that goes into that reality that plays with the different colors and combinations and ideas which we call dreams, is our subtle body. The sense of self that we have in dreaming is the subtle physical body. We're relating through that. It's the mask that we're wearing, that the soul is wearing.

In dreaming, you may think of yourself as being the person you now are having experiences. Sometimes in a dream, though, we're someone else. There's an awareness – somebody's having that dream, someone's participating in the experience. You may be running down a street in a dream with someone chasing you. You might not think of yourself as you are now in the dream, you might be a different person. But there's still a sense of self. That dream is occurring to someone who's in the dream. Someone's participating and feeling it. That's your subtle physical awareness, which can change identities in the dream.

In a normal waking state of consciousness, we're not too aware of our subtle physical body because we're in the physical body. We're so immersed in the physical body and its senses and desires and feelings, its wants and its needs, that we're not too conscious of it. The physical body is a great screen that blocks out the subtle physical and that which lies beyond the subtle physical, the superconscious.

In meditation, we move from the physical to the subtle

physical, or through the subtle physical to the superconscious awareness. Very few people meditate well enough to enter into the superconscious awareness. Once in a while, they might touch it for a few minutes, a few times during their life. Most people's experiences in meditation are confined to the subtle physical, which means that they have left their physical body in meditation in their subtle physical, just as you do in dreaming, only you're awake. And you move through a variety of different planes of reality in your subtle physical body, experiencing them and coming to know them. But during meditation, as you're sitting there meditating, even if your thoughts stop, if there's still a sense of self, there's still a feeling, 'I'm not having thoughts,' even if you're not thinking that. But there's still that feeling, that awareness, that there is a presence. Even if you think, 'I'm God, I'm eternity, I'm endless,' even if you just feel that, there's someone feeling it. As long as there's someone feeling it, there's a sense of self. That self is the subtle physical body, which means you are the subtle physical at that time.

You see, we are the body, we are the subtle physical and we are the soul. We are all these things, and yet we're none of these things. When we're in the physical consciousness, in the day-to-day waking world, we feel, 'Hey, I have a body, I'm alive. My body was born, my body will die.' And there's a sense of self associated with that and that's correct.

When we move into what we term a higher level of consciousness, which is a subtle physical awareness, if you meditate, and you move into a higher plane of being where you go beyond the physical, or eventually if you meditate long enough, for enough years, and you are able to maintain a state of meditation during your waking or dreaming hours – in other words you're always up, or you're always in a meditative state of being – then you're in the subtle physical. But there's still some sense, even if you're very high, there's a sense of, 'I just got into the car.' Everything may be fluid energy, and you don't see anything as being solid and there's light all around you, but there's still a strand of subtle physical connection. You're still in the subtle physical realities or realms because there's still a sense of self, a persona.

The demarcation point, of course, is nirvikalpa samadhi. We would link the lower samadhis, which I've talked about before with you; the lower samadhis are connected with the subtle physical. That is to say, all thought is stopped, you've gone beyond this world, you've gone beyond time, but there's still a sense of having done that. There's still a sense of experience. Salvikalpa and the other samadhis, which Pantanjali and other describe, are part of the subtle physical awareness. Nirvikalpa samadhi, which is nirvana – these are different terms, of course, that we apply to describe these indescribable states – means there's no sense of self.

Now, one of the questions that students like to ask teachers is, "Well, what's the difference between the deep sleep state and nirvana?" In the deep sleep state, there's no awareness per se. There's no sense of self, and there's no sense of self in nirvana or nirvikalpa samadhi. Is it the same thing? No.

In the deep sleep state there are seeds. Something will come forth from that state. Just as a tree has a little acorn, there's a seed in it and the seed may be still for a while, but then it will germinate, grow, and develop a tree. In the deep sleep state, all the tendencies, latent desires, attachments, all of the things that bind you to this world are still present. They're just dormant, they're still, but upon waking, all of those tendencies will come out.

Before you went to sleep, you liked cake, you liked croissants. You went to sleep. You entered into the deep sleep state. Maybe you dreamed for a while. When you came out of the deep sleep state, in which there was no dreaming, and no waking and no sense of self, you still liked croissants. You still liked cake. Nothing changed that much. Everything just rested. It disappeared for a while, but then it returned.

When you enter into nirvikalpa samadhi, into nirvana, it's different. You never come back. You are not the person who went into nirvana. It's something or someone else. It's impossible to describe; it's not too bad. But let us say you might not like cake (Rama laughs). Then again you might. Everything is reshuffled. You're a deck of cards, and you're dealt out the same way again and again. But, you see, when you go into nirvana – not that there's an "into" – the deck is reshuffled. Different combinations occur. You let your being go to God. You merge with God and whatever God wants to send back, if God wants to send anything back, it comes back. And in the advanced spiritual states, of course, you do this many times a day. You constantly change. There's constant revolution in your being upon return, you might say, or as you move into this awareness – all very abstract, but also quite concrete.

The subtle physical body, then, is a body of light. And the physical body is dependent upon it. By that I mean that when there is damage to the subtle physical body, you will see in concordance with that, relating damage in the physical body. The reason you die is not usually because of damage to your physical body but because of something that happened to your subtle physical body. There are obvious exceptions. In the case of a violent death, if someone shot you, or you're in an automobile accident and there was tremendous damage to the physical, naturally you'll die because of physical injury.

But the aging process, the process of decay that we see in the world, takes place largely because the physical is affected through the subtle physical. The subtle physical wears down, and as it wears down the energy, which keeps the physical alive, which comes from the subtle physical, is lessened and lessened. And of course there's a corollary reflection in the physical. The physical goes downhill. If you wish to improve your health, it's necessary to improve the health of your subtle physical body.

The physical body is dependent upon the subtle physical. Now, if your health has descended to a static point, that is to say, if you've gotten very, very sick and your body is very weak and tremendous damage has been done to the physical, it may be almost impossible to reverse that. Once a part has been damaged, it can almost get to the point of being beyond repair. We might be able to stop any further damage from occurring. The subtle physical body can restore the physical unless too much damage has been done. If there's too much damage done, it will restore it partially, but it can't completely restore it. That's what happens in the case of aging. You see, there's a certain residual wearing that takes place on the subtle physical body that reflects in the physical body. When that happens, we can't expect the subtle physical to repair that. That's just the way existence works.

But that's only of great concern to you if you think the physical body is life. If you're totally concerned with the shoes that you're wearing and you think that nothing matters but the shoes that you're wearing, then if something happens to them, you'll be very sad. However, you can just get another pair of shoes or go barefoot. Death is going barefoot, that's all. Your body falls away, then you're in the subtle physical. You spend some time in the subtle physical, you go through some different journeys and lands and have some adventures, and then you go beyond the subtle physical. The subtle physical falls away. It falls back into its own plane or its own world. Then that which is left, which we call the jiva or the soul, is absorbed into eternity for a time – kind of like going to sleep, in the deep sleep state. The soul just merges back with eternity for a while. And then it comes forth in a new lifetime. It takes on a new subtle physical and a new physical body.

What I'm suggesting is that the subtle physical and the physical are related. What happens to your subtle physical affects your physical tremendously. However if something happens to your physical, it won't affect your subtle physical. If you lose an arm, you won't lose your subtle physical arm. This has happened to many people who have lost a limb but still retain the sense or feeling of body beyond where body ends. They lost their arm but they can still feel their fingers. That's their subtle physical that they're feeling through. They just associate it with the physical because that's all they've ever known.

As you meditate more and more you'll become more conscious of the subtle physical awareness. The subtle physical awareness is very important. Without the subtle physical we do not exist in this world. If the subtle physical is weak, we're weak. If the subtle physical is strong, we're strong. If we're not aware of the subtle physical, then we're locked into the physical world of desire, pain, frustration, transitory happiness and pleasure.

The physical world is very limiting. It's like a maze that you're stuck in – and a very small maze. The way out of the maze is the subtle physical. When you become aware that you're not just the pair of shoes you're wearing but you're a whole body. You become conscious that you have an entirely different self, which is light, which is free to travel throughout the universes, beyond time itself, then you're not really trapped by what happens to your physical body or what occurs to you in your physical life. In your physical life you can be working at your job and working at a computer terminal and talking to your boss or your employees, but at the same time while you're doing that you can be in a meditative state and be having experiences in other realities and universes, in and through your subtle physical body.

Just as when you work at a factory – when I was a kid I worked at some factories and we used to put boxes together and put products in them and stuff, over the summers after school, and after a while your body just gets used to it. You can just stack those boxes on a palette and they'll ship them away. And your mind is free to go elsewhere. You can think about something you read. I used to think about Thoreau or what I was going to do on Friday night or whatever it might be. My body was not limited by my physical surroundings. That's what gives us intelligence.

In the same way, you are not limited by what your mind does, by your thoughts or by your physical proximity. There's a step above – my experiences in the factory, when I was freed from the actions of my body, the actions became so routine my mind could wander elsewhere and I could think of all kinds of lovely thoughts. You can put your mind into work, you can put your body into work, and then you can have a nice time with your subtle physical, being aware of countless levels of existence and planes of realities and so on.

Now, there's something beyond that, and that's once again our friend nirvana. In nirvana, you can't do anything. When you're fully absorbed, your body is not there. You can't exactly be working in the factory because for you there is no factory. But not to worry about it. When it happens, it all works out. The universe does everything perfectly.

The subtle physical body becomes stronger through meditation. Meditation is most important. The subtle physical body is purified through self-giving, whenever you give of yourself or you do something remarkable for someone, particularly when you help someone gain more light, spiritual light, or even on a basic physical level. But particularly when there's any kind of transference of light that purifies your subtle physical body. Humility, purity, integrity, truthfulness, honesty, caring, raising your higher emotions–these things purify the subtle physical. Whereas passion, frustration, anger, jealousy, hatred – these emotions damage the subtle physical. The subtle physical is like a delicate, beautiful flower. If the weather conditions are very bad, the flower fades quickly. If the flower has what it needs, a nice environment, it can thrive.

The world we live in is not conducive to the existence of the subtle physical, in a sense. In ages past, in this world, the vibratory energies were more conducive to a healthy subtle physical. Not only were there less people on the planet, with less energy waves, but just the vibratory energies of this universe were very, very different. It was a different time, a different era. This is in past yugas, past cycles of existence. People lived to be very, very old, thousands of years, because the subtle physical was maintained. You might say the energy of the earth was more healing and more nurturing. But as times change, which times tend to do, and the cycle of history ensued, we've dropped through a succession of ranges of consciousness. The level of consciousness of most people of the earth right now is very low. All those energies affect the subtle physical bodies and damage them, and therefore people don't live for as long a period of time, nor as happily as they used to.

Now, you can go above it all. These are weather patterns. The weather on the earth right now, well, we're in a time when there are a lot of storms. It's very tough on the planet, a lot of erosion. There were times when it was sunnier. There were times when the conditions of the earth were more favorable to what we call life. If you can go beyond the weather patterns, it's not a problem. If you can go up above the clouds, no matter how thick they are, there's nothing but sunshine. That's the superconscious. The conditions of the physical or the subtle physical vary, but the superconscious is always perfect light. But the physical factor, the vibratory factors of this time and this era, is that there's a great deal of darkness.

In India, they refer to this as the Kali Yuga. It's the last age of human existence before the cosmic dissolution occurs; this world as we know it ends. This dream ends, and then a new dream will begin, another cycle. But this is the end of the cycle. After this cycle, there will be a complete washing and dissolution and then we'll start off again in a new age with a high vibratory cycle, with excellent conditions for the subtle physical. It will be a very beautiful time. When people talk about a coming golden age, that's what they're referring to. After this final world destruction that will occur, there will be a washing, a purgation, and everything will be cleansed. This dream will end, a new dream will begin. And in that new dream there will be a kind of golden age. A time of beauty and light and so on. There won't be hate and things like that. That will happen one day. It's happened before. This is the cycle of existence.

There was a previous golden age several ages back, when it was just like that. But then after the golden age comes, it won't last. And we'll pass to a lower yuga and a lower yuga and a lower yuga until bam! We're back here again, at the bottom of the barrel. That's the cycle. That's the weather pattern.

But one who can enter into the superconscious can be in the golden age at any time, at any place, in any condition. As a matter of fact, for them, there is only a golden age. You see, the golden age still exists. What I'm suggesting is, it's like a four- or five-dimensional chess game that's going on. There are different planes of consciousness interacting. There are different ways of looking at all of this, this puzzle we call existence.

Most people are aware of only the physical. They're born, they grow up, they marry, they have children, they age, they die, they have experiences. Their subtle physical experiences are mainly limited to their dreams when they dream at night or whenever they're asleep. When you meditate, you're changing your structural awareness of reality. You're becoming conscious of the subtle physical. The following remarks, then, after our brief scan of the subtle physical, are more directly aimed at a person, or directly aimed at a person who meditates and who is seeking enlightenment.

If you wish to attain liberation, or you wish to attain a position of service–you're interested in aiding others in their liberation–then you are a spiritual seeker. Then you are going to go through the stages of development that create enlightenment. You're going to move beyond all weather patterns to the light of the superconscious, which is our true self. But you will become conscious of it. It's inevitable. You can do this slowly or quickly. It's entirely up to you. You must, first of all, bring your physical life together. If your physical life is causing you tremendous pain, then it is going to detract from your awareness of the higher realities.

In the physical world, we will always be distracted to a certain extent by our careers, relationships and so on. But you shouldn't spend too much time on the physical. If you do, you'll short-circuit your awareness. Take the time to organize your life, as I've described on previous tapes. Take your time, pick a good career, don't be afraid to go back to school, spend a few years so that for the rest of your life you'll be in a good career, you'll earn the amount of money you need to exist the way you want to. Have some nice friends, take time to develop them, have a good place to live, work out all the basics: a good car, whatever you need. Be conscious of security, all the different things that one has to have living and working in the world. Even out your physical. Do it right. If you have relationships that are destructive and drawing energy from you, eliminate them. Start to meet new people at the meditation centers and so on, or just wherever you meet them.

We do all those different things to try to balance our life. But don't spend too much time on it. Spend some time, get your physical together, and just get it running and forget about it. Once we set up the software program, we'll let it run. Once in a while we make modifications in it. Initially we have to write a program. We have a new computer and now we have to write the program, which will run on the computer. The program will determine how we're going to process data, how we're going to store it, subdivisions, categories, different functions. We take the time and we do a systems analysis.

The first thing we do is we look at our life, and we analyze it. What do I want? Where am I going? What have I got? How do I want to live? How much money do I want? Where do I want to work? How much time do I want to have–free time? We do a little systems analysis, realistically though, dealing with the conditions of the world as they are. Then from that we determine what it is we want. We write the program and then we start to run it. Once we start to run any program there are going to be a lot of bugs in it. We're going to find that it's not going to go exactly as we planned. But if we work on it, we can work out the bugs in the system.

You decided to go back to school. You thought it was going to be two years, it turned out to be three. We go through these experiences and we make the best of them, happily learning from whatever position God puts us in. But once the system is running, once the program is running, it doesn't take all our time. It took a lot of time to get it going, to work out the bugs and to write it and things. Now we can just let it run. Once in a while we make a structural change, a new person comes into our life, we enter into a new plane of awareness. But get the program running on the physical. Taking care of your body, your health, exercising, being vegetarian, following the vegetarian diet program, not smoking, you know, all the basics. Then we can begin to work, which we'll also do at the same time, but more freely, on the subtle physical.

If you're still working on your physical, I consider you a beginner. If your physical life is not yet together, you're having problems with employment and relationships and all this stuff, you're a beginner. Take your time, straighten those things out. Now let's move to the more sophisticated aspects of the spiritual study. And of course, as you meditate, you'll gain more and more strength to help bring your physical life, emotional life and mental life together.

But now, if you're moving a little further along, if you've worked that out a little bit or you're doing it really quickly because you don't have that much time in life, now you're turning your attention to something else. And that's your subtle physical. If you want to make your subtle physical not only stronger and more vibrant but also become more conscious of it, then there's very little that you have to do. First, you have to spend time with people whose subtle physicals are more evolved than yours are, who have more energy. We do this when we join a meditation center and we go and associate with others who meditate. Being around people who meditate, who seek light and who are channeling light through their being–in other words, when you meditate, light comes through your being. If you're around them and if you meditate together, that increases it.

Secondly, we have to look at where we lose light, what damages the physical: people we spend time with, people who drain us, thoughts that we ourselves think, situations we put ourselves in. We have to eliminate that. We have to think ahead and plan and say, "Now look, last time I got myself into this situation and it wasn't pleasant, and it drained me and I didn't feel well. This time I'm not going to let it happen. I'm going to be a little more clever and anticipate and feel inwardly in my meditation, stretching out my being so I can feel beyond my being, sense beyond my senses," and you can then alter reality. You can change dreams in the middle of a dream, several times, so that you won't even encounter those situations.

Then you need to find an enlightened person. You need to work with me or someone like myself who exists in the superconscious. While we pass through the subtle physical and the physical, most of our time is spent absorbed in the superconscious, and we enter in the physical and the subtle physical just enough to do what we need to do. But the rest of the time we're absorbed in the superconscious. And there's a light that passes through us, which is the superconscious light, that will infuse in you, it will give you, a tremendous charge. This is the kundalini. It's also called the shakti, when it's transmitted.

If you can be around an enlightened person–it's like standing near the sun–you'll get a lot of light. But you have to be aware of it. You have to meditate and purify your consciousness and practice self-giving and just tighten up your life. Otherwise, the light will pass through you or you will not retain it. You can come and see an enlightened person and spend time with them and get a terrific charge of energy. It's very healthy, it's good for your subtle physical, it opens the doorways of your awareness. But then you'll leave, you'll go out into the world and immediately go associate with some people who just have a lot of anger in them and hate, and that will enter into you, or you'll get frustrated or you'll be worried because you don't have enough money to pay the bills, and that will drag you down–all these different things, holes in your being, the light will pass through, you'll lose it. You have to work on accessing more light and then retaining light. If you do those two things, then you will gradually move higher and higher into the tremendous beauty of the subtle physical.

You should be around people who meditate in your free time. Don't be afraid of other people. If your subtle physical is nice and strong, you can be around anyone. But in your free time you should be around people who vibrate at a higher level. It will help attune you. Particularly, of course, be around someone who's enlightened whenever you can.

You should try to have contact with someone who's enlightened not only outwardly, but inwardly. Tap into them whenever you can. Draw light from them. That's what they're there for. They're like tremendous generators. The more you draw, the more you have. Each of us has to draw light in a different way. Someday when you become advanced in your spirituality, you won't necessarily draw light through a person, or a persona that we call an enlightened being; you'll draw light directly from the source. Just as an infant has to take– the infant takes nourishment from its mother in the beginning, then eventually it can eat independently–so we draw light from a spiritual teacher to start with. It's easier that way. Then eventually we can just draw light directly from the superconscious, and then we realize that we are nothing but light, and then we realize that we don't even exist, and then there's no realization, it all goes away. The cycle ends. And a new cycle begins.

Places of power. Just as different human beings have subtle physical bodies that emanate different amounts of energy, so there are physical places that emanate different amounts of energy. If you go to visit places of power, these are places where there's a tremendous charge – a certain mountain, certain deserts, valleys. These are places where spiritual practice occurred over thousands of years, or thousands of years ago, and there's an actual cosmic charge on the land. If you go to these places, then you can access more energy–if you meditate there, that is. Even walking through them, of course, you access energy.

This is what pilgrimages were all about. The idea was you go to the holy place. There's a place, or several places where there's more energy or more light for one reason or another, something connected with the past that happened there. If you go there, you imbibe this light and you take a part of it home with you. You change. Metamorphosis. It's the same as meditating. Sometimes it's good to go to a place of power to meditate. And there are many, many places of power, of course, particularly in the southwest United States. California probably has the most, which is why I live in California, but there are many places that have strong subtle physicals. The whole Southwest does, and there are places, of course, in Europe, and all over the world, India and so on.

At the places of power there are guardian beings. There are spirits or forces who guard the gateways. There's a mystery to places of power that I'll talk about sometime perhaps. And when you go to a place of power there are beings who are there who guard the access ways to the other worlds, the other realities. If they like you, they can help you. They are great warriors, and if they smile on you they will bless you in the same way a spiritual teacher will, an enlightened person. They're enlightened beings, they just don't have bodies. They're the same as the enlightened. It's just that they don't have a body. They have a different job to do, you might say. And they're very brave and free and happy beings. They only exist in the subtle physical. They don't bother to take physical form at all. They're not more advanced than an enlightened person with a body. One is not more advanced than another. It's the same thing. It's just one has the physical body, one doesn't. But they don't work so much with people, as a rule, or a very small group of people. They just exist. They are power and light. And that's really enough.

If you want to work with someone to help you attain enlightenment, you should go to a teacher who is in the physical body. They will help you. Sometimes particularly, they help very advanced souls, people who were perhaps enlightened in their last lifetime who have come in again in this lifetime. And when you come in of course, you lose it, you forget. They help the enlightened person gain their enlightenment again. They draw them back to the places of power. And when the enlightened person who has forgotten, who is in maya, in illusion, goes to the place of power, for some reason they're drawn there, then they help them gain their enlightenment again. They usually work with very, very advanced spiritual seekers. Not too much with beginners. But they'll help you, they'll smile on you, if your attitude is good, if you really care, if you're pure at heart, then they'll help you.

If you can go to a place of power with an enlightened person, with a spiritual teacher, that's the best. You can go to a place of power and not see too much or feel too much. But when you go with an enlightened person, they can open the crack between the worlds for you and help you go through into those other realities. You see, an enlightened person has the power. You're like a kite, but there's not much wind. The enlightened person brings the wind and you fly in the sky, into the other worlds, into the other realities.

Don't be afraid, be brave now. The spiritual path is easy. It's exciting, and it's adventurous. You must become aware of your subtle physical body, which I can't describe to you in words. Let's not get too caught up in description. What matters is that you care, that you love, and that you're going to do everything necessary to perfect yourself while at the same time accepting your limitations, your desires, and your frustrations without getting too taken out about it. It's going to take a long time to perfect yourself. But fortunately, we don't have to wait for your physical nature to be perfected. If we did, we might as well give up now. You will still have desires, you will still have feelings. That will always be going on to some extent in the lower strata in your being. On the lower floors, they will have different things–they may have a tag sale going on or whatever. But if you're up on the higher floors you won't even know about it. There's more light on the higher floors.

Don't be disconcerted if you find that you're doing the same stupid things again and thinking the same stupid thoughts and having the same mucky desires. It's not necessarily essential to stop all of that. It's nice, it's easier. It's more pleasant when you're in those states. But you can simply go beyond them into the higher realities, and then the light from the higher realities will wash down into those places and help you straighten them out. But put your attention to God, to truth and to light. Meditate, be around those who will help strengthen you, avoid those who weaken you, and mainly work on yourself.

Your challenge is yourself. Your challenge is to meditate more deeply, to give more of yourself. Not to blame others or blame your circumstances or your age or your economic condition, but to change those conditions. To change them. That's what yoga teaches us. To change things, not to say, "Well, I can't. Gosh, I'm too old. I'm not capable. My life has been bad." Those are the thoughts of a loser in the game of life.

Your meditation gives you the power to totally change everything you've ever done or been, to develop talents and abilities and strengths far beyond anything you've ever imagined. And it's necessary for you to do that. To do that you need to meditate more deeply, to become conscious of the subtle physical, and to begin to happily and joyfully walk through those other worlds and other realities of consciousness. Who knows what you might find. I'll be there waiting for you, though.

Along with a few friends.

WOMEN, MEN, AND SELF-REALIZATION

It is much easier for women to attain spiritual liberation than it is for men to do so. A woman's subtle physical body accepts light in this world much more readily than does a man's. It seems a curious fact then that throughout the short-lived history of spirituality in this world there have been very few self-realized, enlightened women. There are a number of reasons for this, and whether you are a man or a woman it is essential that you understand these reasons, accept them, and utilize them. As a man you can further the realization of all women when you understand these basic principles. As a woman you can, of course, advance yourself and all other women when you understand these basic principles.

I'd really like to divide this discussion into two sections. The first section will be, I suppose, more historical in the sense that we'll be considering why women have not attained enlightenment, and then in the second section, we will perhaps look at some things that women can do to foster and attain enlightenment. Also there will be some consideration as to what men can do to foster the enlightenment of women.

To begin with, let us establish that there is no difference between men and women on the deepest levels. Each one of us has a soul, a jiva, a self. That is to say, beyond the surface there is a particle of being which is larger than eternity, which is our existent and extant reality. It is neither masculine nor feminine; it's both. Yet in a particular lifetime, in a particular incarnation or series of incarnations, we will manifest as male or female, and just as the physical body of the male and female are somewhat different, so the subtle physical body of the male and female are different. But on the deepest levels there is no difference; we are all one.

However, in self-realization it's necessary to integrate, to some extent, the physical, and the subtle physical with the absolute. We have to work through these terms. If we live in a highly developed country, we have a certain frame of reference through which we view our experience. If we live in an underdeveloped country, we have another frame of reference. We have to deal with the physical. It affects us. In self-realization, the physical and the subtle physical affect us.

The subtle physical body of a woman is very different than that of a man. While both are composed of luminous fibers of light, the subtle physical body of a woman conducts light, or vibrates with light, at a different rate than that of a man. The subtle physical bodies of men are much denser. They're much more tightly packed. The subtle physical body of a woman is much more pliant. In my estimation, it's much easier for a woman to absorb and retain light and to change. In other words, the subtle physical body of a man is more fixed, a woman's is more pliant and that's the most important thing in self-realization, in enlightenment – the ability to make tremendous and rapid transcendences, to constantly change and reshuffle ourselves again and again in the white light of eternity.

Women are essentially much more powerful than men are. The kundalini flows through them much more readily. The problems are really very few. The primary reason why more women don't attain enlightenment is that they have a misunderstanding of their purpose as women. Women think of themselves as being women, and they're not. Women have a preconceived notion of what it means to be a woman, and this notion is incorrect. This notion has been given to them by our society, history, men, and other women. Everything is reversed in this age. Men appear to be more powerful than women, while the opposite is really true. What appears to be light is dark and what appears to be dark is light.

For a woman to attain liberation she has to realize that she has everything she needs within herself. Women have become dependent upon men in our society. They feel that they have to draw power from a man. They build their identities around men or around their children, and in doing so they do themselves and all women, and men, a great injustice. In order for a woman to attain enlightenment, she must realize that her true aspect is power. If she thinks of herself as being feminine–in the sense of the term that "feminine" means weak, gentle, constantly self-effacing, always cleaning up the house for others – then she's misunderstanding her power and her purpose. This is an image that has nothing to do with what really exists.

The time span for a woman to attain enlightenment is a little bit different than that of a man. There are certain times in the life of a man or woman when it's easier to make tremendous transcendences. For most women the best time is from, I would say, around the age of 18 to 35. If a woman hasn't really started on the path to enlightenment before that time it's more difficult. Again, women also develop a great deal of power later in life, but the intermediate stage for most women, from 35 to let's say around 55, is a more difficult time. In other words, if the right wheels haven't been set in motion, it's a much more difficult transit to pick up.

For men it's a little bit different. For men, realization occurs very readily from about 18 to 22. In other words, that's a very good time for a man to start on the path. If a man doesn't start during that period of time, it's more difficult. However, for men a very powerful time is from about 35 to around 55, 60. For women, in other words, the stronger years would run about 17 to 35, 38. Then they'd go through a slack time from about 35 to around 50 or 55, and then from that time forward it would be strong again. Whereas for men, [there is a powerful time] just for a few years from 18 to 21 or 22, then their slack time if they don't pick up the threads of realization would be, let's say, from about 22 to around 34 or 35, maybe even up to 40, and then again a strong time will come for them.

Now there are all kinds of exceptions to this, and certainly if you hear me say this and you think, 'Well, gosh, I'm a woman and I'm 35 and I've just started meditating, does that mean I can't attain enlightenment?' No, not at all. These are general guidelines. Anyone can attain liberation at any age, but there are times when it will be easier. There are sequences in our life when it's easier to do something. The current is going with us. The wheel of dharma is spinning in our direction.

Now, when I say begin [on the path], I mean that for both men and women at around the age of 18, 19, 21, 22, there's an opening, a door opens. A person gains a sense of their spirituality. There's a kind of past life return that occurs when we just remember a little bit of who and what we are. If you start meditating and seeking at this time and continue forward, that's ideal. The subtle physical body of a man and woman is in perfect shape at that age. If you start to meditate at that time, you will preserve that subtle physical and constantly increase its strength. As you get older, you won't get older.

If you haven't done that, then the subtle physical body will begin to wear. With a man, what will occur will be ego. Men, if they don't begin the spiritual process fairly early, tend to fall into the world of ego very quickly. There's this need to fight your way to the top. Men become obsessed with power, which is completely unnecessary and destructive for them – it's better for women to be obsessed with power– and so they [men] tend to fall away. Later at about 40, in their 40's sometimes, the interest will come forward again and they'll become interested in meditation, and that's a very strong time for men–40's, 50's and 60's. But most men, if they don't catch it by around that age, then they'll just kind of dive into the maya and from around 22 to around 40 not much will happen. There are exceptions, of course.

With women, their subtle physical bodies fade much faster in this world. While the strength of a woman is the fact that her subtle physical body is pliant and conducts energy, it's also the thing that is problematic for her, particularly in this age. In this age, in this time cycle of this universe, the destructive vibrations are very powerful. If the energy is very good, a spiritually oriented woman will progress very fast. If it's very bad, it'll be just the opposite. In other words, men are not quite as affected by the vibratory forces of this world as women are. If a woman places herself in an environment of light and she's around an enlightened spiritual teacher, has spiritual friends and all that sort of thing, her growth will be tremendously fast. If she's in the opposite environment, her descent will be very, very quick.

The damage that occurs to the subtle physical body of a woman occurs in several ways. Most of it is sexual. Most women lose their power in sexual relationships or simply by being exposed to the lower sexual energies of men. Sexuality is neither good nor bad, it depends how you approach it, but for most men sexuality is filled with violence. In the act of sex itself, while making love, men become very angry, very hateful; they very often hate the women they're making love to. There's this need to conquer, to assert your identity, and it's because men are afraid of the power of women. They sense this tremendous power, and rather than helping to foster it or accessing it, they want to cover it over. They're afraid of their own impotence.

The unrefined masculine energy enters easily into a woman, particularly during sex or when there's a sexual relationship, because women affix themselves very readily, emotionally, to men, much more so than men do. When a woman falls in love she will think of the man she's in love with constantly. When she does–psychically as she affixes herself to his consciousness–whatever is in his consciousness will enter into her consciousness. If there are a number of very destructive, or let's say high velocity, forces in the man's consciousness, which a man's subtle physical body perhaps can deal with, then when a woman draws those forces into herself by attaching herself to a man who's not very highly developed, who still hasn't worked those things out, they come into her being. While they may not destroy his spiritual potential, they will destroy her spiritual potential. You can look at a woman and quickly ascertain how many relationships she's had and what they've been like by simply looking at her subtle physical body. As a spiritual teacher, I do this constantly.

Now, you must understand, there's no good or bad–men are not better, women are not better. We're all children of God and we're all following the path to light, but we have to understand the operative conditions of the universe. It's men who make the wars. It's men who are interested in hatred and killing, by and large. It's this unstable energy, and it's because men are afraid to be women. They're afraid of their feminine side. If they would accept their feminine side, their female side, their femaleness, then there'd be a balance. There's a lot to sex. Freud wasn't so wrong, in certain ways, from a spiritual perspective.

As a woman, if you're interested in enlightenment, then it is necessary to detach yourself from men until you become much stronger. Now, this doesn't mean that you have to give up relationships and that you can't be married. You can, it's just tricky. Let me give you the average scenario for a woman so you'll understand what I'm describing.

A woman's power is at her height around, let's say, 17, 18, 19, 21 or 22. She literally glows with energy. At this time she's very attractive to men because men sense that there's a radiant power and light and they want to merge with it, they want to be part of it. The man and the woman go out or whatever, and as they become emotionally and sexually involved with each other, the man, instead of accessing that light or helping that light in some way, becomes afraid of that light. It's a threat to his masculinity because he doesn't understand yet what masculinity is. He tries to cover it over or destroy it. Now, needless to say, this is not conscious, but this is what's happening in almost every human relationship. He seeks to cover it over and destroy it, the very thing that could help him in his liberation.

The woman, of course, is in such a state of power at that age that she's intoxicated with it, that without realizing it she allows it to happen. In other words, she doesn't realize that she will only have a few years with this level of energy. While she's at that age she thinks, 'Oh gosh, I'll always feel like this.' There's never the possible thought that this power may go away. Now, the power wouldn't go away if she were very careful, if she kept her emotional relationships to a minimum. If she has relationships and if she has sexual contact, to make very darn sure it's with someone who's nice and who's not abusive, and most importantly to not allow herself to become emotionally wrapped up in a man or in men, then she can retain the integrity of her subtle physical body and through meditation, that power will grow stronger every year. But if she goes and just spreads herself too thin, she'll absorb all this very destructive energy and her subtle physical body will be very, very damaged, and she'll have her power drained, you might say.

Now, there are other factors that contribute to the demise of women in enlightenment. Women themselves allow this to happen. They foster an image of being weaker, or they want to be taken care of, to a certain extent. They want a daddy; they want someone to make decisions for them; they don't want to claim their own power, their own intensity. They choose attachments to the family instead of attachment to liberation.

Women don't support other women. They're jealous and they're vindictive, again, simply because they don't realize that they have enough power within themselves to enjoy other women and appreciate them. It's not necessary to compete over a male. What an absurd idea. Women should be sisters, unite, and pool their energy.

What can women do to attain liberation? First of all, in most cases, it's very healthy to break up patterns regardless of what your age is. We begin with meditation. As you meditate you become stronger and purer and clearer. There are two types of yoga that work best for women. The first is karma yoga, the second is mysticism. In karma yoga, through selfless giving, coupled of course with lots of meditation, a woman accesses her power. Then, as that power increases, the path of mysticism opens itself to her.

For men it's a little bit different. For men, bhakti yoga, devotional yoga, the love-oriented yoga, is the best. It stabilizes their energy and it's just more natural for their earlier years, as is karma yoga for the early years of a woman. Then, jnana yoga works very well for men. Now, men and women can all learn all four yogas, but what I'm suggesting is that there are certain pathways that will be easier.

Women have to be very careful of their relationships with men. It's easier to have someone make the decisions for you, but it's not, because then you're enslaved and you don't draw your own power and you become weak. Women seem to have this idea that they always have to be nice and allow people to walk all over them, and this is absurd. You don't help men by allowing them to do that. All you do is fixate them in a bad state of consciousness. Whenever you allow someone to abuse you, you don't help them, you're not a friend, because they're incurring bad karma. If you truly love someone, occasionally you'll be a little mean to them, if it's necessary. It may seem mean, but it's not because we love them.

You have to learn to be more unattached. There's this idea that women are emotional and men are not, and that's how women act, but actually it's quite the opposite. Men are much more emotional. They love much more quickly than women do. What I'm suggesting is that the way we see men and women outwardly and the way they act in our world and society is not the way they really are inwardly–it's backwards. That's why not too many people in this world attain enlightenment.

As a man you face a number of problems and difficulties, some of which I have already alluded to, as you reach for liberation. If you're a man, the best way to balance your energy is through love. Women need to work on power and claiming their power and bringing that power up–the power of the kundalini from the root chakra–and bringing it right up to the top of the head, and realizing their independence and asserting themselves more and more and not letting others run their lives or ruin their lives.

For men it's a little bit different. Men have to soften their nature. It's necessary to practice the yoga of love and to lose interest in power and conquest. In relationships with women, it's necessary to be gentle and to foster the power of women, to realize that a great deal of wrong has been done, not strictly because of the fault of men. There's no fault in this–both women and men have allowed this to happen. I don't see that men are more to blame than are women for the fact that not too many women attain enlightenment. It's equal. It takes two to tango.

As a man who's working towards liberation, you can aid women, mainly by leaving them alone and by not projecting sexual energy towards them. This lowers the vibration of the man and the woman. When a woman has energy thrown at her, sexual energy, it hurts her subtle body. If she's walking down the street and you look at her and you throw a lot of sexual energy at her, if you desire her, then what you're doing is just throwing all this energy at her, and it hurts her. This doesn't mean that you won't feel sexually attracted to people. That's fine, but there's a way to use it and not abuse it. It's not necessary to look at a person sexually, as a sexual object, because when you do, it fixates you in a particular level of consciousness. You're really not like that; it's just an image that you walked into. The macho image is absurd. What you need to do is learn about surrender and self-giving and humility and self-effacement–if you seek eternity.

It's important to work on the refinement of your nature and to meditate. The thing that will help you as a man the most, is meditation. But even when you meditate, you have to be very careful. You can't let it become an ego fixation. It's not an experience where you're going to conquer the world of meditation. There's no conquest. What you need to do is, you need to learn to be a woman. You need to surrender. You need to take eternity as your lover and just open yourself up to it and let eternity do with you as it will. You need to become stronger, more patient, and when these tremendous surges of energy come over you, you have to just let them come and go without becoming fixated in them.

As a man, you will find self-realization in this age quite easy. This is still the age of men, in a sense, although the age of women is around the corner. It's necessary as a man, more than any other thing– if I could recommend one thing to you–it's to develop a consistency in spiritual offering. The primary problem or difficulty that men have in self-realization is a kind of a low masculine energy that lacks sincerity, the locker room mentality, in the negative sense of the term. It is a lack of caring, being obsessed with oneself and one's own destiny as opposed to a group destiny, the idea of being the maverick: "I'm the fellow who drifts into town and has an adventure and then drifts out." This kind of I'm-just-in-it-for-myself mentality will not lead one to realization. Rather, it's best to meditate on love and on the heart and to just learn to love more and more. This will be a painful process for you because men have, by and large, turned off their emotional selves because they've been told that being a man means you should turn off your emotional self, and if you don't you're a bit of a sissy.

Now, I don't mean you should become maudlin and wrapped up in emotion. What I'm suggesting is, women need to gain control of their emotions, to be more detached and to see life and relationships from a higher level where we love but we don't fixate, whereas men need to open their hearts up and learn to love and practice kindness and allow those emotional whirlpools to open up within themselves. I'm suggesting a tone, a feeling, hopefully through my voice and through the vibratory energy that speaks forth at this time, regarding the self-realization of men and women. There are no special techniques. It's just that everything is backwards–women are powerless and men are powerful. Both are powerful.

The strength of a man's character is expressed through gentleness and through love and ultimately through discrimination. You meditate on love, you live in love, love purifies your nature. It removes the stain of selfishness, slowly but surely. Practice meditation and self-giving and work on humility. It's the most important. For women it's self-confidence. Then, after many years of meditating and love, and when your love has become so large that it embraces all of eternity, then you'll practice discrimination. You'll go beyond love as we know it. We'll never leave it, but we'll experience other things, let's say. Then you'll practice discrimination. You'll dissolve the personal self, which experiences a certain type of love.

Don't misunderstand me. I'm not suggesting that you shouldn't have relationships. You have to be yourself. If you need love relationships, have them. Most spiritual teachers don't recommend that people have love relationships because people get wrapped up in their emotions. They identify very heavily with the physical body; it unleashes the passions and the attachments. But you have to be yourself. You can find light in everything.

My suggestion is not that you don't have relationships or you don't get married or do whatever you want to, but that you bring light into everything that you do and that you realize, very simply, that as a man you have to learn to do it in a new way. The way you're doing it is not working. You have to be less concerned with yourself and your progress. You know, the old scenario, the guy and lady get married and then she works to support him in school, and he succeeds and drains her power and then leaves her and marries a younger woman and drains her power, and so on and so forth. That's really not so good for the guy either because you can never become what you're capable of being as long as you're going around hurting others.

The limited power that you draw from another human being is nothing compared to the limitless power of the force of eternity. You don't need to draw power from anyone, unless it happens to be an enlightened person. In that case, it's no longer a person. It's someone who's merged their consciousness with eternity so that they are now eternity–so you're not really drawing the power from a person, although there may be a body there, but just from eternity directly. They're just an access point, a jetty sticking out in the ocean.

For a man to attain liberation, gentleness is the requisite, and love, for many, many years; and to be very gentle with all beings; to be strong but to have a delicacy in your strength; to just practice meditating with love and to become less wrapped up in others; to not abuse women and to not be what you've been.

For women it's a little bit different. For women, what's necessary is to realize that power is your aspect, to be more supportive of other women in their quest for liberation and perhaps for a short time to step back from men in relationships–not to give them up, necessarily, but perhaps to step back for a while, just so you can become complete and whole. All your life you've gained your identity from the men in your life. Now, perhaps, it would be good, just for a time, to step back and discover who you are and what you're all about, because if men only see you in a certain way they'll fixate you. That is to say, it's like looking in a mirror and you believe what you see. In the mirror, you think that's what you look like, but suppose the mirror was projecting an image that wasn't really you?

For most women when they look in the eyes of both men and most women, the image that's projected back–that a woman is psychically told to conform to–is not really what she is. It's necessary to step back and be, for a while, around women who are more supportive or men who are very supportive or an enlightened person or persons, and discover what it means to be a woman.

It's not easy, it's a difficult search because you have to assume responsibility, you have to become commanding and to assume your power. You need to, in this world, avoid dressing in ways that attract a lot of lower sexual energy from men. It would be wonderful if we lived in a world in which the conditions were all perfectly balanced, where you didn't have to be concerned about this, where you could just be yourself and that would be enough. But that's not the way the world is. We have to deal with objective reality, so it's good to be inaccessible.

You don't have to hide yourself, but one should not display oneself either. If you walk down the street wearing a lot of valuable jewelry, you'll probably get robbed. If you wear it in places with people who won't be that way, then it's fine, or by yourself and you enjoy it and eternity enjoys it. In the same sense, if you push your body forth, there will be people who will throw energies at you that are extremely destructive. You have to decide yourself.

Now, for both men and women, children can be a tremendous obstacle to enlightenment. If you already have children then that's wonderful. You can use those children that you have to help you attain enlightenment by helping them, but it's necessary to not make them your world, to do your very best for them that you can – but not to make them your world. If you don't have children, I would not recommend it. If you have them then we do the best that we can with them, but if you don't have children, and you really are interested in liberation, I certainly wouldn't have them. If you do, don't feel you're doing anything wrong. You must be yourself.

You see, I'm speaking on different levels of consciousness simultaneously. That's why these things I say sometimes appear to contradict. They don't. I'm just giving you openings on different levels of understanding. Something will be true on one level and not on another. You have to accept what is useful for you on the level that you're on. It may change tomorrow. If you've just gotten married and if you heard this tape and you're all excited and you want to have children and you feel, "Oh, well Rama's saying I shouldn't have children. If I do, I won't attain enlightenment." No, I'm not saying that, but it will be much more difficult. I'm not saying that if you have children that you won't be able to attain enlightenment. Not at all.

You have to accept that God does everything perfectly and that you're in exactly the situation you should be in. If you now have children, that's wonderful. Use them as objects of power. By giving to them and being kind to them and nurturing them, you'll help yourself grow and develop. But don't have any more children, unless you really need to–that's what I'm suggesting. It's just more difficult. During the first years of a child's life, and all the years of a child's life, there's a tremendous fixation on the child, which is right, there should be. You have to take care of the child. Your consciousness is tuning to this child, which is fine, but lots and lots of people have had children and not attained enlightenment. Just by tuning your consciousness to the child, enlightenment doesn't occur.

You need to see that your child is eternity, all of existence. If you have children, do the best you can with them. If you have to have them, have them and do the best you can with them. But if you can, open yourself to the possibility that fulfillment can come without having children or any more children, that it's really not necessary, that you can sit and meditate and go into the higher consciousness states and experience completion that way, that the world will have all the children it needs. There are plenty of people who want to have them. It's easier for you that way.

It's the same with sexuality. For women, if you can avoid relationships for a time, just until your own energy is straightened out, that's fine. But if you're in a relationship and it's working, if you're in a marriage and you enjoy it, that's fine. Don't feel the need to pull back from these things–try to improve them. You have to be yourself, but if you find a natural inclination in yourself, for a while, to pull back from relationships, sexual relationships, and just for a while to tune out another person from your life and find out who you are, that might be a very healthy thing to do for a while. Then perhaps later you'll go back into the world of relationships with different motivations. You won't get trapped in them. You'll be able to enjoy them. The same is true for men, but even more so for women because women have been and are more affected by relationships than men are, by and large, because of the structure of their subtle physical bodies.

Don't be afraid to change. Change is necessary and the most basic change that we make has to do with our sexual identity. Sex does not matter. It's not important, unless you make it important. People have placed much too great a charge on sexuality. It's not necessary to be celibate to attain enlightenment. It's necessary to be yourself and if you're yourself, who could ask for more? There will come a time though when you will probably be celibate for a while, on the way to enlightenment, in one incarnation or another. That will be a very fun, lovely time, but it won't be forced. There won't be the need to say, "Oh, gosh, I want to have relationships and I can't because I'm not supposed to." That's nonsense, you have to be yourself.

Then you'll return to relationships, your sexuality, perhaps, if that's what you want to do, when you have sufficient detachment so that it won't be sex anymore. When you're with someone it will be a giving, a pure self-effacement, a transfer of energy. There won't be any desire. You won't even notice it. There'll be no concerns of the personal self or physical satisfaction or fulfillment or anything like that. That will all just go away. Then it can't be harmful. In other words, your emotions won't get wrapped up. You'll preserve complete detachment and every action will be service and self-giving. When you have that attitude nothing can hurt you–if it's not just an idea in your mind but it's something that you can actually do in any circumstance. It's a wonderful thought. People try it, but it's difficult.

You must meditate and ground yourself in the eternal light and begin to think of yourself in a new way. As a man you must think, 'I am not what they taught me. They told me that this is what being a man means and it's not necessarily the case.' Being a man is a very noble thing, a very powerful thing, a very gentle thing. You need to develop your artistic abilities more, to express your feminine side more. It's not a feminine side–it's another part of yourself, but these are categorizations that people who are not too balanced have developed.

As a woman, you have to work on power, independence, self-confidence, supporting other women and not always running to a man for justification, for condolence, for support, and not always looking for the nod of the father figure saying, "Yes this is right," or someone to just pat you on the shoulder. Rather, you have to realize that you have tremendous power in your being and you can bring that power into eternity.

As either a man or a woman or as neither or both you need to harmonize yourself with eternity. Whether you're heterosexual or gay or whatever it really doesn't matter a bit. What matters as a man and woman is that you see that you're not a man or a woman, that you're both, and that you create a balance of both sides of your being. It's necessary to do a little work on the side that you've been neglecting. As you do that, you will become stronger and stronger and stronger.

Regardless of your age, once you enter into the timeless there is no time and there is no age. The age factor will make a difference, but if you can go to an enlightened person and work with them then it won't. In other words, when you're with someone who is enlightened you enter into a timeless realm where the age factor disappears. You can also do the same thing by yourself if you can enter into samadhi. If you can enter into the superconscious completely then there is no age.

If you're not capable of doing that yet, which most people who meditate aren't, then you need to be around someone who does that, and then by being there it's sort of the same thing, you get a free ride.

Then while you're with them in that timeless period the age factor doesn't matter as much. Otherwise it does. It's much harder the older you get. When I speak of, for women in their late 50's or 60's [entering] a very powerful time, that's true, but that will be a much harder approach than it would have been at 18 or 19 or 20 by yourself.

The same is true of men if you miss that beginning at that age. True, the 40's and 50's and 60's are a strong time for men, but if you miss that early training, it's going to be difficult on your own. You can do it, but best to find a liberated being you have faith in and go to them, and when you're with them, you step into the timeless realm when you meditate with them and work with them and then you're 18 again, you see? By being with them, if you learn from them, if you access that light that courses through them, you're 18 again, always. It doesn't matter what the age of the body is.

You can do the same thing by yourself if you can enter into samadhi. If you can be absorbed in perfect light with no self, no mind, no body, no world, time falls away, there's nothing but eternal reality, complete perfect light. If you can do that every day, on your own, in meditation, to the point that there is no difference between you and God and then even you and God fall away into nirvana, then it's not necessary. Otherwise, it's easier for you that way [to work with a liberated being]. These are just a few thoughts, suggestions, and feelings about obtaining liberation as a woman or as a man. There are no ironclad rules. You have to be creative as you go along. What I'm suggesting is a tone, a feeling.

As a woman, you need to feel powerful, to feel strong, to bring the kundalini up from the root chakra, to have it surge up your spine to the crown center, to assert yourself, yet to be inaccessible in a world that doesn't like women and to realize that most men hate women because they're afraid of them. They're afraid of the power of women because they realize that women are much more powerful than men, and there's something in men, in their unenlightened side, that fears that power. It doesn't understand that if it would open itself to that power, that power would enter them and help them in their liberation. They fear that power and they seek to put it down. And there's something in the unenlightened side of women that allows that to take place, that doesn't want responsibility, that wants someone to make the decisions, but ultimately that's not satisfactory because then a woman will be drained, tired and discouraged and just pass from birth to death, from birth to death, with little or nothing to show for it.

As a man it is necessary to become loving and gentle and kind, to be strong as you can be and to be fearless, a fearless warrior, but at the same time to be delicate and to work on your capacity to love purely. To not throw sexual vibrations at someone because of the way they look, not to feel bad because you have desires, but just don't let them be uncontrolled—push them aside. If you're with someone you love, to be as you are, but simply not to project those energies at everyone just because of the way they look because it's quite harmful to them, and it's quite harmful to you because then you put yourself into a very low plane of consciousness. Desire is neither good nor bad. It's like a river. If you get in the river, you have to go where that river takes you. If you get out of the river, then you can walk someplace else, on dry land.

Never feel bad because you have desires, but because you have them doesn't mean that you should give in to them all the time. You have to ask yourself what is right, and when you know what is right, if your desire agrees with what is right, then fulfill your desire. That's detachment. Detachment is the ability not to avoid our desires and not fulfill them, but to just ask ourselves, "Is this right? Is this feeling I have now right? Is it one with the dharma?" If you feel that it is true and it is right, then you can fulfill your desire and it won't be harmful.

But if you're so wrapped up in your desires that you don't care and you just fulfill them—if it isn't with the basic flow of eternal life, with what we call the dharma—then we will suffer, this is our destruction. That's discrimination. Discrimination means we can stand back when the heat of desire is pushing us and say, "Now, is this really right? Is this what God really wants? Is this what eternity wants?" Just to sit in silence and feel what is right and then do what is right. Then sometimes your desires will be correct, and you'll fulfill them and that is fine. It's no big deal one way or the other, but if you fulfill your desires when it isn't the dharma, when it isn't correct, that's when you create bad karma and you have all kinds of problems. That's when you'll suffer like anything. Take the time to meditate, to reach within yourself and ask yourself, "What does it mean to be a man? What does it mean to be a woman? It's not what I thought." Ask eternity to show you and to teach you what it means. Don't be afraid to change. Be open to being something that you haven't been again and again and again— you'll change, until finally you become everything and nothing.

INACCESSIBILITY AND ATTACHMENT

Attachment creates pain and frustration. Attachment is the thing that we seek to overcome in self-discovery. Attachment creates pain, and if you don't like pain and suffering, frustration and misery, you must overcome attachment. Attachment on a basic level means not getting caught up in desires. Desires pass through us like the wind passes through the leaves on a tree. The wind moves the leaves to and from. Desire passes through us and can create movement, a stirring, a rustling within the self.

Desire is neither good nor bad. It just has a simple result. Some people feel in spiritual practice that in order to attain higher states of consciousness, to lead a happier life, they have to overcome desire. It's impossible to overcome desire. It's like trying to overcome the earth or the solar system or God. It's not necessary to overcome anything in order to attain liberation. Enlightenment and liberation have nothing to do with overcoming anything. Rather, they involve acceptance and dissolution. If you fight against your desires, you get ensnared in them. If you don't do anything about your desires, you get ensnared in them. Desires are not necessarily bad. It depends on the desire. Let's take a look at desire and attachment.

There is something that we call dharma. Truth. The idea is that there is a universal movement or motion that is correct. When desire is in concord with dharma, then desire does not create pain. When desire runs contrary to dharma, then desire creates pain.

Let me give you an example. You have many different sides to your being. And each of those sides seeks happiness in different ways. Now, if we go to your absolute self, your highest aspect, we find nothing but light. Your real being is timeless and endless light. It has no beginning, it has no ending. It's static and ecstatic consciousness, beyond description. When you are absorbed in that light, meaning when your attention is fully focused on your own infiniteness, then you feel no suffering, no pain, no desire, no frustration. Everything is perfect perfection. This is the stateless state that all human beings, and all beings, sentient and non-sentient, seek. We call it God-consciousness. No worries, no problems, no second mortgages, no lines at the bank teller's window. Endless, infinite consciousness. It's what they call heaven. And it exists right here and right now. You simply have to become aware of it.

Imagine that you're a very, very tall person and that your head, the top part of your being, exists in that world, in that state. Then let's say that there are other levels of your being that cut through other parts of your body, as if we segmented your body. Your feet and up to your knees is in one segment, from your knees maybe to your waist is another segment, from your waist to your neck is another segment and then from your neck to your head is another segment. Let's say that your head is in the superconscious. It's in the highest reality. It's in that timeless state that we call nirvana, or heaven, or perfection, whatever terms you like. Now, that part of your being doesn't seek to do anything. It doesn't have desires. It's a cloudless sky. Other parts of your being, though, get caught up in desire.

We all have a physical body, and the physical body is moved by desire. We all have a subtle physical body. The subtle physical body can also be moved by desire. But our absolute self is far beyond desire. The part of us that causes us pain, then, is the physical body, the subtle physical body, and of course the mental body. These are the three avenues of self, the three segments below the head. Let's say the physical body is that area from the knees down. Then maybe the next area up would be the mind, and above the mind the subtle physical, and then above the subtle physical, the superconscious. There are various divisions we can make; these are all just divisions that try to describe something that's really beyond words.

Now, desire usually involves the body and the mind and sometimes the subtle physical. The idea is simple. You want an ice cream cone. If you don't receive the ice cream cone, then your desire is frustrated. When your desire is frustrated, you lose the lessons of experience, which means not to get angry because when you get angry it does nothing except cause you to go to a lower bardo. You lose the lessons of experience, and when you lose the lessons of experience, of course, you lose discrimination. Discrimination means that you get so wrapped up in your anger at this point that you forget to ask what is right or wrong, maybe you go punch the wall or punch your friend, or whatever it may be. Suddenly instead of just seeing the beauty of life, because you didn't get your ice cream cone when you wanted it, you've become enraged. Then all of life is ugly, everything is terrible, life is just meaningless. And you can descend further. That's the problem with desire.

Having things isn't bad. There's nothing wrong with having an ice cream cone if you want one. I mean, if you're overweight, you might not want one if you're trying to maintain a certain weight level. But otherwise there's nothing wrong with having an ice cream cone. The problem is that you become ensnared by it. That is to say, if you don't get it you're unhappy. If you do get it, you build it into such an experience that it rarely comes up to your expectations, although ice cream sometimes does. Perhaps we should put ice cream in a whole separate category. But in any case...

So, we think all day about, 'Well, gosh, around 4:00 when I get out of work I'm going to zip down to the old ice cream parlor; I'm going to get a Häagen-Dazs Rum Raisin ice cream cone,' or whatever your favorite is. And we wait for that moment and then we finally get there. They've run out of our flavor. 'Ooohhhh! Nothing else will do, life is terrible.' Or, we've built up the experience so much that when we have it, it really isn't quite as good as we remembered–must have been something wrong with the shipment, and we're unhappy. Or, let's suppose it all worked out. Let's suppose we did get that ice cream cone, and it was the most wonderful ice cream cone that we'd ever had. Fantastic ice cream. But then after a while it's all gone. Well, we can try and repeat the experience and order another and another and another. But we'll find that as our appetite slackens, the sensual experience will suddenly change. It won't be pleasant any longer. We'll be satiated.

Why does this all happen? In other words, we can't be happy from the fulfillment of desire, or if we are, it's only a transitory desire, then it goes away. What's the problem here? Well, it has to do with the nature of the physical. A Chevrolet is not a Ferrari. If you drive the Chevrolet like you would drive a Ferrari, you're going to get into a bit of trouble. It doesn't corner that well, it can't go that fast. It's important to understand that happiness does not come from the physical.

The physical exists and has a sheen and a tone all of its own. But it doesn't make you happy. The physical at its best, meaning your body and its sensations, is quiet. It doesn't distract you. When your body is in pain, when you're ill, when you don't feel well, when you're in a state of desire and expectation, at these times, you notice your body. Otherwise the body is relatively unnoticed. And that's how it should be. But when you focus on things that are in the physical realm, you become fixated or attached to them. Attachment means that you want to hold onto an experience, a person, an idea, a way of being, a self — but there's a sense of fixation. You feel that you want to hold onto it because you enjoy it, and if you continue holding onto it and experiencing it again and again, your enjoyment will last.

Now the problem is, the universe doesn't work that way. Nothing in the physical or mental or astral worlds lasts. Everything is transitory. It's a self-defeating notion. Ultimately, no matter what you hold onto, if it's physical, mental, or subtle, it will change, it will transform, it will go away. You're just setting yourself up for unhappiness.

The nature of reality is freedom. And when you try to block the nature of reality through your fixations and attachments, you create problems for yourself, you become unhappy. Now, if you wanted an ice cream cone — you saw that a part of you wanted to have an ice cream cone and it seemed like an appropriate thing to have — and you had the ice cream cone and enjoyed it and then just kept on going, there's no attachment. If you didn't make that big of a deal out of the ice cream cone, it was one moment in a series of endless moments–you noticed it, you enjoyed it, it was pretty in its way, as all of life is. If you got there and they didn't have the right flavor, it would be exciting to know that life is exposing you to another flavor. If you didn't compare the way it had tasted before, if you took it as a new experience, then you would not be disappointed by the flavor, as opposed to how it had tasted the week before. You see, it's attachment that fixes us in time. We become a body in time. You're not a body in time, you're a limitless awareness.

That's the problem with attachment. Things are not bad. You're not bad. What causes a problem is when you become affixed to things. Now, the reason this happens is that you have been taught or conditioned to believe that happiness comes from physical possessions–money, sexual gratification, owning a big home, artistic experiences, whatever it may be. You feel that it will make you happy. These things don't make you happy. They can neither add nor take away from your state of happiness. You just think they do. For a while they may indeed give you some sort of a temporary satisfaction. But if you understood that what you really want is to merge with eternity and that all of the experiences you seek are attempts to do that, then it will be easier for you.

The primary want in your being is to become one with all of existence, to experience the superconscious–limitless, perfect bliss, ecstasy, stillness, whatever you wish to call it. Our attempt to hold onto people, relationships, things, experiences, careers, all of these things, are attempts to do that. They're fleeting attempts to try, within the transitory, within the physical frame of reference, to experience eternity. There's nothing wrong with experiencing eternity in the physical, transitory frames of reference, as long as you don't think that that will make you happy. Happiness comes from experiencing the superconscious or realizing that we are the superconscious. Then, when you have that understanding, that knowledge, when you live in that world of light all the time, you're free to roam the world, as am I.

I can go anyplace and be happy. I can be in any experience. I can experience any frustration, any loss, any gain, success, failure; it's all the same to me. My body will experience pain and not necessarily like it. My emotions can be painful. My thoughts can be painful and unhappy. But I now live beyond all of these conditions. I am no longer bound by my body, by my emotions or by my mind. I stand far beyond them in light. I am light. I am free to walk in the world, to have sensual experiences, non-sensual experiences, and just enjoy them because I don't pay that much attention to them. I observe my self – parts of my selves — going through them, knowing that life is directing all things. Just as the electrons move around the atom without wondering why, so I move around the universes without wondering or knowing why.

Knowing why is a function of the mind. If the mind seeks to know why, that's fine. But there's a level of knowledge or understanding that we call love, that is beyond knowing why. It just is. When you raise to that level of attention, there is no attachment. And if you see parts of your being fixating, you are able to step beyond that fixation and all the fixations dissolve. As you step in and out of samadhi, in and out of nirvana, all the fixations go away.

From my point of view, there's no attachment. From your point of view, there still is. Parts of my being could easily become attached. No one is beyond attachment, as long as there's someone to be attached. But when we dissolve ourselves in the superconscious, then there's no one to be attached, therefore there's no attachment. That's the way you overcome attachment. Not by stopping your desires, not by ignoring them, but by dissolving yourself in light. By becoming what you really are, in other words.

Dissolving is a way of speaking. You don't dissolve. It would be just as accurate to say that you become what you really are–your higher self, eternal consciousness. Then you don't even notice desire, you don't even notice attachment. If you sit there in light, who could notice? All of the ecstasies that have ever been or will ever be could present themselves in front of you, and you wouldn't even feel them, compared to the pure light of eternity. That's really the way you do it.

The way you overcome attachment, which causes pain, is not by giving up relationships, giving up possessions, or all that sort of thing. You might want to pull back for a while if you've gotten so wrapped up in relationships and possessions and careers. Sometimes it's nice just to shut off the faucet for a while, to just give ourselves a little distance. It's easier that way, if we break contact for a while with things that we've been wrapped up in, so that we can breathe a little bit and gain our balance. But then you go back in. The world is fun. People are fun. Life is filled with beauty. Even in tragedy there's beauty, if you can see the eternal within.

This is what meditation and yoga teaches us. Meditation and yoga teaches us not to try to change the world, because it's always changing. But to observe and to enjoy, to allow eternity to express itself through us freely as it will, and to allow eternity to enjoy itself as it will. Our job is simply not to hold on.

You can't hold onto anyone. You don't own anyone. The idea of holding onto someone in a relationship is absurd. How can you hold on? Everyone is light. And you're light. Light can't hold light. You may think that you're a person who can retain something. But I assure you, death will take away from you all those things that you cling to, and then you will experience great suffering and loss. While now you are alive, you can realize the truth, and if you realize the truth, you will be free. Then you can play in the world and enjoy the world. You'll still suffer at times. You'll still feel heat and cold, pleasure and pain–unless you're completely absorbed in the superconscious, in the highest meditation–you'll feel these things, but you won't be that affected by them; you'll understand them.

A great conductor who is leading a symphony orchestra, if suddenly a fly is buzzing around his head, he's not going to get all excited and mad and start swatting at the fly and upsetting his orchestra. He simply ignores it. He gets on with what he has to do, his concentration is strong enough. Eventually the fly will go away. When you're absorbed in higher consciousness, when desires that could cause attachment pass through you, you simply ignore them. You say, "No, this isn't right. If I become wrapped up in this person or this experience, I won't be happy." Because when you become wrapped up, you get pulled down from the superconscious awareness. Your attention fixes on a physical experience or mental experience.

Now the big attachments in self-discovery have nothing to do with attachments to cars or people or love relationships. Those are the basics. And if you're still working on those, I suggest you work through them quickly because there are larger and more exciting challenges ahead of you. The big challenges, the big attachments, are states of being, are states of awareness. Universes. The big attachment is not to someone else or something else, but it's to ourselves. To the way we see life, to what we believe we are – our understandings, our ideas. And these are the best, the most fun, the most exciting attachments to destroy or to slay. You use discrimination, meaning you can see beyond the surface to eternity. Then you rid yourself of all attachments and then you're free. Sounds easy, doesn't it? Good luck! (Rama laughs.)

You can do it. I did it. If I can attain liberation, anyone can attain liberation. That should give you great hope. It's not that difficult. If you really love light and you really want that and you simply give everything that you have and everything you are for what you believe, it's quite simple. If you don't do that, then how can it possibly happen? If you give 60 percent of your attention to self-discovery and to overcoming your attachments and suffusing yourself with light, then it will happen in 60 percent, and 40 percent it won't be. If you find a path, follow it, and devote 100 percent of your attention to it, then you will become the path itself — in time. It just takes time to become timeless. And it's kind of fun. There's no rush to get there. Going there is a beautiful experience also.

Attachment – the less you deal with it the better. You'll suffer as long as you want to. When you get tired of it, you'll listen. Then you'll give up attachment, give up trying to hold onto people, places, possessions, your old selves. You'll meditate, devote your life entirely to self-discovery while living and working in the world and having a good time, helping as many people as you can without thinking too much of yourself, and everything will be delightful. Till then you'll burn. Such is life. (Rama laughs.) Sorry about that. But — it goes away after a while. Life goes away after a while, and death goes away after a while, so don't feel too bad about it. There's something good waiting for you. If it hurts now, it won't hurt forever, I assure you. Life is light. Just be patient and work like mad.

Inaccessibility. Well, inaccessibility is essential if you live in the world. As you know, we live in a world that has several billion physical beings–people–living in it, all of whom are on varying levels of self-awareness. Many of these beings are what we call in the trade not too evolved, meaning that they're in their very early stages of existence.

Think of the earth as a school, a giant school that runs from kindergarten through graduate school. And then of course there are teachers who teach at varying levels within the school. Those teachers may be at a static level themselves. The teacher may complete college and now teach first grade, and the teacher's not progressing. Some teachers, while they teach, continue to make progress. Then there are those who are old tenured faculty and they keep up their research and attend meetings, but they've just reached a point where they know their stuff pretty well.

Along the path we have different teachers. And these teachers are sometimes people, sometimes they're nonphysical beings, occasionally, that help us. Sometimes they're the other people around us who don't call themselves teachers, they're just human beings we can learn from. Nature is a great teacher. If you need to learn something, go take a walk on the beach at sunset, take a hike up in the mountains by yourself, just listen to the rhythm of nature. Listen to the wind. Go to the desert. There's so much to learn from the pulse of nature, if you listen. You can be in nature and just be filled with thoughts and learn nothing, or you can walk with a silent mind and see all of eternity.

In my estimation, a great deal can be learned from going to the movies. Movies are the art form of the day. The movie is to the 20th century what the novel was in the 19th century. And I personally feel that a great deal about human consciousness can be learned through the arts, through drama, and film today. The cinema is certainly a place to learn about varying states of consciousness, ways of seeing. It's fascinating.

Inaccessibility, then, means we recognize and accept that the spaceship earth has lots of divisions, lots of different levels, and that the vast majority, let us say 90 percent of the people on the earth, are not too evolved. They're still in grammar school and junior high school. And that they fight a lot and they hurt each other a lot and they hurt themselves a lot. Their energy is not very stable. Now, if you happen to be a spiritual seeker, one who is refining their nature and overcoming hatreds and jealousies and fears and all these things, you have to realize that the odds are not necessarily against you, but let's say that the history of spiritual seekers has something to offer or teach us.

From age to age, spiritual groups and spiritual seekers are persecuted and very often killed for their belief in God. That's what history teaches us. We learn to be inaccessible. We learn from history. We learn that it's good to veil the light, to a certain extent, in most cases. If there's someone who will understand and appreciate your spirituality, it's fine to be with them and discuss it. But in most cases, it's good to blend.

Why do people stand out in the world? Well, usually two reasons. Reason one is they stand out because they're very fixated in their egos and they want people to notice them. They think that if people notice them, if they're famous, be it in a small circle of friends or in world terms that will make them happy. This is illusion number 99 in a continuing series of illusions. Some people stand out without meaning to stand out. They stand out simply because they're different, because their views are different, their ways of living are different, or because they're following or performing a task in this world–Lincoln stands out, Gandhi, Kennedy, many others. They stand out as great individuals.

Now, the problem is, of course, when you stand out you draw attention to yourself. When you draw attention to yourself, it's very easy to get wrapped up in attention and wanting more attention, and you become attached to it and fixated and of course you lose your ability to discriminate, and your high consciousness becomes a low consciousness. The other problem is when people fixate upon you, they send vibrations. Whenever anyone thinks of you, a vibratory force is directed towards you on a subtle physical level, on the astral level. When people hate you, that hate touches you.

The classic example is a woman who is scantily dressed and is walking down the street in front of the place where they're building the new building, and all the construction workers whistle at her and yell at her and wave at her and throw a lot of sexual energy at her. Now, she may enjoy the attention, but what she doesn't realize is that on a subtle physical level, the energy they're throwing at her is harming her subtle physical body. Also, maybe later, if she keeps walking down the street and it gets a little darker, someone will put a gun to her head, take her home, rape her, and kill her. I mean, this happens. This is the extreme, but it happens on many levels.

Inaccessibility means that you just don't show up. You blend. The master of inaccessibility is the chameleon. This has nothing to do with what you feel or what you really are. It's just an intelligent way to live. It's the way of the survivor. The way of the survivor is to change as circumstances change. Now, that doesn't mean you should ever abandon your principles. This has nothing to do with inaccessibility. That's being chicken. You should always stick with your principles. But it's necessary, if you wish your principles to succeed in the world, to live and to implement them. You may have wonderful ideas about the world. But if you leave the world too quickly, your ideas will leave with you. Occasionally there comes a time when we have to stand up, expose ourselves to the world, and be accessible to do what's right. And if we die doing so, then we have to do that, if that's what's right, but that's in an extreme situation. Then we're not afraid of death because we see we're already beyond death.

But in most day-to-day living situations for spiritual seekers, it is not necessary to be accessible. You can be accessible by the way you dress, you can be accessible by the way you act — if you laugh too loudly, if you show your enthusiasm too much, if you are too morose— in other words, you shouldn't let people see your feelings. In a nice world, everyone would understand and no one would take advantage of your feelings. However, in this world, very often there are persons who will prey upon you, upon your feelings, your emotions. If they see that you're dejected, they'll make fun of you or try to drain you further. If they see that you're elated, they'll become jealous.

In a spiritual community, it's a good idea to blend. If you meditate very well, if you're doing very well spiritually, don't let anyone know. This is inaccessibility in terms of fairness. You have to realize that human nature goes through many changes, that each one of us has many sides. Let's say you went and saw the spiritual teacher and spent time together, and suddenly you decided to tell all your friends about it and you're very inspired, and suppose you're not even showing off but your enthusiasm is genuine. By doing this, what you'll do is probably not inspire anyone, but you'll make people jealous.

You have to realize, take into account, that everyone isn't perfect yet, that they all are working through different things. And as a favor to another human being, you don't put them in a situation whereby they can do harm to themselves. You anticipate their level and you watch out for them, you care about them. While it might inspire you to tell somebody about your experience when you went and saw the teacher and you had lunch together or something, your friends might become jealous. They think, 'Well, why did so and so go, why didn't I get to go?' Now, true, maybe they shouldn't feel that way, but they do. That's reality. And if you want to walk around on cloud nine thinking, 'Well, it doesn't matter, they put themselves in that situation, I'm not to blame if they want to think those thoughts,' then you're a very selfish human being. If you really care for others, you anticipate how they feel. And while you can't think their thoughts for them, nor should you, in any way that you can be of comfort to them or of service, you do so.

If you're going to visit some poor relatives, you don't wear your most expensive clothing because they'll feel bad. That's humility. In order to be inaccessible, you need to be humble. If you're proud, you won't be inaccessible, you'll want to show off. But you'll be the loser, you'll be the victim.

Inaccessibility is a very good quality. It's good not to tell everyone your life story. It's good not to feel that you need to expose yourself that much, because it's ego. It's good to listen and to learn. It's fun to inspire people, but don't make yourself the central attraction, the diamond in the tiara. It's really not necessary. You'll cause yourself and others more harm.

In the world, very few people will understand meditation and the superconscious, let alone some of the miracles or the siddhas. They'll doubt you or fear you or whatever it may be. It's very good to be quiet and still about what you do. Don't push it. Even if you're very enthused and very inspired and your life is changing—now you've become a vegetarian and you've given up smoking and life is great – not everyone is going to understand. Don't try to give a detailed explanation of meditation to somebody who's working at the plant, unless they're really interested. Just say, "Hey, I meditate, it's relaxing, you know." In other words, speak to people on the level that they're on.

Because otherwise you don't do a service to them. When you speak to people in terms that they can understand, then they respond nicely.

It's very important to be unattached and inaccessible emotionally. Otherwise, you will suffer again and again and again the slings and arrows of outrageous fortune, my friends. The principal thing I see in all of you, all of you human types, is that you are so accessible and so vulnerable and so attached emotionally. It's necessary to love all, not just to love one. When you love one, you make yourself a potential victim. When you love one, you are at the mercy of that one. The only time you should love one is if you love an enlightened being who will not hurt you. And even then you shouldn't confine your love to them, you should confine your love to eternity.

Now, you don't have to love everyone. People who say, "Well, I love everyone," they don't know what they're talking about. Let's go sit them next to Adolph Eichmann or someone like that, you know, Charles Manson, and let's see how long they love. It's an idea, it's a theory: "I love everyone." And it's a nice theory. You don't need to love everyone. Everyone's not particularly loveable in the form that they're currently in. You can love everyone's essence, but it's not necessary that you love the substance.

When you love one person, you're a hostage, you're an emotional hostage. If the person you love, if you're attached to them, feels that you're wrapped up in them, then they will probably abuse you, if their nature is not pure and refined. You've opened yourself up, you're vulnerable. Only open yourself to God, never to a human being. Human beings, you simply cannot trust them. Which is not saying anything bad about them. That's the nature of being a human being – the mind changes, the emotions change. They're wonderful, but they're not stable.

If you deal with an enlightened person, they're extremely predictable. You'll never know what they'll do, but you'll always know it will be good, no matter what it is. Otherwise, when you deal with anyone else, they're very intractable. They love you one moment, they idolize you; the next moment they hate you. They're still bound by their emotions. When you're enlightened, you can just stand back from that. You know that you will always do what's dharma. You have nothing to do with it any more. It's out of your hands. No one else is that predictable.

Don't open your heart up. You can love without opening your heart. That's how you're inaccessible with your emotions. To be inaccessible emotionally doesn't mean that you don't love and care. You'll love and care much more than you do now – much, much more. It simply means that you don't allow yourself to be hurt by anyone, because it won't help you and it won't help them. You love someone, and if they choose not to love you, you can walk away from them and never see them again, if that's what's necessary, and not feel any pain, or if you do it will go away quickly. It's unattachment. It's inaccessible. It's much, much better because then you can really love.

Try not to spend too much time with anyone. Spend time with different people, otherwise you become too accessible. When you become accessible to other people, they hold you back. When you spend a lot of time with the same people, they tend to see you in the same way unless they're very advanced spiritual seekers. Every day they see you and they develop an idea of you and then when they see you they project that idea, they have a dream of you. And you, without realizing it, will conform to their projection. It's very hard to change, if you're around the same people all the time. Try to make new friends. See your friends when you want to, but you should always be making new friends. We've become so fixated in each other. It's not healthy spiritually at all. And you make yourself much too accessible.

Don't talk about the same things all the time, don't read the same books, don't go to the same places. You want to become inaccessible not only to other people, but also you need to be inaccessible to yourself, to the parts of yourself that you're trying to transform. In order to be inaccessible you must break up your routines. Human beings, like birds, are creatures of habit. It's very easy to stalk a person, once you learn their routines. Try not to be a person of routines. Don't be fixated on getting a certain amount of sleep every night, sleeping in the same room, living in the same place, wearing the same clothes, working at the same job, having the same friends, using the same toothpaste, driving the same type of car, feeling that you're human.

If you're interested in learning about inaccessibility and breaking up routines, I think the master teacher is Don Juan through Carlos Castaneda. I think in *Journey to Ixtlan* and *Tales of Power,* there are some very fine discussions about becoming inaccessible and breaking up routines. And through the stories in the books it is very clear why this is advantageous.

You must be very careful in the world. The world is filled with violence. The way spiritual people escape violence is by perceiving it before it comes and avoiding it. That's what God has given us. God has given the highly evolved people not necessarily physical strength–sometimes we have that–but God has given the spiritually evolved people two great gifts to survive. One is the ability to see and sense danger and problems before they occur through our intuition and to avoid them, and also to be very pleasant when we are in a difficult situation. The other is when we get in that difficult situation, God has given us complete unattachment, so we can do whatever is necessary, without any feelings of remorse, without getting caught up in our emotions. If necessary, we can take a life without blinking an eye because we realize that we can't take a life, that only God has that power. If necessary, we can give our own life without blinking an eye because there is no life to give, there is only eternity.

Inaccessibility and overcoming attachments give you a very beautiful life. As you meditate and go deeper within the self, you find that there's radiant happiness everywhere. There's a kind of fulfillment far beyond the muck that most people call love and happiness. But you have to live yourself into that higher level, you have to burn through your different selves until you come to the purified being that you really are, and this is the process of self-discovery. Try to apply these principles in your life. If you do, I think you'll be very, very pleased with the results.

Inaccessibility and attachment.

SPIRITUAL EXPERIENCES, DREAMS, AND VISIONS

The pathway to enlightenment is, for most of us, very experiential. While you may accept the philosophical concepts that are handed down with meditation–a belief in the reincarnation of the soul; the stateless state of nirvana; a sense of dharma, that there is a code of right and that when we follow the highest good we become the highest good; cycles and theories of cosmic evolution; the different lokas and planes of reality–while we may acknowledge that all of these things exist to some extent, what really brings us forward on the pathway to enlightenment is the need for spiritual experiences and visions.

Spiritual experiences fall into many different classifications. The most common type of spiritual experience is the one that you're having at the moment. We call it life. We're not apt to think of life as a spiritual experience. We feel that life, as we've come to know it, is flat or bland. But life for one who has not lived is a spiritual experience. It is not so much that life is flat or bland, it's just that we see it that way. Or perhaps it would be more accurate to say that we don't see it.

Life is energy, constantly moving, changing, recycling, becoming new. The energy of eternity takes on countless new forms and we experience them. We experience them through our senses, through our mind, through our reflections, through our emotions and through our spiritual bodies.

The spiritual experience of life is never ending. As you sit listening to me, you're having a spiritual experience. Later, in the day or the evening, your spiritual experience will continue. Life will precisely direct you through a variety of different experiences. These experiences are not the experience. The experiencer has left and gone someplace else. There are no plans to dream, no visions to keep. These experiences are the beginning and end of existence because that's all there really is.

We sit on an island in the middle of eternity, thinking to ourselves how important we are because we sit on an island in the middle of eternity, not knowing all the while that eternity is an island. We feel we've come to know something, that as perceivers with intelligence we've developed clarity and order and form, but we're only an island. The island of eternity.

We wait. We wait for our loves, we wait for our completion, we wait for the fulfillment of our desires. We wait with hope, apathy, resignation, belief. We become despondent, elated; we wait. We wait for the final experience, the vision, the dream quest that will lead us above the ebb and flow of this life and will place us into that which we have not experienced, that which is new, that which will command all of our attention to the point of complete absorption.

Life is the only spiritual experience there is, life and death. Death is but another part of life. There is no beginning and there is no ending. We're marvelously eternal. And our perception of existence changes as we change, which changes existence. Perception not only defines existence, but it creates existence. It gives it form. Without perception, there is no existence.

When we dream, we create. All of life is a dream or a series of waking dreams. We dream our surroundings, we dream our friends, our relations, we dream our bodies, we dream our dreams. There is no beginning and there is no end. Some days there's not even a middle.

A person tries to understand truth. They seek to come to some kind of resolution about the meaning of life. They seek to explore their own humanity. What is it to be alive? What is it to be? Or not to be? There are no answers. The waves crash on the beaches as they always have, the children play, the aged and the infirm wait for death, and those in midlife are caught up in a cross-current, somewhere between youth and old age, somewhere between birth and death, trying amid all the cruelties and joys in life to find silence and some kind of perfection–perfection in their art, perfection in their work, perfection in their loves, their children, their spouses, their lovers, their disciplines, their vacations–an endless panorama of spiritual experiences.

Now, if you're really a perceiver, you have this broad-based acceptance of life, you're able to look and feel and believe, and yet at the same time you're somewhat withdrawn. You stand back behind the gateways of your eyes and quietly observe the coming and going of eternity, a witness. You allow life to do to you what it will, trusting it always, and observe. But there's not so much a sense of action, of being an actor. Rather, of quietly watching the spring buds emerge; the summer with all its fruition; the beauty of death in the fall, transmigration; and the winter, the preparation for the new life.

It's enough sometimes. It's enough to watch, to sit in front of a fireplace and listen to the crackling of the wood and stare into the flame and to contemplate immortality, without thinking about it too much. To feel that in this moment there is all that will ever be or has ever been. Alexander the Great is walking the earth conquering. Caesar is being murdered. Bach is writing his fugues and preludes. Shakespeare is putting on his latest play. Kennedy is being shot. The world is dissolving in the final cosmic flash. The world is being born out of the molten masses of dreams.

All of the events of all of our lives are going on simultaneously. There is no beginning and there is no ending. There is only this moment, and all the eternities that have ever been or will ever be are contained in this very moment, if you will but look, if you will but look and see that at the moment you are having a spiritual experience.

You are a vision. You are a dream. And we call this waking, waking to life. Slowly like a young fern we unfold, the fronds unrolling, stretching ourselves upward towards the light, feeling the atmosphere of an alien world, reaching for nourishment, for strength, feeling the winds of change, growing without knowing how or why. And it's enough sometimes. Sometimes it's enough just to be, to not think, to not calculate, to not triumph, to not lose. It's enough sometimes to sit in the sunshine, to watch the raindrops, to sit alone and feel this marvelous thing that is existence, that is our self, our body, our spirit. This is a spiritual experience.

A spiritual experience is not something that you have, it's something that you are. We're always trying to get to something, to get to the experience, to have the flash, but it's here, now. It's quiet. The most profound experience is quiet and fulfilling, drenching you with its life, with the knowledge and awareness of countless eons, timelessness, all present in this moment, all futures forwarded to this address–an endless parade, a panorama, of all that will ever be and never be contained within your perception–standing behind your eyes, watching through them.

Who is watching through them? Who is watching through your eyes? Who is that? The perceiver? Not she who feels or thinks, not she who believes or wants or loves or hates. Who is she? Who is the one? The one who has always been this moment. She is a spiritual experience. She is a dream, a vision.

Spiritual experiences are all there are. There is nothing else, there is no beginning and there is no ending. There are no crimes, there are no punishments, there are no absolutions. These are all ways of talking, games that people play, invented to pass the time. But here, with me, alone, the two of us, on top of the mountain today, or perhaps by the ocean or just back from the ocean, surrounded by the spring, far from the wars and war's alarms, far from the noise of the city, far from the newspapers, the political strife–the world of mankind has faded away. When you sit here with me today on the shores of existence, you're in no hurry to go anywhere; the world is forgotten. We seem to have lost our purpose, but it doesn't matter. We've forgotten that there was a past, that there is a future, sitting here today on the banks of existence. No thought, no mind, no belief systems. Perfect stillness. The sound of the waves crashing, the birds in the distance.

Life is a spiritual experience, it is! Today we're here. Oh, you may think that you're listening to this tape in your car, or in your home, or wherever you may be, but you're not. You're really not. You're here today with me, sitting here, listening, watching. Or perhaps I'm with you. Listening and watching. It's just the two of us. There aren't any more, you know, and there really aren't even two; there's only one. There's only the one who's listening, the one who's watching behind the eyes and waiting.

We wait for spiritual experiences. We cause them. We dream them. We dream the self. From a structural point of view, there are naturally different levels of spiritual experiences. While everything is a spiritual experience, we can place order in what appears to be but is not really chaos. The body is a spiritual experience–its perceptions. The body is holy, as are the senses, as are its actions, its gestations, its movements. Desires are holy. Emotions. Everything has its own integrity, in its own time and its own place. But in the world it's hard to know that, in the cities, with others, sometimes alone, with our mind raging and stampeding and thinking and analyzing and calculating and remembering and giving birth to marvelous thoughts that trap us. It's hard to know what matters, what we really care about, what is important.

We've been so influenced. We've been raped repeatedly by the minds of others. Conditioned, programmed, taught how to see, think, believe, taught to cross at the crosswalk, not in between, because it's functional. And it is! It's true. But we hate it, we rebel, and that's a dream, that's a vision. That's a spiritual experience. You see? All methods of perception, all ways of seeing, the terrorist and the savior, they're all one. Each is a spiritual experience. An act of God.

But here we sit, the two of us today, just for a little while, a short time, beyond within, waiting. There are changes, there is transition, or so it would appear outside of this lovely garden that the two of us are in today. But here time is forever. Yet we do note the seasons change. I suppose we could go out into the world and make forays to change the world, but by the time we went out and changed it, the garden might have changed too and we might have missed that. Perhaps it's better to sit in the garden today, the two of us, and sip some tea.

There's a level of experience beyond experience. There's a world of dreams beyond dreams as you know them. We call it the superconscious. It is the home of spiritual experiences of another kind, another order. The waking dreams of life as most people know them are spiritual experiences. Their children, their families, their lives are spiritual experiences. But there is another order of spiritual experience that some of us choose, that some of us are chosen by or that we choose not to choose, therefore choosing. And that's to be in the garden of the heart, in the perfect stillness where the white light of eternity meets the white light of eternity and there's flux and stillness at the same time. This is enlightenment. It can be yours, if that's what you want. It's not so hard.

People complain that enlightenment is a difficult thing to reach. I don't think so. I just don't think that they want to. If you want to, it's very easy. You simply set your sails for the course. There may be storms along the way. There may be people that you meet, but they're all part of it too, the journey is.

We find ourselves looking for that Northwest Passage, the way through to enlightenment. And I tell you that the way to enlightenment is enlightenment. There is nothing else. It has always been the same. The times may change, the technologies may change, the leaders may change, the spiritual philosophies may change, the egocentric liberators who bind us may change. But the path has always been the same, and it hasn't been walked on. It's rather new, still. I think you'd enjoy it. The Sierra Club has not yet walked all of its members down its ways. No, it's only been trodden by a few.

Isn't it funny that in all the history of existence only a few have walked its full length in this world? And you can be one. Oh, you don't know how far you'll walk. You can stop whenever you like. If you come to a nice inn, you can spend the night, marry the innkeeper or his daughter, and stay there forever, or for a time, until you decide to move on again. That's a spiritual experience. We call it a lifetime. One after another like beads on a string, they stretch out before you and behind you. Must you choose the next bead on the string? Yes. No. Is there another string?

I think of telephone networks, of vast interchanges–thousands of calls coming in and out on microprocessors, all on little chips. Little messages, little emotions, passing through wires, through laser beams, crisscrossing eternity. Existence. I think of airports, of places of transition. Places where the planes connect. Realities touch. Watching the passengers leaving the plane and the relatives waiting. Meeting them, hugging them, crying. The businessman who gets off the plane, no one to meet him, thinking about the length of the rental car line. Holding his briefcase and his carry-on luggage for security. Living a life he doesn't believe in, yet not having a choice. So it would seem.

I think of the farewells–the plane leaving, the soldier hugging his girlfriend of one night. The old woman going to her son's funeral, dressed in black. The couple traveling together to New York. The young child with its mother, who will cry all the way. The flight attendants moving to another city, another destination, uniforms in place, their suitcases on the little rack with wheels. And the plane leaves. And those who came to see it off go back to their lives and those in the plane, where do they go, into the sky. Units on a microprocessor. Voices in the night. Spiritual experiences.

Each one, each life is a spiritual experience. And you're having all of them, you are all of them. You are the old woman going to the death of her son, his funeral, and the long processions of agony that follow. You are the soldier and his young lover. You are the flight attendant thinking about getting back to her husband. And you are that endless space through which the planes fly. It's you who's listening to all of this. That's a spiritual experience. It's you who still believe in truth, when there is nothing else and it's not necessary to even believe in it, although it's nice.

I think there might be an end to it one day, an end of this nature and this cosmos. I know there's an end to it. The cycle closes.

The "for sale" signs go up. Last day clearance sale. Then the flash comes. The unexpected light. The radiance beyond radiance, not a physical light, this light. And all the worlds are withdrawn. Everything ends. The void, the dream ends. All that we thought was solid and substantial goes away. Not the ending everyone supposed. No supernovas, just white light. Everything just dissolves, goes away. Just as at the time of death, you will watch this world disappear before your eyes. Everything will become hazy. You'll hear a high-pitched ringing sound, or a buzzing sound. You'll feel light, and then suddenly the world will fade from your eyes. When it ends, it will end that way. With white light and beautiful colors. I've seen the end. It's really not a bad ending. No credits though. Spiritual experience. The end. The beginning.

Now I realize too, that there's a function in a tape. We want information, techniques, methods. We need to have a sense of having gotten something out of it. And this is a good feeling. It creates progress. And this is said without irony or malice. There must be a sense of purpose and order in a world of purpose and order, or in a world of disorder, which lacks purpose. This is the section of purpose and order–in order to give it purpose, sort of a purposeful order.

In order to have spiritual experiences, you must be willing to surrender and give up everything. It's only with the sense of complete abandon that you can have the highest experiences. Which is why, of course, most people don't have the highest experiences. You can judge your experience, its level of intensity, you can predict it by how much you're willing to let go. If you need to cling to your family, your friends, your beliefs, then your experiences will appear to be rather ordinary. The more you can let go, the more you will be.

It's not intended that everyone in this lifetime who practices self-discovery should reach liberation. That's not proper. It's intended that only a few should. And you may be one of those few. And you should always believe, not that you are one of those few, but that you might be. Because you might be. Suddenly your name turns up on the paper having won the lottery. No one is there to collect the check, though.

To have spiritual experiences, it's necessary to alter your understanding, the way you see life. There are lots and lots of ways. If you need a quick spiritual experience, fast for three or four days on fruit juice or protein powder, or something. You don't have to starve yourself. But you will immediately change planes of reality. Then after you fast, you'll find yourself in the world again. But if you need a quick one, that's good.

Prolonged changes in consciousness come about, and of course occur, through intensive meditation experiences. The bottom line in meditation is to have no bottom line. To sit and meditate with your whole being and to reach that stillness. Then of course, when all thought stops, consciousness becomes eternity. You see that it is.

Another way is contact. Contact with light in any form. To meditate with one who is liberated, with one who is no longer fettered by family, friends, conditions, relatives, appointment books. One may keep these things, but there's no one in them. For the enlightened, there's only this garden. And the music, the music of life. The beautiful music. The one who listens.

Contact with such a person produces total chaos in your life. You're moving along at a certain cycle, a vibratory pitch. Your life is progressing. It's predictable, within a basic span of human experience. Suddenly you come upon one who is liberated, one who laughs loudly and frequently. Their vibratory rate is infinite. You reach out to touch them emotionally, spiritually, physically, and as you do, as you open yourself to one who is free, that freedom enters you. The vibratory light that permeates their being, that is their soul, enters your being and it changes your vibratory rate. Perhaps just for a short time; it's maybe initial contact. And you're no longer the same, for a while, like fasting. Then you come down. Then you find yourself in the world again. Then you make a choice–to go back, to consolidate, to change, or to regress and relapse into your former state. Which is not entirely possible, but you can convince yourself that it is. That's a spiritual experience too. Maya, we call it–illusion. One of an endless chain of spiritual experiences, dreams, and visions.

It's unnerving to be naked and to be touched. It's unnerving, I suppose, to have someone who can look through every fiber of your being and not really look but still look through them. To be with someone who's completely unemotional and yet, at the same time, a flood of love. If we have something to hide, it makes us nervous. If we're willing to allow someone to look in, then what's there to be afraid of? Remember, you're eternity. No one can hurt you. No one can take away from you that which you are. They can take away your house, your car, your friends, your family, even your own life, but they can't take away what you are. No one can do that. That is what you are, that is your integrity. This perception is a spiritual experience, a vision of reality, a dream.

We try on different hats in the clothing store of existence–lover, husband, teacher, educator, nurse, engineer, mechanic. We live with others, we live alone, the cycle continues. But where is that spiritual experience that will cause the breakthrough? Where is that moment that we've always suspected existed? Where is that moment with Christ when his 12 disciples were seated around him at the Last Supper, laughing and talking–when you're with the chosen one, the enlightened one? Where has the meditation garden with Buddha gone, with he and his disciples meditating in stillness? Where are all the holy and pure moments that we've always suspected existed? Where are they? They're here with me. I being you, sitting here for you today, on your behalf, since you were ill and couldn't come. In this perfect light, in this still flux that radiates, as I listen to the voice that speaks, with no sense of what it does or why, curious like a child, enjoying light. I am your spiritual experience, as are you mine. This is all there is until there's something else, which there is, all the time.

The urge to take you beyond words, to make you conscious of eternity–I can only accomplish this by awakening your eternal longings for spiritual experiences, for a level of awareness seen only by a few in all of the cycles of creation. You can be one of the few. It's not hard, believe me. If it was, I couldn't have done it. It's easy. All you need is the pure love of God, of life, of those around you. And of selfless feeling, a feeling that it's more fun to give than to receive.

It's more fun to be anonymous. It's more fun to meditate and to still our minds and to lead the special life that we lead, we seekers of truth, without thinking too well of ourselves, on a very even, down-to-earth basis. To be willing to accept pain and pleasure with an even mind, meaning you don't get too taken out by either one. To love those who love us. To forgive those who condemn us. Knowing that we're all the time sitting here in the light, and then there's nirvana, the ultimate spiritual experience, when the world fades away and life fades away and death fades away. No fear of death in nirvana. Only eternal life, eternal being. Not as we've come to know it, but as we came to know it once before.

You forget, my friend, you forget that you spent quite a bit of time at that particular resort we call nirvana. And now, out in the world, you've forgotten. But it's not strange or unnatural. It's nothing that you haven't done before. It's easy. Nirvana is easy. Spiritual growth and development is easy if that's what you want. If you want spiritual experiences, you can have them. All you have to do is want them. You have to be like Dorothy. You have to click your heels three times and want ever so much to be home, more than anything. And then the way will be shown.

Spiritual experiences, dreams, and visions. There are different types of dreams. Naturally, there are dreams in which we wake and find ourselves in another world. This is the dream we call life. Then there are the dreams that we have at night, when we put our heads on the pillow and move into the astral. Most dreams are not too important, in the sense that most of them are numbers that don't answer, parties we didn't attend. But occasionally a dream is not a dream. Occasionally it's not a mindless shuffling from one scene into another, one body into another, one picture into another. And that's a vision, a dream vision. Suddenly, in the midst of the dream, everything stops. Someone comes to us, a spiritual teacher, a being of light, and the consciousness, the quality of the dream changes dramatically. There's a feeling of eternity about it, or perhaps a joy so great that we could have only experienced it in a dream–a joy that was too great for this world that we live in, too great for this mind, too great for this body.

In dreaming, we're in the astral, and in the astral we have a greater capacity to feel, to see and to believe and to understand. After such a dream, you will be different. For two or three weeks, you'll see a pronounced difference in your consciousness. This is how you know it was not an ordinary dream. Upon waking from the dream, you'll be surcharged with energy. You'll find that if you tell the dream to someone, they will experience a part of it too. Don't tell it too frequently to unreceptive persons; it will dissipate its energy and power for you, but don't be afraid to share it. To share is to give. To give is not to lose, it's to grow.

Some people say you shouldn't share your spiritual experiences, dreams, and visions with others. I think that's nonsense. It's a very selfish attitude for a person who cares only about their own realization, and one who cares about their own realization will not have such a realization, or they'll only have the realization of selfishness. Never be afraid to share a meditation experience, a dream, or a vision. When you do so, you must do so without egotism, without a sense of being special. You had it because you were special, because you were better than others? More advanced? No. You have to feel you had it simply because it was there, it was a gift, which you didn't deserve, nor were you not worthy. It came, it opened your life, and then when you tell it to another, you must tell it not to make them jealous but only to inspire them. Keep it very simple, very humble and very pure, as it was. Don't tell too many people.

And then write it down. It's most important to keep a journal, a journal of your spiritual experiences, dreams and visions. These are moments out of time, and you need to record them because they're few and precious. By keeping such a journal and keeping it by your meditation table, you will find it's nice, occasionally, to sit down, before meditating or after meditating, and read over some of them. You'll find that you can go back to them. On a dark day when you can't meditate too well, when your thoughts are turbulent, when you open up the journal, you'll read back about a dream you had, a vision, a spiritual experience. Something with your teacher, something by yourself, when the world fell away and time stopped, and there was time out of time, and everything was quite right.

Beyond words, yet you put it in words. It will bring the vibration back to you. You'll be able to touch that place and go back there. It's very important to keep a journal. You don't have to write down everything that you do or every meditation that you have. It's better not to; leave them alone. But whenever a special meditation occurs, a special experience, a special dream, type it up or write it down and keep it in your journal. It will grow and it will aid you.

We're imprinted by the world, by our civilization. We have to re-imprint ourselves with a higher imprinture. We need to publish our experiences to the skies. We do this in our journal. No one reads the journal but us, so we don't have to impress anyone with our style. We don't have to hope that someday someone will discover it, publish it, and think how wonderful we were. We'll let it leave the world when we do. Therefore, we're free to write as we really are. Because no one would read it but ourselves–we're writing for ourselves–then the journal will be free of egotism. We won't be writing for a future audience. We can be truthful, honest, and clear. We're writing it to God. Try to keep a journal. It's a very important thing to do in the early stages. Very important.

Try not to hold onto any type of spiritual experience that you have. Very often we have a very powerful experience and then we fixate on it, and in doing so, we lose the purpose of the experience. The purpose of the experience was not the experience itself. The purpose of the experience was to loosen a defined state of being that we were in. Then we cling to another state of being which was the experience and we fixate on that. The purpose of the experience is not to relive the experience. To see the movie once was fine. If the movie comes to town again, it might be fun to see it again. But we don't have to follow the movie from town to town. Let's see other movies. Or take a break from the film.

Try not to cling. Enjoy the experience. When you have the spiritual experience, if you're sitting meditating, you may feel different sensations flooding your body, you may see different lights, hear sounds – ignore them. Be neither attracted nor repulsed, because as soon as you become caught up in them you'll stop the experience, unless it's an extremely powerful experience. Let go. Let the experience take you where it will. Don't try to understand what they mean; they don't mean anything, they are their meaning. Don't worry about the color of the light you saw, the sound, the ray of energy. These are all mental fixations, ideations. You're trying to move into the superconscious, beyond the known, into the vast ocean of light. Let it be. Later, if you want to, you can think about the experience. But during it, just let it happen. If your mind starts to fixate, make the mind quiet. Let go.

If you have an experience and you're afraid–suddenly you find yourself letting go and dissolving, experiencing something new, don't feel bad. But realize the next time that you don't want to do that. You stopped the experience. But a spiritual experience will never hurt you. God is trying to open a new page in a book to show you something new to read, a new picture to see. The next time the fear comes back, remember, 'Well, last time, I remember I was afraid, I held on and I stopped myself. I've meditated, I've worked for a long time to have this beautiful awakening, and I stopped it. And I don't want to have that happen again. I love the experience. This time when the fear comes, I'm just going to shush it away, push it away. This time I want to feel eternity. I want to know it, as it really is. And nothing is going to stop that, nothing. Not myself, not my thoughts, not my fears. What's the worst that could happen to me? I might become enlightened. I might become happy. What's the worst that could happen to me? Do I think

I'll lose my mind? Am I afraid that after the experience I'll be deranged, I'll be crazy?'

That's not how it happens. It's only light. It's like pure water, it can't hurt you. You have to trust. In order to have a great experience, a great vision, you have to trust God completely. You have to trust that light of eternity and know that it only, only, has your welfare in mind. Unless you can let go, there will be no experiences.

A great deal of what we do in self-discovery, along with our meditation, is to learn to let go, to break our bonds with the past, to give up that which binds us. Only you know what binds you. You don't necessarily have to leave a person or a family or a marriage, but you have to leave the part of yourself that clings to it. Sometimes it is necessary to leave these things, only because we've outgrown them. They were fine at the time, then we move on. Sometimes they're working–well, why should we leave them if they're happy? But sometimes we change and we move in a new direction. We feel eternity beckoning. We know that we could stay in the life we're in now, with the people we're with, and that would be a lovely life. But the vision calls us on.

The pathway to enlightenment is, for most of us, very experiential. While you may accept the philosophical concepts that are handed down with meditation–a belief in the reincarnation of the soul; the stateless state of nirvana; a sense of dharma, that there is a code of right and that when we follow the highest good we become the highest good; cycles and theories of cosmic evolution; the different lokas and planes of reality–while we may acknowledge that all of these things exist to some extent, what really brings us forward on the pathway to enlightenment is the need for spiritual experiences and visions.

Spiritual experiences fall into many different classifications. The most common type of spiritual experience is the one that you're having at the moment. We call it life. We're not apt to think of life as a spiritual experience. We feel that life, as we've come to know it, is flat or bland. But life for one who has not lived is a spiritual experience. It is not so much that life is flat or bland, it's just that we see it that way. Or perhaps it would be more accurate to say that we don't see it.

Life is energy, constantly moving, changing, recycling, becoming new. The energy of eternity takes on countless new forms and we experience them. We experience them through our senses, through our mind, through our reflections, through our emotions and through our spiritual bodies.

The spiritual experience of life is never ending. As you sit listening to me, you're having a spiritual experience. Later, in the day or the evening, your spiritual experience will continue. Life will precisely direct you through a variety of different experiences. These experiences are not the experience. The experiencer has left and gone someplace else. There are no plans to dream, no visions to keep. These experiences are the beginning and end of existence because that's all there really is.

We sit on an island in the middle of eternity, thinking to ourselves how important we are because we sit on an island in the middle of eternity, not knowing all the while that eternity is an island. We feel we've come to know something, that as perceivers with intelligence we've developed clarity and order and form, but we're only an island. The island of eternity.

We wait. We wait for our loves, we wait for our completion, we wait for the fulfillment of our desires. We wait with hope, apathy, resignation, belief. We become despondent, elated; we wait. We wait for the final experience, the vision, the dream quest that will lead us above the ebb and flow of this life and will place us into that which we have not experienced, that which is new, that which will command all of our attention to the point of complete absorption.

Life is the only spiritual experience there is, life and death. Death is but another part of life. There is no beginning and there is no ending. We're marvelously eternal. And our perception of existence changes as we change, which changes existence. Perception not only defines existence, but it creates existence. It gives it form. Without perception, there is no existence.

When we dream, we create. All of life is a dream or a series of waking dreams. We dream our surroundings, we dream our friends, our relations, we dream our bodies, we dream our dreams. There is no beginning and there is no end. Some days there's not even a middle.

A person tries to understand truth. They seek to come to some kind of resolution about the meaning of life. They seek to explore their own humanity. What is it to be alive? What is it to be? Or not to be? There are no answers. The waves crash on the beaches as they always have, the children play, the aged and the infirm wait for death, and those in midlife are caught up in a cross-current, somewhere between youth and old age, somewhere between birth and death, trying amid all the cruelties and joys in life to find silence and some kind of perfection–perfection in their art, perfection in their work, perfection in their loves, their children, their spouses, their lovers, their disciplines, their vacations–an endless panorama of spiritual experiences.

Now, if you're really a perceiver, you have this broad-based acceptance of life, you're able to look and feel and believe, and yet at the same time you're somewhat withdrawn. You stand back behind the gateways of your eyes and quietly observe the coming and going of eternity, a witness. You allow life to do to you what it will, trusting it always, and observe. But there's not so much a sense of action, of being an actor. Rather, of quietly watching the spring buds emerge; the summer with all its fruition; the beauty of death in the fall, transmigration; and the winter, the preparation for the new life.

It's enough sometimes. It's enough to watch, to sit in front of a fireplace and listen to the crackling of the wood and stare into the flame and to contemplate immortality, without thinking about it too much. To feel that in this moment there is all that will ever be or has ever been. Alexander the Great is walking the earth conquering. Caesar is being murdered. Bach is writing his fugues and preludes. Shakespeare is putting on his latest play. Kennedy is being shot. The world is dissolving in the final cosmic flash. The world is being born out of the molten masses of dreams.

All of the events of all of our lives are going on simultaneously. There is no beginning and there is no ending. There is only this moment, and all the eternities that have ever been or will ever be are contained in this very moment, if you will but look, if you will but look and see that at the moment you are having a spiritual experience.

You are a vision. You are a dream. And we call this waking, waking to life. Slowly like a young fern we unfold, the fronds unrolling, stretching ourselves upward towards the light, feeling the atmosphere of an alien world, reaching for nourishment, for strength, feeling the winds of change, growing without knowing how or why. And it's enough sometimes. Sometimes it's enough just to be, to not think, to not calculate, to not triumph, to not lose. It's enough sometimes to sit in the sunshine, to watch the raindrops, to sit alone and feel this marvelous thing that is existence, that is our self, our body, our spirit. This is a spiritual experience.

A spiritual experience is not something that you have, it's something that you are. We're always trying to get to something, to get to the experience, to have the flash, but it's here, now. It's quiet. The most profound experience is quiet and fulfilling, drenching you with its life, with the knowledge and awareness of countless eons, timelessness, all present in this moment, all futures forwarded to this address–an endless parade, a panorama, of all that will ever be and never be contained within your perception–standing behind your eyes, watching through them.

Who is watching through them? Who is watching through your eyes? Who is that? The perceiver? Not she who feels or thinks, not she who believes or wants or loves or hates. Who is she? Who is the one? The one who has always been this moment. She is a spiritual experience. She is a dream, a vision.

Spiritual experiences are all there are. There is nothing else, there is no beginning and there is no ending. There are no crimes, there are no punishments, there are no absolutions. These are all ways of talking, games that people play, invented to pass the time. But here, with me, alone, the two of us, on top of the mountain today, or perhaps by the ocean or just back from the ocean, surrounded by the spring, far from the wars and war's alarms, far from the noise of the city, far from the newspapers, the political strife–the world of mankind has faded away. When you sit here with me today on the shores of existence, you're in no hurry to go anywhere; the world is forgotten. We seem to have lost our purpose, but it doesn't matter. We've forgotten that there was a past, that there is a future, sitting here today on the banks of existence. No thought, no mind, no belief systems. Perfect stillness. The sound of the waves crashing, the birds in the distance.

Life is a spiritual experience, it is! Today we're here. Oh, you may think that you're listening to this tape in your car, or in your home, or wherever you may be, but you're not. You're really not. You're here today with me, sitting here, listening, watching. Or perhaps I'm with you. Listening and watching. It's just the two of us. There aren't any more, you know, and there really aren't even two; there's only one. There's only the one who's listening, the one who's watching behind the eyes and waiting.

We wait for spiritual experiences. We cause them. We dream them. We dream the self. From a structural point of view, there are naturally different levels of spiritual experiences. While everything is a spiritual experience, we can place order in what appears to be but is not really chaos. The body is a spiritual experience–its perceptions. The body is holy, as are the senses, as are its actions, its gestations, its movements. Desires are holy. Emotions. Everything has its own integrity, in its own time and its own place. But in the world it's hard to know that, in the cities, with others, sometimes alone, with our mind raging and stampeding and thinking and analyzing and calculating and remembering and giving birth to marvelous thoughts that trap us. It's hard to know what matters, what we really care about, what is important.

We've been so influenced. We've been raped repeatedly by the minds of others. Conditioned, programmed, taught how to see, think, believe, taught to cross at the crosswalk, not in between, because it's functional. And it is! It's true. But we hate it, we rebel, and that's a dream, that's a vision. That's a spiritual experience. You see? All methods of perception, all ways of seeing, the terrorist and the savior, they're all one. Each is a spiritual experience. An act of God.

But here we sit, the two of us today, just for a little while, a short time, beyond within, waiting. There are changes, there is transition, or so it would appear outside of this lovely garden that the two of us are in today. But here time is forever. Yet we do note the seasons change. I suppose we could go out into the world and make forays to change the world, but by the time we went out and changed it, the garden might have changed too and we might have missed that. Perhaps it's better to sit in the garden today, the two of us, and sip some tea.

There's a level of experience beyond experience. There's a world of dreams beyond dreams as you know them. We call it the superconscious. It is the home of spiritual experiences of another kind, another order. The waking dreams of life as most people know them are spiritual experiences. Their children, their families, their lives are spiritual experiences. But there is another order of spiritual experience that some of us choose, that some of us are chosen by or that we choose not to choose, therefore choosing. And that's to be in the garden of the heart, in the perfect stillness where the white light of eternity meets the white light of eternity and there's flux and stillness at the same time. This is enlightenment. It can be yours, if that's what you want. It's not so hard.

317

People complain that enlightenment is a difficult thing to reach. I don't think so. I just don't think that they want to. If you want to, it's very easy. You simply set your sails for the course. There may be storms along the way. There may be people that you meet, but they're all part of it too, the journey is.

We find ourselves looking for that Northwest Passage, the way through to enlightenment. And I tell you that the way to enlightenment is enlightenment. There is nothing else. It has always been the same. The times may change, the technologies may change, the leaders may change, the spiritual philosophies may change, the egocentric liberators who bind us may change. But the path has always been the same, and it hasn't been walked on. It's rather new, still. I think you'd enjoy it. The Sierra Club has not yet walked all of its members down its ways. No, it's only been trodden by a few.

Isn't it funny that in all the history of existence only a few have walked its full length in this world? And you can be one. Oh, you don't know how far you'll walk. You can stop whenever you like. If you come to a nice inn, you can spend the night, marry the innkeeper or his daughter, and stay there forever, or for a time, until you decide to move on again. That's a spiritual experience. We call it a lifetime. One after another like beads on a string, they stretch out before you and behind you. Must you choose the next bead on the string? Yes. No. Is there another string?

I think of telephone networks, of vast interchanges–thousands of calls coming in and out on microprocessors, all on little chips. Little messages, little emotions, passing through wires, through laser beams, crisscrossing eternity. Existence. I think of airports, of places of transition. Places where the planes connect. Realities touch. Watching the passengers leaving the plane and the relatives waiting. Meeting them, hugging them, crying. The businessman who gets off the plane, no one to meet him, thinking about the length of the rental car line. Holding his briefcase and his carry-on luggage for security. Living a life he doesn't believe in, yet not having a choice. So it would seem.

I think of the farewells–the plane leaving, the soldier hugging his girlfriend of one night. The old woman going to her son's funeral, dressed in black. The couple traveling together to New York. The young child with its mother, who will cry all the way. The flight attendants moving to another city, another destination, uniforms in place, their suitcases on the little rack with wheels. And the plane leaves. And those who came to see it off go back to their lives and those in the plane, where do they go, into the sky. Units on a microprocessor. Voices in the night. Spiritual experiences.

Each one, each life is a spiritual experience. And you're having all of them, you are all of them. You are the old woman going to the death of her son, his funeral, and the long processions of agony that follow. You are the soldier and his young lover. You are the flight attendant thinking about getting back to her husband. And you are that endless space through which the planes fly. It's you who's listening to all of this. That's a spiritual experience. It's you who still believe in truth, when there is nothing else and it's not necessary to even believe in it, although it's nice.

I think there might be an end to it one day, an end of this nature and this cosmos. I know there's an end to it. The cycle closes. The "for sale" signs go up. Last day clearance sale. Then the flash comes. The unexpected light. The radiance beyond radiance, not a physical light, this light. And all the worlds are withdrawn. Everything ends. The void, the dream ends. All that we thought was solid and substantial goes away. Not the ending everyone supposed. No supernovas, just white light. Everything just dissolves, goes away. Just as at the time of death, you will watch this world disappear before your eyes. Everything will become hazy. You'll hear a high-pitched ringing sound, or a buzzing sound. You'll feel light, and then suddenly the world will fade from your eyes. When it ends, it will end that way. With white light and beautiful colors. I've seen the end. It's really not a bad ending. No credits though. Spiritual experience. The end. The beginning.

Now I realize too, that there's a function in a tape. We want information, techniques, methods. We need to have a sense of having gotten something out of it. And this is a good feeling. It creates progress. And this is said without irony or malice. There must be a sense of purpose and order in a world of purpose and order, or in a world of disorder, which lacks purpose. This is the section of purpose and order–in order to give it purpose, sort of a purposeful order.

In order to have spiritual experiences, you must be willing to surrender and give up everything. It's only with the sense of complete abandon that you can have the highest experiences. Which is why, of course, most people don't have the highest experiences. You can judge your experience, its level of intensity, you can predict it by how much you're willing to let go. If you need to cling to your family, your friends, your beliefs, then your experiences will appear to be rather ordinary. The more you can let go, the more you will be.

It's not intended that everyone in this lifetime who practices self-discovery should reach liberation. That's not proper. It's intended that only a few should. And you may be one of those few. And you should always believe, not that you are one of those few, but that you might be. Because you might be. Suddenly your name turns up on the paper having won the lottery. No one is there to collect the check, though.

To have spiritual experiences, it's necessary to alter your understanding, the way you see life. There are lots and lots of ways. If you need a quick spiritual experience, fast for three or four days on fruit juice or protein powder, or something. You don't have to starve yourself. But you will immediately change planes of reality. Then after you fast, you'll find yourself in the world again. But if you need a quick one, that's good.

Prolonged changes in consciousness come about, and of course occur, through intensive meditation experiences. The bottom line in meditation is to have no bottom line. To sit and meditate with your whole being and to reach that stillness. Then of course, when all thought stops, consciousness becomes eternity. You see that it is.

Another way is contact. Contact with light in any form. To meditate with one who is liberated, with one who is no longer fettered by family, friends, conditions, relatives, appointment books. One may keep these things, but there's no one in them. For the enlightened, there's only this garden. And the music, the music of life. The beautiful music. The one who listens.

Contact with such a person produces total chaos in your life. You're moving along at a certain cycle, a vibratory pitch. Your life is progressing. It's predictable, within a basic span of human experience. Suddenly you come upon one who is liberated, one who laughs loudly and frequently. Their vibratory rate is infinite. You reach out to touch them emotionally, spiritually, physically, and as you do, as you open yourself to one who is free, that freedom enters you. The vibratory light that permeates their being, that is their soul, enters your being and it changes your vibratory rate. Perhaps just for a short time; it's maybe initial contact. And you're no longer the same, for a while, like fasting. Then you come down. Then you find yourself in the world again. Then you make a choice–to go back, to consolidate, to change, or to regress and relapse into your former state. Which is not entirely possible, but you can convince yourself that it is. That's a spiritual experience too. Maya, we call it–illusion. One of an endless chain of spiritual experiences, dreams, and visions.

It's unnerving to be naked and to be touched. It's unnerving, I suppose, to have someone who can look through every fiber of your being and not really look but still look through them. To be with someone who's completely unemotional and yet, at the same time, a flood of love. If we have something to hide, it makes us nervous. If we're willing to allow someone to look in, then what's there to be afraid of? Remember, you're eternity. No one can hurt you. No one can take away from you that which you are. They can take away your house, your car, your friends, your family, even your own life, but they can't take away what you are. No one can do that. That is what you are, that is your integrity. This perception is a spiritual experience, a vision of reality, a dream.

We try on different hats in the clothing store of existence–lover, husband, teacher, educator, nurse, engineer, mechanic. We live with others, we live alone, the cycle continues. But where is that spiritual experience that will cause the breakthrough? Where is that moment that we've always suspected existed? Where is that moment with Christ when his 12 disciples were seated around him at the Last Supper, laughing and talking–when you're with the chosen one, the enlightened one? Where has the meditation garden with Buddha gone, with he and his disciples meditating in stillness? Where are all the holy and pure moments that we've always suspected existed? Where are they? They're here with me. I being you, sitting here for you today, on your behalf, since you were ill and couldn't come. In this perfect light, in this still flux that radiates, as I listen to the voice that speaks, with no sense of what it does or why, curious like a child, enjoying light. I am your spiritual experience, as are you mine. This is all there is until there's something else, which there is, all the time.

The urge to take you beyond words, to make you conscious of eternity–I can only accomplish this by awakening your eternal longings for spiritual experiences, for a level of awareness seen only by a few in all of the cycles of creation. You can be one of the few. It's not hard, believe me. If it was, I couldn't have done it. It's easy. All you need is the pure love of God, of life, of those around you. And of selfless feeling, a feeling that it's more fun to give than to receive.

It's more fun to be anonymous. It's more fun to meditate and to still our minds and to lead the special life that we lead, we seekers of truth, without thinking too well of ourselves, on a very even, down-to-earth basis. To be willing to accept pain and pleasure with an even mind, meaning you don't get too taken out by either one. To love those who love us. To forgive those who condemn us. Knowing that we're all the time sitting here in the light, and then there's nirvana, the ultimate spiritual experience, when the world fades away and life fades away and death fades away. No fear of death in nirvana. Only eternal life, eternal being. Not as we've come to know it, but as we came to know it once before.

You forget, my friend, you forget that you spent quite a bit of time at that particular resort we call nirvana. And now, out in the world, you've forgotten. But it's not strange or unnatural. It's nothing that you haven't done before. It's easy. Nirvana is easy. Spiritual growth and development is easy if that's what you want. If you want spiritual experiences, you can have them. All you have to do is want them. You have to be like Dorothy. You have to click your heels three times and want ever so much to be home, more than anything. And then the way will be shown.

Spiritual experiences, dreams, and visions. There are different types of dreams. Naturally, there are dreams in which we wake and find ourselves in another world. This is the dream we call life. Then there are the dreams that we have at night, when we put our heads on the pillow and move into the astral. Most dreams are not too important, in the sense that most of them are numbers that don't answer, parties we didn't attend. But occasionally a dream is not a dream. Occasionally it's not a mindless shuffling from one scene into another, one body into another, one picture into another. And that's a vision, a dream vision. Suddenly, in the midst of the dream, everything stops. Someone comes to us, a spiritual teacher, a being of light, and the consciousness, the quality of the dream changes dramatically. There's a feeling of eternality about it, or perhaps a joy so great that we could have only experienced it in a dream–a joy that was too great for this world that we live in, too great for this mind, too great for this body.

In dreaming, we're in the astral, and in the astral we have a greater capacity to feel, to see and to believe and to understand. After such a dream, you will be different. For two or three weeks, you'll see a pronounced difference in your consciousness. This is how you know it was not an ordinary dream. Upon waking from the dream, you'll be surcharged with energy. You'll find that if you tell the dream to someone, they will experience a part of it too. Don't tell it too frequently to unreceptive persons; it will dissipate its energy and power for you, but don't be afraid to share it. To share is to give. To give is not to lose, it's to grow.

Some people say you shouldn't share your spiritual experiences, dreams, and visions with others. I think that's nonsense. It's a very selfish attitude for a person who cares only about their own realization, and one who cares about their own realization will not have such a realization, or they'll only have the realization of selfishness. Never be afraid to share a meditation experience, a dream, or a vision. When you do so, you must do so without egotism, without a sense of being special. You had it because you were special, because you were better than others? More advanced? No. You have to feel you had it simply because it was there, it was a gift, which you didn't deserve, nor were you not worthy. It came, it opened your life, and then when you tell it to another, you must tell it not to make them jealous but only to inspire them. Keep it very simple, very humble and very pure, as it was. Don't tell too many people.

And then write it down. It's most important to keep a journal, a journal of your spiritual experiences, dreams and visions. These are moments out of time, and you need to record them because they're few and precious. By keeping such a journal and keeping it by your meditation table, you will find it's nice, occasionally, to sit down, before meditating or after meditating, and read over some of them. You'll find that you can go back to them. On a dark day when you can't meditate too well, when your thoughts are turbulent, when you open up the journal, you'll read back about a dream you had, a vision, a spiritual experience. Something with your teacher, something by yourself, when the world fell away and time stopped, and there was time out of time, and everything was quite right.

Beyond words, yet you put it in words. It will bring the vibration back to you. You'll be able to touch that place and go back there. It's very important to keep a journal. You don't have to write down everything that you do or every meditation that you have. It's better not to; leave them alone. But whenever a special meditation occurs, a special experience, a special dream, type it up or write it down and keep it in your journal. It will grow and it will aid you.

We're imprinted by the world, by our civilization. We have to re-imprint ourselves with a higher imprinture. We need to publish our experiences to the skies. We do this in our journal. No one reads the journal but us, so we don't have to impress anyone with our style. We don't have to hope that someday someone will discover it, publish it, and think how wonderful we were. We'll let it leave the world when we do. Therefore, we're free to write as we really are. Because no one would read it but ourselves–we're writing for ourselves–then the journal will be free of egotism. We won't be writing for a future audience. We can be truthful, honest, and clear. We're writing it to God. Try to keep a journal. It's a very important thing to do in the early stages. Very important.

Try not to hold onto any type of spiritual experience that you have. Very often we have a very powerful experience and then we fixate on it, and in doing so, we lose the purpose of the experience. The purpose of the experience was not the experience itself. The purpose of the experience was to loosen a defined state of being that we were in. Then we cling to another state of being which was the experience and we fixate on that. The purpose of the experience is not to relive the experience. To see the movie once was fine. If the movie comes to town again, it might be fun to see it again. But we don't have to follow the movie from town to town. Let's see other movies. Or take a break from the film.

Try not to cling. Enjoy the experience. When you have the spiritual experience, if you're sitting meditating, you may feel different sensations flooding your body, you may see different lights, hear sounds – ignore them. Be neither attracted nor repulsed, because as soon as you become caught up in them you'll stop the experience, unless it's an extremely powerful experience. Let go. Let the experience take you where it will. Don't try to understand what they mean; they don't mean anything, they are their meaning. Don't worry about the color of the light you saw, the sound, the ray of energy. These are all mental fixations, ideations. You're trying to move into the superconscious, beyond the known, into the vast ocean of light. Let it be. Later, if you want to, you can think about the experience. But during it, just let it happen. If your mind starts to fixate, make the mind quiet. Let go.

If you have an experience and you're afraid–suddenly you find yourself letting go and dissolving, experiencing something new, don't feel bad. But realize the next time that you don't want to do that. You stopped the experience. But a spiritual experience will never hurt you. God is trying to open a new page in a book to show you something new to read, a new picture to see. The next time the fear comes back, remember, 'Well, last time, I remember I was afraid, I held on and I stopped myself. I've meditated, I've worked for a long time to have this beautiful awakening, and I stopped it. And I don't want to have that happen again. I love the experience. This time when the fear comes, I'm just going to shush it away, push it away. This time I want to feel eternity. I want to know it, as it really is. And nothing is going to stop that, nothing. Not myself, not my thoughts, not my fears. What's the worst that could happen to me? I might become enlightened. I might become happy. What's the worst that could happen to me? Do I think I'll lose my mind? Am I afraid that after the experience I'll be deranged, I'll be crazy?'

That's not how it happens. It's only light. It's like pure water, it can't hurt you. You have to trust. In order to have a great experience, a great vision, you have to trust God completely. You have to trust that light of eternity and know that it only, only, has your welfare in mind. Unless you can let go, there will be no experiences.

A great deal of what we do in self-discovery, along with our meditation, is to learn to let go, to break our bonds with the past, to give up that which binds us. Only you know what binds you. You don't necessarily have to leave a person or a family or a marriage, but you have to leave the part of yourself that clings to it. Sometimes it is necessary to leave these things, only because we've outgrown them. They were fine at the time, then we move on. Sometimes they're working–well, why should we leave them if they're happy? But sometimes we change and we move in a new direction. We feel eternity beckoning. We know that we could stay in the life we're in now, with the people we're with, and that would be a lovely life. But the vision calls us on.

You see, the vision is the vision of self-giving. It's the vision that we can lead a personal life for ourselves and enjoy ourselves and make people happy. Or we can dedicate our life to a higher principle or ideal and move beyond the personal life to a more cosmopolitan awareness, where it's not the two of us walking down the street together, just loving each other and sharing our little world, but where we're able to laugh more freely, love many, and work for many and enjoy many. This is attached love versus unattached love. One is not better than the other, it's just different, and sometimes we move from one to the other, kind of like a seesaw, until one day we see that unattached love is just much more fun.

The couples walking down the street, arm in arm, they love each other, then they quarrel. They make their plans, their dreams. They go on a vacation together. They dream their lives. They dream their children, their world. Or we can walk down the street by ourselves observing. Perhaps with many friends, talking and laughing. Not having to create the special world between the two of us, which is ultimately our trap, our rebirth. That's a spiritual experience, a dream, a vision. There are so many of them. At every stage of life, in and out of life, the word of thumb, I suppose, the rule of mind, the matter of the subject is endless. Mixing metaphors dancing.

Consider wisely, oh nobly born, oh you who must cross the threshold of life and death again and again, oh you who is in the bardo–remember, life is the bardo. This is the bardo now, not after death, now. Remember, oh nobly born, choose well, because what you choose you will become. If you choose spiritual experiences, dreams and visions, then you'll have a life that's quite dissimilar, quite beyond that which most have. It will make special demands, but they're lovely demands. Or you can choose the mortal coil, which we've all chosen many times and there's nothing wrong with it. It's old and comfortable, but it lacks luminosity. It lacks the pure intensity, the completion, the moment in time out of time, when everything is one and there's nothing but light, that transcendental light that is the beginning and that is the end, that is everything. That all-powerful light.

So, oh nobly born, listen well. Neither be attracted nor repulsed as you cross the bardo. No matter what you see, hear or feel here or in any world, know that it is your self-form, that it is an extension of your being. Whether it be the most powerful experience or the most subtle, finite or infinite, be neither attracted nor repulsed. Instead, meditate on the clear light of reality, the clear light of the void, the pure gentle white light of existence that is existence. Feel that, become that.

All these other things are spiritual experiences, dreams, and visions that rise forth and return to that light. Focus on that light and enjoy the experiences as they go by. Whenever you cling to one–a person, a world, a reality, a plane of being, a lifetime, a cosmos, a cosmology–then you will rest there for some time until you let go again, until the tide loosens your ship which has been stuck on the sand beds and you wash free again and you sail onward, in search of the light.

ZEN, TAOISM, AND BUDDHISM

There are many different pathways that lead to spiritual awareness, consciousness, and perfection. Certainly three of the most frequently traveled pathways are the pathways of Zen, Buddhism, and Taoism. Today I'd like to talk to you a little bit about these ways, not so much from a historical perspective but from the perspective of one who, in other lifetimes, has practiced and taught these three ways. If you'd like historical information on the evolution of Zen, Buddhism, or Taoism, there's a wealth of information at your local library or in a metaphysical bookstore.

Naturally, if you're interested in Taoism, I would suggest that you read *The Way of Life* by Lao Tzu, the founder of Taoism. I personally prefer the Witter Bynner translation. It's available in paperback.

For Zen, there are many, many books, the Suzuki books and others. I remember a time a number of years ago when you could go into a bookstore and maybe just find four or five books about Zen–*Zen Flesh, Zen Bones*, Suzuki on Zen and Alan Watts. Now there are many, many more to choose from.

As far as Buddhism is concerned, there are many different books on Buddhism, on Mahayana Buddhism, Vajrayana Buddhism, and Hinayana Buddhism. There's a wide variety. Buddhism itself, of course, has evolved and changed quite a bit since the time of Buddha. There are different sects, which are basically different Buddhist religions. Just the evolution of Buddhism, from which Zen also sprang forth, or the evolution of Christianity for that matter, is fascinating to study–to see how an enlightened person will come into the world and present a way, as did Lao Tzu with Taoism or Buddha with Buddhism or Christ with Christianity, and to observe how that way will be modified and changed by the needs of the people and their consciousness level over a period of several thousand years.

But my interest is the essence of these teachings, not so much what's happened with them historically or the books that have been written about them, detailing them, or the descriptions of people who have had experiences in the monasteries or experiences living a more secular life. Rather, my interest is the essence of the teaching–the way, as it were.

Taoism is the way of water. The most frequent element or symbol referred to in Lao Tzu's writings is the symbol of water, and it's the primary symbol that we find throughout *The Way of Life*. In essence, Lao Tzu suggests that we behave like water. Water, of course, is the symbol of consciousness, pure consciousness. He suggests that we flow like water does. Water always seeks the easiest path, the common level of life. When it reaches a spot where there is a blockage, water finds the easiest path around the blockage. Or, if it can't find a way around the blockage, it continues to assemble. The water gets deeper and deeper until finally the level increases and it flows over the blockage. It uses itself to go beyond whatever it needs to go beyond.

Water gradually wears down even the hardest rocks and stones. The Grand Canyon is living evidence of the power of water over a period of time. The power of water may not manifest immediately. We don't see these effects right away. We see the little stream of water flowing and we say, well, look at this massive mountain, obviously it's much stronger than this water. Then suddenly, over a period of time, the mountain goes away and the water remains. Water can be very powerful, like a tidal wave, the ocean. It takes on so many different forms. Lao Tzu says that the way of life is water, to be fluid.

He often uses the analogy of the tree. The old hard tree breaks and falls when the wind blows. It doesn't survive. The young tree bends and therefore need not break. He advises us to bend and not break. Lao Tzu doesn't seem to hold too much stock with words or phrases or teachings. Rather, he says that the way of life is ancient, timeless. It is existence, which he calls the Tao. It is a mysterious source, beyond understanding, and all of us are a reflection, if not that source of life ourselves.

Taoism is the gentle way. It's the way or the path of least resistance. Taoism is something that Lao Tzu found easy to reconcile with the world of human beings, which is interesting because with all the nature imagery associated with Taoism, one might think that it was in some way antithetical to contemporary life. But a great many of the sections of *The Way of Life* are taken up with political discussions and how the way of the ruler, the way of the servant, the way of the merchant, the way of the householder and the way of the army interact with the Tao.

Lao Tzu always points a finger directly towards us. He says that we must begin with ourselves. It's impossible to bring order into the world unless we bring order into ourselves first. The enlightened person, he says, who has managed to bring order into themselves, will have a tremendous effect upon all those around them, both those they see and those they don't see, because their effect is both visible and invisible. Rather than running out and trying to change the world, Lao Tzu suggests that we change ourselves.

"Existence is beyond the power of words to define. Terms may be used, but none of them are absolute. In the beginning of heaven and earth, there were no words. Words came out of the womb of matter." So begins the writings of Lao Tzu. "If name be needed, wonder names them both. From wonder into wonder existence opens."

The essence of Taoism, in my estimation, is really expressed by these few words, "From wonder into wonder existence opens." Taoism is the way of the child, or as Lao Tzu finally refers to himself or others who follow the way, the way of the fool, the way of someone who doesn't have to have pomp and circumstance, who doesn't need to be noticed. The primary quality that Lao Tzu seems to embody is humility, which is the image of water–seeking the common level of existence, without struggle. Or if there is struggle and there is strife, being silent, being at the center of being.

Taoism is not particularly a popular way in the West, and not really so much in the East. Lao Tzu recognized that this would happen. When he writes, he writes, he says, to the few. He says, "Most follow the passing way." The crowds, the masses are attracted to the popular teacher of the moment, to the popular philosophy that tells them what they want to hear. But very few, he realizes almost sadly but with inevitability, recognize the way of life itself, the way that withstands all time and all change.

Lao Tzu's way of life, his Taoism, is not a religion, although perhaps it has been made into one by some people. Lao Tzu's way of life occurs in any spiritual philosophy, if it's real. Because if a spiritual philosophy doesn't conform to Taoism, then it's not truthful. Taoism has no rules. It's a suggestion for perceiving life in its wholeness, without unnecessary categorization, yet while enjoying the beauty of categorization.

Taoism shows us how to deal with life and death by realizing everything here is transitory but its substance is eternal. Lao Tzu says, "A sound man, immune as to a sacrifice of straw dogs, faces the passing human generations." We should not weep, cry, or be upset when those we love die, or when we see the generations pass, the multitudes, because all these are forms of the infinite creation. They are not real. They are not eternal. The death of nations, of the world, of all the worlds, does not affect eternity in any way. Just as when water is frozen into a form as ice and then it melts–the ice is gone, but that which it was all along, the water remains–so at the time of death, there is no death. The spirit simply changes form. It becomes something new.

Lao Tzu was worried that some people would attack him or his philosophy and say that it was the way of nothing–quietism, giving up. His only concern was that this observation was very, very inaccurate. Some people think that Taoism means not doing anything, just going on with your life as if nothing had happened, and that has little or nothing to do with Taoism. Taoism means stretching your being. As Lao Tzu says, it is becoming both a man and a woman and joining within yourself, to be the heavens themselves, to stretch your awareness beyond the breaking point until all opposites are reconciled within yourself. Taoism is Tantra, the reconciliation of opposites, where all things join together in perfect unity and at the same time have beautiful diversity.

Buddhism is a very scientific approach to self-discovery. Buddha gave a number of talks, lived to be quite old and spent many years with his disciples. When we push away the mythology and myth that's been connected with his life, when we just examine him as the man who attained enlightenment, his own life was fascinating. He was a prince, had a wonderful family, and like many of us was confronted one day with pain and suffering. He saw the pain and suffering of others, and suddenly the fulfillment of his own life for its own sake was no longer sufficient. He recognized the need to aid and put an end to the pain and suffering of others.

He decided to use himself as an experiment. He was very much like an Einstein. He said, "Well, before I go out and tell people what to do, I have to find out myself. If it doesn't work for me, how can I hope to show anyone else?" Left his family, he left his kingdom, and he began to wander throughout India. He studied with many different teachers, learning from each one. Each teacher showed him something new about the enlightenment process. Then one day he had learned all he could from teachers because none of the teachers he met were truly enlightened–they all had learned something about the way. He went and meditated under the Bodhi tree, and over a period of time, through his meditations, attained liberation. He saw his past lives, the triple universe, the seven higher and lower worlds, and of course was absorbed in nirvana.

After his absorption in nirvana, his consciousness returned to this world and he set off to teach, to show the way. He presented the four ways, the four rules, the four causes. There is pain, this world is filled with pain, he said. All pain comes from attachment. There is something beyond pain, which is nirvana, an end to pain, infinite bliss, perfect consciousness, and awareness. And there is a way, a pathway, to reach nirvana, which he called the eightfold path. He divided the way into eight sections: right actions, right thoughts, meditation, absorption, many different things.

He formulated a scientific approach, which was not really at all in conflict with any other true way. You'll always notice that all the ways agree. Some have different terms, different methods. And there are different methods. Different roads do lead to Rome. But once you're there, the roads are forgotten, unless you're showing others the way.

All of the great teachers have come into the world to reestablish what we call the dharma, the truth, the true way. A teacher will come, an enlightened teacher, perhaps in a generation or not for thousands of years. He or she will show us the way again to truth, to light, to immortal consciousness. These teachers are higher beings who take incarnation into this world to help their brothers and sisters, their friends. Then after their death, the way will be forgotten again. What they said will be corrupted or simply not understood. Because when a liberated teacher is among us, what they teach us are not just a series of words that can be written down in books that others can understand–that's part of it–but it's to be in their physical presence and meditate with them. That is what they show.

There are no books or words that can describe that, although videotape is a possibility in the modern age, perhaps, but still, the level of meditation when you're with them is what stops your thoughts, what brings you into eternal consciousness and awareness. So the way is lost, ritual replaces it. People begin to worship statutes. They worship all kinds of things. They make up rules and prohibitions until another enlightened teacher rolls down on the planet and says, "OK, let's forget all this ritual, let's go back to the essence, to the truth."

Each teacher will say exactly the same thing. The teachers, of course, always speak on the level of the audience. It depends on the culture they've incarnated into. They might be able to say much more, but they're bound by the language of the time. They're speaking so the people with them will understand.

Buddha spoke to those who would listen, for many, many years. He and his disciples traveled throughout India, teaching about the transitory nature of existence, to become absorbed in the eternal. Buddha wouldn't answer a lot of questions. He didn't like to speculate on the nature of God, on the nature of truth. Very often students would approach him and ask him these very convoluted questions, and he would just repeat his four noble truths or discuss the eightfold way. He felt that such speculations don't help us. All that we need to know is that which will take us to truth. To understand what got us in the condition now will not necessarily alleviate the problem. You may know why you're in pain now, but the simple knowledge will not necessarily show you the way beyond pain. It's interesting information. Sometimes it's helpful. Buddha says that all suffering is caused by attachment, therefore here's a simple analysis of the problem without a lot of history.

Now when Buddha says "attachment," he speaks of the same thing that Lao Tzu does. Lao Tzu says we have to flow like the river and not get stuck. Well, attachment is getting stuck. Liberation is being unstuck. Many people think that liberation is simply being attached to a spiritual set of ideals and rules, and that has nothing to do with it. Liberation means that we are not fixated on any reality. All of eternity flows through us and with us. We are it. Liberation can adopt and accept all forms or no forms. It's not a philosophy, a creed, or a way. It is existence, in its absolute and its finite form.

Buddha pointed out that all pain and suffering comes about through attachment. Physical pain comes about through attachment to the physical body. We identify with our body. We think it is our self, and when the body hurts, we feel we hurt, whereas if we could see that the body is an outer cloak, that it's not that much a part of us, if we recognized our larger self, our eternal body, as it were, then the pains of the physical body wouldn't disturb us so much, or the pleasures.

We become attached to possessions, to persons, to experiences. There's nothing wrong with possessions, persons or experiences, or with having a body. But our attachment causes us to suffer. When someone we love leaves us, when we lose a possession, when our house burns down, whatever it might be, at that time we suffer. Whereas if we recognized all along that these things were transitory and they had only come to us for a while, as we have only come to them for a while, and they weren't meant to last, then there would be no sadness. Because we would know that life is fullness, that every absence will be filled.

If we didn't derive our happiness from the things and people and places of this world, if our happiness was based just upon pure being, then we could have all the things in the world and be happy, or none of the things and be happy. Or if we had all the things and then they went away we'd be happy. We'd enjoy the things of this world, but not be bound by them. We won't be slaves to our possessions, to our friends, to our loves, to our careers. This was Buddha's point. Not to give everything up but to give up attachment, which we do through meditation and by purifying ourselves—meaning right action, right thought, by leading pure and simple and happy lives, doing all we can for others without a sense of self-importance. Of course, on a more advanced level, Buddha was discussing becoming attached or fixated into states of consciousness, even very advanced states of consciousness like the samadhis, the lower samadhis.

It's easy to become fixated, to think of ourselves, in other words, in a certain way, as opposed to being the thin air. Sri Ramakrishna always used to use the analogy of the smoke. He would say that when the smoke blows through a building, it leaves soot all over the walls. Similarly, when a person who's not liberated or self-realized or God realized or enlightened passes through this world, it leaves its mark. Their attachments leave a mark, just like the soot, and it gets deeper and deeper and deeper and darker, until it's very hard to see the light of the soul. Whereas with the enlightened person, they're like the thin air. When the smoke passes through the thin air, it leaves nothing. That's enlightenment, to be the thin air, in a way of speaking, or we could just say to be pure light.

Buddha stayed away from religious concepts, not necessarily, because he didn't believe those things, but he just felt that thinking about these things only leads us farther away from the truth. In his day there were many pundits who would have debates over spiritual philosophy for hours and days on end—the learned philosophers. But they didn't know much about the truth; they just knew a lot of words.

Rather than seeing his own students get caught up in all this sort of stuff that was popular at the time–these philosophical debates on the meaning of certain Sanskrit phrases and words–he would say, "Forget all this nonsense about God and about this and that." He didn't say they didn't exist. He'd say, "Forget about it, let's not discuss it. Let's just look at the problem and let's solve it. The problem is we're in pain and suffering, we're bound, we're attached, we don't see truth, we don't experience the bliss of nirvana, the joy of life. Now what can we do about it today, because there is only today? Well, what we can do is that which will free us, and that which will make others free." He was very conservative in his spirituality, much more so even than Lao Tzu was. Both were extremely conservative spiritual teachers, in my estimation.

Zen was a reaction. Just as Buddha came into the world and spoke against the fall of Vedanta–Vedanta was once a high and pure way but it became ritual. Enlightened teachers taught the way of Vedanta, but then it was corrupted. Buddha, upon obtaining liberation, looked at the corruption of Vedanta and spoke against it and presented a way that again was the original Vedanta, which he called Buddhism. Buddhism was corrupted. It lost its essence, it became ritual, and Zen was a reaction to that. Zen was an attempt to go back to the purest teachings of the Buddha – enlightenment without strings.

Now when I speak about Zen, I have a problem, in the sense that the Zen of today has lost the essence, in my estimation, of what I call "old Zen." Just as Zen occurred, or came about, to correct the problems inherent in Buddhism, so Bodhidharma [the founder of Zen] wanted to show that the way still existed, and wanted to get back to its essence. In the same way, today, Zen has lost its zip, if you will, or its nothingness, and has become ritualistic. It's established in monasteries with strict codes of koan study and things like this. These are all fine ways, there's nothing wrong–when I say something's been corrupted, I don't mean that it's corrupt in the sense that it's corrupt like criminals are corrupt. I mean that it has become ritualized, the enlightenment has been forgotten.

There are certainly, in every major faith, advanced spiritual seekers and teachers, but the vision of the founder, that eternal, omniscient, omnipresent vision, has been somewhat lost. This happens, this is existence. There's nothing wrong with it, it just occurs. When I talk of Zen, the Zen I'm referring to is not what you would see today if you were to go to Japan to a Zen monastery. Oh, there might be an old monk or two who practices the old way, but most of it is an entirely different way. It's not a bad way, it's just a different way than old Zen.

Old Zen is the way of nothingness, the way of having a good time. In the old days, in old Zen, Zen was not really practiced so much in a monastery. The Zen master, not that he would probably call himself a master in those days, usually lived up on top of the mountain or the hill or in the forest or sometimes in the village, but usually outside. He would usually study with a small group of students, men, and women. They would spend a lot of their time just simply walking around in the woods or in the cities, or they would come over to his house and he would teach them, with a great deal of humor and laughter, about the nature of existence.

Old Zen was very funny; there was a great deal of humor and happiness. Zen today seems to be much drier. While there's a certain amount of humor, it seems to lack that total intensity because humor is one of the primary tools for liberation. When one laughs, one ends fixation. When you laugh at your own state, the state dissolves. When you laugh at the world, the world dissolves. Old Zen was also, of course, disciplined meditation, without the need of sticks. When you get to the point where you have to hit someone with a stick, you've kind of lost the point, in my estimation. I appreciate the thought, but it's really not necessary. The stick is love.

Old Zen was the reduction of concepts to absurdity–the koans, the magical phrases that are used in Zen today. "What is the sound of one hand clapping?" "What is the form of your original face?" You know, all of these one-liners that the Zen masters throw out and the students respond to. Today they're very fixed. There are classical responses to them and they call these koans. The idea is that you go and see your Zen master, maybe once a day, and you're working on a particular koan, "What is the sound of the forest at night?" Something like that.

You go back each day and you repeat the answer that you've managed to get together. The idea is that when you have the right answer you'll make some kind of a breakthrough to a new plane of consciousness. You'll see something. There are no right answers, though. Today, there are books that give you the right koan answers. But there are no right answers. It has nothing to do with what you say, it's how you say it. It's the moment, and old Zen, of course, was the study of the moment, to see that the moment is eternity.

The Zen master would do literally anything to break down the concept of what the study was, because the study was Buddhism, and everyone had fixed ideas about how to attain enlightenment through Buddhism. So the Zen master would present conflicting codes all the time, not that he necessarily believed in them but just to shake this fixation that people had on how to realize God, how to attain liberation.

In addition, the Zen master was constantly attempting to break up concepts that people had about what it was to be a spiritual teacher or what a spiritual teacher is like. They're very fixed ideas. We have a traditional image, so the Zen master broke with the traditional image. Now, the Zen masters of today, of course, have their own image–Gucci sandals and things like that, but in the old way it wasn't like that. There was no way to be, there was no way to dress. Each Zen master was a complete character, yet they all said the same thing because there was really only one Zen master. That's all there has ever really been or will ever really be. And that's your self.

Zen is the way of splitting–splitting the self again and again and again until there's nothing left. Reshuffling the deck of cards, each card being a part of your being. Dealing out hand after hand, then walking away and leaving the cards on the table where they sit and stare at each other, sometimes changing places.

Zen doesn't believe in the reconciliation of opposites because from the point of view of Zen, there's no point of view, therefore there are no opposites, therefore there's no Zen. All there is is dishwater. Timeless, eternal, perfect dishwater. Waiting for the dishes that will never come. The Zen mind is mindless, yet it embraces everything.

Zen is discipline. The discipline of living life, the discipline of taking a breath, the discipline of not knowing and not trying to know. The enlightenment of Zen is called satori, and it's thought of as a quick enlightenment. But satori is not a final state. There are really two types of satoris. One satori is the satori of instant enlightenment (Rama claps his hands loudly). In a flash, enlightenment comes (he claps again). With the clap of a hand, enlightenment comes (he claps again).

With the clap of a hand, this world dissolves (Rama claps loudly). With the clap of a hand there's nothing but eternal consciousness (Rama claps three times). Three times the hands are joined. The threefold world dissolves and disappears (Rama again claps three times). Three times the hands are joined, three times all of existence appears (he claps three more times). Three times the hands are joined, the mind stops, the world dissolves. Everything is as if it's always been.

Satori is a brief flash. After some meditation, while working in the field, while talking with someone, while making love, while meditating up on the mountain having renounced all people, suddenly the light breaks through, and for a short timeless time we experience eternity in its unmanifest form. This is satori. It's comparable to salvikalpa samadhi.

There's another satori, though. After one has the Zen awakening, the Zen satori, which does not last, which comes for a period of time, a moment, day, a week, but then fades and we see signs of it for perhaps 28 days or 34 days, then it goes away. Yet we're different. But after this happens again and again and again and again, we reach a point where there's nothing but satori. In other words, it's a different level or a different kind of satori. It doesn't fade, it just is, which is like nirvikalpa samadhi, nirvana.

Zen is a very viable way. It's one of my favorites. I play it with my students all the time. Of course, I had many incarnations as a Zen teacher. I like it because it's so incongruous yet makes complete sense. It drives my students up the wall, and then once I get them up the wall I leave them there and go out of the room and move on into another lifetime.

Zen is the fastest method I know of, aside from mysticism of course, of dissolving the fixations that people have about spiritual practice and about themselves. And like mysticism, it's a very happy way, although it works very differently than mysticism. With mysticism, we're using the intensive mystical kundalini to literally, with a dose of radiation, just blow apart the subtle structure of a being and rearrange it.

With Zen, we do it more through sleight of hand. With Zen, it's not so much done with power as by a very subtle and delicate shift in consciousness, which shifts the world. It's kind of done from the inside out. But both mysticism and Zen have this beautiful quality of happiness and laughter, which I think is so important and so necessary in our modern, contemporary age.

If you were to go to Japan today, I don't think you'd find many Zen teachers. You'd find a lot of people who teach Zen though. And what they teach, I'm sure, is very fine. It's the new Zen. And perhaps it's better.

A short lecture on enlightenment.

THE OCCULT BODY, THE AURAS, AND
THE CHAKRAS

The occult body is a field of attention. A human being is composed of various parts: the physical body; the subtle physical body or the etheric body; the occult body; the psychic body; the mind; the ego; the life force; and of course the jiva or the soul or what they call in Buddhism the anatman, that eternal spark which is the ultimate perceiver or non-doer. The occult body is not a body in the sense that it has a shape. It's shapeless. The occult body is a field of attention. It's an avenue of awareness. It's a wind tunnel that connects the different realities.

Now certainly there are what we call "occult bodies." It is possible to create these occult bodies. They're extensions of your own bodies; we call them allies or helpers. An advanced spiritual aspirant is capable of creating many different bodies and can utilize these bodies to help aid others in their liberation. But the occult body, more than anything, is a field of awareness. You might say it's a way of being. The occult body is power but power that is not directed in an obvious manner. The word "occult" means hidden, that which is unseen.

There are various forms of spiritual practice. Naturally, in some forms of spiritual practice we see that which is apparent. When someone loves God, is truthful, is kind to others, compassionate, we can see what appears to be the cause and effect. But the occult body is part of the realm of mysticism and it works through the occult fields.

Just as there are different radio frequencies – shortwave, longwave, television, microwave – so in the cosmos there are different planes of awareness, different frequencies of being. Some of these frequencies don't relate to human beings at all. Some do. The principal planes that relate to human beings are the physical plane, which is part and parcel of the physical body; the vital plane or the plane of energy, the life force; the mental plane or the plane of thought and ideation; the plane of self, the sense of self, the ego, the "I"; the occult plane which is the plane of mysterious power, effect without cause; the psychic plane, which is the plane of beauty and psychic oneness and awareness; and finally the superconscious, the undifferentiated pure light of being from which all things come forth and to which all things return.

The occult plane is neither good nor bad, neither emotional nor unemotional. It's an expression of pure intensity. We go down to the beach on a cloudy, stormy night when the wind is blowing and there's a tremendous gale. The white caps are foaming, the winds are rising and everything is swept by that wind. The surf pounds the sand. That intensity, that tremendous, awesome power is similar to the occult reality. The occult reality is a place of force and power.

Many different beings live in the occult world, but the occult world is not a world for the lightweight. By that I mean that the occult world is a world of warriors. It's a world of power, survival of the fittest, I suppose you might say. The beings in the occult world help some people in their spiritual evolution. But very often they destroy people. The occult reality is like a wild jungle and to go into that jungle you have to be very strong. You'll be dealing with untamed tigers and lions and elephants and all kinds of things. Unless you are very confident of your power, it's a good place to stay out of.

Many people tamper with the occult. I have a number of different students who have in this life and in other lives practiced witchcraft and different forms of what I would call lower occultism. And when you practice lower occultism what you're doing is opening a door. Imagine that there are many doors within yourself and they lead to different worlds, different realities, and when you open the door that leads into the occult realm, it doesn't necessarily close. As you journey into the occult realm, as you explore that plane of reality, things that are in the occult plane and realm explore you.

You travel through the occult plane, through this different spectrum or band of existence, in your occult body. The occult body is your extended awareness. For example, if I choose to, I can send my occult body anywhere, to any universe, to any plane of existence, to any place in this world. And my occult body can produce effects. I can gather knowledge and see. It's like having a kind of mobile video unit out there. I can communicate, transmit power, prevent things from happening, start things – all without leaving my room. I can sit here in my room and create effects without appearing to create effects. This is all done through the occult body.

Now, the occult body can be used for positive things. In my case, I use the occult body to locate students, people who seek enlightenment, who I could work successfully with. Many people might seek enlightenment but I wouldn't be of any help to them. I wouldn't appeal to them as a teacher, even though I'm enlightened. The shoe wouldn't necessarily fit. But there are many people on this earth who live in many far-flung lands. Some are my students from past lives or some have worked with other teachers, but they could work successfully with me, meaning that I can be of some service to them along their way, which is of course what I live in this world for.

Now, for me to find those people is very difficult. The world is very big; we only have a small amount of time in any given incarnation. So how could I find those people? I could travel the world and put ads in magazines, but maybe that day they wouldn't look in the magazine. Or maybe they're just in such a state of inner slumber that the thought of meditation and self-discovery hasn't even occurred to them yet. Even though they have an advanced soul, they're wrapped in maya. What I – or any spiritual teacher – do is to use my occult body to work for me. My occult body can be out traveling, producing effects and creating changes, waking people up, giving them spiritual experiences, guiding them in some way to see a poster or an ad or something like that. People who are receptive, whom I could be of some service to, can be helped tremendously by my occult body. I don't have to necessarily be consciously aware of what it's doing.

The mind is limited. It's a small computer, a little home computer. It can only process a certain amount of information. It has a limited storage facility – 64K. However, there are other parts of our being that can do much more. Now, the mind will not necessarily be aware of what the other parts of the being do or will only have glimpses of it. In order to become aware of what the other parts of our being do, we must move into the superconscious. From a point high on top of the mountain, we can look down and see everything that's happening in the valley, on any side. When we're in the valley, sometimes it's hard to see just past the next line of trees. From a high altitude, from the superconscious, you become aware of what the many sides of your being do.

Very often, I use the occult body in dreaming. The occult body is the body of dreaming. At night when I'm asleep for a few hours, I use the occult body to travel and visit, to give people spiritual experiences, to learn, or simply to have a good time, just to play. Because I love to play, just to play in the occult realms. Sometimes in the occult realms, I have to fight sorcerers and witches and nonphysical beings that are harmful. I also have many friends who are in the occult realms, who exist in these planes, nonphysical beings who help me terrifically in what I do. We work together as a team. For humanity.

Very often, my occult body will travel in dreaming when I'm awake. For example, I might have a student who's in, let's say, Japan. I might be physically awake at that time, but my occult body, if my student is asleep, can enter their dreams, can converse with them, can communicate with them, teach them or simply have fun with them. I have literally thousands of occult bodies. Being an advanced teacher, who's been a spiritual teacher for many, many lifetimes, I've accrued the power to manifest hundreds and thousands of occult bodies simultaneously. Or you can say that hundreds and thousands of occult bodies have learned how to manifest me. Either one would be correct. I use the occult body just for fun, to give people beautiful spiritual experiences, to help find people, in other words to aid people in their spiritual evolution, to help them in their overall advancement.

Now, the occult body can be used in other ways that are not quite so progressive. The occult body can be used to injure someone, to gain power over them, to steal their power or to destroy them. A lower occultist, someone who practices voodoo, has learned to manipulate energies and to send their body of dreaming to do harm. Whenever I encounter such a person I "destroy" them. It's like a psychopath who, no matter what you do or say, is bent only on doing harm to others. They do not know reason. A person who has opened themselves up to entities and has been taken over by these lower occult beings has really lost their mind and all they do is destruction. Such a person must be destroyed. In other words, when I say "destroyed," I don't mean that you kill the person, but I mean that you remove their powers. You take them away. You destroy that part of them that has any affinity with that world.

Very often, it's necessary to actually destroy beings. I've done that many times, in the occult world. If I see a negative being harming one of my friends, it's necessary to destroy it, to vaporize it. You can't kill it; it will change form, but it's like destroying a virus or a bacteria, something harmful that seeks to destroy the life force in someone. You can't be emotional about these things. There is no emotion in the occult world. In the occult world there's only power and various uses of power. If your heart is pure, you will use that power only for the greater good of all and never to further or advance yourself. If you are impure, then you will use the power in impure ways, and a person who uses the power in impure ways will suffer tremendously.

Many people practice what they call channeling. They get in touch with spirits; they communicate with nonphysical beings. This is the occult. They're dabbling in the occult reality. But always remember when you do these things you're opening a doorway that will not necessarily close when you want it to. When you communicate with spirits and forces you're linking your energy with theirs. They may appear initially to you to be very progressive. They may give you interesting information. But always remember, they can see. Some of them are quite knowledgeable. And they can see what you want. They can tell what your desires are. If they fulfill your desires, then they begin to gain control over you, over your mind.

Very often, we read about some lunatic in the paper going and killing someone. Like the fellow who killed John Lennon, for example, or the "Son of Sam" as he was called in New York. These lovely people tell us that they heard voices that told them to kill a certain person and that they listened and they followed what the voices said. These [voices] are occult beings. These individuals were practicing occultism. Now, they may not have been part of a coven of witches, necessarily, but inwardly they were talking to nonphysical beings for a long, long time and there were transactions that occurred with them.

Many of the invisible friends in childhood are not imaginary; they're actual. These beings really exist. Normally they will not have a transaction with you unless you seek them. They don't particularly like light, the lower ones. If you meditate every day and if you're a happy, progressive person you need never even think about the occult. You can throw this tape away because the occult doesn't really apply to you. And I do not suggest that you look into the occult.

I had many incarnations where I worked with the occult, particularly in ancient Egypt and Atlantis and in other cycles. But occultism in those days was a high science. Today occultism is your local fortune-teller, your witch. This is not occultism. These are people who dabble with forces that they don't understand, with powers that can destroy them and eventually will. Occultism is a beautiful art when you understand it and it's definitely an art. It's much like ballet. It involves perfect form and movement. You have to be able to move perfectly through the occult realms. Many things will tempt you and if you can still be tempted then you will give in. But if you realize that

347

the only thing that matters is light and that that's your real essence and substance, then you're free to play with occultism, to use the higher occultism.

Many of the pyramids were built with occult power. People didn't do a lot of it manually; it was all done with energy, with fields of attention. You can move the stars around, rearrange their patterns, project alternate bodies to different locations. Walk on air. Walk on yogurt. You can do all kinds of things with the occult attention. But it's definitely an attention. If you want to develop your occult attention, do a lot of fasting. Fasting is very good for developing the occult attention. I don't recommend that you develop the occult attention. I'll tell you how because I think all knowledge is useful; some of the knowledge that is most useful is the knowledge we never use. But occultism is a slippery path. It's a slippery mountain pass, and it's a long way down.

Moving into a slightly lighter area, perhaps – the auras and the chakras. The subtle physical body, which I've discussed in our tape on the subtle physical, is composed of strands of luminous light, millions of them networked together. The subtle physical body is the body that lies just on the other side of the physical; it supports the physical. Now, the subtle physical body has a number of different junctions within itself where the strands of light that are the essence and substance of the subtle physical body connect together. We call them chakras. Most people are familiar with the seven chakras. If you open up books on yoga and self-discovery, you see little paintings where they show – it looks like an outline of a human body and there's a line that runs from the base of the spine to the top of the head. This line is an astral tube called the shushumna, and there are two little tubes on either side, the ida and pingala. Normally they show seven junctions, seven train stations where the trains stop. These are the chakras.

The chakra at the base of the spine is the chakra of the kundalini. The chakra around the spleen is the chakra that endows life force. Sexual energy flows through this chakra, and also creative energy. The chakra at the navel center, around the area of the navel, is the occult chakra. That's the chakra of occultism and is used in the production of the occult bodies and the transfer of occult power. That's the chakra that the occult body enters and leaves through when it does its work. The chakra in the center of the chest, of course, is the heart chakra, which is the central chakra; there are three above and three below. It's the center of psychic love and oneness and beauty and it leads to the psychic planes, the higher astral. The throat chakra is connected with higher creativity and particularly spiritual vision.

The chakra at the forehead, the third eye, as it's referred to, which is between the eyebrows and about an inch above, the agni chakra, is the chakra of timelessness. When you meditate on this chakra, you'll find that it's very easy to go into a timeless state of being. It's also the chakra of the occult siddhas. Many of the powers are connected with this third eye, and the third eye also has to do with discrimination, being able to determine that which is real or unreal. Just as the physical eyes show us things, so the third eye is the eye with which we see the soul.

These six chakras are all connected by the shushumna, the ida and the pingala. But the top chakra, the crown center or the thousand-petaled lotus of light, as it's called, is not connected to the other charkas; it's separate. That's the chakra of the superconscious awareness. Each chakra is a floor in a building, a doorway to a floor in a building. There are seven floors. And if you meditate on each chakra, you will have different experiences.

There are other chakras. There are chakras in the hands, in the palms of the hands and in the fingertips. The chakras in the palms of the hands can be used for manipulating what they call the shakti. Shakti is the kundalini energy when it's taken outside of the body and transferred from one person to another. It's very easy to move the kundalini in the form of shakti through the chakras in the hands and bring it into people, either by physically touching them – you can put your hand on their body and transfer the energy – or just shoot it out. That's what you'll see me do very often when I meditate and I'm doing what they call the mudras. I raise my hands and hold them in different positions. I'm not simply moving my hands on a physical level, but let's say that on a subtle physical level I'm moving energy, fields of energy, through everyone who I'm meditating with in a variety of different ways.

The chakras in the fingertips and in the hands are connected with healing. The healing energy, which comes from the second chakra primarily, what we call the spleen chakra, the chakra of generation and regeneration, will move through the hands and it's amplified by the chakras in the hands, if they're open. It increases the power of that healing energy. There are many chakras, hundreds of them, in different places in the subtle physical body. There are some very strong chakras in the feet. As you progress in your meditation, you'll gradually become more and more aware of the different chakras in your being.

Some people feel that they should spend their time meditating on the chakras. I really don't think so. I think it's a great waste of time for most people to meditate on the chakras. Because when you meditate on a chakra, you're fixating. I will take exception to the heart chakra or occasional chakra meditation. If you meditate and start your meditation each day by meditating on the heart chakra, you'll have a very progressive, beautiful meditation. It will bring you into the higher psychic planes, which will bring purity into your being and love and light. Occasionally it's fun to meditate on some of the other chakras. But I'm suggesting that you should not spend your whole meditation focusing on the chakras because it's a bit of a fixation. Spend maybe five or ten minutes or 15 minutes at the beginning of, let's say, a 45-minute meditation session meditating on the chakras. And then, after you've done that, stop – stop focusing on the chakra. Now just feel light, feel love, ignore your thoughts and let go.

If you fixate on the chakras too long you will develop certain powers, you'll open certain doorways to other worlds. But very often you'll create more problems for yourself than you'll solve. If the powers come prematurely, they can be very painful. It's necessary for your body, your being, to become purified through meditation and through self-giving and by associating with the holy – persons who practice advanced forms of spirituality – and by wanting that more than anything. You'll gradually become pure, meaning you'll lose your lower motives. You'll care more for the welfare of others than you'll care for yourself. When you've reached this level of attention, when this is the way you feel, then you'll find that the chakras will open by themselves. Also, the chakras are, to a certain extent, superfluous, in the sense that you can open up all of the chakras and not attain liberation. The chakras are access points. They're gateways to other worlds. Liberation really has nothing to do with these access points. Liberation means we've gone beyond the access points into pure light itself.

Don't make gods out of the chakras. The chakras are places of joining together. They're meeting places. Each one has a power, and that power will work on its own. It's not necessary for you to associate certain colors with the chakras and memorize the yantras or mantras that go with them and all this sort of stuff. All this pragmatic knowledge won't really do much for you. It may make you feel better in a superficial sense. But what you really need is the knowledge of pure bliss and oneness, which will come when you stop thought. When you meditate, when you stop all thought, time goes away, the world goes away, life goes away, death goes away and there's nothing but a big smile. Nothing but eternal joy. You can meditate on the chakras for hundreds of years and not achieve that.

The chakras are useful; they're like an automobile. The auto will take us from one place to another. But the auto has its limitations. It can't fly, it can't talk to us, it can't give us a foot rub. At least not the models I've seen. Don't be overwhelmed by the chakras. The chakras are like the organs in your body. When your body is healthy, they function properly and efficiently. You don't have to think about your heart or your lungs or your liver. If your body is healthy, if you're in good condition, then everything functions perfectly. To keep everything functioning perfectly you have to attune yourself to light, love, and humor. Then the chakras will work the way they're supposed to. But if you fixate on the chakras, very often you can enlarge them, in a way of speaking.

It's hard to put this into words. But imagine that you made your heart too big for your chest. It would be very painful. If you developed one leg much more than you did the other, you'd be imbalanced. People who meditate too much on the chakras very often create an imbalance, not in the chakras themselves, the chakras won't exactly get larger or smaller, but let's say that the chakras are fields of attention, fields of awareness, and you're formed by these fields of awareness. The fields of awareness are in a certain balance; there's a certain structure. It's like the DNA. Now, when you start to mess around with that balance, you're messing around with the structure of your being. If you don't know what you're doing you can get yourself in a lot of trouble. If you do know what you're doing, you won't do anything, you'll let eternity do everything.

It's fun to try meditating on the chakras a little bit. Meditating on each chakra will not hurt you, don't misunderstand me. I'm simply suggesting that people who meditate on the chakras every day for several hours a day, let's say on the same chakra, day after day, month after month, unless it's the heart chakra or any of the higher chakras, really, but if you're meditating on the navel chakra or the two lower chakras for excessive periods of time, you will bring energies and forces into yourself that are very strong and very powerful but not necessarily very pure and happy. You can fall into deep depressions, be filled with frustration, anxiety. It's fine to meditate occasionally, meditate for a few minutes each day, on your navel center or on one of the other centers. But to spend hours and hours on the chakras will produce effects, and those effects cannot necessarily be erased very quickly.

If you open the doorways to the lower astral, then you'll find these beings will seek you out, they'll come to you in dreams, and many of them are terribly unpleasant. I've had people come up to me and say, "Oh Rama, can't you help me, I'm being followed by these entities. They're in my dreams, they're controlling my life, they're taking over my body." Now, I'm sympathetic, certainly. And I always try and do what I can for these people, which is, of course, limited by how much they really want to be helped. If they say, "Take them away" outwardly, but they are still intrigued and want to hold on to them inwardly, there's not a whole lot anybody can do. And while I feel sorry for these people to a certain extent for having gotten involved, at the same time I realize it was they who got themselves involved. The entities don't come and just take someone over. Some part of you has to want that. And if that's what happens, then there'll be an effect for that want.

The auras are the colors of the subtle body and they're strikingly beautiful. Once again, people want to figure it all out. They want to say, "Well gosh, if I see this color, it means this, or this color means this." Not necessarily. The colors of the auras, which are the reflections of the subtle physical body or the outskirts of the subtle physical body, don't necessarily have meaning, any more than different planets have meanings. You can go to Mars or Jupiter and perhaps Venus or Mercury. And what is the meaning of the planet as opposed to another planet? Well, the term doesn't really apply, so it's kind of an incorrect way to look at it. A planet is what it is and you can have different experiences there, but it doesn't necessarily have a meaning as opposed to or separate from another planet.

The colors of the aura are connected with different spectrums, different bands of awareness. The color of the superconscious is gold, not a dull gold but a very shiny, beautiful light gold. Light blue or blue is the color of the vastness or infinity. It suggests a very advanced state of consciousness. Red is obviously the color of spiritual transformation and power. Green is usually connected with renewal. Usually when you see green in someone's aura, it suggests that they're accessing a lot of newness. They're making some changes in their life that are connecting them with the newness of life.

The chakras emanate or support the auras. The chakras are the power vortexes. But don't spend too much time worrying about what color your aura is or what color somebody else's aura is because the auras change color constantly. As you cycle in and out of different levels of consciousness, the auras change. But if you meet an enlightened person, you will see, if you have the ability to see on a subtle physical level, a beautiful golden light around them. Oh, you may see many other things – purples, magentas, violets, greens, blues, whites, all of the colors, because all the colors are beautiful. But you'll see this light gold light, this beautiful shimmering gold light. It's very hard to see at first. But as you develop your sensitivity you'll see that it's everywhere. It's like the giant net that brings forth all of the worlds, sustains them and then one day takes them away.

Now, I'll do an experiment with you. This is something unique. I've never done this before. Today is the 22nd of March, 1983, and I'm sitting here in my home. It's about 12 after eight in the evening. The sun has already set. This time and this place that I am in right now will always exist. Each moment of time exists eternally. While we move from moment to moment, the moments that we pass by always exist somewhere. This moment will always exist. And the tape that you're listening to will remind you of this moment because it was crystallized – this tape is a photograph of this moment.

Now, what I'm going to do is show you how the occult body works. I could talk to you for hours about the occult body or if you came and saw me meditate or went out into the desert with me, you could see it a little bit. But it's not necessary. I can show you the occult body and the influence of the occult body from where you're sitting listening, and that's what I'm going to do right now. Because all time is divisible. In other words, it doesn't really matter when you listen to this, if it's two days after I make the tape, if it's a hundred years hence. The occult body that I'm going to be using will be available as long as this tape is available.

What I'd like you to do is just for a moment, unless you're driving an automobile, in which case you can just kind of listen along – just sit up nice and straight, don't lie down and close your eyes. Do this now, if you would be so kind. Now what I'm going to do is reach out and touch you with my occult body. I'm not going to touch your skin or your body, but I'm going to go inside your being. You're going to feel a variety of different sensations, perhaps see something, perhaps not. What I'd like you to do is to close your eyes – this will work best if you're alone, but it'll work anyway – and just be very still and listen to my voice. Your eyes should be closed at this point. Now what I'm doing right now, through all time, beyond time, is reaching out with the occult body. It's a body of beautiful light and I'm reaching inside your being, and you should be able to feel me reaching right inside your being, feel me going right up and down your spine, and I'm turning you. That is to say, I'm taking a higher level of attention, and I'm spinning it inside you. And you can literally feel a shifting. Now, just listen. We're going to have a moment of silence on the tape while I do this, and you just feel what I'm doing.

[Several seconds of silence on tape.]

Now that I've done that, which is kind of preparation, I'd like you to open your eyes for a moment and just look around you. And as you look around you, I'm going to play with the colors of your room a little bit, with the intensities and the hues, the brightness. Again, if you're driving, my friend, please keep your eyes on the road. You may see some unusual things on the road, but keep your mind on your driving. Okay, a moment of silence again. I'm going to play with what you see around you. Don't look too hard. Don't fixate. Don't try and "look" at anything. Gaze. Just relax your eyes a little bit, just gaze. I'm not hypnotizing you; it's not necessary. I'm just reaching out with my occult body. It's sort of like in the phone ad where they say, "Reach out and touch someone." Here we go.

[Several seconds of silence on tape.]

Very good. I've just changed your level of attention. I've demonstrated to you that there is no time. I've made a transference through my occult body to yours, which will help you. It will raise your energy level. It may heal certain parts of your being that you had problems with. You see, I, like all spiritual teachers, am always available. Whether we're in the body or out, there's always someone here, if you reach out to us to help you. We're beings of light, as are you, it's just that we're conscious of it and we can use that light a little more strongly. You'll be able to do that one day too. But this simple demonstration of power is to show you about the occult. It's very difficult to talk about; I find it much easier to show you. You'll notice at the end of this tape that you will feel very, very different than you did in the beginning.

Also, one last thing I'll do for you. This is an unusual tape, I admit. The next time you go to sleep, or within the next few times, if you would like that to happen, I will visit you in dreaming. If you listen to this tape particularly before you fall asleep, or as you fall asleep, it will help you synchronize your being with mine, and I'll visit you in dreaming and I'll tell you some interesting things about yourself. And maybe I'll take you flying with me. In the other realms.

You see, as an occultist, I have nothing that I can tell you. As a spiritual teacher, I can tell you a great deal. But when I practice occultism, higher occultism, when I help you gain enlightenment through that, there's very little I can say. I can show you, but I don't have much that I can say. And as I'm talking right now again, of course, I'm showing you, I'm reaching out. Not through the tape, the tape is a mere medium. The tape is like a crystal. You look inside it and you see it reflects something, it refracts it. Let us just say I'm making you aware of my occult body and I'm giving you a little practical demonstration. Here I'm going to put my finger – right – on – the back of your neck. Right there. And I'm now bringing the kundalini energy right in through your spine, from the top down. You can feel it flowing right down. Now I'm letting go. This is mysticism. And I think you've had enough for one tape.

Spiritual Teachers And The Enlightenment Process

I would like to address what I consider to be the most difficult topic for a person who seeks enlightenment to deal with. There are different types of spiritual teachers. The ultimate spiritual teacher is life. Life is constantly teaching us, if we'll only open our eyes and observe.

Because we have so much, such a large self, such a developed personality and persona, we don't really see. We see ourselves. We're always basing everything that we see in life on a comparison with our own views, our feelings, our ideas. It's only after the self has been swept away that we can really see. Otherwise, everything is colored by our own perceptions. But when we are no longer a separate finite individual, then all there is, is the universal, real perfect sight, perfect seeing, perfect perception, untainted by personal want, desire, gain, past recollection, sorrows, hopes, ambitions.

Life is the teacher. We are part of life. We are the teacher. Our own body, our mind, the aging process–all of these things are teaching us. We learn to listen to the wind. The wind is a wonderful teacher. You could learn much more from the wind than from myself, unless I happen to be the wind, which I am some days. The earth, the water, all of the elementals, the things that go to make up this universe teach us. Each has a force, a power.

Human beings teach us all the time. We can observe them; they're all our spiritual teachers. Observe people when they're happy and understand why. Observe them when they're unhappy, angry, hateful, and jealous and understand why, with no judgment, no recrimination. Just with understanding. This is how you study consciousness. You observe. You sit and watch, quietly. You don't think about yourself or worry about yourself, your problems, your ambitions, because you won't see correctly if you think of these things. You must push them all aside, just as when a physician is performing an operation. The surgeon is in a critical moment, he can't be thinking about other things. All his attention must be on the operation. You have to place all of your attention on that which you study, to learn it. And the more you can do this, the more complete will be your knowledge and your learning.

Every moment, every day, is an opportunity to learn, to observe what I call the theater of the soul. The orchestrations of eternity. If you're by yourself you can watch yourself, watch nature, watch your house, watch the time pass, watch the moon rise, the sun set. Each time of day teaches you something, each time of day has its own mood. The morning, noon, the afternoon and the sunset, the early evening rounding around until midnight, after midnight, the sunrise, the early morning–each has a mood, each a power. Naturally, if you're completely caught up in your thoughts, in your ideas of what's important and not important, you won't learn. You have to be still, you have to learn to listen. Listen to nature. Observe human beings. There's a lot to learn there.

Practice meditation. Stop your thoughts and learn from meditation. Practice self-giving. Self-giving is a wonderful spiritual teacher. And observe what happens. It's like lifting weights or working with your body. If you do it on a regular basis, your body changes, it becomes stronger. When you practice selfless giving on a regular basis, you change. Oh, if it's very sporadic, you won't see too much. If you lift weights once a month, not much will happen. But if you do it every day, if you exercise every day, it's amazing how fast the body can change. If you don't exercise every day, it's amazing how badly the body feels, how quickly one can regress.

Practice compassion. Compassion is a wonderful teacher. Compassion means loving without attachment. Caring, not trying to lead other people's lives for them, but being helpful and useful when you can, without feeling that you're important. You can always learn. There are so many teachers. The birds teach us when we watch them fly. Love teaches us, hate teaches us, everything. There are so many teachers. Anyone who says they don't have a spiritual teacher is so wrong. You have infinite teachers. Everywhere there are teachers–books teach you, movies teach you, There's so much to learn if you'll only watch and observe.

Naturally, there are human teachers, teachers who specialize in teaching us not simply factual information as they do at the university, but they teach us how to learn about life, how to be independent, free and strong. These are spiritual teachers. A spiritual teacher teaches us about spirit, about the formless and how that relates to this world, to the form. There are different classes of spiritual teachers. But from my point of view, there are only three classes–some people make larger divisions–unenlightened spiritual teachers, enlightened spiritual teachers and harmful spiritual teachers, or ignorant ones.

Unenlightened spiritual teachers are persons who have a type of knowledge that they may have gained in past lives or in this lifetime. They themselves may not be really capable of doing everything they can see or know. For example, your teacher may say, well, lead this kind of life and you'll be happy and free. And they themselves may not be able to lead that kind of life completely. But they're not hypocrites, not at all. We must be more cosmopolitan in our view because what they say may be true. Now, if they pretend to lead that type of life and don't, then they're hypocrites. Your coach, if you're a runner, may be able to help you run very fast and to win the Olympics. The coach can't necessarily run very fast himself or herself. They don't need to, to be a good coach. Certainly, it would be helpful if they had run themselves, so they would understand what it's like. But they don't have to be the fastest runner in the world to be able to help you run. They just have to have the knowledge of how to run and be able to transmit it.

These are unenlightened teachers. They may be able to do some of what they teach; they may not be able to do all of it. They're sincere and they are not capable of leading you to enlightenment. Only an enlightened person can do that or God will do that directly. The unenlightened can only take you to the beach, but they can't bring you across the ocean. God can do that directly, if that's the will of eternity, or God will do that through the voice and the guidance of what we call an enlightened person.

In my estimation, there are very few enlightened teachers in this world. If we were to believe everyone who says that they were enlightened, I suppose there'd be thousands and thousands of enlightened persons. And I suppose there are thousands and thousands of enlightened persons, perhaps millions, and billions. It depends what you mean by enlightened. I'm rather traditional in my classification of what liberation means–full liberation, beyond the samsara, beyond birth and death, no self left, just a caretaker personality to go through the world. Nothing but light inside. Incarnation after incarnation of spiritual practice until the self is completely refined. Absorption in nirvana, continuously inwardly and outwardly, sometimes completely, and so on and so on.

In my estimation, at this time, there are twelve fully enlightened teachers in this world of which I am one. It's important to note that a fully enlightened teacher is not in any way, shape, manner, or form better or superior to anyone or anything else–to a blade of grass, to a person wrapped up in ignorance, to the cosmic beings. We're all the same. But there are different hallmarks in our evolution, in a way of speaking.

Think of the fully enlightened teacher as the twelfth-degree black belt in martial arts. Maybe there are just twelve of them in the whole world, so you may study with many different teachers. The first teacher you have may just have a brown belt; they can show you some basic moves. Your next teacher may have a black belt. Well, once you've come up to the level of the teacher, now you have a first-degree black belt also, now you need, if you want to continue to progress, a second-degree or third-degree or fourth-degree. You work your way up. You wouldn't begin your study as a beginner with a twelfth-degree black belt. You might start even with a third- or fourth-degree, perhaps, if you were fortunate. But the twelfth-degree black belt would be reclusive and only work with people who were more advanced. Oh, he'd drop in on the beginner's classes, perhaps, from time to time, or maybe even just teach one for fun. But his art is a very advanced art and could only be understood and appreciated by those who were in the higher ranges, who had their eighth- or ninth- or tenth- or eleventh-degree belts. Others wouldn't understand the subtlety of the moves. As a matter of fact, they might even think that the fifth- or sixth- or seventh-degree black belts were more proficient because they made more noise, because they were more obvious. But the twelfth-degree black belt will be a master of inaccessibility. Only those who are very, very advanced will recognize him, and they will be drawn to study with such a person and learn.

It's not necessary to study with a self-realized person, for most people. Most people should content themselves with the best teacher they can find, and feel and know that when the time comes you will be directed to a self-realized teacher–when it's necessary. One should not be so egotistical to think that it's necessary simply because one wants it to be. Life knows what it's doing. Trust it. When you are ready, you will be directed. But perhaps you need humility, perhaps you have to wait. When the time comes, the door will open.

Now, I say there are twelve and they're really all the same. In this earth, at this time, eleven of them are men and one is a woman. However, we're trying to change that, even it out a little bit more. That's history.

Then there are those who claim to be enlightened, who take the power of others, who dominate them, who create cults. And some of them are very, very impressive. One must be very careful. Some of them have maybe made it up to third- or fourth- or fifth-degree black belt. They can be very impressive. They can speak the language flawlessly and they can do a very high kick and you might think that's all there is. Perhaps they can manifest a few occult powers, a couple of siddhas, but their realization is not completely rounded. Unfortunately, the great danger, of course, is that people get stuck in their knowledge. Knowledge is as much of a trap as ignorance, and it's very easy to get stuck in knowledge. It's very easy for the fourth- or fifth-degree black belt to stop, set up their little school, teach, and not go any further. In order to progress spiritually, continually, you must have tremendous humility and realize that your own knowledge is only knowledge if you continue to progress. Otherwise, it's stagnation.

You should always seek not to be around those who have less knowledge than you. You may feel better, you won't be threatened, you won't have to do anything and everyone will admire you. But between you and me, let's face it, you know you still have a long way to go, and I know that too. And if you fight against that, then you'll be unhappy. If you accept that with humility, then you'll grow and you'll remember why you started all of this. But you definitely cannot fool me. I know, I've done everything that you've done. I've gotten stuck in all the places one can get stuck, made the mistakes, had incarnations of delay and then learned the way, remembered it again. There's nothing you can do that's wrong, but you can delay your progress and your happiness or the happiness of those you could help and reach if you wouldn't be so stuck on yourself.

The false teachers set up cults. They have people worship them. They say, "I am the guru, I am God, and I can do no wrong. I am a perfectly enlightened being! Everything I say is wisdom. I am above maya." Only fools talk this way. No one is above maya, not even the enlightened. And they're convincing. Because a person seeks truth. They want to know what's right. They're very sincere.

You go to these teachers, they speak knowledgeably, you might even feel some sensations when you're around them, a little bit of power. And if you don't know better, you might think they're enlightened. And they'll tell you wonderful things about yourself to flatter your ego. But you will see, while you may experience a lot of growth with these people in the first year or two, after a while it will slow down to a snail's pace. Then you'll discover, hopefully, if you have the humility to realize that eventually, that it wasn't they who gave you the growth, it was you. It was your own aspiration. You were so happy to attribute all your wonderful growth to that teacher, but it wasn't the teacher at all. The teacher didn't have that much power. All the teacher did was fool you and took credit for what you did.

There are a lot of these teachers. Oh, and they have vast followings. But they lack integrity. They lack humility and purity. They've forgotten. They no longer care. They surround themselves with a small group of people who are not a threat and if you disagree with their policies, if you don't like what they say, then they'll throw you out of their community. They make rules such as, "Well, no one in the community is allowed to speak to someone who's been asked to leave, or associate with them, because they've been taken over by evil forces, the devil," whatever it may be. "They'll drain your energy." I mean, they make up the most wonderful rationalizations. And people believe them. It's astounding, the damage that these idiots do. They can be very persuasive and very convincing.

When you work with the fully enlightened teacher, you are dissolving all the time. You won't feel wonderful all the time but you will change constantly. And as time goes on, the changes will become faster and faster. Now, naturally, a person has something to do with it. A person can resist the process and therefore slow it down, not meditate, not participate. Naturally then, you have to assume some responsibility for your lack of spiritual progress. But even so, when you meditate with an enlightened person, if you're in the room when they meditate or outside with them, you will change. The radiance is too strong. It's like going into a particle accelerator, standing in front of radioactive isotope. It's going to affect you, it has to.

When you meditate with a person who's truly self-realized, you will see them surrounded by a glowing golden light and you may see other lights. But the sign of realization is the golden light; it's luminous and very light, very refined and it doesn't necessarily have to be flashy. And you will feel a still presence of eternity–if you listen. Oh, some people come to the enlightened teachers and they see and feel nothing, obviously. Christ was crucified. Do you think that the people who pounded in the nails, who laughed and jeered, saw anything? No, everyone doesn't see enlightenment. You have to be sensitive to it. There are people who come to see an enlightened teacher and they've meditated for three or four or five years or they've done what they think is meditation–they've just been dabbling actually. And they say, "Well, I didn't see anything, I didn't feel anything, how could they be enlightened? I'm so wonderful, I'm so perceptive, I'm so knowledgeable, I can tell an enlightened person instantly." What vanity.

Very often it's hard to recognize enlightenment unless you're very advanced spiritually. You have to sit with it for a while because it's subtle, it's not obvious. It's very subtle. Occult power is obvious, it's flashy; the siddhas are obvious and flashy, but enlightenment is quiet. An enlightened teacher uses the siddhas and is flashy sometimes, but ultimately they're just very quiet. They take on all forms, all personality structures are at their beck and call, they use whatever one they need to help their friends progress. But when they're by themselves or with people who they love who have great purity, who they can be close to because it's not painful to be with them, they're like little children, they just laugh and play with the universe. They can be the most awesome, powerful beings in the world. And then just like children. There's an innocence there. A humility. At the same time, they're not afraid to confront someone, to take on the whole world if necessary, to yell at someone, anything to help the person with their enlightenment process. But what happens is light. They are light; nothing but light flows through them.

Sometimes I think it's easiest to tell if a person is enlightened when you're not with them physically, but you have to be somewhat receptive and meditate well. Sometimes it's easiest just to sit at home and meditate on that person. If you have a photograph of the person to look at for maybe a minute or two, then close your eyes and just try and have contact with them. Now, first you have to be able to stop all your thoughts. If you can't do that, you can't really tell. But if you can stop all your thoughts for five minutes or so when you meditate, clear yourself completely, then when you focus on them you'll have a very profound experience because you'll be right with them, in the room with them wherever they are. You'll just feel a quietude. Don't look for flash. And don't be fooled by their appearance.

Truly enlightened people are characters. They're the most unlikely looking people. Everyone has an image of what an enlightened person will be like and I assure you it won't be like the image unless they're just playing images one day. Each one is different and they change constantly, there's no set form. Each time you see them, they'll be a different person. There'll be some repetitive patterns, some repetitive caretaker personalities that they use. But then if you were to go and see them with another group of people you'll see them in a different way. They're dreamers, enlightened people. Whatever dream the people happen to have they're with they enter into that dream and become it. And they do it so cleanly and completely that no one can tell. Then once they're within the structure of the dream they try and teach the people to go to the high end of the dream or then to change dreams or go beyond dreaming to nirvana.

I have seen so many wonderful people go to false teachers and have their lives ruined. They place all their faith and trust in them, give the teachers their possessions, leave their families for the teachers, only at the end, possibly to realize–if they can, if there's enough of them left to realize anything, after they've been so psychologically brainwashed–that they've made a terrible mistake, that the teacher was selfish all along, played piety, made rules, made demands upon the students that the teacher didn't live up to. The teacher wasn't interested in the growth of the students, the teacher didn't place the welfare of the students above and beyond their own. Oh, they may say they do and quote the right scriptures. But the test is always kindness.

Real spiritual teachers are exhausted all the time. They're beat. This may not fit with your picture of enlightenment, but they have to be, they're always working for others. Oh, when they're absorbed in complete meditation, they dissolve, they disappear, they're gone, no forwarding address. Nothing but light. But when they move into the field of action, into this world, they have to use every moment for the welfare of others, either in conditioning themselves so that they can be of more use or in actual service – both are service. There is nothing else, nothing else matters but to serve eternity.

Enlightened people usually have a pretty good sense of humor. They think life is pretty funny and that death is even funnier. And they can do some interesting things for you. The spiritual books tell us this. They say that there's lots of good things you can practice to help you attain enlightenment, to become conscious–meditate; do good works; don't eat too much; don't eat too little; travel to holy places; be a vegetarian; exercise enough; don't be attached; practice love; think of God as much as you can, of eternity; live in the world, if you live in the world and make the world a better place; don't be attached to the world; let the world come and go; be absorbed in eternity. They tell us many different things. They give us creeds to follow, ways. But if the books are any good, they tell you one thing ultimately–all of this is fine, but it won't cause enlightenment. It will prepare you. It will clear the ground, which is necessary. And we do this for many, many lifetimes. But for enlightenment really to occur you must have contact with the enlightened, with the holy.

Most of the enlightened are recluses, to be honest with you. I certainly am. There's nothing that the world holds for us anymore. Oh, it's beautiful to be at a shopping mall or a field of flowers. It's all lovely, it's all infinite forms of the self. But we tend to stay by ourselves because there's no place to go or nothing to do anymore, unless we're out teaching. It's fun to go for a walk in the hills, but there's really not any need for contact with people anymore. We have nothing to say to them. What can I say to someone? "Hi, how are you? Did you have a nice day? Hope you're feeling better."

Oh, I can teach the sophisticated processes of rebirth, how to attain enlightenment, how to have more fun with your life, how to avoid pain and misery, how to enjoy pain and misery, but there's really nothing to say anymore, because there's only eternity, there's only light. Once you have attained liberation, there's only light. You're a member now of a different race. It's a different species. You look at human beings and you watch what they go through and you love them and you do your best for them. But they're all just blown about by the wind of the samsara, by their emotions, by their ideas and their attachments.

You've become eternal. You're a member of the staff of the school and you see the students come and go every year and the new ones come in with their ideas and expectations, some go out and have experiences, get married, have children, careers, some go to graduate school, a very few elect to become teachers themselves. Some become poor teachers, some wonderful teachers, some go beyond that to enlightenment and then come back and teach. Some become enlightened and go beyond. There are so many variables, so many possibilities. But you've become eternity, you're the eternal watcher, when you're conscious of this world, and much of the time you're not, you're absorbed in eternity, in nirvana, beyond form and dissolution and death and rebirth.

So what can one say? But what the enlightened can do for you is change you. You see, it's very hard to attain enlightenment on your own. You have to meditate perfectly, you have to give perfectly. You can't fool yourself with your self-styled humility and purity and integrity, which is usually just a laugh. Well intentioned, but it doesn't go very deep – because you have no sense of what deep is.

But you see, an enlightened person has countless powers of transformation that they use with their students, both when they're physically with them and when they're not. Actually, the largest part of the teaching that I or any enlightened person does occurs when we're not physically with our students. It's necessary to be with them, hopefully once a week or twice a week. When we're with them physically, when we gather in the meditation hall or we go out in the desert for a hike or we go to a movie together, whatever it may be, the radiance and the light is moving into everyone. It's very strong in the physical proximity of the teacher and it creates an opening. In order to work with a teacher, you have to have what we call an inner connection. Once the inner connection is fully developed, you don't have to physically be with the teacher. You're always with the teacher. You're with each other.

Now, remember, the teacher is only an intermediary. You see, we don't want to get into teacher worship because that destroys everything that we work for. If you think the teacher is some remarkable being who attained enlightenment and you can't, that they're different, that they ate a better breakfast cereal, then you've kind of misunderstood. It's a convenient way of avoiding enlightenment yourself. It's like saying, "Oh, the teacher's an avatar, a wonderful being. She went to the right schools, she ate the right breakfast cereal, came from the right family, that's why she or he attained enlightenment and I didn't, and what can a poor soul like myself do? I'm lucky just to be around such a person. Oh, let me worship them, they're marvelous!"

What trash! It has nothing to do with enlightenment. All you're doing is saying, "They're special and I'm not. That way I don't have to do the work." Hey, they were just like you. I'm you. We just kept going to school, that's all. We didn't quit. And we worked harder and harder. Even when it was difficult, even when it was easy, we just kept working. When we made mistakes, we made them. And then we got over them and went back in and worked some more. It's just a lot of work, that's all, to attain liberation. But if you love the work, it's not so hard. It takes time. But you've got all of eternity, you know.

Then there's truth. Truth in everything and truth in nothing. And to get to that truth, you need to learn to be still and sometimes to be active. You go and see the teacher whenever you can, at every opportunity to be around an enlightened person, you'll travel thousands of miles to do so. Because those hours or minutes you spend together are eternal. Being in the physical presence of a teacher, in this vortex of light–it's a power place, the teacher is a power place and you go to it, and when you're there, at a power place, everything changes. You may not even be all that aware of it when you're there, but later, the next day you'll see you're different. You've been opened up to another plane of consciousness. Oh, you might just think it's some accidental process, you just sat in the light. But I assure you when you're with the teacher, when I'm with my students, I'm doing a thousand different things on a thousand different planes of consciousness, sometimes simultaneously, to create those openings for all those people who are there.

Then, when you leave, the rapport doesn't end. By being with the teacher you create an inroad, you open a little doorway. The idea is not to get stuck on being physically with the teacher, but to go home and meditate, to learn to have contact while you're at work, to tap into that source. Remember, the teacher's a doorway, the teacher is an absence, not a presence. You see a body and you hear them talk and you see a bit of a personality. But that's all a front. It's a prop. It gives you something to look at and focus on. The teacher is an absence, the teacher is a nothingness, a wonderful nothingness that you can walk through. And then there's nothing but light, there's no teacher, no you, just light. Or there's you and light. But we're just light. Eternal vortexes of light. We can't be separated from the rest of existence. You can't either, but you're not aware of that yet. You can think it, but you don't know it, you haven't lived it or outlived it.

You have to develop an inner connection with a teacher. It's necessary to love. This is how the whole process works. In the beginning, you come in contact with a teacher and you decide they have something to offer you. You study with them for a while. But there comes a point in time when you have to kind of commit yourself, not to the teacher, but to what the teacher believes in. If the teacher's an absence, how can you commit yourself to an absence? A real teacher will never ask you to do this. Real teachers don't ask for commitment because they know, how can you ask for it, it has to come on its own. How can you demand love, it has to grow in its own way. Real teachers are wise. They know the human species very well. Oh, they play dumb a lot so people can still relate to them.

Then, of course, there's the emperor's new clothes or the false teachers who say that when they make mistakes they're playing dumb so people can relate to them when actually they're just dumb. (Rama laughs.) It's tricky! It's very tricky! You have to have a pure heart to tell and even then you can be fooled. I've been fooled. In this life, I studied for many years with a teacher who claimed to be fully enlightened before my own realization returned, and gave the teacher my heart, mind, body, and soul completely. I was fooled. But it didn't hurt me. My own aspiration kept growing and increasing. And then I started to go into samadhi, day after day, night after night, year after year, dissolution after dissolution and the realization came back from other lives. Of course, I've been a spiritual teacher in hundreds of lifetimes.

But see, you can be fooled. Never feel that you're above illusion. Once you're enlightened you're not going to be affected by illusion as long as the enlightenment is complete. But even then you can get stuck when you're not sitting there absorbed in samadhi, but stuck is eternity too. There's as much light in ignorance as there is in knowledge. Just a different form. Not to worry so much about it.

You develop an inner connection with a teacher. It's really essential. You can only do it through your hard work and your integrity and your caring. And the teacher always sees. Remember, if you're dealing with someone who's really enlightened, they see everything. Oh, not the time you spent this afternoon by yourself, they don't have a knowledge of the things you do, but when I look at someone, I see the composite that they are, all their past lives, presents and futures. Not in terms of events, I don't know what you did when you were in Egypt two lifetimes ago. I can look it up if I want to, but who's got the time? It's not necessary. Because what I can see is the result, your current state of evolution, the strands of being that you are and how to turn them around and inside out and redo them over and over again, so that they become more and more refined, until enlightenment is a reality for you.

There's this great concept that people have that if you go to an enlightened teacher and if you sit down with them and meditate, that that's all it takes. "Oh, I'm just going to sit here with my beloved teacher and that's all it will take." I really hate that phony devotionalism, tacky stuff. The really saccharine spirituality bothers me. It lacks clarity and humility and laughter. Real devotionalism doesn't have to be very demonstrative. If you really love somebody, you don't have to say it, it shows. You don't have to fold your hands every time the teacher walks in, you should do whatever you want to with your hands. Because the reason most people fold their hands is that it's a ritual. Better to sit still. Love is always understood, it doesn't need outer signs.

You sit and you meditate with the teacher, whenever you can. And that's how you learn. You ask questions, hopefully dumb questions sometimes unless you're too proud to ask dumb questions. You ask anything you can, that you really want to know. And if there's nothing you want to know, you sit and you listen with humility to the questions of others and you learn by listening and watching. The whole time with your teacher, when you're with a teacher though, you should meditate. It doesn't matter what the teacher's doing. Don't over focus on the physical body of the teacher. If you go someplace together, don't have everybody stare at the teacher. Don't be so dependent on the physical. The awareness is what you're interested in.

Sometimes I take my students to Disneyland and we play in the world of Disneyland mysticism. Hopefully they don't all stand around and stare at me, they should go off and have a good time on the rides. I'm there meditating the whole time with them, generating a field of light to make Disneyland into a slightly different experience. It's not necessary for them to watch my body, what's the difference? I have a body like they do, so what?

You see, a real spiritual teacher makes you independent, not dependent. They're not interested in worship. They're not interested in making you happy, actually, in a way. Happiness is a nice state but it's transitory. You're happy today, you're unhappy tomorrow. They want to give you something more solid. But they realize that they can't do it for you. Oh if you want a father figure or mother figure, go out and find one. But a real spiritual teacher is your friend, he's your buddy, he's your comrade. They deserve respect, only because if you don't respect them you won't respect what they say. And you need that respect to access the light. But they can't do it for you. You can't just go to the teacher and smile and love them and that will do it. Well, that's nice, it's nice that you love them and it's nice that you smile. But you have to work out your own realization with their guidance and help. But simply being there is not enough. It's nice to be there. If you have to be somewhere, you might as well be with the enlightened. I mean it does rub off. Keeping company with the holy definitely transforms you, but it won't cause enlightenment. But it might get you started. But then you have to, over a period of time, realize that, well, time to change! Time to die! Time to be reborn in this life, over and over again.

You have to take up the cause of the teacher, whatever it is, if you really believe in it and work with the teacher, help them with what they do with their work in the world, and by doing so you'll stop thinking about yourself and your enlightenment and your happiness and your unhappiness and you'll get absorbed in the work, and the work is light and the light will enter you and you'll be transformed. It's work, that's how it all happens. And the work is all done because of love.

The whole basis of the relationship is complete trust and love, which develops not all at once. I never trust those quick loves, to tell you the truth. They come and they go. Real love grows over a period of time. As you work with a teacher and you see your life change, when you see that their motives really are pure and you throw your suspicions aside, then the love begins, the connection begins, you learn each other's names. If your spiritual teacher does not know your name, you're in hot water. It means that you're on the outer periphery of the student body, which is maybe where you belong for a while. But if they don't know your name, personally, then they're working with you, perhaps very profoundly, inwardly, but you haven't reached a close level of contact yet. You have to give them something to help them know your name. And the way you do that is by being fantastic. You have to be a fantastic student. You have to glow, you have to meditate well, you have to do profound acts of self-giving. Then they learn your name. There's a reason to learn it. Until then you're an interesting commodity. You're someone they're working with, but you're with the twelfth-degree black belt and you're still out in the first or second degree. There's no need to know your name, they can just show you some basic things and you have to work on them.

Most of the teaching is not done physically as I suggested before. It's done inwardly. When you meditate, you should always think of your teacher if you work with an enlightened teacher first. Don't focus on them the whole time. Some people like to focus on a teacher's picture when they meditate. It's neither a good nor bad practice. I don't recommend it to my students only because I know that most of them would start looking at my picture when they meditate and they'd become dependent upon it and it would be kind of culty in my opinion. It does work, but I don't think people should do things just because everybody else does them. It has to be something that you want. I don't think it's wrong if you like to do it, if you like to meditate on a picture of your teacher, but you shouldn't do it the whole time throughout the whole meditation, that's ridiculous. You might want to look at the picture for a couple of minutes to begin with and if that helps you connect with their consciousness, then you can close your eyes and meditate. But I don't even think you need the picture, personally. I think the thing to do is to chant their name, maybe seven times, nine times before you meditate, either silently or out loud, think of them. Think of the last time you saw them or a neat meditation you had with them and that will access their consciousness, then close your eyes and meditate.

You see, it's so easy to get stuck in the image of a teacher and forget that they're not the body, they're light. But your teacher will guide you in all your meditations, if you choose to be guided by them. The teacher will visit you in dreams. Very often I go out and visit my students or just people out in the world in dreams, in my dream bodies, and give them instructions, show them things. However, if the teacher gives you a particular piece of advice that's important in a dream you should always check with them to make sure that you didn't fabricate it with your own mind. I've had students who say, "Well, gosh, you came to me in a dream and you gave me my spiritual name." Or a mantra or something. And it's been nonsense. I didn't do that at all. Whereas other people have had dream experiences that have been very valid and very real where I've actually come in my dream body and visited them and shown them different things.

A lot of the things that I have to teach people I can't teach on this earth. Their minds can't understand it, so I come in dreaming. In the astral I can explain things, most of which they usually forget by morning, when they wake, which they should. The physical mind can't contain it. But other parts of their being will remember. They'll just vaguely remember that we talked. It doesn't matter, you don't have to remember, it's all stored inwardly, for when you need it.

After a period of time, when you're really getting closer to enlightenment, you have a closer association with the teacher. It has to happen. You need to spend more time together. And that happens of its own accord. The teacher will tell you. You don't have to try and sneak in, the teacher will see you in the meditation hall and just give you some work to do, perhaps initially just to check you out, help you grow a little faster, when that's necessary. The teacher may choose to ignore you for a long time to just see if you're humble, to see if you're interested in sticking around, without being patted on the head all the time. If you're going to complain all the time and want attention, the teacher will have nothing to do with you, if it's a real teacher. Oh, they'll let you stay in the community, they'll meditate with you and see you, but they don't want to work closely with you because you still have such basic things to work out. You don't need that close contact. The close contact is only useful for people who are at the more advanced end of the spectrum.

Also remember, enlightened people are terribly sensitive to everything. While they go out in front of hundreds of people and meditate and do public meditations and things like that, that's different, they have their shields up. But as Ramakrishna said, the paramahamsas, the liberated souls, only associate with the pure of heart closely. It's just very uncomfortable otherwise to be with someone who's all caught up in ego fixations and still has hostilities, even if they're subconscious. You'll notice that the people that the teacher often surrounds himself or herself with are not necessarily heavyweights, in terms of meditation ability. A lot of the people who work in our offices and I spend time with, aren't my best meditators, they're not the most advanced people in the community at all. Actually, most people can meditate a lot better than they can and are more spiritually advanced. But they have purity. They have developed that side of their being and it's very easy to be with them. They don't have a lot of subconscious, mean motivations. That's all worked out. They're progressing in their own way.

There are so many sides to this teaching process–thousands, millions, so many dimensions to it, planes. It's really quite exciting. But it's not necessarily the way it appears to be. All you have is your heart to follow and your intuition. Everything else is unsure, which is what makes it exciting. My recommendation is to learn as much as you can, from all your teachers. Life is your teacher, death, your friends, your family, everyone, everything. Don't try and run away from yourself, it doesn't work. You go with yourself wherever you go.

Find the best teacher you can find, whoever you feel is not only a good teacher, but someone you feel comfortable with. Someone might say, "Oh yes, Rama, wonderful, he's an enlightened teacher. But gosh, I just don't feel comfortable with him, I feel more comfortable with *beep*," (Rama laughs) with someone else, whose name we won't mention. Why won't I mention it? Well, you have to do some work, I mean there has to be some adventure here. If I give you the names and addresses of the eleven others, maybe they don't want you coming to their door. Maybe the test, part of the test, at least to get in, is that you have to find them. It's hide and go seek. And then you have to believe them. I mean, I could just be making all of this up. Maybe I'm not enlightened. Maybe it's an extra double bluff, where I'm just saying all this so you'll just think that I am, you see? Who can tell? You can tell. You can tell and your heart can tell. That's the only way you know.

You must trust yourself and trust life. Life will never let you down. It will put you through some unusual experiences, but you need them. You must trust life and you must listen. And don't be hasty, there's no rush. Find whomever you feel is the most advanced being in this world you can study with, you need a physical teacher, and go and see them and spend time with them. You may be uncomfortable with it sometimes. You may not like all the people who are there. It doesn't matter, learn to love them. Don't look at their faults, look at the good part.

When you admire a spiritual quality in someone else it will become stronger in your own being. Everyone has limitations, you have limitations, I have limitations. So what else is new? Look at the bright spots. Look at the sunrises and the sunsets. Look for the beauty, we all know about the horror. Follow the light. And if you're not meant to have a fully enlightened teacher at this time, be humble, accept that! It's not time, it wouldn't help you. Do you think God is going to hold that back from you when it's time? Eternity does everything perfectly. When your hour comes up, it'll be there. Until then, there are other things to learn, don't complain.

Learn from the wind, the tide, the books written by teachers. Don't depend on books too much though, please. You know, people over-read. They read too many spiritual books and it's confusing. They get too many ideas. Find a few good ones and read them again and again. I have 12 that have influenced me profoundly and I just read them again and again. Oh, I like to dabble and read this and that, but I'd rather read a good novel, to tell you the truth, or go to the movies. But it's hard to find books that are high enough, is what I'm suggesting. Most of them are very dogmatic.

If you're fortunate enough to find a fully enlightened teacher and recognize them and you get in the door, then you've just begun. Now you're at day one of school and you've got a long way to go. Do well with that. Be excellent. Have spiritual dignity and poise. Avoid "in" groups. They'll just slow you down. There are no "in" groups. The "in" groups are the "out" groups in spiritual practice. The cliques–all they do is hold themselves back. The people who do the best are independent individuals, who love others and see others, who make friends, but who are too busy growing to get wrapped up in these little personality cliques.

Try not to associate with the same people all the time in your spiritual group. It gets rusty fast. You hold each other. If you're seeing the same people all the time, when you see each other, you see the way you were the other day. You hold each other back, you fixate each other with your ideas. You should be introducing new people into your life constantly. Oh, if you have a few people who you just click with, that's wonderful. But click with them, don't be a clique.

You have to change constantly and always be new in this process. And you have to realize that you're working with someone who's enlightened–you've never seen him yet. You've only seen the part that they have chosen to show you. Remember, they're more in control of the situation than they let on. Enough said. Spiritual teachers and the enlightenment process. Good luck. You'll have it.

ADVANCED MEDITATION

There is no end and there is no beginning. There is only eternity. Eternity can be warm, assuming the shapes we love, the petals of the beautiful flowers of existence. Eternity can be cold and ruthless–the solar systems and worlds which begin and end, the winter of our death and then the spring of our rebirth. As human beings, we try to understand, in the brief span that we're given here in this world, why we're here, what we should do while we're here and where we'll go from here. And, of course, we wonder how much time we have.

At first glance, we appear to be people. The world appears to be physical and solid. There appear to be universes, stars, planets, our planet, seasons, different species of animals, plants, protozoa, bacteria–the visible universe. There are many universes, countless universes, and many of them are invisible. As you know, we call these the astral planes, but they are as real as this world is and they're filled with beings and forms that have life spans, as do the beings and forms in this world. They too wonder about the nature of existence, where they've come from and where they're going to and how much time they have.

Meditation is wondering. It is both wondering and wonder at the same time. When we meditate we quiet the mind and open ourselves to our limitless possibilities. As a human being you are capable of a higher level of perception than you may now be cognizant of. You are not really who you think you are. There are many selves inside you, not just one. In introductory and intermediate meditation, we seek to know ourselves. We get a sense of the countless selves within our self, the different forms that they take. We become acquainted with them. We find that some selves agree with us, some don't. Those that don't seem positive or helpful we push aside. Those that seem progressive we enjoy.

Meditation means the cessation of thought. For years, we practice meditation, like any art, and we get better at it each day. In the beginning it's just enough for us to sit down and focus our attention for twenty minutes or twenty-five minutes, to chant a mantra for a minute or two to start, practice a couple of gazing exercises, concentrate, and to try and still the mind as best we can–and if we can't stop our thoughts, to ignore our thoughts and just let go and feel. Feel beyond our thoughts.

Our thoughts will swim around and talk to us while we're sitting there, make fun of us, ignore us. We'll think about everything that one can think about. But if you pay no attention, if you don't look in the direction of your thoughts, you meditate. Your consciousness expands. You are no longer focusing on the thoughts, but now you're increasing the spectrum of your focus. As you meditate, as a singular meditation evolves, you'll find the nature of your thoughts will change.

At the beginning of a meditation session your thoughts will be relatively earthbound; you'll think about yourself, your world, problems, difficulties, and anxieties. Then as the meditation evolves, your attention, as it passes into higher realms of consciousness, will cause a resulting change in your thought patterns. Your thoughts will become more pleasant, more creative. You'll think about positive things you can do, good feelings will start to flood your being, feelings of hope, joy. You'll have visual experiences–you may see flashing lights, hear bells, feel energy changes inside your body, have a sense of being weightless, as if you're floating, and feel altogether pleasant.

Sometimes you won't feel pleasant during a meditation session. Sometimes it just seems like it's an uphill run. But then when you get to the top, the view is rather beautiful and breathtaking. You should learn not to judge your meditation. Just meditate, do your best, set a minimum period of time and meditate. When that period of time is past, stop meditating. If you're inspired to keep going, keep going by all means, but don't meditate less than a specific time. If you're a beginner, it's good to meditate for twenty minutes or a half an hour twice a day. If you're more advanced, 45 minutes to an hour, two or three times a day.

It's really not necessary to formally meditate longer than that. Naturally, if you're going to a meditation session with your teacher, as my students do with me, we may meet for three or four hours. During that period of time, some will meditate, doing the defined meditation session when I formally meditate. Others will meditate the entire time that I'm there. Others will meditate even before I arrive. It depends on their level of attention.

We have longer meditations, we have spontaneous meditations. After you've been meditating for a while, you'll just be sitting in a room, your living room, talking to a friend at a restaurant, working, and suddenly you'll feel yourself enter into a meditative state.

You'll find that it will always come at the right time; it will never interfere with your work or with anything that you have to do on the physical plane. Sometimes these meditations occur because our soul is reaching to the infinite, even though our mind is not conscious of it. Sometimes they come because a being, a spiritual teacher, or something or someone else is reaching out to us and filling us with something, giving us an inner present.

For most people this is meditation. Getting up in the morning and as soon as you get up or whenever you get up, meditating and never leaving the house until you've meditated. Your mind is most receptive at this time, even though it may seem more difficult to meditate because you're a little sleepy. Still, the mind is quiet, you haven't been thinking, so you'll find it easy to meditate. Meditate then for half an hour or an hour. Then, don't think about your meditation. Go out into the world, do your best all day, try to think higher thoughts, try to be kind and compassionate, but don't let people take advantage of you. Then at noon, try and meditate again for a few minutes.

I always meditate every day at noon, the time when the kundalini is the strongest. If you have to work at noon, at least try and think about eternity, think about your ideals, what you're trying to do with your life. Feel the pulse beat of the universe. It's very strong then. Try to meditate at sunset or in the early evening. It's very easy to meditate at sunset; there's a feeling of peace and there's a transcendental awareness from about 4:00 in the afternoon on. It's a very high energy time, from about 4:00 until about 8:00 or 9:00. Try to meditate then, before you start your evening. If you've been out in the world or working, that meditation will clear off all the energy you've picked up during the day, the unhealthy energy, and it will balance you and progress you.

Some people like to meditate for a few minutes before they go to bed. You won't really gain quite as much from this meditation because you'll be sleepy, you won't absorb as much. But you can gain something.

One who practices basic or intermediate meditation is learning to still their thoughts; trying to get on a regular schedule with meditation, which may take a while; getting used to meditating a couple of times a day and never missing; learning what the different basic experiences are like; and of course, dealing with the resulting changes that occur in your life from your forays into the infinite.

As you meditate and you move from the introductory phase to the intermediate phase, your life will begin to tighten up, you'll change again and again. You'll become smoother, more collected and crazier, in a positive sense. You'll begin to be yourself. There'll be an ease to your being, a deeper joy to your life. You'll see your own eternality. You'll remember a little bit more of who and what you are. And you may never go beyond this point in this life, if you just can meditate regularly.

Try to meditate with a group, hopefully with an advanced teacher, once a week or so if your lifestyle permits that or by yourself. Just reach to God, and you'll feel God and you'll feel eternity. Light will come into your being and you'll have a remarkably beautiful life. The world won't necessarily change but your understanding of it will, and therefore the world will change. A tree won't appear to be a tree anymore, a person a person, an experience an experience, because you'll see level upon level within it and beyond it. Your attention will no longer be confined to the physical body and the physical world.

If you never go further than that, then you've advanced to a very nice, safe place. And when death comes, it won't frighten you. And when life comes, it won't frighten you or excite you. You'll care more for those around you and you'll be able to do more for them, because as your own awareness advances, everyone who comes into your field of energy is positively influenced. This is as far as most people get.

Then, of course, there's graduate school. Graduate school is advanced meditation. Advanced meditation assumes certain things. It assumes that one has meditated for many years, five, ten, fifteen years, and learned to meditate well. You can meditate for an hour, stop your thoughts completely at some point in the meditation, even if it takes you half an hour or forty minutes, and enter into a timeless state of existence. You've worked out the basics in your life. You become a very nice person.

You can't really go into advanced states of meditation if you're holding a lot of baggage in your hands. You're too heavy. Over the period of years that you've been meditating and studying and practicing, you've let go of your attachments. You can live in the world and have friends and family and possessions if you like. But you don't take them all too seriously because you know that death removes everything. And you feel that death is every moment, as life is every moment. You enjoy, but you don't fixate. If it all goes away tomorrow, that's OK, you trust God implicitly. The universe will always do what's right for you. You have this feeling.

Emotional storms may pass through your being, upsets; the sea of life is not always smooth. But these things don't affect the deeper you. You have a link, you've established contact with your deeper self. You no longer envy others. If someone gets the larger piece of cake, you're happy for them. They'll get fat and you'll stay thin. You feel a comradeship, a kinship with life, a deep love of nature and existence. Like the whales that we see here off the California coast this time of year in February and March, it's just enough sometimes to play. As I'm speaking to you now, I'm looking out a window and there's a whale playing in the surf about 150 yards out beyond the beach. Every once in a while it surfaces and it just plays in the waves and goes back under.

The self plays among the waves of existence. It surfaces, it comes up for a while, and then it disappears again. We are that self, playing in the waves of existence as my friend the whale is–I've just spotted it again, breaking through. In deeper meditation, then, we're no longer concerned so much with putting our life into order. We live in a spotlessly clean house, our papers are in order, there's no extra accumulation in our closets. In other words, you lead a totally tight life. Your relationships are as good as they can be, you don't feel the need to possess anyone or be possessed by them. You've learned to love, to share, to be fair, and to be humble. Your only real concern in life is either being absorbed in eternity or working for the welfare of others. And there's still time to have plenty of fun. You're very busy, reflective and the thousand voices of existence speak through you. This is the preparation.

Anyone who really practices advanced meditation has spent quite a bit of time, of course, doing karma yoga. You have to work for others. Usually such a person will live in a spiritual community where they have the opportunity to give to others, as the personal family doesn't mean as much to us. The personal family is a fixation. Not for you, perhaps, but for people who are advanced meditators. You can enjoy your family and your friends and your career, and that's fine. There's nothing wrong with that.

A person who practices advanced meditation has gone a step further. It's like joining an order of spiritual aspirants. The family, career, money, the things that most people strive for don't mean that much to you. You may have them, you may not. But usually such people don't have families anymore. They're usually not married, some are. They usually don't have children, some do. But the chances are, if they've become an advanced meditator, they will not marry or have children because it demands too much time. This isn't selfish, it's just that God is directing them in another way. If they become an advanced meditator after they've had children or married, they may choose to leave their family, feeling that it was a nice stage that they went through and now eternity's pulling them in another direction. They know that God will take care of their family as God would if they died, which they have, because in advanced meditation we die and another self is born.

Or, they may choose to stay with their families and see that it is the dharma for them to be with their children, with the person that they married, and that they can practice selfless giving right there. It's a wonderful opportunity to raise their children without trying to make them into anything special. They're not trying to make them into spiritual aspirants, but just let them be and give them what they need to love and be kind.

But, you see, when you enter into the world of advanced meditation, you no longer fixate on an individual. It is not your husband or your wife or your child or your parent that matters anymore. I realize this may be hard for either you to accept or for the child or the parent or the husband or wife to accept, but if they truly love you, they'll understand.

I was raised in the Roman Catholic Church, and it was understood that if you became a priest or a nun, your family would understand that. You'd chosen another way of life. You weren't expected to marry or have children. You wouldn't see your family too much because you'd given your life over to God. That was understood. Well, people who practice advanced meditation have done that. It wasn't a hard choice to make. No one forced them into it. As they progressed spiritually, those things just didn't matter. It's easy.

Now, you shouldn't be afraid that if you meditate, you will suddenly feel that way. Meditation will give you a clear mind and a solid purpose and a wonderful life. As I said before, most people won't go beyond that. It's only by your personal choice, something in you will elect to go to a higher level of power and knowledge. Then you'll choose a different way of life and it will be fun for you. You won't miss anything. You don't even have to force yourself to give anything up.

Such a person can live in the world on their own, which is unusual, or they join a spiritual community. Spiritual communities come in two packages basically. One package is the ashram where everyone lives in the same building or on the same grounds, like a monastery or convent. You get up in the morning, early in the morning, usually, and you meditate, and then you may work in the community, helping to sustain it, or outside of it. You go to work all day and you come back in the evening, and there may be a group meditation or private meditations. You get together with your friends and spend time. It's a big family; it's like a kibbutz. The single-family unit is nonexistent because you just feel that it's selfish for you to devote your life to one person. You don't just love the one—you do love the one but you love the many also. Your politics have changed. You've become a larger being. If everyone felt this way there would be no wars, no hatred, because you don't have to rush to defend anything because you love everything.

The other type of community, of course, is like the one we have here at Lakshmi, and that's where we have a spiritual community but everyone lives where they want to. Many of the people in the center live in the same area. I recommend certain areas to live because of their power, and most of us live near each other and we see each other at the supermarket, or whatever. People get together and go to the movies or on hikes or meditate together, but everyone maintains their own independent domicile. Some students live alone. Some share places with each other. And in that way, not only now but as they grow older, there's no loneliness. There's no loneliness because when you meditate well, you feel eternity. How could you ever be lonely? You just feel God's love for you and that sustains you. It's totally clear; it's part of every aspect of your being.

Of course, whenever you want to do something at night you just call up one of your friends and get together, or a group of them have dinner together, whatever. There's so much love between people, there's just not a sense of absence. That's what a spiritual community is for. You join it, it feels right, it's a group of advanced souls who have had many, many lifetimes, many incarnations, in which they practice spirituality, who now work together and play together and enjoy their lives in a very different, but very fulfilling way.

Meditation is a way of being, and it assumes so many shapes and forms. But there is a spirit that guides us, if we will listen. It speaks softly. In order to hear it we must still our thoughts and meditate.

Advanced meditation is the entrance into the superconscious. When you can successfully stop your thoughts for a period of time, you've started to move into advanced meditation. In advanced meditation, we not only pass through other planes of consciousness or awareness but we become them.

There are primarily two levels of what we call samadhi. Samadhi is a Sanskrit word for the advanced states of meditation. There's salvikalpa and nirvikalpa samadhi. Some people say that there are a few other levels of samadhi, which are beneath salvikalpa samadhi. But from my point of view, it's sufficient to say that there are two.

Salvikalpa samadhi is a rare experience for most people who meditate. It not only means stopping all thought, but the awareness of this world vanishes totally. Unless you've had many high births, unless you've practiced self-discovery for many lifetimes, it's unlikely you'll experience salvikalpa samadhi in this lifetime, unless you have tremendous intensity, unless you just burn and ache for God, for eternity, for absorption, or unless you study with someone who is enlightened.

If you study with a fully enlightened teacher, a liberated one, then that person is samadhi. They are just a being of light and when you meditate with them, particularly in person, they have the power to give samadhi. That is to say, when they meditate with you, if you meditate well, they can actually bring you into some of the lower levels of samadhi at will. But they will only do that, of course, if you've developed yourself sufficiently so you can retain that light.

You have to be somewhat formable. You can't be too rigid anymore. If you've done your homework and meditated for a number of years, then they can transmit samadhi to you. You can experience it on your own, but you have to meditate very, very intensely with complete willpower and purpose for long periods of time. That's why most people go to a teacher.

I am a multilevel teacher. I teach introductory, intermediate and advanced meditation. And of course, I run a spiritual community called Lakshmi, named after the Indian goddess of beauty, purity, and prosperity, which opens its arms to people who are beginners, people who are on the intermediate level and advanced seekers.

My specialty is advanced seekers. I've had many, many lifetimes as a teacher, but what I really have to offer are the fine points that a person needs in advanced meditation. While I enjoy teaching people on the basic and intermediate levels to work them up to those levels, my real talent, again, is for the advanced students. You could say I'm like a ninth-degree black belt in martial arts. While I can still teach a beginner's class or an intermediate class, my real skill is not even teaching the first-degree black belt, let alone the lower belts, but those who are in the fifth, sixth, seventh and eighth range. But I'm happy to do either, personally.

The way advanced mediation is taught, the way I teach it, the way all enlightened people teach it, is through transference. We transfer light and power to someone else. We teach someone how to hold that light, how to eliminate their attachments, the holes in their beings through which they lose light. We teach how to become selfless, pure, and humble and just generally how to have a heck of a lot more fun with their lives. But the way we do it is all inwardly. We use the powers that we have developed in previous lifetimes, or in this lifetime, to bring a person through a series of altered states of consciousness, different planes of existence, very quickly, to expand their being, to dissolve their selves. It's a very, very complex, sophisticated process, which I really can't describe to you in words. It's something that you may have experienced if you've ever worked with someone who is enlightened. If you've sat with them and meditated with them, you have a sense of what I'm speaking of. Otherwise, these will just sound like words. You can do your best to imagine it, but it's nothing like it.

Advanced meditation is taught, then, in most cases, by a self-realized teacher, one who is liberated, enlightened–not through words but through transmission. That transmission does not have to take place physically, that is to say, the student doesn't have to be sitting across from you. But it's easier if they are because the vibration of the teacher is strongest in the physical proximity of the teacher. Once the student has spent some time with the teacher and learned the frequency, you might say, the student can be thousands of miles away and tune in and gain quite a bit. But it's still a good idea, whenever possible, to be in the physical presence of the enlightened teacher because it's not physical. You can hear the ocean from quite a ways away, but if you're standing right in front of it, it's easier. Then of course you can just jump in, like my friend the gray whale, who seems to have vanished from sight, which is not a bad thing for all of us to do–you can just be absorbed.

Advanced meditation has an awful lot to do with nothing. You become friends with nothing. First, you experience salvikalpa samadhi. Salvikalpa samadhi means that there's no thought, no form. As you're meditating there's no idea of this world, time goes away, and as you sit there meditating, there's no sense that you're sitting there meditating. You become consciousness itself. But there's still a slight sense of self. There's still a vague feeling, 'I'm eternity, I'm God, I'm all of existence.' You become that. Your awareness has merged with the transcendental awareness and it is the sense, without having to think about it, without you as a perceiver or a person thinking about it, that you are the transcendental awareness. This is salvikalpa samadhi.

If you experience salvikalpa samadhi even for a few minutes, you'll never be the same because to enter into salvikalpa samadhi, the human self, the old self, has to die in a sense, or be reborn. You're composed of an aggregate of different forms and energies, and those energies are held into focus or line by your past life development, what we call the samskaras. These are lines within your being. When you enter into samadhi, these lines dissolve gradually so you become less formed. You're freed each time you enter into samadhi.

For years and years, you enter into samadhi every day in order to attain liberation. For years and years you enter into samadhi every day and each time you enter into samadhi for five minutes or five hours, whatever it may be, it's as if your inner being, your substance, has melted down in the core of eternity. And eternity fashions a new self, which you find yourself with when you come out of samadhi. But you never quite come out. Each time you come out a little less, you might say, or your real self comes out a little more. There are different ways to talk about it. None of them will be exactly what it's like, except to say it's an experience of such absolute beauty, radiance and completion, such life, such depth, such joy, such indifference and such love, that nothing else is really like it or worthwhile in comparison, yet it gives shape, color and meaning to everything. In other words, there's nothing you should be afraid of. It's not going to take away your humanity. It will give it to you. But you will become more cosmopolitan, more conscious, more infinite.

Nirvikalpa samadhi, of course, is the pearl in the oyster. Nirvikalpa Samadhi–there's nothing we can say about it. I use the term "nirvana" interchangeably with it, meaning that you've gone off the board, you've gone off the map, there's no way to describe it. You've attained liberation, you no longer are bound by the cycle of existence. You can't be born and you can't die anymore. You just are, and yet you're not at the same time. There are all these paradoxical ways of discussing it, suggesting that it's beyond discussion, though it happens to some of us. It happened to me and to not me. You just become eternity.

When you're absorbed in nirvana, there's not even a sense of self as eternity. There's no way to describe it. Then you're liberated. Liberated while living, what they call a jivan mukta. And when death comes you won't be reborn, unless, of course, you're reborn, in which case you won't be reborn as other people are. You'll be reborn as a liberated being. While a number of years will go by after you've been reborn–if that's what happens, if you choose to be reborn to come back to help others–a number of years will pass and you may look like everyone else. But then one day you'll be drawn to the light, you'll meditate, you'll study for many years and then your liberation will return without you having to try a whole lot, in a way. It comes back. You dissolve again. It was never really gone; it was just dormant. It was sleeping for a while. But then your old personality comes back, all the selves from before and then liberation, of course, that which is beyond.

There's not really a whole lot you could say about liberation. The closest experience you can have of it is to come meditate with someone who is liberated. Many people claim to be liberated. Oh God, if we were to believe everybody who said they were liberated and self-realized, I mean, it's an endless list. According to "moi," as Miss Piggy would say, there are currently on this earth 12 beings who are self-realized. Eleven are men, one is a woman. Most of them are in the Far East, most of them you've never heard of and probably never will. They work with a very small group of advanced students. A couple don't even have students. They have friends, I suppose, but they just meditate a lot.

Liberated souls are a rare commodity in this world. They're no better–it's just you, a little later, in the next act or in the next play. But if you yourself seek to learn advanced meditation, that's really how it's done. You devote your life to such a person, you have to, but they will never ask it. A real liberated teacher never asks for a commitment from a student. They realize that that's absurd. How can you ask for a commitment? That's looking at it the wrong way. There's no commitment–a person wants to be there and they want to learn everything they can.

When I was a graduate student and I was studying English literature, working on my Ph.D., on my Master's, there was nothing else I wanted to do in the sense that I wanted to find the best teachers and learn all I could with them, study everything that was possible, learn the art. It was fun. I suppose you could call it commitment. I never thought of it as being commitment, it was just what felt right.

When you find a teacher, you devote your time and energy to what they believe in. If they think you should all go to the movies, you all go to the movies together because obviously you feel they see something beneficial about going to the movies that night, maybe just to have a good time. Or if you should meditate for five hours, you all meditate together. You surrender not to them but to the infinite, which operates through them.

Now, here, of course, as you know, I'm always a stickler on this point, this is where the abuse of power manifests with the phony spiritual teachers and phony gurus who tell you how to run your life and what to wear and what to eat and all that sort of stuff, what to do with your money. They abuse. People who don't realize that, of course, listen to them and ruin their lives. They [phony gurus] make themselves objects of adoration and worship. Real spiritual teachers aren't interested in adoration and worship. They like respect only because they realize that that respect will actually help the student. When you respect something you do better with it or for it. If you respect your teacher, you do better. You feel, "Gosh, this is someone very knowledgeable, I have to give them my best. There's a lot to learn from them." If you don't respect them, you're not going to give them the time of day.

Respect is good only because it will help you. But a real liberated teacher or liberated person, what can you do for them? They've got everything; they are everything. They don't need to be worshipped, they don't need to be adored. It's nice if you love them and you should because they love you. They're lovable. They're children playing in a very, very unusual world filled with vortexes of dancing darkness and light. A sense of eternity, that's what you need, a sense of timelessness beyond time and within time. If a spiritual teacher says something that doesn't make sense to you, you should always listen to yourself and not to the teacher. A little common sense would end all cults. Of course, one person's cult is another person's spiritual organization. There are many sides to it all, I suppose, I don't know.

Advanced meditation. I'd love to find some people to teach advanced meditation to, I've been looking for many years. I travel all over the world, lecture, and meditate, and I'll continue to do so. I'd love to find some people eager and enthusiastic about the higher aspects of the rebirth process, who have already put in the time and the energy to reach that point where they're ready for the advanced study. But there aren't many in this world. There are a few around. Once in a while I run into another one. But it's a very limited league at this time in this world. The next best thing to do is to work with those who are not quite there yet to bring them up to that level.

What I'm suggesting then, is that advanced meditation requires a level of complete dedication to existence. Complete dedication is not forced, it's easy. You don't think of it as dedication. The sign of a spiritual person, an advanced spiritual person, is that they don't think they're an advanced spiritual person until after liberation, and after liberation, you can say whatever you want because you don't really care, because it doesn't matter, because you're no longer a person. But on the way up, there's a way to do it. In other words, you've got to shine, you've got to work.

I remember in college, I had a Doctor Klein. He was a biology professor I studied with–he was a marine biologist, he was great. He used to tell us what it took to become a successful research scientist and how, for someone who became a successful research scientist–you know, there were so few positions available, there was a sequence they had to follow. At a certain age they would start. They'd do really well in college and really well in graduate school, they'd get a post doctorate. If they married, they'd hardly ever be home with their family, and even when they came on at a university, if they got a job at a university, they'd have to shine because there'd be four or five other people and only one or two would be able to stay, so they'd just have to work intensely all the time. You have to pay your dues; you have to be an apprentice, putting in 15, 16, 17, 18 hours a day. You have to do the same thing if you become a physician. If you become a physician, my God–medical school, internship, years of residency.

Anything that you want to bring to perfection–if you want to be a ballet dancer, if you want to be a first violinist with the Chicago Symphony or the London Symphony, you give it your whole life, it's all that matters.

Now you don't have to do that. There are lots of people who are happy–they listen to music, they play a little music, they study and go to college. There are lots of people who have a wonderful time in life just going to college and learning. College is a wonderful place. A handful go to graduate school, five or ten percent. And of those, how many go all the way? Do you see what I'm saying? It's a small number. You shouldn't worry about being in a small number because if you're supposed to be in a small number it will be fun, it will happen by itself. You'll just be inspired. If you're not, then that's not the track life wants to take you on at the moment.

The people at the top are not happier, they just have more responsibilities. Yet there is a way beyond this life and beyond death, and that is the path of liberation, and in order to be liberated, you have to enter into the world of advanced meditation. One path leads back to this world, to rebirth; one path leads beyond. Your soul stands at a crossroads, trying to make a decision. Flipping a coin. A nice image for the soul, I think.

I'm just trying to say that advanced meditation is not just a little bit of meditation; it's not just sitting and meditating. That's not advanced meditation. True, you have to sit there and be able to still all your thoughts and move into the superconscious awareness. But the reason you can do that is because you not only practice meditation for many years in both the good times and the bad times, when it was easy and difficult, but because of the type of life you lead, which doesn't mean it's a strict life. It doesn't mean that you necessarily have to be this or have to be that. You don't necessarily have to be celibate or necessarily have to not be married. There are variables.

It's not what you do, it's the intensity of your feeling that determines how far you go in the spiritual life. If you were that dedicated and that committed to sports, to medicine, to music, to business, to whatever it may be, if you take that same total level of dedication that anyone had to get to the top in any field, and apply it to self-discovery, the same thing happens. Except that when you get to the top in anything else, it washes away, it's transitory. You've devoted your whole life to working and endeavoring, and then you'll die and you'll lose it all, whereas here you'll never lose it. It loses you. The only thing that stays with you forever is your awareness.

To some of us it makes sense. We don't even know why. We're drawn towards the light like moths to the flame, and into the flame we go and burn up and then suddenly we become someone and something else, all the time. But you have to excel. You have to be exceptional. You have to be impeccable. You have to care about nothing but light, all the time. Then, of course, you put that caring into action, not in a sloppy way but in a perfect way, in order to enter into the world of advanced meditation. It's a very strict school.

The other schools, introductory and intermediate meditation, are easy schools. But advanced meditation is like graduate or professional school; it's much more demanding. In one year of graduate school, you might learn what you learned in five years as an undergraduate. But if you've done a good job as an undergraduate and if it's what you want to do, it's fun. You're ready for that level of professionalism.

But don't even think about advanced meditation until you've meditated for many, many years, burned your bridges behind you and the bridges in front of you and you can feel that your life is very stable. You've got your physical life together; your economic life together, in most cases; your emotional life is tight; you no longer feel the need to have someone in your life, rather your interest is in serving people. And you don't just think these thoughts because they sound correct, this is how you genuinely feel. When you wake up in the morning, all you think about is, 'What can I do for my spiritual teacher, or our spiritual journey that we're on, our community, or for others?' Or whatever the thought is, for God, it's the same thought, just taking different forms.

It's not an obsession, although you're definitely obsessed. It's just the way you feel. It's not right, it's not wrong; it just is how you feel. You feel that way all day long. You feel that way all night long. You don't care about anything else the same way. You're the same as the research scientist who has just given up his life to do that, the doctor or the artist, for whom nothing matters more than their art. You don't have much of a personal life, is what I'm suggesting. If you want a personal life, it's definitely not the world of advanced meditation. Advanced meditation is if you want a personless life, one filled with people and with love and with beauty but without that fixation. It's if you're brave enough to stand alone, even when you're surrounded by others. It's if you have the courage to live your convictions, even when things aren't going your way, even when you make a fool out of yourself. Even if you fail a thousand times, you get up a thousand and one times and each time try to be more creative, and at the same time you accept your destiny and accept what God gives you.

People who are advanced meditators don't worry about liberation and self-realization anymore. They're not trying to become liberated. They, instead, are interested in the welfare of others and aiding others in their liberation. They know that when it's time for them to be liberated it will happen. They're not even desirous of liberation anymore, that's just another attachment. There is no liberation. There is no bondage. These are just ideas in the mind. They're children, children of light. They're ageless, timeless, and wonderful. We call them saints, sages, fools, different names. They glow, those who practice advanced meditation, they glow.

Then, of course, there are the old hardcore teacher types like me who just sit around and tell jokes, realizing that what's the difference anyway, it's all timeless, and looking for someone who wants to play a good, fast tennis game sometime. If there's no one around to play a good, fast tennis game, then you teach them how to hold the racket and how to get the ball over the net, as patiently as eternity, and just wait. And if no one ever comes, that's nice too because what's the difference? You're the finite and the infinite, you're the beyond and the near, everything and nothing.

Advanced meditation is life. It's the pure acceptance of life in its totality. It's climbing up to the highest point and beyond and observing the view. It's being alone with yourself and facing the immensity of eternity, and even at its most awesome, even when it's most frightening and terrifying, embracing that which terrifies you and frightens you and loving it because it's God, you're God.

It's not being afraid to stand alone and do what's right, through life or through death, and realizing that you never had anything to do with it anyway–not because you were good or wonderful, it was just the way it worked out, the way the cards were dealt. There is no sense of self, but a great love for all, and total trust. You must have total and impeccable trust in eternity. Whether you have it or not, eternity's in charge so you might as well trust, you'll feel better.

Advanced meditation. Never leave the body without it.

DREAMING

You are a dream. You are a dream of eternal consciousness in the waking state. You are a dream of varied and infinite realities in the sleeping state. You are the dream of death in the deep sleep state, and you are awake in the superconscious state. Dreaming is reality.

All of life is a dream. There are no unimportant dreams. Dreaming is the borderline between life and death. It is the most sophisticated of all spiritual arts. Dreaming is existence. This world, this earth, the people upon it, the ages that have past, the stars, the moon, the experiences that each one of us has, our loves, friendships, hopes, dreams, ambitions, frustrations, from the moment of our birth to the moment of our death, that which we call the experience–our experience in this world is but a dream or a succession of dreams.

Normally when we use the word dream, we think of something that's insubstantial. Dreaming is something that happens at night. It's the dark side of the moon. When we dream we have experiences that don't seem to relate to the world we're in. Sometimes we may dream of a person or a friend, we may find ourselves in unusual circumstances or usual circumstances. Sometimes it would appear that the subconscious mind brings us a message in our dreams, tells us something about ourselves or others or the nature of reality.

Most people tend to forget their dreams. You might remember a dream that was very frightening or very beautiful, perhaps a very zany dream where you went through many different experiences, which were very disconnected. Some dreams bring us into the waking consciousness. The final dream that we have at night, before we wake up, is the easiest to remember.

Sometimes in a dream we will be ourselves. The person you are now will have a dream odyssey, an adventure. You won't be aware that you're dreaming. During the dream, you'll feel that you are wide awake, that you are having a solid experience. And if you're Susan, Susan will be in the dream as the central character or as an observing character.

Sometimes we will dream another self. In the dream, we will be another person. We'll have another identity, another name, another set of ideas, different conditioning. Sometimes we won't be present in the dream at all. It's as if we're watching a movie and the only presence, or consciousness, is that of the observer, the witness. We're watching the dream move back and forth, the characters, the players speaking, talking, acting.

Dreams bring us our fantasies. Things that could never happen in this world that we might want to happen, happen in our dreams. The person we loved who went with someone else can come to us in a dream and be ours for a time. Our worst nightmares, of course, come true in dreaming. All the things we fear can come to us and terrify us.

Most people don't regard their dreams very deeply. Dreaming seems to be an offbeat experience in our human cycle of existence. We don't question the fact that we have to sleep or that we have to breathe, that we have life. We don't question the fact that we need to dream. Science tells us that it's healthy to dream. If we deprive a person of dreams, if we keep waking them up every time they start to dream and then let them fall back asleep, if a person doesn't dream enough, they begin to exhibit abnormal behavior when they are awake. It seems that dreaming is a very healthy experience. It purges us. It allows us to process, or cycle through, many different emotions and experiences, radical feelings and tendencies, which would perhaps enter into the world of the waking experience otherwise, and which might not be socially acceptable. In dreaming, we can do what we want to. We can break all the rules and not hurt anyone, including ourselves, and then we can enter into the rational orthodox world after awakening.

There are other levels of dreaming, and that's what I would like to chat with you about for a little while, if we can dream along together. There is of course, the yoga of dreaming, in which we become aware that dreaming is not ephemeral. When we dream at night, what is actually happening is our subtle physical body, our astral body, another body of ours, is traveling. It's traveling into different worlds, different dimensions that our physical body can't see or perceive or enter into. And at night we travel to these worlds. There are countless astral worlds and we have experiences there. Some of the worlds are lower worlds, hell worlds, worlds that are infested with demons and horrible forms. And in these worlds, we see our worst fears. They do exist. Other worlds are heavenly worlds, beautiful worlds, worlds of color and light.

When we enter into these worlds in dreaming, we rarely remember them afterwards. We can remember the horrible worlds because we can relate to them. If we see a horrible creature or being or an unkind person, if someone's chasing us, those things can happen in this world it seems. But for most people, which is indicative of the spectrum of consciousness that most people experience, it's very hard to retain the higher astral dreams. When you move into a world of pure light, of ecstasy, various shades of spiritual coloration – since most people experience so little of that in this world, what we would call the world of the waking – there's no point of relation. When you wake up, you lose it because there's nothing to join it to in this world, whereas in this world there's hate and fear and violence and aggression. These are the dominant themes of the world of men and women. The perception of beauty is extant, but not as developed, so it's easier for us to retain the lower dreams.

Also, many people don't climb into the higher astral regions that frequently because they're bound by their desires and tendencies. As you are in the waking world, so you are in the dreaming world. If you're still attracted to the material worlds exclusively, if you're bound by fears and personality structures, then in dreaming you'll also be drawn to those worlds. Your hidden desires will manifest.

Dreaming is like going to Disneyland. This is why I like Disneyland. Disneyland is conscious dreaming. Walt Disney was quite a dreamer, and he created a world, as a matter of fact he even calls it the Magic Kingdom, where you can go to the Haunted House, Fantasyland, Tomorrowland, different dreams, and you can go and sit on the rides and have experiences. Well, this is what we do when we dream at night. We visit different lands and different realms.

In the yoga of dreaming, in which there are two primary stages, we begin by learning how to dream. At night, when we go to sleep, we meditate first and we plan to wake up in the dream, to become conscious during a dream that we're dreaming. You'll be asleep and you'll be engaged in a dream, perhaps you'll be walking through Times Square in New York City or visiting a friend's house. And of course you're unaware that you're dreaming. Then suddenly, you say, "Wait a minute! This is a dream! I'm dreaming. I know my body is lying asleep somewhere and this is a dream. And as a dreamer, I can now change realities at will. Now that I've brought my attention into this dream and I'm no longer locked into the movie where all I'm aware of is what's on the screen, I can actually realize I'm sitting here watching it. I can change movies."

It's like being in one of the Cineplex theaters where they have eight different movie screens, eight different little theaters, and you can get up and leave the theater and walk into another theater. And then another and another. You can choose what you want to dream. That is to say, you can travel and have conscious experiences in the dream state. You can go and visit a higher being in another world, see your friends, visit those who have left this world. You can dream your way to wherever you'd like to go or be.

You can dream yourself to a physical location. For example, let's say you're sleeping, and something's going on 100 miles away. Well, you can actually go there in your dream body, see what's physically taking place at that time, then come back, wake up and remember, know what was occurring 100 miles away during those hours of your sleep. Experiments have been conducted at several universities where people have demonstrated this ability, which is of course old hat to Tibetan dreamers. People have been able to report conversations exactly that were occurring at great distances, which they could not have possibly witnessed without going there in their body of dreaming.

In the first step of dreaming, we set up dreaming. Oh, there are dream exercises that you can practice to help. Before you go to bed, you should sit up and meditate on something that you're going to do in dreaming. Meditate for a while and have a nice meditation, and perhaps at the end of meditation, and perhaps for a few minutes at the beginning, you'll think of a place that you'd like to go in dreaming, where you'll become conscious. A power place perhaps, where you've been, and you'll go there in dreaming and become conscious that you're dreaming. You might go and meet someone in dreaming and you'll think to yourself, "Well, I'm going to go see so and so in dreaming and wake up in my dreaming when I meet them." And if you hold the image of the person in your mind, particularly if you focus on your third eye, the agni chakra, between the eyebrows and a little bit above, during your meditation, it will be relatively easy for you, with practice, to accomplish this. Now, there may be many, many months and every night you'll be practicing dream yoga and you won't get there. But if you don't give up, eventually you will.

That's the first state of dream yoga, and that's to become conscious in the dream world. Then the next step is, of course, to see that the waking world is the dream. Once we're in the dream world and we wake up there, then we see that this other world, this waking world, is just another dream and that there's no essential difference between the two. When you're asleep at night and you're in a dream, it's perfectly real. It is reality. Oh, later when we awaken and the dream fades, we say, "Well, gosh, it was only a dream." But in the dream world, when you wake up, if you recall the waking world, which has now faded, you'll realize that the waking world is only a dream. Eventually you'll see that there is no difference between the dreaming world and the waking world. Both are dreams. All are dreams.

Now, there's something that lies beyond the threshold of a dream. Beyond the threshold of a dream is waking, eternal waking, which is the superconscious. The superconscious awareness is beyond dreaming and sleeping, in deep sleep, beyond what we would call normal waking. It's a state of eternal, timeless consciousness, in which there's no sense of form or self as we've grown to know it. And with no self, there are no dreams. Perfect peace, perfect light, the awareness of your own immortality, beyond discussion. All dreams come forth from the superconscious and all dreams return to the superconscious. The art of dreaming is a pathway to enlightenment, one of the many. Dream yoga.

There are other ways to look at dreaming. We view and see life through levels of attention. By that I mean that as you're listening to my voice right now, you are having a series of perceptions. These perceptions are conditioned by your sense of selfhood. The way you regard yourself, the way you see the world and life, is something that you have constructed. Just as in a dream, we will have a completely defined reality – we go to Disneyland and we're going to go on the Pirates of the Caribbean cruise, and we'll ride the little boat and there'll be pirates all around us, doing the things that pirates do. We'll enter into a complete world for a while, with its own conditions, its own laws, its own gravitation. Each dream is a world in itself. The state of awareness that you are in is a dream. Now, when you're in the dream, you don't necessarily see that. It's only on stepping outside of the dream that we become aware that we were in a dream. When you're in something, you don't have proper perspective, is what I'm suggesting. Or we could say that you do have proper perspective, but it's only the perspective of the dream.

The art of the perceiver, of the dreamer, is to see and understand that all of the ways of seeing life that we have, within any given lifetime, are dreams, and to be able to step outside of our dreams and see them as dreams, which is of course another dream. This world is made up not of people, places, things and conditions, but of different dreams. It's a dreaming vortex. When you were a child, you saw the world in a certain way. You no longer see the world as you did when you were four. You may forget what it was like to be four. How you viewed life: your emotions, your feelings, the sense of taste, touch, smell, sound. But the world you're in now, the glasses you look through, are very different. When you were a child you were in the dream of childhood. Then you were in the dream of adolescence. Now you're perhaps in the dream of being an adult. Then there's the dream of old age. There are dreams within dreams. There's the dream of romance, there's the dream of marriage, there's the dream of the family, there's the dream of success and of failure, the dream of war and peace, the dream of art, accomplishment.

What I'm suggesting is that life is like a giant computer, I suppose. The computer is nothing without the software. The computer is just a big piece of metal, tubes, transistors, chips, diodes, and it sits there and it doesn't do much. What gives the computer life is the software, the programs that we run on the computer. Now, there is no such thing as a program. A program is a dream. We dream a context in an alphanumeric sense. We create a reality through designing a program. This is why I think computer programming is so fascinating and such a good art for a person who practices meditation, because it's advanced dreaming. When you write a program, you are practicing dreaming.

We write a program. Oh, perhaps to generate a list, a database, accounting package, a game, whatever it may be. We create a reality. There was nothing. And then we put one point in the center of a blackboard, and then there's one point. Then we put another point there and we draw a line between the two. Then there's a third point or a fourth point; we draw lines in different directions. We develop a decimal code. We gradually construct something. There was nothing originally, except our open perception. But then we put the pieces of a giant jigsaw puzzle together, and a picture forms. And we look at the picture, and if we look at it long enough, we believe that it exists independently of our perception of it, which is not the case at all. It is our perception that gives everything life.

When you die and your perception of this world ceases to be – which occurs every night when you enter the deep sleep state, where there are no dreams – this world goes away, it doesn't exist. This world does not have an existence that is independent of your being.

You create the world through dreaming. For example, I can sit in a room, as I am now, open my eyes and see a fireplace, a table, the sun has just set. I see the ocean, plants, a couch. I see these things. That's a dream, just as if I had fallen asleep and I'm having a dream and I see these objects. Now, I can change levels of attention. I can close my eyes and meditate for a moment and all of this will go away. And I can move through many, many different dreams without changing my physical environment. I can open my eyes and everything will become light. In other words, the couch will not be solid. The plant in front of me will not be solid. I will see the light moving in vortexes and swirls. I've moved into a dream in which things are not solid. I'm perceiving reality on another level, where nothing is solid. More of an atomic level, I suppose you might say. I can move into a world where everything talks to me. The flowers can talk to me, the couch, the life force in everything–I'll sense its meaning. That's a different dream. I can go beyond all of this. I can move into the superconscious. And suddenly the couch and the room and the ocean and all these things will go away, as if they've never been. There'll be no memory of them. They will all be eternity, without form.

There are countless dreams, countless ways to see life. However, for most persons, there are only a few. There's the dream of infancy, childhood, adolescence, the world of maturity and old age. And the subdivisions are few–desire, frustration, hope, anxiety. It's as if you've got a video player and you only have about 10 or 15 cassettes for your whole life; they last for a certain period of time. And there are little adventures that take place within each one. Meditation is the art of dreaming. Instead of just having those few cassettes, you can have thousands of them, and some of them are much, much more beautiful.

Life is not so simple. In its essence, life is simplicity, but it's also total complexity. You can have the freedom to change levels of attention, to move into these different dreams at will. Simply because you see life in a certain way doesn't mean that that's the way life is, that's how life is. Another being in another reality who's not physical doesn't see the world the way you do at all. Who's right? Are they or you? Neither. They're different dreams. Some dreams are more limiting than others. Some dreams are unhappy dreams. Some dreams are happy dreams. Some dreams are neither happy nor unhappy, they just are. The art of dreaming, then, is the art of changing dreams. The advantage that a dreamer has, one who's mastered the art of dreaming, is that at will they can change dreams. If they find themselves stuck in a certain level of attention, stuck in a certain way of seeing life, at will they can change that. You can change the channel. Everyone else has to just watch the same channel. But you can change the channel. A very advanced dreamer, of course, can not only have access to thousands of different realities but can go beyond all static realities, to infinite consciousness, to the superconscious awareness from which all these things come forth to the source.

There are places in this world where it's easier to change levels of attention, it's easier to dream – dreaming in the sense of when you're awake, in the waking state or in the dreaming state. Places of power. The American Indians used to go to places like this to dream. They were called dream quests. When a young man reached a certain age, or if at any point in life you had to make a decision, you would go to a place of power, a high hilltop, a lonely desert, a place by the ocean. It was usually relatively inaccessible. There were spirits and forces. The magnetic energies and subtle physical energies of the place of power were different. There were beings that existed there, guardians who would help you. You would go to the place of power, perhaps fasting for several days, three or four days first, to cleanse your body and develop your attention, to draw it away from the world, which is synonymous with food. You would focus your attention on eternity. You would go to the dreaming place, and you'd stay there and spend the night there. And at night you would be able to dream different dreams. Someone would come and visit you in your dreams, perhaps an ancestor or a spirit would come and tell you something that you needed to know, where your tribe should travel to, what you should do. You'd be given secret information by other beings; advanced beings in other levels of reality would come to you. The gateway between this world and other worlds would open.

Then there are those whom we call the enlightened, who are always dreaming. They are dream vortexes. They are moveable places of power. When you are with one of them, it's the same as being in a place of power. You can dream more easily.

When you go to a place of power, it's easy to change levels of attention, to change dreams – changing dreams not simply by going there and falling asleep and dreaming of "Darby O'Gill and the Little People," but in the sense that while you're awake, if you sit and meditate there, you'll find it very easy to change levels of attention. When you change levels of attention during meditation you can change levels of attention permanently.

You see life in a certain way, you're caught in a web, a maze that you constructed. You're in a program that you've written, and you can't get out of it. All you can do is experience again and again the same thing, the parameters of your life. But when you meditate, meditation raises us up for a while and we go beyond our world. It's like taking a vacation. When you take a vacation, it's easy to change. You leave the frame of reference, your place of conditioning. You go away for a while and it's easy to start over, to make changes in your life.

Now, the trick is, of course, when you come back, to realize that you haven't come back. And that the place you're returning to never existed before. If you take a vacation, go away, make a lot of good resolutions about how you're going to change your life and then come back home, then you'll fall back in the same patterns. Your conditioning will pull you back. But when you go away on a vacation, if you realize that when you come back you're not coming back, but you're going there for the first time, that the place you came from, where you lived before, no longer exists. It was a state of mind, and when you've now stepped out of that state of mind that's ended, and now you're going back, not to memories and experiences that you've had there before, but you're going there for the first time, then it's easy to maintain one's new dream or one's new level of attention.

Of course, we try to have nicer dreams and more beautiful and more complete levels of attention as we progress in meditation. Each time you meditate, in each meditation session, what you're doing is going through the bardo. You're trying to dissolve your current self and create a new self, a more refined self, a more beautiful self, a new dream.

When you go to a place of power, it's a dreaming vortex. It's like a supermarket of dreams. In the cities, in the places, the haunts of human beings, the same dreams are being dreamed by others and you're influenced by them. Your consciousness is like a blank video screen. There's nothing on it. Then a show comes on. A cassette is inserted and we see a program. The people around you dream very vivid dreams. Your parents, your teachers, the people who love you, the people who can't stand you–everyone is dreaming. They're all watching these programs on video. Now, your little monitor screen picks them up, because everyone is psychic. In other words, if everyone is dreaming the same dream, you're influenced.

In Nazi Germany, everyone dreamed the dream of the master race, an insane dream. Hitler was the dreamer. But his dream was so strong that it affected others. He touched their weakness, their subconscious desire to be superior and to destroy others in the name of that superiority. He influenced others because he was a very powerful dreamer. He had great power. And the dream spread. Now, as the dream spread through more and more people, more and more people kept dreaming the same dream, the weak were influenced.

You can be programmed by others. This is conditioning. Conditioning isn't simply that you're taught a certain language and a set of rules of conduct in a given society. That's a kind of programming, but that's a very superficial programming. The real programming of an individual, the real conditioning of an individual, is dreaming. When you are born, you have no dreams. Dreaming comes from the vibratory fields of attention in this world. Everyone who is here is experiencing a dream. If you would imagine that everyone on the street–let's say you go out onto a busy street, and there are hundreds and hundreds of people walking around to and fro, like Third Avenue in New York at noon. Hundreds of people walking around. But they're all asleep. If they're all asleep and they're walking around in a dream, and you were awake and you saw this, you would see that each one has a different dream. If for a moment you could access their dreams, if you could look inside each one, you'd see that they're all having these different dreams. And one will look at a restaurant and another will look at the same restaurant, and they'll see it in very different ways. Their dreams are different. Yet there are certain conventional patterns.

That's how it really is–everyone is dreaming, they just think they're awake–to one who is enlightened, who is waking, who is wakefulness. There are certain basic dreams that people have, and you've been imprinted. These dreams have been shown in your screen of your consciousness again and again, to the point where you don't know that they're dreams. Meditation allows you to change that because the dreams are not particularly nice dreams, they're not very healthy, that most people dream in this world: greed, suspicion, fear, desire, very limited dreams. Not a good show at all. When you meditate, you rise above that.

The key is stopping all thought. When all thought stops, or even detachment from thought, if you can just detach yourself and pay no attention to thought, which is the dream, then you can change it. Each time you meditate, you modify the dream structure. But then, after meditation, when you go out and see someone, or even if there's no one physically around, the people in the next house, in the next city, on the other side of the world, all their dreams are so strong, they're always affecting you. They're making inroads in your consciousness. As you try and change, it's hard, because everyone is at a basic level of attention; there are just a few basic dreams, and you're being influenced by them. You have to be very, very strong, you have to meditate very deeply, and that's why it's so important to find other dreamers, other people who meditate, and associate with them because all of you are entering more and more into the dreamtime together, and you're building up an alternate vortex of energy. If you live in a world of alcoholics, it's very hard not to drink if everybody drinks. Only the exceptional person can step outside that and say, "Wait a minute. Everybody's doing it, but that doesn't make it right. Nazi Germany–everyone's killing the Jews. But that doesn't mean it's right, even though they all say it's right. I have to go deeper to ascertain what is right, I can't accept these things."

You meditate and you find yourself in a world that's very barbaric. It's very primitive in its value systems and beliefs. And you say to yourself, "This isn't right, I can't accept this." But you will find that you will be pulled into other people's dreams. Whenever you have a relationship with someone, they dream you. And unless you're very, very strong, it's hard not to be dreamed. Two people fall in love. Well, they each have a dream of each other, they see each other in a certain way. They don't really see what each other are like at all. They have an image that they hold in their mind. Their mind is a screen and they project this image. And what they will do is, depending upon how powerful they are, they will assert this dream, and the other person will, without realizing it, begin to conform to the dream, depending upon how much personal power the dreamer has.

What I have to offer you as an enlightened being, my suggestion, in other words, is to see dreaming as a way of going beyond dreams. That's the yoga of dreaming. The old analogy of the Indian story is that we're going to take this thorn—we have a thorn stuck in our foot and we'll take another thorn, pry the first thorn out and throw both away. Through dreams you can go beyond dreams. "Through time - time is conquered," as T.S. Eliot, says. The idea is that we're going to have subtler and subtler dreams. Each dream will be more expansive, more complete, until finally the dream is so void it's the dream of eternity, of God realization, of nothingness, of everythingness. It'll be easier to step out of that dream into the waking state.

We're in a very deep dream, it's very thick, we have no idea that we're dreaming, then we dream subtler and subtler dreams, where more and more awareness comes in each dream. Finally, we reach a dream that's so subtle that there's very little difference between that dream and the waking state because it's the dream of the waking state, and then we move into the waking state, which is the superconscious awareness. That's the yoga of dreaming.

Also, in dreaming, it's easy to lose the old self. You're being chased by someone and that's yourself—your dream of yourself. Your dreams are chasing you down the street, kind of a nightmarish image of a person running. If you're a great artist, maybe you could do a picture of it and send it to me. You're running down the street and all your dreams are chasing you.

How are you going to lose your dreams? Well, the best way to lose your dreams is to hop into another dream. They can't follow you, or it will take them a while. Then, just as you come out of that dream and your old dreams are about to snag you, move into another dream and then another dream. If you go through enough dreams quickly enough, you'll lose your old dreams. And you'll end up in a new dream. Then of course, you'll have to lose that dream.

This is what I do when I meditate with people, particularly at a place of power, but at our regular meetings too. I bring people through a succession of dreams. They may not be conscious of it, but I have the power to change people's levels of attention. And I bring them through maybe a thousand levels of attention in an hour. Then they walk out free from their old dreams, not realizing it because now they're in a new dream, and in the new dream, of course, they've adjusted to their current level of reality and they've forgotten their old dreams.

I don't dictate the dream. I'm not programming people into a particular dream. Let us just say that it's kind of like I'm the Sears Catalog or the Whole Earth Catalog to your self. I just present you with thousands of different dreams, dreams that you might not have seen before. It's a videocassette catalog. There are thousands of movies that you can rent. You only knew about five; I'm going to show you a thousand. Now you will pick. I'll teach you how to pick, but I can never pick for you.

As a spiritual teacher, there's a certain code that I follow, and that is never to influence a human being in any way. The only thing I will do is teach you the art of dreaming, how to stretch your level of attention, make you aware of the thousands of different dreams. But you must make all the choices yourself. I assume no responsibility. The management is not responsible. You pick the dream, you try it out and see what it's like.

Now, my opposite is a person who's developed great power, as have I, or you could just say the power came after countless incarnations and meditation. My opposite is a person, like a Hitler, who has the power to change people's levels of attention. But he's a Darth Vader, you see. I'm sort of your Obi-Wan type. You know, I'll teach you about the force–Yoda, the ways of the force–but then you have to do it. Whereas your Darth Vader will program you. Your Hitler will say, "Alright, this is what you will believe." And their powers are so great, they can enforce that, they can imprint you. Whereas, I do just the opposite, I show you how to erase the tape, then offer you a wide selection of other dreams that you can dream which are nicer dreams, and show you that they're all really the same. The dream of horror, the dream of beauty, it's all the same in the sense that they're all just dreams. Then I will suggest, if you're really interested in our special catalog, which we keep under the counter, that there's something else. Of course, in the special catalog there are no dreams listed. It's an empty catalog. But that's only for particular customers who have been with us for a long time. We show them that catalog. It's the dreamless catalog.

So then, if you attain enlightenment, what that means is that you are dreamless. Or, you can come in and out of dreams if you choose to. But you'll always remember that they're dreams. Very often as an enlightened person, if you're a teacher, you'll experience the dreams of your students and your friends. They'll pull you into their dreams and you'll allow them to do it. They dream you. But you realize the whole time that they're dreaming you and while you're appearing in the dream for their benefit, you yourself are not affected by their dream. The smoke comes through the air, it doesn't affect it. If the smoke comes through the building, it will leave soot on the walls. But for the enlightened person, the smoke will come through the air and the air may appear to be cloudy for a while, but then the smoke will vanish and there's no trace. The air is clean. Enlightenment is the clear air.

Dreaming is the art of meditation. It's one of the mystical paths to enlightenment. There are other pathways. Each pathway is a dream. At the end of the pathway, there's something else. We can't say what it is, because there are no words.

Try to become more conscious of your dreams. Not so much even the dreams that you have at night, but the dreams that you have during the day. Realize that you are separate from them, that they are videotapes that you're watching. When you meditate, what you're doing is popping out the cassette for a while and seeing what it's like not to be plugged into anything in particular. Then as you meditate, the more deeply you meditate, the longer you can stop your thoughts or detach yourself from them, the larger the range of new dreams you have. The important point in meditating in the advanced states and dreaming is not going up. Going up is easy. But it's coming back and choosing the right dream. That's what we call the rebirth process. I did a tape about that, "The Tibetan Rebirth Process."

That's the art of dreaming. And of course, the art itself is a dream, which you can step into or out of, as you see fit. God is dreaming all of this. God is the dream of nirvana. Nirvana is the dream of God. Beyond the dream, there's waking, the dream of waking, and beyond the dream of waking, there's something that's even beyond dreams. Our special catalog under the counter. But first you have to become a good customer. After you've rented all our best videos–and we'll be glad to–and you've seen them and viewed them and you can do that at will, once you can change all the levels of attention, then we'll show you our special catalog.

Just one more word about places of power–it's very important where you live. Because where you live, the energies of this world, make it easier or more difficult to dream. In certain places dreams are very manifest and very strong. You should always pick a place to live that's good to dream in. One of the best places to dream is by the ocean, because it's a formless dream. If you have ocean on one side of you, if you live along the beach, it's very, very good because the vibratory forces of the human beings can only be on either side of you or behind you. But you've got ocean out there; it's easier to dream. The wind comes in. The vibrations move across the ocean. You get more formless. There's not as much of a locked-in vortex around you.

It's easier to dream by the ocean or on very high mountains. Very high mountains do the same thing. You're up above the vibrations. The vibrations don't tend to go into the upper atmosphere. That's why flying is so much fun, in a plane, particularly if you're not in a big commercial plane. Even there it's good. But if you're in a big commercial plane, with 300 people on it, each one of those persons is dreaming something and you feel those dreams. You're in a locked little space with them. But if you're in a private plane or if you fly yourself and if you're by yourself in a plane, you put it on autopilot, it's very, very easy to meditate, to change levels of attention.

The dream vortex has a limited physical radius, just as radio waves do. Radio waves don't go on forever, they go a certain distance and stop. Dreams, as projected by people, depending upon their personal power, will only carry a certain distance. The vibratory field of the people who live next door to you will project for maybe a hundred yards or two hundred yards. If the person is very, very powerful, if he's a politician, and he's dreaming about running for president and if his dream is strong enough, that dream will touch people all over the country.

Your dreaming is what you do in life. You dream your career, you dream your wife or your husband or your friends, you dream your death. We set it all up, is what I'm saying. But I'm suggesting that the way you set it up may not be the way you really want it to be. The cassettes you have–you think you have the choice, the ten cassettes; you think that that's all there is. And I'm suggesting that there are millions of them. It's an unlimited video rental library. There are many more than you realize. But you're not aware of the titles. You assume or take for granted, "This is life. Hey, this is what everybody experiences, this is the range of human experience, and I can pick and choose in this. This is the range of existence." But it's not.

The dream energies, the fields of attention that influence you much more than you realize, have a limited distance that they travel. In other cycles, there were even fewer. When there were fewer people on the earth, it was easier. Now that the earth is getting so crowded–there are three billion people on earth, there's three billion different dreams–it's harder. That's why it's good to go sometimes to a place where there aren't many people. A remote place, physically, it's easier. But then again you don't want to be limited to that place. You have to become strong enough so that you can go into downtown Los Angeles, where there are some pretty wild dreams, let me tell you, and not be affected.

Being a recluse is not necessarily desirable. It's good to take some time to go to a place distant from people. That's why the ocean is so good. Because if you're at the ocean, particularly late in the day, let's say, or in the winter or sometime when it's not crowded and there are not a million dreams on the beach, the dream of the body consciousness, when it's kind of lonely–you haven't gone a thousand miles away to be in a forest, it's not necessary, because the ocean is in front of you. When you go on top of a mountain, if you go to Mt. Palomar or Mt. Shasta or one of those places, when you get way up high, Colorado–this is why they had the caves up in Tibet, the yogis living in Tibet, because you're above that level. Now, it's harder and harder to get away from people. It's very difficult to just find a place where there's not an airplane or a person, but it's not really necessary.

There is something that you can do. And that's to live in a place of power. There are certain places that are dreaming vortexes. The energies are very strong in a place of power because people meditated there many thousands of years ago and the energy of the land itself – not the physical, but the subtle physical energy that surrounds it on the astral plane – is very open. Dreams come in and out faster there. The southwest United States is a very good place to dream. It's easier. On the East Coast and the Midwest, the dreams are fewer. There's less choice. It's harder to dream there. New dreams. The West is the new open horizon buffeted by the Pacific Ocean, and particularly California, which is on the ocean. If you live in that little coastal strip, it's very easy to dream there.

People came thousands of years ago here to dream, the Indians, and long before the Indians we know about, a race of very powerful dreamers dreamed here. They meditated here. And their force, their fields of attention are still here. There are subtle beings here that help. Certain places are dream vortexes. The people who live here won't really notice, who don't meditate so much. La Jolla, most all of San Diego, certainly, but La Jolla is a dream vortex. Malibu is a dream vortex. These are places where, particularly along the ocean or up in the mountains above it, it's very, very easy to change dreams. Mt. Palomar and some of the other ranges, the Anza Borrego desert, Joshua Tree, these are places, where, if you live there, it's very easy to change dreams. You'll just find you'll go through changes faster living in a place like this. The energies cycle and recycle constantly. It's very disconcerting sometimes. In other words, it's as if you're in a place where the weather changes constantly. It's raining, it's sunny, it's raining, it's sunny. In Malibu, La Jolla, places like that along the coast of California, you'll find that the dreams can change constantly. It's easier for you to view the different cassettes of existence in these places. It kind of counterbalances the civilization vibration.

Always try to live near water, if you can. Water is like a giant radiotelescope. It reflects and mirrors vibratory energies. If you can live near a lake or an ocean, it's really worthwhile. Try to live by water if you can. Living on a mountain is fine too. Now, not all mountains are dreaming vortexes. Not all places by the ocean are dreaming vortexes. There are specific ones. Each one has a different tonality, a different pattern and a different power. If you're really interested in dreaming, until you become absolutely adept at it, it's good to live in such a place or, if you don't live in one, to go there occasionally on pilgrimage. To go to the places of power and meditate there. And then when you come back, remember you're not coming back. You never come back – a new self and new world, and there is no back.

Dreaming. At the end of the dream, there's wakefulness.

GODS, GODDESSES, AND CARRIER BEINGS

There are many sides to the inner life and the outer life. And what makes life and self-discovery exciting is love. Love is the strongest force in the universe. It's not the only force in the universe, but it's the force of attraction, the force of balance. Love is the power that keeps the universe functioning. As individuals, we experience a limited type of love. We experience love between each other, sometimes love for country, love for beauty, love for food, love for God. But it is only a small particle of the universe. We experience only a small particle of love and truth. What we know as love is only a shadow, a glance of what total love really is.

Throughout the ages, prophets and enlightened persons have talked about love, and they've said that the way is love. These words have apparently fallen on deaf ears because while the world does seem motivated occasionally by love, most of the time it's by desire. I suppose we could call desire a type of love, but there's so little light in it. There's so little self-giving in it. Beyond the spectrum of love that we experience is a radiance of love, a complete, harmonious, endless and perfect love. And this love is engendered, is awakened, not simply by our own actions. This love is engendered very often by the gods, goddesses and carrier beings.

The universe has many stages. This is one small stage we're upon now. There are countless worlds. Not just worlds in a sense of material planets like our own, but there are planes of existence, dimensions. Each dimension contains billions of galaxies. They're endless because existence is eternal and infinite and the infinite has no end. There are different planes of being. We can say that God has different dreams and in each dream there's something else. In other planes of being there are other evolved forms of life. Many of these forms of life are not physical, they're etheric. And there are different types of beings who have etheric bodies. Most commonly, we talk about the gods and goddesses, very advanced beings with superhuman powers, who live far beyond our earth and who human beings occasionally have interaction with.

Today I'd like to talk with you a little bit about some of the different types of beings that you as a meditator, as a spiritual seeker, will encounter on your journey to enlightenment. There are essentially two classes of beings and many subdivisions–those who are more evolved than yourself and those who are less evolved than yourself. From my point of view, whether they have physical bodies or subtle physical bodies or they're just idea forms – they don't even have a subtle physical body, what some call the causal forms – it's really all the same. What matters is not the type of clothing that one wears but the kind of person that one is. If a being manifests as an etheric god or goddess, as a human being, as some other form of life, as a tree, a branch, something that we don't see in our world, in our planet, or as a lower form, there's God within all. All are God.

Yet there is diversity, and this is where discrimination comes in. Beneath our world, not in a physical sense, there are many lower worlds, countless lower worlds, where beings on various planes of evolution exist. Now when I say "below," I mean that these worlds are darker, not as happy. They receive less light. There are worlds above that are more luminous where no one has a physical body, where all are luminous subtle physicals. There are worlds that some refer to as the causal worlds, where everything is an idea form, an ideation, no body at all, just intelligence. All of these forms and beings are transitory. They are all whirled around by maya and by the wind of the samsara, by the winds of existence. They all come and go just as the flowers come and go in the springtime. They return into that eternal mist of creation and then they come forth again. None can die, but all pass through the cycle of death and rebirth. The timespan varies; just as there are certain insects that live only for a day, their entire life cycle is a day. Our lives are a day unto some of the beings who live for eons– so we appear to them.

There are noble beings, higher beings, who assist and help spiritual seekers, more than they realize. These beings are not usually disincarnate human beings. These days it's very popular for people to use what they call "guides." They reach out into the astral regions for these guides who they feel are disincarnate human beings – human beings who perhaps made a lot of spiritual progress and are not reincarnating or not incarnate right now. They reach out and try to be directed by these beings. In my estimation, this is a relatively dangerous practice.

Sometimes, of course, they reach out for beings who are not human in form, meaning they haven't had a cycle of human incarnations. And it's just like dialing phone numbers at random. You never know who you'll get. Very often the lower beings will impersonate higher beings. A person will be trying to channel, to have one of these beings come inside them. Mediums do this sometimes. And you may assume it's a higher being and it may show the signs of that, but perhaps it's not. These beings can be very clever. Just as someone can feign to get in your apartment and pretend to be a nice person, if you can stop them at the door it's a lot easier. Once they get inside your apartment it's very difficult to get them out sometimes, if they are very strong, perhaps almost impossible. It's very important to discriminate. While it's true that God exists in everything, we don't walk around drinking strychnine or eating arsenic, although there is as much God in strychnine and arsenic as there is in yogurt or milk.

All things are not good for human beings, all parts of the creation, in the sense that there are different vibratory levels and human beings have a specific vibratory level and this creation – the world as we know it, all the universes, that which we call existence, the part we see with our eyes or with telescopes or microscopes – has a certain vibratory energy and has variance within it. Saturn vibrates at a different rate than Mercury. One person vibrates at a different rate than another person. One universe vibrates at a different rate than another universe, but all these vibrations are within a certain scale. But there are other universes that do not vibrate in the same way ours does. And to open yourself to some of these universes, to cross planes, can be very destructive to your physical and mental being because they vibrate at such a different rate that it's quite destructive to human life.

Many people, when they invoke the lower beings through voodoo or these various practices or mediums or automatic writing and things like that, make a terrible mistake. They bring these beings from the astral world; they open a door that's supposed to stay closed. It's not meant to be opened. There is a ward in the hospital. There's disease there. It's contagious so they seal it. And only people who are properly equipped can go in and out. Now if someone opens the door to that ward and starts to bring the people out, the disease out, it spreads and it can be lethal.

There are worlds, which are not meant to be tampered with by human beings until they are very, very advanced and very strong. I raise this point only because so many people practice this channeling stuff. It's quite dangerous. Simply because you're naive and innocent does not mean you will be protected. I'm naive and innocent in many ways and people say bad things about me and try to do bad things to me sometimes. Christ was naive and innocent. The people in Auschwitz were naive and innocent.

You are eternal. No one can destroy you. But they can sure cramp your style in any particular life. Please don't feel that simply because your heart is pure and you're channeling and opening yourself up to different nonphysical beings that only the right ones will come calling. It's not true. Most of what we call mental illness is actually possession. Someone has opened a doorway to another plane of existence. And this plane of existence, it's not bad, it just doesn't fit with our life. Strychnine isn't bad, it is what it is. But you shouldn't eat it.

There are worlds, darker worlds, unevolved worlds. I suppose you could call them hell worlds. Some art reflects some of these worlds, if you've seen some of the paintings by Hieronymus Bosch and others. The painters, without realizing it, are seeing these worlds, some of them. They are worlds of constant warfare, constant hatred, constant violence and strife, constant unhappiness. We see a degree of that in our world here.

You see, the earth is an interesting place – earth meaning not simply this planet but this system, this cycle, all of the galaxies and so on – because you get a little bit of everything here. Sort of the smorgasbord of existence, all the planes touch in the physical. You see some of the highest and some of the lowest and everything in between. That's why our world is such a world of contradictions. There are some worlds where there's just light. There are some worlds where there's just darkness. We're in the middle, consequently it's a mixture. You get a little bit of everything.

There are lower beings and you should not deal with them. If they ever come to you, lower entities, then the best thing to do is to meditate, to pay no attention to them whatsoever, to meditate upon the clear light of reality, to just feel God and eternity. They can't stand light. They'll leave. Naturally, if you have an association with an enlightened teacher you should think of the teacher and meditate on them or contact them. Usually you don't even have to outwardly contact them. If you just think of the teacher, you'll see an energy will come immediately and chase these nasty little things away, or nasty big things as the case may be. Or if you have a close association with a higher non-physical being, cosmic god or goddess, they can come and help you and chase these things away.

Some people have had the experience of being physically restricted by these beings, the lower ones. You wake up from sleeping and you can't get up. Your body won't move. You feel as if you're being held down. But they go away after awhile. You see, these beings rely on fear, as do most tyrants, and misinformation. They try and make you afraid, and when you're afraid you become powerless, but they can't really hurt you. The only cases in which complete possession occurs are either when a person wants that; they constantly seek these beings to come inside them. Well, it happens sometimes. They make deals with them. Sometimes these beings will come and they'll promise you all kinds of things, and they can deliver–Mephistopheles. But there's a price that you have to pay. In other words, as they say out on the street, "If you want to play, you gotta pay." And it's true.

When these beings come, they promise to get you a person you desire, money, fame, and they can do it sometimes. Then you have to be willing later to pick up the check. And the check is that once they give you what you want, they'll take you over, drive you out of your mind. Sometimes they can kill. Some of them are very strong and very virulent. But they won't hurt you, they can't, if you meditate and if you're not interested in them. If you meditate every day there is a force, a shield of protective light, around your being. You don't have to think it there, it's already there. If you aspire and if you're not subconsciously attracted to these beings and forces, it's not a problem.

Now we might wonder why some people are bothered by them and others are not. Well, when you're bothered with them it's usually because you had an association with them in past lives. For example, a number of my students in their past lives have practiced witchcraft and things like that, different forms of occultism, which all of us practice in one lifetime or another, I suppose. When they reincarnate a part of them is drawn back to that study. They want to use the allies and different forces to do their bidding, and naturally I teach people not to do that but to seek light and enlightenment instead and not worry about all that silly stuff. But because there is a subconscious draw, they come back. The person may not think that they are interested in such a thing, but another part of them may be. Remember we are very complex. We have many, many selves.

I think the best way to deal with any of the lower world forces is not to deal with them at all, to keep your mind centered on light. Not to worry about them; they can't hurt you, unless you want them to. But just to pay no attention because there are too many higher beings to play with and have fun with who aren't harmful, who are helpful. If you know people who channel, who deal with entities and spirits and guides and all that stuff, I'd stay pretty far away from them if I was a real seeker. Not that they're doing anything wrong. They're doing what they want to do. But it is catching. It's kind of like a disease. These forces are very powerful. And after a while a person won't realize it but they will no longer be thinking their own thoughts.

How can you tell that your thoughts are your own, where they come from? It's very difficult. So many people who deal with these lower beings think that after they stop channeling, or whatever, the beings have left. But once they open that doorway, it's very hard to seal it to that other world. Once that doorway to that other plane opens, it opens all the time. Very often these beings will then begin to put thoughts into the minds of people and people will believe them. And after a while the voices of the beings will become louder and louder inside a person's head. This happens when somebody goes to do something really dumb like they try and kill somebody because they say, "Well, the voice told me, the voice told me to kill so and so." And the psychiatrist will say, "Well, this is mental illness, schizophrenia, the person had a latent this or that." That's not it though. These are beings that that person started to transact with on some level and then the person lost their ability to discriminate and started to listen to the being.

The only other instance in which possession can really take place is when a person is just very psychically weak. Now when I say "psychically weak," I don't mean when you had a bad day. I mean a person who has no power whatsoever. If you are listening to this tape you wouldn't be in this class because you wouldn't be interested in these subjects. We're talking about someone who's quite far down in terms of consciousness, not just a little depressed or a little out. But someone who has no personal power at all. Such a person wouldn't even be interested in meditation or anything like that. But you'll observe this occasionally. They're just very weak. They're manipulated by everyone and everything and they're very easy for a more powerful organism to affix itself to and enter into and take over.

Most of the destruction that takes place in this world, when you have a Hitler or someone like that, Mussolini and these different sorts, occurs through possession. These beings come in. They take over. They plant thoughts. They have no love. They seek to destroy. They get a weird delight from it. And a way many of these people became successful was by making deals with these beings. But deals aren't necessarily conscious. It's not as if you sit down and write up a contract. Allegorically that may be how we see it. It takes place sometimes inside, sometimes in dreaming. But a lot of successful people have been helped by both lower and higher beings.

The best way to deal with lower beings is not to deal with them at all. Don't be afraid of them. If you meditate and you seek, they can't hurt you. They can scare you. And then you learn to laugh at them. If you see one sometime, if you're meditating or whenever, and you see some horrible form, just laugh at it. Say, "Oh, come on, can't you do a better one than that? I'm not impressed at all." Then they go away. See, if they see they can't bother you or hurt you or affect you, they just go away. They get very frustrated. It's not going to work with you so they go pick on somebody else. But they do exist and we shouldn't pretend that they don't because sometimes if we underestimate our opponents we make a grave error, and also if we overestimate our opponents we make a grave error.

So realize that they are powerful. They can be very harmful. But if you don't invoke them, you shouldn't be bothered by them. And if they do come around, if you meditate, if you think of light, if you invoke a spiritual teacher, a powerful person, a powerful being, they'll be chased away. But if you still have a subconscious draw to them, they'll keep coming back. You have to be willing to go through your own being and find out if there are parts of yourself that are still interested in that sort of stuff. See that dealing in those levels and those worlds is antithetical to your own health. It isn't what you really want; there's no fun or light in there. The little powers that you'll get are nothing compared to the power of enlightenment, plus there's no happiness in it. When you realize that, you'll lose interest and then you'll evolve to a higher state.

The higher beings, of course, are just the opposite. These are the gods, goddesses, carrier beings and allies. There are different classes of beings, if I can use that term. We talk about angels, gods, and goddesses. They do exist. There are countless luminous beings. Very often you'll see them or one of their worlds when you meditate. Sometime when you meditate, you'll see what appears to be almost like a fairy world of castles and buildings. They're all made out of light.

They're very luminous. They're not really substantial. It's almost like a luminous fog. You're looking into a higher loka, a higher sphere.

The beings there come in two forms: they either have what we call astral or subtle bodies–same word, same term–or causal bodies. Now the astral beings – the higher ones or those who have subtle bodies, same thing – these beings are easier to see. If you meditate and if you're very pure, they'll come to you. They can't stand impurity. They won't come. Very often when I meditate you'll see lots of them all around me because they love the light. Their food is actually light. They don't eat like we do. They don't have to worry about losing weight (Rama laughs), only losing light. And they're very beautiful. There are two types. The first type is just the very innocent form, it's kind of the "E.T." consciousness, I suppose, these beautiful little beings. And they can manifest in any form that you like, sometimes as fairies or winged horses or, oh, all kinds of things. Most of the things that people have seen in this world, like winged horses and things, are nonphysical and some people have seen them. They're beautiful happy beings. But they won't go into a place where there isn't a lot of beautiful light. They're uncomfortable there. They vibrate at a very, very high rate. These are the carrier beings, that's what I call them. They carry messages and light back and forth between the planes, and they're lovely. They're like young, pure children, actually kind of silly some of them. And they exist in what we call the psychic regions or psychic realms.

Then of course there are the gods and goddesses. I'm not sure it's an apt name, but let's say much more powerful astral beings with subtle bodies. In this class, we would put some of the well known: Kali, Vishnu, Shiva, and others. Many of these gods and goddesses have different names in different cultures. In one culture, we might call her Lakshmi, in India. In another culture, we might have another name. The names vary, but the beings are the same. These beings can help you in your evolution. And sometimes you'll be drawn to a particular being or maybe several. You may have had something to do with them in your past lives. In a Greek life, you may have prayed to Diana. In this life perhaps it's Lakshmi – same being.

When you pray and meditate on these beings, very often they will help you. They won't necessarily help you in the sense of solving your life's physical problems. They won't necessarily interfere with fate. They won't make you a lot of money or cause you to have physical health or prevent an accident. They're not necessarily supposed to interrupt those things. Those are your karmas, your actions. You need those experiences for your growth and development. What they can do, however, is manipulate consciousness. Oh, occasionally they do make changes in destiny, I suppose. But it's not that frequent. Most of the time the changes that they cause are in the advancement of your awareness.

I don't think you should program yourself in trying to meditate or pray to the cosmic deities or beings, the higher beings. If you find that you're drawn to one without knowing why and you meditate on them a little bit each day or maybe repeat a mantra that is associated with them, if that happens by itself, that's fine. It's not something you need to do. You can just meditate on light, you can just work with your teacher, meditate on God.

You see there are different access points in this study. Some people like a human teacher and that's all they need to work with. Some people don't want a human teacher, they just want to work directly with the source. And that works well for them. Some people like to work with gods or goddesses or carrier beings. Some people don't want to work with anything in particular, but they like a mix. They have a spiritual teacher; they pray to a certain goddess; they of course orient to God directly, to nirvana, the unmanifest; they love the carrier beings, the little astral beings that come and visit, come in dreams. You don't have to choose one and you shouldn't try and figure out, "Well, what's the best? What would be the best ones for me to meditate on so I'll make the fastest progress?" That's not how it's done. It's all done through love. It's not a formula because one being won't be more helpful than another. One orientation isn't more helpful than another. What's most helpful is for you to have the right orientation. When you have the right orientation it all works very, very nicely.

Then there are the allies. Now if we can leave the old, luminous worlds for a moment here–as I've been sitting here making this tape, it's fun. As I talk about the different classes of beings they've been appearing in the room. It's marvelous. I'm sitting here by myself – I guess I'm not by myself (Rama laughs). When I've been talking about the astral beings, the room has been filled with them. Then, of course, when I started talking about the gods and goddesses and the other lokas, immediately there was an access-way there. When I was talking about the lower worlds, a few of them were sliding around. It's fun. You'll like being enlightened. It's certainly never dull.

Then as we enter into another plane, there are the allies, the occult beings. These beings are very difficult for humans to understand because they're really a part of us. We have different sides and different natures. Each one of us has a psychic nature, a superconscious nature, an occult nature, a physical nature – the different sides to us. And we have occult beings. In other words, a part of your being is in the occult dimension, a part of it is in the psychic dimension, a part of it is in the physical dimension, a part of it is in the superconscious dimension; part of you exists in all the worlds. It is as if you have limbs that extend into these other worlds that you are not conscious of.

The allies are powerful beings or aspects of ourselves that exist in the occult worlds, and spiritual teachers use them to help their students. The allies are absences. They are like antimatter. They are the exact opposite of anything. There is a polar opposite to everything. Just as we're in one universe, there is a polar opposite to this universe and the allies are part of the polar opposite universe.

Very often, I use the allies in my work. They are very powerful and I can use them to help people all of the time, but I can't really say that they are separate from myself. You could say that it's my opposite side or that I'm their opposite side. It's hard to find words for this, but they exist and they're quite helpful. All spiritual teachers have them.

Everyone has an opposite side. But in order to harness that opposite side you have to go through a very rigorous training program spiritually. Because the opposite side will destroy you unless you are very pure and quite powerful and quite lucky. Part of the spiritual training process that really isn't offered so much on earth any more – it was more in the ancient Egyptian mystery schools and in Atlantis – had to do with harnessing the opposite side of one's being. But it's hardly taught anymore at all because it's not really necessary. It's something from another cycle, another time. But some of us went through those schools and we developed those parts of our being, you might say.

Now then there are the guardians. Enlightened people don't work by themselves. There's no such thing as "by yourself." Otherwise it would be a very lonely universe out there. Enlightened people are part of a team and they work in concourse with a group of nonphysical beings, and these are, at least in the case of most spiritual teachers, what we call the guardians. There are places in this world, on this earth, that are access-ways to other dimensional planes. Now, you can move from one reality into another everywhere, but there are certain places where it's easier. If you want to go hang-gliding there are certain places where there's lots of wind and it's easy to hang-glide. Other places–no wind, no hang-gliding. These are what we call places of power. People go there to meditate. And when you meditate in a place of power it's easier to have an advanced meditation.

An enlightened person is a place of power. They're a mobile place of power. They come to you. A place of power is an absence. It is where it's easy to go through. Now, I suppose this might sound mad to someone who hasn't dealt with all of this, but then again it seems to be that the human world is rather mad with its cruelties and injustices and all that sort of thing. But anyway, there are places, and quite a few of them in the southwestern United States, where there are doorways to other worlds. But God in Her infinite wisdom has not left the doorways open. There are particular beings who guard these doorways, and I call them the guardians. It's interesting, if you read in Navajo and American Indian mythology, you'll find references to these places and to the guardians.

The guardians assume different forms. But if you ever see them, at least in the Southwest, most of them look like Indians, their subtle physicals, like strong, beautiful, virile warriors. These are great beings who are very beneficent. When you go to a power place, if you yourself are either quite innocent and pure or noble, that is to say you're trying very hard with your inner life, you're really doing your best, they can help you. The way they'll help you is, well, they can come to you in dreams, they can just open a doorway for you. They'll let you see in a little bit deeper. But they're quite detached.

Now these beings are very strict in their discipline. You see, there are different classes of spiritual teachers. Some spiritual teachers are kind and munificent and they pat you on the head. Some yell at you and give you a hard time so that you'll become perfect. But some are very aloof. They feel, and I can't say that they're wrong, that in order to become enlightened you have to work your way up. And they're not really interested in you until you get close to the top. They feel that's your problem.

Sometimes one of our parents, perhaps our mother, perhaps our father, is very kind to us, very easygoing, loving, we can't do anything wrong. Whenever we make a mistake, they help us to try and correct it. Perhaps the other parent is very stern. Well, these are different faces of existence. One isn't better than another, they take different places sometimes. Sometimes we need the sternness. It helps us develop. It makes us reach in a way we wouldn't otherwise. This isn't a cold indifference, but it's a knowledge that it's tough out there on the street and that the strong do survive, and that we need to become strong. The great warriors at the gateways, the guardians, are like that. They have very good senses of humor, I must say. But they're very detached. They won't acknowledge you until you've come a long way up. And even then it will be in a challenging way. They'll help you as they've helped me. But you have to prove yourself worthy, otherwise they don't really want to spend the time. Not because they feel there is anything wrong with you but simply because it's not their way, it's not their job.

The guardians help enlightened people. Let's say that you were a self-realized person your last life, or very spiritually advanced, extremely – which everyone likes to think and you can tell if you really were, perhaps, if you don't think that way, you shouldn't think that way. If you think that you were perhaps a very advanced being in your last life, chances are you weren't. But if you feel that probably everybody else was, then you might be. The humility is always a sign. But best not to think about it one way or the other, in my opinion. In any case, in my own experience I was helped by these beings and still am. I work with them even with my own students. We work together for their liberation. I've been self-realized in many lifetimes and in each lifetime when you come in, it's kind of like parachuting in. You don't know exactly where you're going to land or what's going to happen.

When you come into this world you lose your realization for a while. The maya pushes it away. Part of the way you get it back is that the guardians help you. The guardians do not physically incarnate. They're enlightened beings who don't take incarnation anymore. I'm an enlightened being who takes incarnation. The guardians and I are the same. I am one of the guardians and vice versa. But some of us take form to work in the world, some don't. We all like to work in the world and aid people in their self-realization. That's fun for us, as someone once did for us. That's just passing on something nice that was passed on to us. That's the way life should be.

In my own case, I had no idea what enlightenment was or self-discovery. I grew up in a world of high schools and junior high schools and the 60's and the drug culture and who knows what all. But I was brought, I was pulled, to certain places. I was pulled to places in Colorado, to places in California, a few places in the East too. Without knowing why, I was drawn to these places. When I would go to these places I was very high. I was drawn to read spiritual books, to meditate. At the time I didn't realize what had happened was that the guardians had pulled me to their places of power and when I was there, they were working on me. They were helping brush aside all this junk, this maya, so I could see again. Each time I would go back to one of these places, a part of me would return from a past life. And gradually my realization came back over a number of years, of course meditating and seeking and giving and so on, living in spiritual communities and things. But the guardians brought me back. That's the agreement we have. When one of us comes in to take a body, the others will bring us back.

Now, of course, I take my own students very often to these places of power where the guardians are because when we go there, these vortexes of energy, not only can I help them and the place itself can help, but the guardians sometimes help. Sometimes they just look on with bemused laughter because they get a kick out of beginners. But once in a while they'll come by as some of you have seen, some of my students have seen, and do some interesting things, interesting manifestations and things. But they are great warriors with fabulous senses of humor.

I suppose the only beings that I haven't talked about, aside from human beings–and I think we know enough about them today–are the causal beings. Now, there are different systems. I'm not big on systems myself but people like them and I suppose it's convenient to talk on them. According to one system of the different classes of beings, there are physical beings; above the physical beings there are subtle physical beings, astral; above them are the causal beings and then above the causal beings there's just the unmanifested reality, nirvana. Now as far as I'm concerned I really don't see an appreciable difference between the causal and the subtle beings. I'd class them all as nonphysical beings. But some people do make the distinction.

The causal beings are ideations. It's very hard to talk about them. They're beings of pure energy and they take no form whatsoever so there's really not much to talk about. Physical beings have a slower vibratory rate. That's why we have matter. Now a physical being also has an astral being, it also has a causal being. We all have these different bodies. We all have physical bodies, astral bodies and causal bodies. We also have the occult body. We have different parts of ourselves and the causal is the ideation. It's pure intelligence. It doesn't need a body, of any form.

The causal does exist. The causal is like salvikalpa samadhi. When you move into salvikalpa samadhi, that plane of consciousness, that is the causal. And above that is nirvikalpa samadhi or nirvana. Some people hold the idea that you have to go through a lot of incarnations in the earthly cycle, then through the astral incarnations, then through the causal incarnations and then you don't incarnate any more. It's not exactly that simple.

There are causal incarnations. There are astral incarnations. There are physical. But you can hop back and forth. You can have a lot of astral incarnations or causal incarnations then come into the physical and so on. It's not that simple. But sometimes people do do it that way. There is this gradual evolution. However, some people begin their celestial journey in the causal and choose to incarnate in the so-called lower planes, not that it's class distinction or anything, from time to time. That's what I did. I began causal and then I've taken incarnation in the astral realms and in the physical realms and so on. Remember, we're all eternal. And not one of us is superior to another. The lowest astral being is in no way inferior to the highest causal being. It's all the same. It's all God's dream. We call it lila, the play of the dance of life.

But it's interesting to know what's around you. There's a lot more around you than you might realize. As you meditate and progress, you'll see these beings and they'll help you. You can always determine what kind of being you're dealing with by how you feel. If suddenly you're in your room and you feel something, a presence there, if it makes you uncomfortable or frightened in any way or you just don't feel right, you're dealing with a lower being, one that's beneath your level of evolution. If the room is bright and shiny or somewhat happy – you might become afraid a little bit just because it's unusual – but if something is good there, then you're dealing with one of the higher beings. If it's just plain powerful, it's neither good nor bad but it just is, you're just thrown into that vortex of energy, then you're dealing with one of the occult beings.

The occult beings don't give a fig about humans. They're not interested at all. The only reason they come in is when a spiritual teacher uses them. It's the opposite universe. It doesn't usually come into this world. If you feel uncomfortable with a being of any type that you encounter in your travels, pay no attention. Let it go by. And if you move into light, your vibratory rate changes and shifts, if you meditate or invoke a higher light, they go away. They have to.

But it's a wonderful, wonderful universe. We're all in the play of existence, and you should extend yourself and begin to learn. There's so much to see and so much beauty to comprehend in such a short human life. The beings will help you, usually without your knowledge. Sometimes they'll come in dreams and appear and give you information and tell you things. But be very careful.

Always remember, you have to discriminate. Never trust the package. You have to see what's inside, and know that if there's truth in something that someone says, that truth will resonate with a deeper truth within your own being. Don't believe things just because they're attractive. If there's great light in it and it will do a great good and there is no harm to it, then it's healthy. Otherwise, pay no attention.

DHARMA AND KARMA

Dharma is the truth. Dharma is the truth throughout the ages. There are two types of dharma, universal dharma and individual dharma. To understand one, it's really necessary to understand the other. They can't be separated, although human beings try to.

Universal dharma is existence. We begin with the assumption that there's a primal cause for all things, there is an omnipresent reality or being that we call God, the self, nirvana, eternity. This omnipresent force or reality is existence. All of the worlds, realities, beings, experiences and times that we call existence come forth from and are directed by this reality.

Human beings like to think of God as a big person. We identify through the medium of ourselves, so we explore and come to know, to some extent, our own tonal ranges. We know that human beings think a certain way, feel a certain way, see life in a certain way. And so we assume that eternity or God must do that, and we are, in fact, correct, to an extent, since God exists in all things, at all times and all places and at the same time is beyond all times and places and things. God exists as human beings. The aspect of God that is each of us does see and feel existence in a certain way – the way we see and feel existence.

But God is not limited or bound by the human mode of perception. God may be a tree: growing, experiencing wind, heat, the passage of time in a very different way. God is in a stone that experiences a different type of awareness. You may look at a stone and say, "Well, there's no life there." But a physicist will correct you. A physicist will point out that there is as much life in a stone as there is in a human being. While the stone may not be, or appear to be, animate to you – it doesn't get up and walk around and move and talk and dance and perform– the molecular structure of the stone is in a constant state of motion. The atoms, the electrons, the protons, neutrons, sub-atomic particles, the worlds within worlds that exist within a fraction of an ounce of a stone, are galaxies; they're fathomless. And who is to say that those atoms and those electrons don't have consciousness, don't have awareness, simply because we are not aware of their awareness? Yet are we not made up of the same thing? Are we not made up of galaxies of universes, of sub-atomic particles that whirl and whirl together to form a certain aggregate which we call a human being?

Everything has awareness. Simply because a person does not see that does not mean that awareness does not exist. It was only a hundred or two hundred years ago that human beings were unaware of bacteria and viruses and their effects. The plague would roll into town and devastate 90 percent of the population, and people would have no idea how or why. That which was invisible was the causative agent, the bacteria, or the virus. Today, through the marvels of the microscope, we know about the existence of these things. Simply because we don't see something, we're not currently aware of it, doesn't mean that it doesn't exist. In spiritual practice and in all learning, we have to constantly be open to vision and revision. We need to be able to see beyond the known, to expose ourselves to that which we are not familiar with.

At the same time, as new information and knowledge and data, new ways of seeing life enter our being, we must be able to push aside outmoded ideas, ways of thinking, ways of examining existence, which we find are incomplete. Young children, of course, find this very easy to do because they don't have a lot of concepts and ideas. A child learns one, two, or three languages very quickly. The child can accept technology because the child is not wrestling with conditioning. The child hasn't been programmed.

In spiritual practice, we all become children again. We erase the tapes that were made before and we create new tapes. Any information that was valid we retain. But as we meditate, we explore the unseen. Meditation is the microscope, it's the telescope, it's the ultimate research tool. And we see that, just as there is a physical universe, so there are nonphysical universes, countless universes. Most human beings can't see them with their eyes. Well, most human beings couldn't detect the bacteria or the virus, which didn't suggest that these things didn't exist. Of course they did. These things had a tremendous effect on all human beings. Simply because one isn't aware of something does not mean that one is not affected by it.

Meditation enables us to see in new ways. When we're able to calm our minds and still our thoughts, we discover that we have other parts of our being, which enable us to perceive in alternate modalities. We have a facility to see into what we call the subtle physical universes. The subtle physical or astral universes, as they're popularly known, are like the sub-atomic worlds, unseen but active. These are the other dimensions which you enter into, of course, in dreaming.

In meditation, we consciously experience the subtle physical worlds. We see that some subtle physical worlds are high and beautiful; their vibratory rate is much finer. Then there are lower subtle physical worlds, with a very slow vibratory rate. The physical world as we know it is somewhere in the middle. It's an access point, a joining of all vibratory fields. It's not the center of the universe, it's not the most important of the planes; it's another world in a succession of worlds, another dream in a succession of dreams.

Meditation unlocks the doorway that leads to immortality. In the subtle physical world there are beings who progress through incarnations just as the people do here in the physical world. But there's something that lies beyond the subtle physical worlds and the physical world. We call this eternity, nirvana. It's the ocean from which all the waves come forth. It's the ocean through which all the fish pass. It's the ocean, which is the heart of life. This is God. How and whence it came from, who knows? Existence simply is. Our mind can run around in circles trying to understand it, but whether we understand it or not, that won't alter existence. It will be as it is and has been, whether we understand it or not. In meditation we come to understand existence. But there are no words for these expressions. Because in order to understand existence you must become it, you must experience it directly, firsthand for yourself.

When you meditate, you move beyond the realm of your awareness, the realm your awareness is focused in. If you focus exclusively on the physical world, this world, in time–your body, your emotions, your feelings, career, friends–if your attention is centered on that which happens from the moment of birth to the moment of death and the time in between, your attention is in the physical plane.

If you've meditated for some time in this life or other lifetimes and developed your facilities of seeing, you can perceive the astral worlds, which are less time oriented. And while you are in this physical world with your physical being, your astral being, your occult body, as we call it, is able to explore and have experiences in countless astral worlds.

But the deepest part of your being, your third body, is the body not of ether as is the astral being, the subtle being; nor is it a body of matter; nor is it the life force that animates these bodies, which we call the kundalini energy; but rather it is that which is the ocean, which is timeless, birthless, deathless and immortal, which all things arise from and all things return to. In higher meditation, in advanced meditation, we experience *that*, the superconscious. In introductory meditation and intermediate meditation, we experience the astral. Our knowledge of the astral colors our understanding of the physical. Our knowledge of the superconscious, which we experience in advanced meditation and samadhi, colors our knowledge of everything.

With this as a basic cosmology, with the recognition that there is time, place and position in the physical world; that there's an astral world or countless worlds, subtle worlds that have their own conditions, that are not physical; other dimensions, which we also exist in since we have a part of our being that is nonphysical, that is etheric; and [that there is] the absolute reality, which is eternal awareness, nirvana, the ocean, which is our real essence – with this understanding we can begin to contemplate dharma.

Dharma is the truth. And there are three types of truth. There's the truth of the physical world; there's the truth of the subtle physical world, the astral world; and there's the truth of the superconscious. Truth means everything is in place. Everything fits.

Our understanding of truth will change as we change. Truth to most people means alignment. If the sun is out and I go outside and say to my friends, "The sun is out," then I have told the truth. I have seen what is and reported it accurately and fairly. I have been a mirror of what is. If I say to my friends, "The sun is no longer out," then I have lied. I am not properly mirroring what is. My mirror is bent out of shape. In order to reflect truth, one must be a perfect mirror.

In meditation, we clean the mirror of the self. The mirror of the self has been covered up with layer after layer of dust. And almost nothing reflects. The mirror in the physical world is not as delicate as the mirror in the subtle physical world. In order to perceive that which lies beyond the physical, we must first understand the physical. Then we can move into the subtle physical. As long as the first mirror is obscured, we will never see the second mirror, let alone the third mirror, which is eternity itself, which is both the mirror and that which we see in the mirror.

Each human being has a part of themselves that is a mirror, which reflects truth. They also have a conscious awareness, which tells them if they are being honest. And no one can ask more of you than to be honest. If you can be honest, then you've done all that you need to do.

If a person's attention is centered in the physical world and they're honest about their physical experiences, about position and place, if they tell the truth and if what they see as being right or perceive of is right, if that's what they do, then that's honesty, then they are living dharma. If a person's attention is in the subtle physical worlds, or mixed between the subtle physical and the physical worlds, they will perceive a different set of rules or truths. Not only will they know the truths of the physical world, but they'll know the deeper elements, higher truths. And if they follow those truths, they are following the dharma. If a person perceives the superconscious, if they merge with that, then they've gone a step further and they've become an extension of the truth.

The superconscious is the ultimate truth. It is God. When you can no longer separate yourself from God, when you've merged with God, then you no longer need to tell the truth, to think about the truth, or even to show others the truth. You are the truth. You are the way and the light.

When a person does not follow the dharma, when they deceive themselves, then they suffer. They're out of alignment. The mirror does not properly reflect what is. All suffering comes about because a person is not a perfect mirror. Now, when I say suffering, I don't mean suffering in the sense of physical pain. Physical pain is a transitory experience, as is pleasure, which occurs to the body in time. Pain is something that cannot be avoided. However, it can be lessened, and pain doesn't really have to hurt. There is always going to be a certain amount of pain and a certain amount of pleasure that the body will experience in the physical world. But this is neither here nor there. It's only important if all your attention is focused on the body. If your little toe is in pain and you focus all of your attention on it, then that little pain will become the entire world for you and all of life will be pain. If you ignore it and put your attention elsewhere, then you won't even notice.

However, the emotional pains exact more damage to a person. They're more problematic. The emotional pains come from attachment. When we're attached to something, when an emotion surges through us and if we listen to it and follow it, we experience pain. We desire something, we want something, something didn't work out, we get frustrated – we feel pain. We love someone, we fail ourselves, we fail others–we experience pain. There's always a certain amount of pain in loving.

If you wish to go beyond pain, the way is the superconscious. The only way you can completely end pain is to be absorbed in eternal awareness. When you are absorbed in eternal awareness, there is no sense of this world, a world in which there must always be some pain. There is no sense of pleasure, there is no time, there is no space and there is no condition. In the highest strata of meditation, all of this falls away. You have merged with the superconscious, which is birthless, deathless and timeless. If a candle is held up to the sun, we don't see the candle, the flame cannot be distinguished. All the pains and pleasures of this world, all the transitory frustrations, in the intense light of the superconscious are not seen. They exist, but like the fish underwater, they're unseen.

Meditation, then, is a conscious entrance into the superconscious awareness, until we are so immersed in it that we are basically unaware of this world. That's samadhi. When we say that someone is absorbed in nirvana, this is what we mean. You can't find them; they're no longer there. Oh, you may see the body, their body may still be here, but their spirit has departed and has merged with the cosmic all.

Dharma is following the truth. When you follow the truth you will see that there is a way beyond pain for your frustration and suffering. When you negate the truth, you create karma, what most people call bad karma. When you follow the truth, you create what they call good karma. Karma and dharma cannot be separated.

Karma is a Sanskrit word that means action. Most people think of karma as a cause and effect process. The idea is that whatever I do produces an effect of some type. This effect is karma. Ultimately, this effect works its way around to me. If I'm a good person and I help people, good things will come back to me. If I harm others, hurt others, if I don't follow the dharma, if I don't do what's right, then I create bad karma. The only way one can distinguish good karma from bad karma is through the dharma. Dharma is the line that separates good and bad karma. What they call adharma is bad karma; dharma is good karma.

Now good and bad only exist in the relative worlds. Notions of good and bad, evil and salvation, pleasure and pain, these are all what we call pairs of opposites. To the human dualistic consciousness – meaning the way you see things because there's a personal form, a personality – there appears to be opposition or complements. To a person who lives in this world, there is, of course, light and dark, sound and silence. But if we erase the person, if the person no longer exists, then there are no pairs of opposites, there's no sound and silence. If there's no one to perceive it, it's not there. This is absorption and meditation. What's there is absorption. Karma only exists in the worlds that are worlds, which have conditions. When a person is liberated, there is no karma, meaning that they have gone beyond the pairs of opposites. They are in the sun itself, they have become the sun, the candle flame is unnoticed. Karma becomes meaningless.

Most people think of karma in physical terms. I saved someone's life, someone will save my life. In a previous incarnation, I did a lot of good things and now, in this incarnation, a lot of good things are happening to me. There is certainly a subtle cause and effect in the physical plane, but it really isn't specific to a person. That is to say, if you give a lot of money out, that doesn't mean a lot of money will come back to you. Or if it does, it won't occur because you physically gave money out and there was someone keeping a record somewhere, in the sky, noting what you did and then making sure that in the express mail the next day you received back what you gave out. That's not the way karma works.

Karma has to do with fields of attention. There is basically no physical karma, or we could say that all physical karma is an outgrowth of a field of attention. It works the same way, it's just that the causative principle is somewhat different. For example, let's say that a person, perhaps yourself, is walking down the street. And you see a small child who's lost. Now, if you help the child find their parents, doing this will place you in a different state of awareness because it's the dharma. It is the dharma in the world that we help one another, that life fosters life. That's a correct reflection in the mirror. We see ourselves as we really are. Whenever you do anything that's right, or that's dharma, then what will occur is that you will go up a level in the school of consciousness. The school of consciousness has thousands and millions of levels, and your consciousness is always climbing in and out and changing levels.

Most people's consciousness follows a relatively small spectrum. Let's say there are a million floors in the building. Well, you may be in the first hundred thousand, the second hundred thousand, the third hundred thousand, fourth, fifth, sixth, seventh, eighth, ninth or tenth. There are ten levels, there are a hundred thousand gradations in each one, let's say. Now, in each lifetime you will be in a particular level, and most people will never leave that level. They will experience some of the hundred thousand gradations within that level, but it is unlikely that they will climb up to a higher level or drop down to a lower level. There's so much gradation, just within the level that they're in, that it's unlikely that they'll change. There are different levels of attention or cosmic awareness. Whenever you approach the dharma, when you do something that is the dharma, when everything lines up, then you will raise up to a higher level of attention within your overall level. Whenever you do something that is not the dharma, the reflection is not clear, it's misshapen, and you will drop several levels.

Most people will rise and fall throughout their lifetime, again, within one level, within the gradations. As a matter of fact, over a course of many births and deaths, as their soul reincarnates from lifetime to lifetime, they will only rarely move to a different level. You may have 50 or 100 lifetimes within the same basic level, experiencing the different gradations. Gradually the soul will work its way higher, but rarely does the soul go through a full transit. Rarely will the soul jump to an entirely new floor and experience all the variabilities and new gradations within that structure. I don't mean to confuse you with all this kind of rhetoric, but it helps you get a schematic understanding.

What I'm suggesting is that spiritual evolution is a relatively slow process, or let us say that it has a grace all of its own, but it's not as quick as many people might think it is. There's no rush, essentially, since there's nothing but time.

So then, what karma does, is it determines your level of attention, your field of awareness. Karma is not simply physical, it doesn't involve just your physical actions but also the thoughts that you think and the emotions that you become affixed to. All of these things determine what your state of awareness is. If you love and you're kind and you give of yourself, if you meditate, you'll develop a very pure consciousness and you'll always follow the dharma. You'll be able to see what's right and follow it. If you only follow the dharma, you only create good karma, then your level of attention will constantly rise. Of course, if you do the opposite, if you don't listen to your inner voice, if you hurt others, if you don't follow what the dharma is, if you practice adharma, then your consciousness will descend and you'll drop down.

All effects in this world are based upon vibratory forces. That is to say, the things that happen to you in the physical world and ultimately the things that happen to you in the subtle physical world, in the universes that have some form, all of these events are predicated upon the fields of attention. Think of it in terms of freeways. I'm driving down the 405 freeway to San Diego from Los Angeles; I will be able to experience what's on the 405 freeway. If there are signs on the road, I'll see them, the cars that are there, and so on. If I take the 10 East out to Palm Springs, of course I'll be on a different freeway. Instead of moving down along the ocean and experiencing what's between Los Angeles and San Diego, I will experience what's between Los Angeles and Palm Springs. I'll go through the mountain ranges and the desert, the high desert and so on. Our experiences are determined by the freeway that we're on. Now, while I'm on the freeway, I can think whatever thoughts I want and feel whatever feelings I want, but still, on a basic physical level, what will occur to me is predicated upon the freeway that I'm on.

Well, let's say that the overall levels of attention, those ten floors I was talking about before, or however many you'd like, are freeways. OK, I'm going to mix my metaphors here, so let's see if we can make a salad. And these freeways take you someplace and they go to different places. Now, while you're on the freeway, there are many possible experiences. Hopefully you'll have a smooth trip. You might hit another car, you might be hit by a car; you might have a conversation with a friend, you may drive alone. There are many variable possibilities, but all those variable possibilities are within one construct, which is the 10 freeway or the 405 freeway.

Your karma determines what freeway you're on, your level of awareness. Your level of awareness is determined by the dharma that you followed, and you will draw to you experiences according to your level of attention. Whatever happens to you in this world happens to you not randomly, but because you have drawn it. That's what karma really is. Karma is not someone keeping a record book, saying you should have this experience because you did this to someone else. That has nothing to do with karma; that's a very pedestrian understanding of the workings of the universe. It all has to do with the vibratory fields of attention. If you're in a good, open state of consciousness, then you will draw certain things towards yourself. If you were not, if you were in a frustrated, depressed consciousness, then you will draw other things towards yourself. That's karma. Your karma determines the state of awareness. The state of awareness, then, will determine what happens to you. In other words, it all takes place inwardly.

Now, you are probably only aware of the freeway that you're on, and you think that everyone else is on the same freeway. But that's not the case. What I'm trying to suggest is that there are many freeways, and they go different places. One place is not better than another, they're simply different. However, eventually you can reach a point where the freeway ends and the ocean begins or you can ride the freeways forever. Rebirth, reincarnation, is just changing freeways. For a hundred lifetimes you'll ride the San Diego freeway, then for a hundred lifetimes you'll move to the 10 freeway, and so on. You'll gradually change.

It is possible within one lifetime to totally change levels of attention. That's my business and the business of spiritual teachers. I have about 900 or 1,000 students. Now, most of my students are on a specific level of attention. They're on a certain freeway. What I do is, in their lifetimes I work with them, try and have them rise up to the higher aspect of it. Back to our mixed metaphors, if there are ten floors in the building and there are a thousand gradations within each floor, what I try to do is, when I meet a person–perhaps they're in the lower ten gradations of the floor–I try to bring them up to the top ten. And to do this, to bring a person through a full level of attention in one lifetime, is a marvelous feat. If I can do that, or if I can do that in concourse with the individual, then perhaps it would have been a hundred or a thousand lifetimes in one. Instead of them having to take a thousand lifetimes to work their way through all this different stuff, we can do it in one incarnation, which means in their next lifetime they'll move into the next level of attention. It's easier for most people to have a major transition in levels of attention with death because it's hard to break out of their conditioning.

Occasionally I meet a person, hopefully yourself, who has enough drive and patience and a good enough sense of humor, who cares enough, who can within one lifetime not just change gradations, but change freeways. It is literally impossible to take someone who has just started incarnating, who is just on the most basic of all our floors in the building, and bring them from the first floor to the tenth floor in one lifetime.

In a sense, people who have just started, if they have any inclination towards spirituality, are easy to work with, because one of the things that holds you to a specific floor is what we call the samskaras. The samskaras are the past life tendencies, conditioning. You've taken that 405 freeway from San Diego to L.A. for a hundred lifetimes now. You're so used to it that you don't really want to leave it. It's hard for you to even conceive of the fact that there's another freeway, you've built up such a pattern. The samskaras are the ways we see existence. You're so used to believing that the world is physical, that there's life, that there's death, and so on; you're so used to seeing things in a certain way, you've done that for so many lifetimes that it's very difficult for you to have a total transit, a complete transition to another floor.

A person who's in their very early incarnations will find it easier to make that transit because they don't have all that conditioning. Someone who is in their first five or ten incarnations has almost no conditioning at all. It's very easy, if they were to work with an advanced spiritual teacher, to move very quickly. But usually such a person is not interested in self-discovery. Their level of attention is like that of an infant. It's very, very basic. They're not drawn to the higher life. It's only usually after thousands of lifetimes that a person will begin to become interested in self-discovery.

Your progress in the process of reincarnation, or within a given lifetime or within a given moment, is dependent upon dharma. Dharma is correctly reflecting what is true, being a good mirror. When you follow dharma, this arbitrary line, then you will create good karma. Good karma means that your own consciousness will expand. And as your consciousness expands, it will bring you into a different level of attention. You'll be on a different freeway. On that different freeway, there will be different experiences. If you don't practice dharma, if you practice adharma, if you do what is untrue, if you don't do what is right, if you don't follow the will of your soul, if you don't do all that you are capable of doing, then you will drop down to another freeway, one that's not quite as nice. And you'll have a different set of experiences there.

Then there is that which is, of course, beyond the freeway–the ocean, the desert, the sky and eventually we want to get out of the car and move to another level of experience. We go back and forth, actually, we go up in the sky for a while, then we find our self on the freeways of existence. But even when you're on the freeway of existence, if you're enlightened, you'll still be in the sky. You can sort of do both at once.

How do you finally get off the map? What is this thing that finally breaks you through? Because you see, the problem with karma is that – let's say you create nothing but good karma. The good karma will raise your level of attention. You'll go higher and higher and higher. But even then you're bound by it. You can be stuck in your own goodness, which doesn't mean that you should go off and practice untruths. How can you break out of that? Because even the best freeway is still a freeway. Even the best level is still a level. Well, that's the tricky part.

In order to even ask that question, of course, or to understand the answer, you need to be at the top level of attention. You need to have practiced self-discovery for many lifetimes, have thrown off your conditioning; you need to meditate impeccably and be pure of heart completely. When your motives are spotless, when you will not be swayed by that which is untrue, then you are ready for the final stages of the reincarnation process, to go beyond karma itself, and to no longer practice dharma but to be it.

Don't judge the purity of your heart by what you think or the emotions you feel or even, to some extent, by the actions that you perform. Sometimes certain parts of our being are still working out transitory desires. In other words, don't be too judgmental of yourself. Don't say, "Well, gosh, because I do this or don't do that, that means I'm not very evolved," and so on. The purity of your heart and the level of your soul's evolution inwardly is not necessarily in harmony with your body and your mind and your emotions. What will tell the story is not what you think or feel, but how you live.

You may wake up in the morning and meditate, and then after meditation have a lot of terrible thoughts. You may get depressed or discouraged or frustrated. You may get angry at someone. The sign of spiritual evolution is not that these things don't pass through you. The sign of spiritual evolution is that you don't follow them. That even though, suddenly, hate is surging through you – although actually you don't hate anymore after a while – but let's say some very strong emotion is passing through you, the sign is that you are not affected by it. You won't follow it. Suddenly I'm angry at my friend. But that anger will never go anyplace. I'll step out of the way. I won't get on that particular train. Don't feel because you have moods or desires that you're not necessarily an evolved being. The test, of course, is whether you follow dharma.

The dharma is, for an advanced spiritual seeker, to remain unaffected. If you were depressed for a long period of time, it won't bother you. If you're elated, it won't bother you. Because you're not looking at these things, you're not looking at the candle flame, you're looking at the sun. These are of little or no consequence. What you do physically, what you think, what you feel, is of very little consequence, if your attention is absorbed in eternity. It doesn't really matter how your toe is feeling today. It's your overall awareness. While the toe does contribute to that, if your awareness is strong enough, it really doesn't matter. This is the higher dharma.

Don't be too concerned about what you see, do or feel. Don't worry about yourself so much. As you fixate upon your body, as you fixate upon your mind and your emotions, then you lock onto them, you become attached to them, and then you're on those freeways and you're stuck. You must experience what's there. Some freeways are nicer than others but they're all freeways. You can do a lot of driving.

Or you can go beyond all such relative states and conditions. To do that you need to focus your attention only on God–God beyond the world and God within the world, God beyond people and God within people. You need to care about, in other words, nothing but light. You can be very active in this world, working, participating in society and relationships; you can do all of those things and not be bound by them. But in order to do that, you have to think and feel and care about nothing but light and the spreading of light.

In past ages there was renunciation. The way out was to leave it all behind, leave the kids, leave the wife, leave the husband and just go up in the hills and meditate. The idea was that it was easier to break your fixation with these things if you weren't around them. True, you still carried the attachments with you, yes. But sometimes it's easier to break an attachment, an addiction, when you're not around it. If you're an alcoholic, it's very hard, if you're in a bar, to not drink. If you're away from liquor, it's easier. Then eventually, if you overcome that particular inclination, then you can go to a bar and have a glass of milk and not be affected. But initially it's easier to break with separation.

In the olden times, in other cycles, in the previous three cycles of existence, in this particular creation, there was more renunciation.

However, in this cycle renunciation is not the way. In this fourth section of the creation, the final one, the way is to live in the world but to be unaffected, be unattached. It's actually been that way really in almost the last two [cycles].

That's why I say it really doesn't matter whether you have relationships, whether you're celibate or not, whether you work, whether you make a lot of money, whether you're famous, whether you're infamous–these things don't matter. Now, the only reason I can say that to you, as a spiritual teacher, as a spiritual master, is with the assumption that they don't matter because your attention is fully engrossed in the consciousness of eternity. Therefore these things have little effect. They have a tremendous effect if your consciousness is not absorbed in eternity.

I'm suggesting that there are two ways to look at it. One way, in terms of self-realization, is that everything counts a great deal. The condition of your body, the condition of your mind, the types of emotions you feel, everything counts. Another way is that these things are relatively unimportant. This is what we call tantra. The pairs of opposites are relatively unimportant. What matters is something larger, a bigger picture.

Now, to get to that bigger picture, it's kind of a catch-22. You have to work your way through the levels to some extent. It does matter what you think and feel, how your body feels. But then eventually we go beyond it all– beyond light, beyond darkness, beyond karma and dharma – to absorption. When you're fully absorbed, which is an enlightened person, it really doesn't matter what you do anymore.

This is what the Zen masters always had fun with and used to confuse the heck out of the local people. You know, the Zen master would come into town and break all the rules. But he wasn't breaking the rules. There were no rules. Once he reached the top floor and beyond, once he was absorbed in eternity, then it didn't really matter what he did in the sense that he was no longer affected by it. He wasn't even that conscious of what he was doing, his consciousness was so absorbed in eternity, he was so drunk with immortality, that what he did or said no longer created that much of an effect on his consciousness. However, for a person who has not attained that level, who is still bound by karma, karma hurts or karma liberates. But for a person who's gone beyond all of that, it doesn't matter. You're no longer affected by the gravitational pull. Someone might observe your body and say that it is, but from your point of view you don't have a body anymore. Your body is light.

Think of karma, then, not as action. Action is a result of karma, not the other way around. That is to say, what you do is determined by your awareness, and as your awareness changes, what you do will change. Your awareness is karma. Your awareness is created not by what you do but by how you are. If you meditate, if your heart is open, if you think of nothing but eternity or as much as you can, if that's your concern, then your spirit opens, it evolves. You change freeways.

It is possible, if your attention is pure, if you care for nothing but light and truth, to not just change within a level but to change full levels, to go all the way to enlightenment in a lifetime–again, not from the very beginning, but from quite a ways. If you work with an enlightened teacher and if you care for nothing but truth, you can do this. Such people are rare. I keep looking. But such people are rare. It can be done, but it's not a strain when you do it. It's a natural inclination. It's fun. That's going beyond karma and going beyond the lower dharma, which is right or wrong.

The lower dharma–there's left and right, right or wrong, good and bad, and there are these things. There are laws in countries that must be followed. But then there's something beyond all of that. We tear the picture away and we find that there was something else on the other side. And that's the higher dharma, which of course there are no words for. That's what you will become engrossed in, in the superconscious.

Some thoughts on karma and dharma on a windy afternoon in March.

TANTRA AND THE LEFT HANDED PATH

There are dark and gloomy days in the path to self-discovery. There are days when it seems that we'll never be able to see the truth. I like to talk about self-discovery in very optimistic terms. I suggest that meditating will inspire you, open up new vistas and new horizons, bring you into different levels of attention and show you worlds beyond your imagination, much happier worlds than the worlds you now exist in, worlds of form, formlessness, voidness. I speak about the ecstasy of samadhi and the superconscious states, the peaks of self-realization.

Eternity is everywhere. It's always with us. Our failure to see and access the pure joy and radiance of life is owing to a lack of awareness. In any situation there is beauty. Even at the moment of one's death, there is beauty. And we can see that beauty and understand the loving kindness of creation when we're in a high enough consciousness. Then everything is one, and what occurs in the physical world is but a dream. We're not affected by it. It doesn't really matter if our fortune is good or bad. If we're in a high enough state of consciousness, we see that it is only a passing dream. We draw happiness and radiance from the eternal sun of self-knowledge, from the pure bliss of existence itself. This is true.

But then there are days when we don't see it that way. There are days that in spite of our best intentions we become confused, deluded, frustrated, angry, depressed. We just can't seem to raise our kundalini, our energy. The past overshadows the present, and the future looms before us as an empty road through what appears to be a barren desert. We try all of the traditional methods and means, the four paths. The path of love–we try to love, but it's not working. The path of selfless giving, where we really want to go out and do something for the world, for humanity, for our spiritual organization – it's not working. We're not inspired. We can think the thoughts but they lack heart. When we practice mysticism we try and raise the level of attention through drawing on the power and energies of the elementals, of the earth and the ether–doesn't seem to be working. Jnana yoga, the highest form, discrimination–it seems empty, barren, lacking in emotion.

When everything has failed you, when it seems that none of the paths are good – which they are, but it doesn't seem that way at the time – what does one do? When you've seen all the best movies in town, you've tried all the best people in the neighborhood, you've pushed yourself through a mirage of sexual experiences, creative experiences, work experiences, love experiences, drug experiences, whatever it may be. You've tried everything and still come away with a feeling of emptiness, but not the higher emptiness. Loneliness. Sadness. A feeling that is accentuated by the knowledge of what could be.

You see enough to know how beautiful and perfect life can be. You've had moments where you've seen it. You've touched it. But now it's faded away, which makes it all the worse. You know you're feeling sorry for yourself, but it doesn't seem that you can extricate yourself from the trap of feeling sorry for yourself. You know you should be self-giving; you shouldn't be worried about your state or your condition, that it's all relative. But it still doesn't matter. At the moment you hurt, and that's what matters.

What can you do when all the remedies fail, both spiritual and worldly? What can you do? Well, at such a time, there is a form of yoga you can practice that will enable you to destroy everything, including yourself and your conceptions. And from this destruction will arise a creation, a new force; an energy will enter your life. This yoga is, I suppose, the most dangerous of the yogas. But then again, you get to a point where it really doesn't matter. One can get to a point where nothing is working. We're headed off the cliff, plummeting to the bottom, so why not try one last thing? When you've sunk as low as you can get – or so you think because there's no end to the depths to which you can fall as there is no end to the heights to which you can rise– when you feel, as my grandfather used to say, "lower than a snake's ass," at such a moment, when everything and nothing works, it's time to practice tantra.

Tantra is the left-handed path, meaning it is the road less taken. Tantra comes from the Far East. And it has to do with the pairs of opposites and oppositions. It is a difficult yoga to practice in the sense that when you practice tantra, it's very easy to not practice tantra and think you're practicing tantra. Practicing tantra itself is never dangerous or problematic. The only problem that occurs in the practice of tantra is when you don't practice tantra but you think you're practicing tantra, and you fool yourself and you get caught up in powerful vortexes of negative energy which pull you into the lower bardo regions of awareness, down into the mud.

What can one do at such a time? Well, before I enter into a discussion of tantra here and take up more of your time, I'd like to tell you what tantra is not. Tantra is not sexual yoga. When the word "tantra" is used in the West, very often people immediately associate it with some kind of sexual yoga in which you use sex as a vehicle for attaining enlightenment. Sex can never bring about enlightenment. Only enlightenment brings about enlightenment.

The tantras are the ancient sacred books of India and Tibet. And the tantras detail specific means for attaining liberation. When I speak of tantra yoga, I'm speaking of a type of yoga that is best practiced by persons who live in society. It's a yoga for the last yuga. Tantra means the avoidance of a set or defined form of spirituality. Tantra is intuitive self-discovery, which initially sounds very good and very attractive. We feel that the path of love, the path of mysticism, the path of self-giving, the path of knowledge, the four paths, are very demanding. And they are. Then of course, there is the fifth path that I respect but do not teach, and that's the path of asceticism.

Tantra is the sixth path. It's a hidden path only because people don't look where it is. Tantra appears to be fluid. It appears that we don't need the discipline required in the other paths. If one is somewhat lazy, it immediately seems like a great idea. "Boy, I'll practice tantra and I don't have to go through all those other forms and practice all those different methods." And so on. Such a motivation will not bring you success with tantra. Tantra is for the desperate. Unless you've really experienced pain and suffering, tantra won't work. Unless you've really experienced exultation and ecstasy, tantra won't work. Tantra is for extremists, but balanced extremists.

Tantra is not for the person who is lacking in self-control. Tantra is for the person who has self-control but doesn't care anymore– that is to say, the person who is able to abandon self-control and its fixation. Tantra is not for the weak. Tantra is for the very, very strong practitioner. And it is only recommended for someone who has a very developed will power, a terrific sense of humor and a sense that nothing else matters but God and self-realization. It's only with those understandings that we can readily approach the subject of tantra. Again, I suggest that tantra is for the person who is pure in heart. If you still have greedy desires, if you still think that material success will bring you happiness, if you think that worldly possessions will fulfill you – relationships, people, places and things, fame, fortune, all of those things – if those things still matter to you, you definitely should not practice tantra. Tantra is for the person who has reached the point in their spiritual practice where they realize that these things are not important, but still, in spite of that knowledge and firm belief from the heart – not just because it sounds nice, but you really feel that way, all the way through your being, and you ache for God, you ache for liberation, but still in spite of that, you find yourself getting stuck. That's the candidate for tantra.

Tantra is for someone who practices all the paths because all the paths are encompassed in tantra. Tantra is a way that can only be practiced by someone who's truly, truly dedicated, literally fanatical, but at the same time who is not caught up in the trap of fanaticism. A person who has dedicated their life to self-realization, not in name but in action, someone who is actually ready to travel to the farthest ends of the earth for truth and will actually do it and will leave everything – family, home, whatever – for truth. But in spite of that feeling, in spite of that readiness, one still is getting snared again and again by one's own games, by one's desires, by one's desire for liberation.

How does tantra work? Well, tantra has to do with the reconciliation of the pairs of opposites. A bit of spiritual theory: the paths that lead to self-realization set down prescribed methods and ways, and if you've listened to my discourses on the four yogas, you're familiar with the basic principles of each of the yogas. All of the four yogas, however, recommend that you avoid certain experiences. In tantra, there is no avoidance. All of the yogas say that there is something right that you should do, that there are certain practices that, if you practice those practices, you'll make spiritual progress. There are certain things that, if you avoid them, then you will make spiritual progress. You kind of combine the two. And each of the four paths shows the way.

Tantra is different than that. Tantra would certainly acknowledge and suggest that there are certain things that are helpful, and those things would include all of the recognized and established methods of self-realization. Tantra is not at all in disagreement with meditation, self-giving, purity, and humility. All of these things, of course, are understood and accepted. Tantra simply changes one small factor, and that is that there's nothing that you shouldn't do. Everything can be used as a tool for liberation. The basic assumption of tantra is that God not only exists in the superconscious reality, which everyone is trying so hard to get to in spiritual discovery, but, excuse me, God also exists in the lowest forms of existence, in the darkest regions and confines of the human consciousness. God exists there as much as any place else, just in a different form.

In tantra, one does not seek experiences that most people would consider to be unspiritual and try to see truth in them. That has nothing to do with tantra. In tantra, we don't try to guide our life in a specific way. We let the winds of existence blow us where they will. Our concern is not so much in directing our life as in living our life and observing and seeing that every experience that life gives us, every situation that we're put into, is a pathway to perfection.

In this world, we see the pairs of opposites. Ultimately, there are no oppositions. In the superconscious awareness there is no division. From that perspectiveless perspective, there is only eternity in all of its radiant perfection. From the point of view of the mind, the relative world, there are pairs of opposites: dark, light; hot, cold; pleasure and pain and so on. Most forms of yoga counsel the spiritual aspirant to not get involved with the physical world, to not get too caught up in it. Instead, what one should do is to fixate one's attention on the subtle physical and on the voidness of nirvana, to become absorbed in God and to ignore the world. In the path of tantra, we enjoy the opposites because we don't see them as opposites but rather as either complements or as one and the same.

In tantra, we accelerate our spiritual progress by not trying. A person who practices tantra yoga will naturally meditate, will practice selfless-giving. When I say not trying, I don't mean that you won't meditate every day or that you won't give from the heart. Tantra is not for the lazy. It just means that on a dark day, in a dark time, in a dark world, in a dark moment, you can actually use that darkness, you can use that depressive force, you can use that frustration, that delusion, to propel you into the heart of light, into God.

How is it done? Tantra and adventure are very, very connected. Perhaps the greatest enemy for one who's journeying along the spiritual path – after you've overcome doubt, fear, anxiety and so on, after you have your house in order and you've taken charge of your life and your emotions – perhaps the greatest enemy is complacency. I've seen many of my students, and also people who I used to study with years ago, do very, very well spiritually for a number of years. In the initial years of self-discovery there's great enthusiasm and love. You see your life changing constantly. But then you reach a point, or you may reach a point, where things begin to get a little dull. In other words, the process of self-discovery has just become another state of mind. It isn't really, it never is. But this is how we see it. In other words, we've gotten stuck in our self-discovery just as we were stuck in the world.

Tantra is a means, a way, of reconciling everything. It's neither here nor there, forward nor backward. It's a state of awareness. The winds of eternity blow, and in tantra we have complete faith in the winds of eternity. The key to tantra yoga is to feel that you are not the doer, that you cannot possibly act, that anything that you choose, you didn't really choose – eternity chose for you. All that you have to do in existence and life is to accept.

In bhakti yoga there's a sense of "I'm loving God, I'm serving God." In karma yoga, there's a sense of "I'm working for the welfare of others. I see God in everyone and work for them." In mysticism there's a sense of "I am impeccable. I am bringing forth the powers of eternity and working with them." In jnana yoga, there's a sense of nonexistence of the self: "I don't exist, nothing exists, the relative world doesn't exist. All that is is nirvana." In tantra, there's a sense of surrender. True, all of the yogas do lead to this sense.

The highest aspect of all of the yogas culminate in a sense of surrender to eternity: "Let thy will be done." But tantra is really that way from the beginning. There's the sense that, "What can I do? I'm a poor, puny human being. How can I possibly attain liberation? How can I possibly rise above the samsara, the illusion of birth and death, of pleasure and pain? Here I am, stuck in the middle of the relative world in a traffic jam, and there's nothing good on the radio. And I'm dying every day. My body's aging. My life didn't turn out the way I thought it would. When I try to feel and communicate, there's little feeling and even less communication." At that point it's necessary to break out of the framework with which we view experience.

So then, in tantra we come to feel that that very frustration is the means that eternity is using to break us out of our conditioning. If, for example, you feel that you shouldn't eat an ice cream cone – I don't know why you'd feel that way – but if you feel that way and you feel that it's a very unspiritual thing to do, yet you're drawn to the ice cream cone and you find yourself eating one in spite of your intent, if you follow any of the other paths you'll be miserable. You'll try and accept it as an experience that God is having through you, but still you'll know that you've failed. In tantra, you'll order a hot fudge sundae, and in every bite of that hot fudge sundae you'll see and feel God vibrating. The path of tantra doesn't mean that you will go out every day and seek that hot fudge sundae. But whatever comes your way you will accept as being normal, natural, and perfect. There are no rules for you to break. Since everything is God and everything contains God, you see God in everything; everything is a step towards liberation.

Tantra works well for people who are engaged in relationships and sexuality. Most of the yogas say stay away from sex, stay away from relationships, they're a terrible trap. And indeed they are. Sex itself, meaning the experience of making love, is really not that much of a deal one way or the other. Very little energy is transferred, for most people. However, the problem with sexuality is emotions. Most people become emotionally involved with someone when they have sex with them and it brings up their ego, their attachments, all kinds of illusions about love and nasty things that will ultimately make you very unhappy. If you listen to the songs on the radio you will quickly ascertain that for every one song about the joys of love, there are a hundred songs about the miseries of love. This is attached love, sexual love. It always seems so promising in the beginning. But what happens is, sexual activity brings up everything in our being that's impure. Remember, sex itself is just an action, it's just part of the dream. It really doesn't matter, in my estimation. Of course the principal path that I follow is tantra. Some days.

Many people have been somewhat confused about my stance on sexuality, and I assure you, if you think you're confused, you should try being me. But you see, I think confusion is a wonderful state of being. We're all in states of being, different parts of our being are in states of being, and confusion, I think, is one of the finer states because a person who is confused is definitely making spiritual progress. The person who sees life as being completely clear – if you understand everything, everything is in a state of balance, you're suffering from complete illusion and delusion. You've fooled yourself into thinking that everything is balanced. Nothing is balanced in the universe. The universe is completely chaotic. That's what makes it work so well. It's chaos that's predictable. It's the most orderly chaos that there is. Uniform chaos is much more orderly than order. This is a perspective that a person who practices tantra has.

Sexuality then, for the person who practices tantra, is a marvelous chance to experience illusion. Illusion is just another way of seeing things. There are no illusions because there is no self. Everything is voidness, and voidness is just another illusion. So why not? Why not, if you find yourself having sex, pay no attention to it? Why not, if you find yourself, I don't know, whatever your moral prescription is, when you do the opposite, why not realize that it doesn't matter? There are no rules. Nothing you can do will take you to liberation, therefore, nothing you avoid will help you along the path to liberation. What will actually help in your realization is this realization–that there is nothing that will bring you to liberation, nor is there anything that will hinder your liberation. Everything is liberation. This is tantra.

Tantra does not seek any type of experience, nor does it avoid it. The perspective of tantra could be that everything that I experience every day, from brushing my teeth to sleeping, aids me in my liberation because there is nothing but liberation. Who's to say what's right and what's wrong? This is why tantra is such a difficult path to follow. You see, tantra is not for a hedonist at all. It won't work. If you're heavily attracted to sensual experience, tantra will definitely not be of any use to you. Tantra is for the person who has gone beyond the rules. They've learned the rules so well and practiced them for so long, that now they can go beyond them.

You're learning to play the piano and you're learning the scales. You learn to read music and you practice for years and years and you follow all the rules. Finally a day will come when you're so good at playing the piano that you can – not necessarily even break the rules, you're not interested in breaking the rules – but just go beyond into unexplored territory. You can start to improvise. That's tantra. Improvisation. Now, there are those who are lazy. They don't want to learn the scales, they don't want to practice. They can't possibly employ tantra. Tantra is for a person who has reached a point in their spiritual evolution where everything looks the same. Such a person is free to do absolutely anything since they see that the rules no longer apply to them. Not because they're special, but because the rules were just another way of looking at life.

In other words, the Ten Commandments have a social purpose, for people who still need a social purpose. Once you've gotten to the point where you're very, very good, you don't have to worry about commandments. If your intentions are noble and pure, if you don't want anything but light and goodness, then it's extremely unlikely that you're going to break the rules. You don't need to worry about the rules. The rules are only for people who still need them. The rules are for persons who are so unsure or lack the discipline necessary to live in the world or in society or to practice an art form or self-discovery, you know, they need those rules. Those rules are good; they help you. Someone is saying, "Listen Charlie. If you do this you're going to get in trouble and you'll suffer. If you do this you'll feel better." And those rules are true, and they're logical and sensible. They've been set down to help you. But you can reach a point in self-discovery where the rules don't mean anything anymore. You would never violate them. That's not your interest. But in spite of the fact that you've followed the rules and now have no interest in doing anything else, still something's lacking in your life. You're still in the samsara. You have enough knowledge, but your knowledge isn't complete. Tantra is good for such a person.

Tantra involves radical change, a change in states of awareness. Remember, I said the principle danger for people who practice self – discovery for many years, obviously aside from egotism, is complacency. You can't be complacent. You must do new things and have new experiences. But you see, people who practice spirituality for a long time have grown to the point where they don't really want much to do with the world because you go out into the world and the world is grungy. People of the world are so fixated on basic things – pleasure, pain, the senses, things like that–and to be around them at times is almost painful. A person who practices self-discovery for many years works out a very simple lifestyle where they kind of dodge the waves. But they get fixated in it. They forget that God is in those people who seem to be low-vibe as much as God is in an enlightened person. They got trapped by spirituality itself.

Now, you can't get trapped by spirituality itself – again, if I can come back to this point – until you've really done it correctly. This won't work for you. Tantra won't work unless you've been trapped by spirituality. You have to be trapped by spirituality before you can be liberated from it. Spirituality, self-discovery, is a tremendous trap. It's one of the biggest traps there is. But you must be trapped by it because you are now trapped by the world and the world appearance. You need to get out of the trap of the world appearance and get stuck in the trap of spirituality. It's a healthier trap, it doesn't hurt as much. Then you need to move from that trap to the trap of tantra, and then from there back to the world because tantra means to come back to the world. It's a circle.

Self-realization is a circle. We run away from the things of the world because they seem to harm us. We leave them, we progress spiritually, now we need to go back into the world again, into careers, into relationships, into all of those things and see God in all of them. That's tantra – that in spite of your advanced spirituality and in spite of your high consciousness, when you think you should be up on top of the mountain just contemplating all day, you'll find yourself in the middle of a traffic jam, you'll find yourself talking to someone, you'll find yourself working in an office. That's advanced yoga.

Advanced yoga is not withdrawal from the world. That's a preliminary state, which is important to go through, when you pull back. And still a person who practices tantra will pull back at times because God is in pulling back too. But the person who practices tantra embraces life in the world, in its formlessness and in its form. Tantra is the yoga of this age. Remember, all of the other paths exist in tantra. Tantra does not disagree with any of them. That is to say, one day you practice jnana yoga, the next day bhakti, karma, this or that because tantra yoga is not going to disagree. Tantra yoga is all yoga. It includes all yoga, but it does not exclude anything. The other yogas include but they also exclude. Tantra includes without excluding. One sees God in everything.

On the dark day in a dark time, when everything is frustrating and depressing, what you need to do is first to meditate, to just sit, even if it seems you're not meditating well, and think of all the beautiful and wonderful experiences that you've ever had in your life. Just take five minutes and quickly review, holding each image just for a moment in your mind – the beautiful places, the power places you've been to, experiences in nature, people you love–bring it all together. Just take five minutes and scan very quickly through the good experiences in your life. By that I mean what you would consider to be the spiritually evolved experiences, the higher moments, when you've touched a deeper reality. And by doing that you'll reawaken something in yourself. Then, once you've done that, even if you still feel terrible, do something. Break your patterns. Instead of going to work that day, roam a shopping mall–this is why I love shopping malls – and see that all the people in that shopping mall who could care less about self-discovery and spirituality are God.

Go to a movie. And see that God is the movie. Go to Disneyland. Go away for the weekend. Just buy a ticket someplace. Surprise yourself. Put it on your charge card and go with a friend or by yourself to the mountains someplace, to a ski resort even if you don't ski. That's true tantra! Be a little bit crazy. Break out. Remember the things that made you happy in those past years that gave you that high moment. Were they experiences with people? Were they experiences in nature? What worked? What brought you to the path of self-discovery? That was your tantra. Don't go back to those same places. But grab onto that essential energy that you used and use it again, only in the next step, in the next phase.

If going into nature gave you wonderful experiences, roaming through the fields and hills, don't go back to the same fields and hills. Go to some new ones. Whatever it was that brought the magic for you, bring it back again. Invoke it by remembering it but then doing something. Be radical! Because there is nothing radical. You only think so. And then you'll catch fire again because you'll see that what happened was – the reason you feel so miserable is because you put spirituality into a form. You boxed it. You franchised it. You sold it around the country. You decided that spirituality was a certain way, and then you programmed yourself to being on that way. And perhaps it was for a while. But then you got stuck in the way, and now you're unhappy because you're not doing what your soul wants.

Your soul wants experience. It wants the world. You're a human. And you're eternal and the two are the same. Don't run away from your humanity. That's what you're trying to do. Don't be afraid to go back in now that you've been out for a long time, and experience a little pain and a little suffering and a little transitory joy – because God exists in those things too. And your avoidance of them, of these experiences, is a fixation, and it binds you to this world, it binds you to the personal self.

It's kind of crazy, this tantra stuff. In other words, after many years of meditation, self-discovery and devoting your life to God, studying with a teacher, different teachers, or just being by yourself but really working on it, and you finally give up everything. All the things that you're supposed to avoid, then you find out that there's nothing you're supposed to avoid, yet there are things that are good to avoid. I mean, you shouldn't run around killing people or eating meat[1] or doing things like that. That's not what we mean by tantra. Again, there's no need to break the rules. The rules have become your life. They're your discipline. But we don't have to think about it anymore. You're a free perceiver. Go out into the world and have experiences. Have adventures. It's the adventure that is tantra, that energy, that kundalini. Don't be afraid to be with new people. Change it around. Because you've gotten stuck. That's why you feel that you're in a dark

---

[1] Editors' note: Later in his teaching cycle, Dr. Lenz advocated a healthy, balanced diet that optionally included meat.

time on a dark day in a dark world. All the other forms work, all the other yogas work, but you're stuck in them.

Tantra, then, is for the advanced spiritual practitioner who is ready to push aside spiritual practice in the name of spiritual practice. Good luck.

LIBERATION AND SELF-REALIZATION

Self-realization is liberation. Liberation is self-realization. There is no beginning and there is no end. Nothing is final. There is no absolute. There is no highest point, nor is there a lowest point. These configurations are ideas. Ideas are primitive constructs, symbolic representations, reflections in a mirror. We see the world through thought, not only in the sense of individual thoughts that we think, but thoughts that have a mass, that have collected, that have formed composites.

There is no way to see the world. In this world, and in other worlds too, there are views. What we see in a view is not necessarily what is in the view or all that is in the view. We have to separate to some extent the perceiver from that which is perceived, or we have to lose all distinction whatsoever.

We see life in terms of physicality. We see a world with buildings, trees, mountains, oceans, people. We are cognizant of time, the sense that there is mutability. Time is change. It's the separation of eternity from itself. When eternity is separated from itself, we see it appear in different forms. Time is not a movement in space. Space is a movement in time. There is no deterioration and there is no creation. There are projections, moments of existence. Each moment is perfect.

For example, if we were to look at an apple and we saw the apple as it was growing, and we watched the different stages of its growth, and we watched it ripen and fall from the tree and then we watched it decay, and we watched the seeds from that apple root themselves into the ground and grow. A huge tree eventually came forth from that apple and the tree provided a place for birds to have nests. One of the birds in that nest one day was flying to the court of a king and it flew in a window and took a precious gem. When the king couldn't find the gem, which was a symbol of his authority, the people said that it was a sign from the gods that the king should not have ruled the kingdom. The king was overthrown. His family had to leave the kingdom; they left in poverty. But the king had a son and one day the son grew up and he came back to the kingdom and he reclaimed the throne. He married, had children himself, and one day one of those children was out by the apple tree, the old ancient apple tree. And a windstorm had blown down a nest and in it he found the jewel, and as he looked into the jewel he saw himself, all the lives that he had ever had or would ever possibly have, all the creations of God stretched out infinitely, all times, past present and future for all beings – worlds unimagined. And he saw that each part of this was a part of himself – that the world and all the worlds were his body, that all the beings that peopled it were his mind, and that his soul was nirvana, which was all of this and more. And seeing this, and seeing us listening to this story, he came to see that there was no time, that the tree had never grown, that the apple – the first apple from which all this came forth – was still sitting in a garden, by a river.

Reality does appear to exist. There does appear to be birth, youth. People appear to have children, but all of it is a dream. These are isolated moments that are only connected by perception. There is no separation.

Self-realization is that awareness. Not the awareness that this world is a dream – that's a part of self-realization – not the awareness that there is time because there is time and that's part of self-realization. Not the awareness that there is no such thing as time, that there are only isolated incidents, but that, in other words, the apple is full-grown in one picture, the apple is only partially grown in another, the apple has ripened and fallen and its seeds have taken root in another picture. The seeds have grown into a giant tree in another picture; the bird has built its nest in another picture; it has taken the jewel, in another picture, from the king. The king and his family, homeless, wander poverty-stricken in strange lands in another picture in our album. The son of the king comes back and reclaims the kingdom in another picture. Further in the album we have another picture, and this is the new king's son, going to the old gnarly apple tree and finding the jewel. In another picture looking into the jewel and seeing all of the universes, all of the worlds, all of the dimensions, all times, all places. In another picture, seeing that there was something behind all that, and beyond it all, which we call nirvana, the self, God. In another picture, watching us listening to all of this. In another picture, being back at the beginning. None of it had taken place. It was all a dream, and on waking from the dream it all went away.

Now, time is our turning of the pages of this vignette, of this collection of photographs. Each one of these events is happening independently. There is no cycle of growth and development. Rather there are moments of perfectly manifested reality. They appear to be in sequence because we place them in sequence. A flower never unfolds. The sun never rises. All of the moments are independent and only seem to be connected by a causal chain, which we call time, because we are time and it is we who are connecting them with our consciousness. They all exist independently. The moment of the apple at ripeness exists. It's separate; it's like a house you can go into. Next to it is another house and another and another. The apple falling, the child with the jewel, each moment is a reality in itself.

Everything always exists, in other words. Everything that has ever been or will ever be exists. What we do is that we, as a body of perception, take a tour and we visit different things, and as we visit them, we say that they "are." When we leave them, we say that they "no longer are." But everything always has existed and always will exist. The awareness of this is part of self-realization but is not self-realization.

Self-realization is not a state of being, although all states of being are contained within it. Self-realization is like the thin air – only you have become the thin air. There is no sense of form. There's no sense of being a person. When you close your eyes and meditate, there's no sense that you are meditating. All there is is the thin air.

It's like going down to the beach on a windy day and there's no one there. It's too windy and cold. All the bathers have gone away. We walk down to the beach; we sit out looking at that ocean and we decide to meditate, so we fold our legs, a half-lotus position or a lotus cross-legged position. We sit up straight; we close our eyes. At first we have a sense that, 'I'm sitting here on the beach meditating. I can hear the wind. I can hear the seagulls when they cry as they go by, whirling in the wind. I can hear the sound of the water slapping against the shore not far away. I'm here alone on this beach, in the wind.' Then, something happens. The sense of being there on the beach goes away. The wind is still there, but no one is there to listen to it. Instead of hearing it as a separate wind, as separate from anything else, we don't perceive that. We see that it never was separate. There never was a beach. We were never sitting on it. The sea gulls were never – or always – were flying. Nothing is distinct and separate.

It's like water. We look at water and we can't separate it from itself. We pour more water into it. It's all water. We take water out from it. It's all water. The water can assume different shapes. It can be frozen. It can be like an ice cube and it seems hard and solid and independent, but then it melts and it's nothing but water. Fluid. The waves of the ocean arise and have a separate birth, crashing on the shore, but then back into the ocean they go. They never left it.

There is no movement in nirvana. There is no sameness, and one does not consider it to be timeless because one is not one. It is you, my friend, who go away. What we discover is that it was not the waves or the birds or the wind that were standing out and being separate from existence. It was we who were standing out and being separate from existence.

We take an eraser and we erase ourselves, kind of like one of those "Road Runner" cartoons, in which suddenly, in the middle of the cartoon, the cartoon would appear to stop and the hand of the artist would come onto the screen. And he would erase the Road Runner, a kind of surrealistic moment when something that was not supposed to be in our view comes into our view and changes everything.

This is self-realization. We erase ourselves. We go away. But we don't really go away and we don't really erase ourselves, since we were never there to begin with. We weren't there to begin with, in that what we are or conceive of ourselves as, is a perception. We've decided what we are. That's the dream. But when the dream fades, it's not that we don't exist. How could we not exist, since we never existed? It was only a dream. Dream after dream after dream. That's life.

The perceiver of the dream, the one before whom the dream is unfolding, is what we call the self. When we speak of self-realization, we don't mean the realization of the dream. The realization of the dream, or the different dreams viewing the movie, is what we already know. Oh, we could view different movies. We view youth, we view maturity, we view death, war, peace, space exploration, love, self-giving, selfishness, vanity. These are the different movies, the little videocassettes that we can pop into our screen and view. But this is not self-realization. True, one does not exist without the other, I suppose. But self-realization means the awareness, not of the movie, watching the movie, but of the self that watches.

Who or what is this self? This is our topic in self-discovery. Yes, the movie is a part of the self too. The movie comes out of the self and returns to the self. But it's a different part of the self. It's like a wave. Frozen in time. None of the waves are really moving, you just think they are. As a surfer is poised on the wave, on his board, cutting quickly to the left, he'll always be there, in that moment. He's never left it. He had no birth. He didn't go to school. He didn't purchase the board. None of those things ever were. Only that moment when he's cutting quickly to the left, frozen in time, a snapshot, a photograph, frozen reality, melting. In another picture he may be on the shore with his arm around his girlfriend. In another picture he's an old man in the hospital, dying. But these are not the same person. These are movies that the self is watching.

We can freeze a frame, and when we freeze the frame we see a moment. We stop on a singular image. We stop the movie and watch him on the crest of the wave. But that's what it really is, you see. Life is composed of singular images. A movie is composed of tiny little singular images, and they go very quickly. When they go quickly they appear to have form, they appear to be solid and substantial. They appear to have movement. What we call life is movement. And this is the samsara.

The samsara is the movement of life, and you, an individual self, a form, a moment on a wave, are bound. You are bound by the frame. You have forgotten that you are watching the movie. You've become so engrossed in the movie of your life that you've forgotten that you're sitting there watching. You're in the movie, now you're participating in it. Self-realization means taking a big step backward. This is liberation, being liberated, and turning our attention to that which we are, the self, while enjoying the movie at the same time. Pass the popcorn please.

Life is a film, a theater, the theater of the soul. We play different roles on different stages. At death we walk off stage, at birth we walk on stage. Self-realization is that timeless, perfect awareness. Well, what is God then? God is that which watches. God is neither masculine nor feminine, although God can assume any form. God is that eternal reality that is in everything, the world of time, space and condition, pleasure and pain, birth, growth, maturation, decay and death. Spinning, spinning, spinning in this world, always spinning. Beings caught in this samsara, in this web of existence, spinning from birth to death to rebirth, again and again, thousands of incarnations in time, in a cycle of existence, a cycle of plays. Then one day the plays end, the screen goes blank, there's nothing. Everything returns to its original formlessness. Then another dream begins.

But who is it who's dreaming all of this? Ecstasy. Pure ecstasy. Joy beyond understanding. Bliss beyond the dry dullness of the mind's philosophical ranging. Light. Light beyond any light in this world. The substance and the essence of all existence is this light, the transcendental light. Self-realization is the awareness of the finite, of the physical world, of the movie, the moments in time – the bird taking the jewel, the king being banished, the son returning – this wonderful movie, seeing it and understanding it in all of its glory. Self-realization means, then, meditating on the beach and watching the birds and the waves and the sound of the wind blur and fade, until we can no longer distinguish one from the other. They become one sound, one resonance, which we find that we are. We can no longer distinguish ourselves from the bird or the sounds of the waves or the wind. There's not even a sense of being able to distinguish anything because we've forgotten that one could distinguish, that one could remember, that one could be. There's nothing. Nothing in particular, that is. Or everything, or beyond everything and nothing, which are concepts of the mind, which is sitting in a body on the beach, contemplating all of this. While not too far away a child is looking into a jewel, seeing all of the worlds stretching out endlessly.

To become conscious of God, to become God's consciousness, to become God, to be God and to be beyond God, God being beyond God, God having an existence, separate from the creation. Going beyond God to that from which God came forth, which sustains God, to which God will return. To be that, to merge with that, to lose oneself and find oneself endlessly again and again in that – self-realization – no ego, no desires, no weight problems, no tax forms, no death to die, no life to live. Not an empty extinction. How could being the entire cosmos and all of its wonder – in all of its stages and cycles, and yet being that which is beyond them all, the invisible – be extinction? Extinction? Extinction of what, of whom? How can that which has never been be extinguished?

None of this has ever been or will ever be. All is an appearance. All is an illusion. Illusions are truth. All illusions are real. We say "illusions," meaning that they're shadows. I'm in Colorado; I'm walking through a field. I look up at the sky and I see a huge cloud moving across, very swiftly across and above. And then I look out and I see its shadow moving quickly over the land. One after another the clouds drift through Colorado, casting their shadows on the ground, moving quickly. The shadow covers a cow and moves on. It covers an old farm house. It goes across the highway, past the barbed wire fences, moving endlessly. Illusions are shadows moving endlessly across the ground.

The shadows are quite real, but they're shadows. They have very little substance. Oh, for the moment that they're there they appear to have a lot of substance, I would agree. Then again, who am I to agree? The shadow passes. The light is there again. Was the shadow ever there? No. The shadow was never there; the light has always been there. The moment with the shadow, when the shadow was there – well, light had never been there because the shadow was timeless. Only you create time by joining these events together. But they don't join together. There's no separativity.

Liberation from the finite. Liberation from the things that make you unhappy? Well, things don't make you unhappy. People don't make you unhappy. You make yourself unhappy. Because you are in the cycle, you're stuck. You're stuck in time. Liberation from time. Liberation means no rebirth. Now, does that mean you don't reincarnate? Well, you never did reincarnate. It's a way of talking, I suppose. Oh, you may have had countless lives and many more stretching before you, and what else have you got to do with your time? What does that have to do with liberation? I'm not sure there was a question. Was there? I've forgotten.

I knew there was some reason that we were talking about all this. Seems to have slipped my mind. What mind? I'm not sure. That word came from somewhere. Must have been an archaic language that they used in another time, on some planet someplace. They all went away, those people, though. I remember that. Oh, there were a lot of them; they thought they were important. And they were. And they went away. Gee, they didn't give us a forwarding address, I'm sorry. They moved out. Yes? One of them was your sister? And your father and your mother and all your friends, your relatives, people you met, experiences you – all of them – yes, they did live here for a while, yes, I remember them. Uh-huh. No, no, the city folks, they all moved, yes. Country folks too. Oh, the military? They went too, yes, uh-huh. You were worried about the bombs falling? Well, they couldn't fall. Oh, I suppose they did. But then they went away. The earth, yes, we had it in a file here. I think it was in one of our cabinets. Let me look for you – uh, earth, let's see, solar, yes, no, I'm sorry we've thrown that file out. Uh-huh? Yes, well, if we find it we'll call you, OK. Where are you staying? Nirvana? Is there someplace else? Oh good, yes, OK, we'll find you, no problem, we'll just, uh, the computer will take care of it.

It's a good model, it's a new one. It has everything in it – all of existence, all of the cycles, all of the stages. This computer is so good, as a matter of fact, that it has all of the past, present and future on one chip. All of the other possibilities on another chip. All of the impossibilities on a third chip. The fourth chip, well, that's the fourth dimension, the superconscious. Oh, yes, we've got that too, uh-huh, we've got that. God? Yep, God's on another chip. Yep. We've got it all. The computer itself? Oh, yes, self-replicating DNA. We grow them. Out back. Yes, that tree that used to be the apple tree? Uh-huh? Yeah, some kid found this jewel, and we got it and we looked inside of it and we saw all of this happening, so we decided that it was. In one facet of the jewel we were sitting here having this conversation, I was explaining how the computer worked. Uh-huh. Then some guy came in and he brought the beach with him. Suddenly it got very sandy here, and we were all sitting around and the waves were coming through. Fortunately we had the computer waterproofed. I can't tell you, I was very nervous about that. Uh-huh? Yes, sure! Well, it's been nice seeing you too, and listen, you know, drop by some time again in any one of the possible futures the computer can construct for you. Yes, well, who do we buy our computers from? Oh, well, we grow them. Uh-huh, yes, they grow out of the heart of being. No problem, sure. We'll call you, thanks.

The awareness of liberation is not liberation. The awareness of time is not liberation. The awareness of place, space or condition is not liberation. The smoke from the fire passes through the building and the soot affixes itself to the walls. The smoke passes through the air and keeps going. Liberation. You can't say what it is, but you can sure say what it isn't. And yet everything is in it. If you choose to be free, if you choose to be liberated, if you choose to be what I am, then you've chosen freedom.

You can do this. That's my sole purpose in life, just to sit here today and tell you that you can do this. In any life. You can do this in one of your past lives, in a future life, or right now. I prefer now. You have to refine your being. You have to go through all the stages and steps of erasing yourself. Through service to others, with purity, humility, integrity, by going through the things that life gives you to go through, happily.

You have to loosen the grip of time gradually. You've fallen asleep in bed with someone you love. Their arm is around you. And veeerrryy quietly and slooowly you have to get up out of bed – you don't want to wake them now. You lie there for about 15 minutes listening to the sounds of the night. And then veeerrry quietly you lift the sheets and just slide – oops, they moved a little bit; we wait a few more minutes, listening to our heart beat. They're dreaming next to you, they're dreaming. Who knows where they are or what they're seeing or what they're feeling? They've forgotten all about you. Such is love.

And you slip out of bed – oh, you did it! Now tip-toe very quietly, put your hand on the doorknob, turn it slooowly, open it, you're out in the hall. Close the door behind you, slooowly – liberation! You're free! From those who loved you. Isn't that liberation? Well, now you're in the hall, true. Well, you've got to go somewhere; you could go to the kitchen, outside.

Liberation, what did you expect it was going to be? What did you think? What do you think, they're going to put a crown on your head and put robes around you? And what do you want anyway? Just who do you think you are? That's the question. It's not enough just to walk down the hall? You can go back into the bedroom if you want to, I mean, if you like that sort of thing, I suppose, if you're one of those. Is that what you really want? Well then go ahead. We've got it on the computer chip. The bedroom scene. Do you want us to play it again? That's the one where you were a person. Do you remember when you were a person? When you still had a life? Yeah, those were the good old days, weren't they? Oh, we had a hell of a time, didn't we? Fought battles together, grew up together, listened to music, went to parties; we worked. God, do you remember all the work we did, all those years in school, sitting in the classroom listening to the teacher? Then we became teachers. Do you remember the time and the worlds where we taught them? God, Atlantis was only yesterday. Let alone Los Angeles. Remember that incarnation in Los Angeles?

Well, you've taught in a lot of places now, and we're glad. You've helped many beings, who didn't exist, to attain liberation, which they never lost, since they never had it, since they never were. We think the work you've done is wonderful. We've got this gold watch here. And you know, we've managed to take our entire computer, with all of existence, with all those chips, and we've reduced it into this watch here. This watch is so good that it never stops. It's what we call perpetual motion. We finally found it. Well, it was here all along. It was the universe; existence is perpetual motion. Galileo wondered about it, da Vinci – we've got it right here. It's a Rolex, of course.

Timelessness and time, life and death. Your existence is passing before you, grains of sand in the hourglass. The Wicked Witch of the West has you in her castle and she's turned the hourglass over and the sand is running through. Will you be rescued, will you be liberated or will you die? The only way you can beat death is liberation. If they rescue you in time, if the Tin Man, the Cowardly Lion and Toto and the Scarecrow get there in time, you'll be rescued. If not, the Wicked Witch of the West will have her way and her day, and she'll get those ruby slippers. But if you can click your heels three times and with your whole heart want to be home, as little E.T. says, "home" or "aum," then you can get out of the castle, you can go home. And all the friends that you had, all the adventures in Oz, will go away, and all your good friends. You'll cry, Dorothy, as you leave them, and they'll all go away. The Tin Man, the Scarecrow and that wonderful Lion and the Wizard himself and the Munchkins and the evil witches and Glinda the Good Witch, they all go away.

Well, you know you have to go home, even though you could cry and stay forever, you have to go home. So, with them all gathered around you and the Wizard up there in the air someplace in that wonderful balloon, you click your heels three times, and the mother you loved and the father you loved and the children and the places and the moments of this world all go away. You don't know why, but you know you have to go home. It's an eternal longing. It's Marvell's drop of dew, wanting to go back to the sky. We're drawn by a force we don't understand – through worlds, through experience, and then click your heels three times. There's no place like home.

And then, when we're home, "Well, God, it was a dream, it was a dream; Oz, I dreamt it," Dorothy says. "Didn't it really happen Auntie Em? You're all still here!" You see that's nirvana. You must understand. It's Dorothy at home. She went to the Emerald Kingdom for a while but at home, all the characters are still there. The fellow who looked like the Scarecrow, the fellow who looked like the Cowardly Lion, the fellow who looked like the Wizard and the Tin Man, they're all there still, just in a different form.

Self-realization doesn't imply loss, gain, or even transition. It's only a settling. The separate sounds on the beach, the bird, the waves, the wind – they all come together again. They blend, they harmonize. The moment of the wave with the surfer cutting to the left, the moment with no surfer and no wave. The ice has melted, the water is all. And beyond all of this, beyond these discussions, these ideas, these analogies, these images, the child is gone, the jewel is gone, the computer outgrew itself and went away. Took itself out for lunch. Everything gone away. Self-realization and liberation.

(Rama chants AUM seven times.)

Lead us from the unreal to the real.

Lead us from darkness into light.

Lead us from death to immortality.

Lead us from the real into the unreal.

Lead us from light into darkness.

Lead us from immortality to death and back again, again and again as you will.

You are the Self, you are my beloved, you are eternity. I am Thine and Thou art mine. But I can't own anything, and I can't be you and you can't be me. That only happens in time, and there is no time when we really love each other. That's the magic of love. When we really love each other, there is no time, don't you understand?

Love. Love is self-realization. Love is liberation. The only way beyond time, the only way to unravel the knot of existence, is to love.

RAE CHORZE-FWAZ INTERNATIONAL

By:

Rama

Rama ~ Dr. Frederick Lenz
president

AMERICAN BRANCH

TANTRIC MYSTICISM

Tantra is a reconciliation, a joining together. In this universe there appears to be opposition. Opposition is a point of view. Everything is one. There is only one eternal reality. Yet there are two – man and woman, sun and moon, dark and light, morning and evening, day and night, forward and back, in and out. Tantra is the reconciliation of opposites, seeing that opposites are complements.

Mysticism is the experience of eternity, beyond the body. In mysticism, a person experiences the spirit world, the alternate planes of reality. Mysticism also is the study of the physical world, but not from the physical perspective. The study is inside out. Everything is viewed from within.

In most studies we use our world, this earth, this island in the middle of eternity, as our measuring point. The island is a certain length. We use that length as our compilation factor for measuring the distance from here to the next star. On the island, a tree grows a certain way. We will measure trees that we find elsewhere in the universe by the tree that grew on our home planet, on our island. People are a certain way, life is a certain way, death is a certain way.

Everything in this world is a template which we use for measuring, judging, quantifying, classifying and amalgamating everything else. When we extrapolate, we extrapolate our theories and our philosophies based upon our physical lives, including the life of the body; the life of the world that we perceive through the body and the senses; the subconscious workings of the mind and the conscious workings of the physical mind – thought analysis, abstraction, inductive, deductive methods of reasoning and logic, free association, the computer functions of the brain – memory, recall, projection of possible futures; emotion as regards the body, emotion measured by the body – my body wants, my body feels, my body feels love, my body feels self-pity, sorrow, courage. The body is the primary measuring unit; it's the angstrom by which we quantify the physical world. All of our excursions are made through the body. Even our mental excursions are made through the body by using the body's knowledge and the body's experience, by drawing on the body's resources.

Mysticism has nothing to do with the body from the body's point of view. In mysticism, we have stepped beyond the body. Or it might be precise to say we never considered ourselves to have anything much to do with the body anyway. We were never really in the body. The body is another interesting piece of furniture in the house that we happen to be walking through. This gives us, not just a different perspective, but a series of different perspectives because our angstrom, our measuring unit, will not be the body or this world but all of the worlds, all of the planes of being. Rather than coming from one culture and viewing and measuring everything in our explorations of the world by our culture, we're much more cosmopolitan. We have the views at our fingertips of all cultures.

We all know that when the white race came to America, they thought of the Indians as little more than animals; their religions were nothing – ritual dancing. The systematic extermination of the Native Americans was permissible because from the limited point of view of the white race it was impossible to understand what the Indians were all about, why they didn't build cities, why they had no interest in building cities. The depth of their religion, their communication with the spirit world, their poetry, their culture, their legends, which are as complex and evolved as the legends and symbologies and systems of any other culture. Their religion is as complex as the religion of any culture in this world. But because they [the white race] were looking through a glass darkly, they didn't see. What they saw were not Indians but animals, something worthy of extermination. Vermin. A pestilence.

This view is the view of people who have bodies. People who have bodies, who orient to the body culture, view existence with the same limitations. A person who had experienced cultures throughout the world, a Margaret Mead perhaps, an anthropologist, would have come here, had she come first, and discovered a delightful race and lived with them in peace. She would have shed her own skin, her own cultural milieu, to look inside the hearts and minds of the people without judgment, just to observe, using her experiences in different cultures, sort of a polyculturalism, to understand the culture in front of her. She could use the Samoans, the Egyptians, the Aborigines, people who live in the Netherlands, the British. Any group could be used as a frame of reference, using that frame of reference for understanding, giving you multiple possibilities. The computer doesn't have to run on one language, it can run on many languages, many possibilities. She [Margaret Mead] would also be able to drop all of these ways of seeing and just look. Perhaps engage in the dance with the Indians, perhaps take part in their religion and be it.

This is mysticism. In mysticism, one has experienced billions of alternate planes of reality and brings them to bear and use in understanding. One is a world traveler, an intergalactic, inter-plane traveler. Tantra, then, is something that has to do with any plane of reality or any culture because it studies not the differences within a culture but the nature of cultures themselves. It observes that in any plane of reality, there is opposition, there's contrast. And it is the study of this contrast, the ultimate reconciliation of opposites, accepting that opposites are opposites and they're also complements, neither and both, and then something else. This leads to liberation.

Mysticism is the exploration and the direct experience of consciousness. In other words, tantra is theory. Tantra's a theory, a philosophical way of seeing. It's more of a mental or super-mental yoga. Mysticism is an experiential yoga. In mysticism we're experiencing countless planes of reality, jumping in and out of cosmic doorways, having spiritual experiences, being filled with light, experiencing the ecstasy. Transmutation. Whirling through different vortexes, gyres of existence. Whereas tantra is a quieter, more philosophical understanding of existence. Tantra takes you to the very root of knowledge. In mysticism we're out running around in the desert or in the mountains; we're exploring; we're experimenting, experiencing. We experience in tantra too, but it's a different type of experience.

Tantra is the search for truth in the finite. Finding the infinite in the finite, seeing God in everything. Mysticism is the experience of God in everything. Tantra is seeing, feeling and ultimately becoming one with God and everything. Mysticism is experiencing, feeling and ultimately becoming one with everything.

Tantric mysticism is then the combination of these two practices. Or I could say, perhaps, is the culmination and is the particular art that I teach. I discussed in our tape about tantra, "Tantra and the Left-Handed Path," quite a bit about tantra and how it works, particularly in everyday situations. In the tape on "The Yoga of Mysticism and Power," I've discussed some of the more specific and practical aspects of mysticism – how it works, different planes of reality, the general, basic introductory rules to the study – as I have in the tape on tantra.

However, tantric mysticism is not just taking some tantra and some mysticism and putting it together. Because a synergistic effect occurs when we marry the two; they produce an offspring, which is greater than both. As you know, synergism is the combination of two radicals, two factors. And when the two are combined, they become stronger than they were as two separate cells. The sum of the parts is greater than the parts because the synergistic effect is to increase the power. The two atoms put together produce 10,000 atoms of power because they affect each other and cause a type of chain reaction. They create a new structure, kind of a new DNA.

Tantric mysticism is a very sophisticated form of spiritual practice and it is not intended for beginners. Beginners can practice it, think about it; it's a nice perspectiveless perspective. Tantric mysticism is something that a person would practice, or any being would practice, after they had mastered most of the other yogas. As you are probably aware, I have classified the different yogas. There's the yoga of love, the yoga of selfless giving, the yoga of discrimination and the yoga of mysticism and power. It's my feeling that all of the pathways that we see in the world, the religions and so on, are combinations and recombinations of these four yogas, no matter what they call it – Buddhism, Hinduism, Taoism, Zen and so on. These are the four primary colors from which all the other colors come forth, in spirituality.

There is a fifth path that is a little bit different, that I don't personally deal with. This is the path of austerity. I have practiced this path myself in other lifetimes, but I don't particularly recommend it. It doesn't go well with the era. And it's a very difficult path. That's the path of negation, whereby through excessive pain one breaks contact with the world. Self-inflicted pain, prolonged fasting, things like that, asceticism – to an extreme point. But it doesn't bring realization. It can bring you very high. But finally to come to realization, as Buddha realized and many others, you can fast for 50 days and go through these powerful practices, the austerities, but ultimately they're an extreme. They don't lead to realization. You have to come back from them into the world to a broader-based yoga to achieve self-realization because of the fixation and attachment.

Tantric mysticism then is awareness itself. It combines the fun of mysticism, that beautiful joy and laughter that we experience in mysticism along with the tremendous discipline and precision in mysticism, with a broad-based, heart-oriented, love-oriented reconciliation that we find in tantra. In tantra we have this beautiful love, this Chaucerian acceptance that all is good, that there's good in the hearts of all, that all are God's creations, from the saint to the thief. God works through all. This is a very Christlike compassion, yoga, whereas mysticism is discipline, precision, the precise use of power. Mysticism is a very practical form of spiritual discovery for a person who has to live and work in the world. Tantra is an internal realization that also works very well in the world.

Tantric mysticism is something that a person would practice after many, many lifetimes of spiritual discovery, after they had already mastered the four paths in other lifetimes. I saved my discussion of it for the last tape in this series. This is the 28th tape. After listening to "Introductory and Intermediate Meditation," "Purity and Humility," "The Yoga of Love," "The Yoga of Selfless Giving," "The Yoga of Discrimination," "The Yoga of Mysticism and Power," "Spiritual Absorption in Nirvana," "Death and Reincarnation," "Samadhi and the Superconscious States," "The Caretaker Personality," "The Tibetan Rebirth Process," "Living and Working In The World," "Pleasure, Pain and the Senses," "How to Achieve Spiritual Balance," "The Subtle Physical Body," "Women, Men and Self-Realization," "Inaccessibility and Attachment," "Spiritual Experiences, Dreams and Visions," "Zen, Taoism and Buddhism," "The Occult Body, Auras and the Chakras," "Spiritual Teachers and the Enlightenment Process," "Advanced Meditation," "Dreaming," "Gods, Goddesses and Carrier Beings," "Dharma and Karma," "Tantra and the Left-Handed Path" and "Liberation and Self-Realization," finally we come to the 28th tape. And as you know, the Buddha sat underneath the Bodhi tree for 28 days. His enlightenment took 28 days.

Twenty-eight is an interesting number: four sevens. There are seven higher and seven lower planes of consciousness, according to some systems. And of course, there are the four directions. Four is the number of mysticism. Seven is the number of yoga. Seven is the number of the superconscious. The seventh chakra is the chakra of liberation, the crown center. The fourth chakra is the heart center, three above and three below. The center of love.

Tantric mysticism is a surprise. It's everything and nothing. It's hide-and-go seek with yourself. It's all of the tapes – everything that we've said, and then all the things that I could never say. Tantric mysticism is experiential and reflective. And to need it is life.

To try and bring about your own realization, to be liberated, to merge with light, to do all these things, all you have to do is to be yourself. Not the self that you necessarily know at the moment, but your eternal self. From the vegetable kingdom, we bring you the onion. Consider it. More vitamins and minerals in the onion than in any other vegetable. "Good Housekeeping" tip. The onion has layers, layer after layer after layer. We peel off one layer and there's another one – tantric mysticism. In tantric mysticism, which is a rather exacting discipline, by the way, we peel the layers of our self back, one after another after another. We do this by using everything. Everything. And sometimes by using nothing.

Tantric mysticism is the practice in which we use all the other yogas. Because none of them contradict what tantric mysticism is. If you practice any of the other yogas or any of the other pathways, they won't tell you to do everything, to practice all the other pathways, because you're following theirs. Tantric mysticism accepts and endorses all the other pathways, yet it is a pathway too. In tantric mysticism we can use anything that will help us, either in our self-realization, aiding the self-realization of another, or just in generally having a good time, which is part of self-realization too.

Yet tantric mysticism is a study. It's not a kind of unitarianism where we're just clumping a lot of different things together and exploring them. It has its own set of – I wouldn't call them rules – but I would say etiquette. There's a spiritual etiquette to the practice. And it can't be written down. It can't be spoken. It's up in a cave in the Himalayas somewhere engraved in the air.

To learn tantric mysticism, well, life teaches you tantric mysticism. All the time, if you'll only watch. Watch the seasons change. Walk in nature. Watch the people change. Walk in the world. Watch yourself change. Look in the mirror of existence and look beyond it. It's best, though, to learn tantric mysticism from a teacher. A teacher of tantric mysticism will use anything and everything to bring you to enlightenment: Zen techniques, koans, Hinduism, the *Bhagavad-Gita*, the wisdom of Krishna, the wisdom of the shopping mall and the valley girl, your own life, your own death, sex, money, negative emotions, positive emotions.

Yet there's a purity that runs throughout tantric mysticism. The two fundamental building blocks of tantric mysticism are purity and humility. Meditation clears the way and makes the way possible. Selfless giving is the practice that burns away the layers of the onion.

Meditation makes selfless giving possible. Purity and humility keep meditation and selfless giving clear. Love radiates through the entire practice because we do all of it only for love. Love is the fuel. Discrimination keeps us on our proper course. While purity and humility make sure that everything runs well, discrimination shows us the way. Mysticism and power enable us to do battle with existence, finally reaching to spiritual absorption in nirvana where we become absorbed in everything.

But do we stop there? Do we stop with absorption? No. Why? That's why we have death and reincarnation. We can be absorbed in nirvana, but then we can come back into the world to play because we are reincarnation. Life isn't bad. Death isn't bad. Because we're everything and beyond everything. But the difference is, while we're in this world, we're absorbed in samadhi, we experience the superconscious states, we're in the world but not of the world.

To do this we use the caretaker personality. The caretaker personalities are the different forms, the different selves that we take on without a sense of being a specific person or a specific entity. We take on different personalities. We play with them like we do with clothes. This is what we call the Tibetan rebirth process. Using tantric mysticism, within this life we go through thousands of incarnations. Tantric mysticism is the fastest path of all the paths. It's not better than any of the others, but it's for the person who wants to, in one lifetime, go through thousands of births and deaths. That's why we have to use everything to do that. It's the yoga of totality.

We do all this, of course, while living and working in the world. We live and work in the world because we use that, because it's part of our yoga. Naturally we have to accept our body, pleasure, pain and the senses. And we use them for realization because God exists in pleasure, God exists in pain and beyond both – God as She who experiences through the senses, God as the senses.

But still, pleasure, pain and the senses can take us away from all of that. We have to have a sense of spiritual balance. We have to achieve it because we can become so wrapped up in pleasure, pain and the senses, in our emotions, in our attachments and our entanglements, that we forget, that we get lost in the maya, in the illusion, in the shadows.

To do this we become conscious of the subtle physical body, which is beyond the physical body. The subtle physical body is our astral self, and in it we can go above the confines of the senses and pleasure and pain. Naturally we have to become aware of the differences. There are tremendous differences in the subtle bodies of men and women. Men and women really realize God in very different ways. It's necessary to learn these differences, to become conscious of them, because when we learn them and know them, we not only can further our own realization, our own awareness, but we can also further the realization of others.

We live in a world with both men and women. All of us are actually men and women. We're both. Yet we find in a particular incarnation that we have to deal with the society, with the history and with our own composure. But to live in the world, you must practice inaccessibility. Because while you may love spiritual light and be aware of it, there are those who would hurt you or you would sometimes hurt yourself. The world is not overly fond of light, I'm afraid, the people in the world, that is – parts of them. So to practice self-discovery, to live in this world, you must learn inaccessibility.

Attachment is the trap, of course. Attachment is to be bound, to think of ourselves as a finite self in a body and not to be the free sky. Unattachment is to be the sky. The birds come and go. We don't fixate. Attachment is limitation. From attachment comes pain.

Spiritual experiences, dreams and visions carry us beyond all of this. It's good to have a knowledge of the traditional ways – Zen, Taoism and Buddhism -- to become conscious of the different layers and strata of reality, of your occult body; to know the workings of the machine, the auras and the chakras. And to know how to deal with an enlightened person, how to recognize one. Advanced meditation, of course, takes us beyond all these things. All the things we've discussed so far are words and ideas – ways. But in advanced meditation we move beyond all of this. Advanced meditation is dreaming – dreaming different dreams, different creations.

There are those who will help us with our advanced meditation and our dreaming. There are higher beings, gods, goddesses and carrier beings. There are also lower beings who can hinder us. We need to know who's out on the street. And the system works through dharma and karma. Dharma is the truth, the shining, immutable existence. Karma is the mechanism, the way it all functions. Tantra is the reconciliation of dharma and karma. All leading, of course, to liberation and self-realization.

Which brings us finally to tantric mysticism. What is tantric mysticism? I can't tell you. I hope you don't feel that you've wasted your money on this tape. I definitely can't tell you though. Oh, I can tell you everything that's part of it, I just did. But tantric mysticism is a great mystery. I can't tell you but I'd love to show you. I think I have. Maybe I haven't. Tantric mysticism is all there is. Yet it has a lot of etiquette. And the way you learn the etiquette is first by wanting to, and then by trying. And as you try, don't be afraid to make a fool out of yourself. If you fail a thousand times, try to fail a thousand and one times. Never give up. There's no going back, and if you go back, go forward. Because there is no forward and there is no back. The way in is the way out. And the way out is the way in.

The way you really learn tantric mysticism, in other words, is by studying with a tantric mystic. You're a budding tantric mystic. But you need to go and be with a tantric mystic because the way you teach tantric mysticism is etiquette. It's nothing that you say. When I teach my students tantric mysticism, I do it in several ways. I do it closely, when I'm talking to an individual, spending time with them; I do it in a group sense, when one can disseminate information to many, and actually at that point, the closer experience would interfere with the process; and [I do it in] the more formal side of the training – books, tapes, talks. Naturally I do it mostly through meditating, by opening up that doorway and helping people walk through it. That's the mysticism side.

Tantra is rebirth. It's the reconciliation – how to deal with the fact that you're all of reality and that you still have a body that has its demands. It seems silly, to be in nirvana for a while and then suddenly find yourself here again. That's tantric mysticism. Tantra shows you how to do that. Mysticism shows you how to get out of it and still have fun with it all.

I teach a great deal through dreaming. Most tantric mystics do, since we're really dreamers, we're poets. I visit people constantly in dreams and explain things to them in dreams that I couldn't explain in this world because in this world everybody's so busy measuring by the angstrom of the body. But in the dream worlds, you're used to that. Then I can come and show you interesting things. You won't remember when you wake up. How could you? The physical mind can't contain the things. But your inner being knows. Remember, you're not just the physical mind that measures by the body. You're eternity.

See, the tantric mystic sits at home a lot, because by sitting at home they can visit people more. They're not bound by their body. They're working through countless planes of being simultaneously both in the past, the present and the future. Because who's bound by that? The tantric mystic is not bound by the past, present or future. They can slip into a past, move into the future and go beyond time, all at once. This is tantric mysticism. You're dealing with the unlimited power of existence and with a happy, humble, sunshiny day that exists at the moment. There's no end to it. Veil after veil will be pushed back. The onion will be peeled again and again. And as fast as you peel the layers, of course, there are more, until finally you get tired of peeling onions and you're crying so much that you go do something else for a while. And then you come back to it. Tantric mysticism. Circles in circles and beyond.

The way I teach tantric mysticism is by doing it in front of people, in other words. That's how it's taught. I live it myself. It's my practice. It's my wayless way. I don't think most people will be able to practice it, personally, in this world, because they won't be interested. Those who are interested will find it very easy. And it leads very quickly to liberation. It's the shortest path. Not the best. Some people like the longer route and that's nice. What's the rush? Of course, for those who follow the short path, there's no rush either. There's only the short path, which seems to get shorter every day.

What is tantric mysticism? Well you'll have to tell me. I'd like to learn myself. That's the fun about it. It's self-exploration, without rules or convention, but with lots of etiquette. And if you'd like to learn the etiquette, then come see me. Meditate with me. Journey with me, in the body or out of it. While I'm alive or after I'm no longer here. It doesn't really matter. I'm always glad to drop by and teach people tantric mysticism. Oh, if I've been dead for a thousand years, it doesn't matter. How can I die? I was ahead of myself in time all the time anyway. I can easily dream myself back to teach the study to anyone. Or, go to someone else that teaches the same thing. You'll find it's me. And then you'll find that I'm you, and that we're one.

Tantric mysticism. It's the study of everything. Yet it has a tremendous amount of etiquette. There's a way to it, but it's invisible. Yet you can feel it. And you know when you're on course, and you know when you're off. But, of course, you know that off course is on a different course.

The waves break on the beach. Why don't you go listen to them and learn from them? See what they have to say. Stop trying to know everything and figure it all out. You can't. Don't you understand, silly? You can't know it all! You can be it all. You are it all. But you can't know it all. Who'd want to? A lot of clutter, if you ask me.

I'd rather meditate. Wouldn't you? And be absorbed – in perfect light. Or find myself in the world, struggling away, or appearing to struggle. Working away while really not working. Giving everything. Knowing that there's no one and nothing to give. It's a feeling, an essence, an expressionless expression, this tantric mysticism, this life. Life is tantric mysticism. It's the highest yoga without being too high. It's the lowest yoga – well, somewhere it's still in the middle. It pops in and out of different places, at unexpected moments. That's what makes life an adventure.

Tantric mysticism is completely unpredictable. But then again, aren't you? Aren't you capable of doing it all at once, without knowing how or why? Of finding your way back to nirvana? I'm waiting for you there on the luminous edge of existence. You know, I'm always in the desert. I send my double back, my other self. I'm always waiting for you, hoping that you'll be really interested, that you'll try completely. In every life I wait for you. I've always been waiting and I always will. And then when you come and join me, you can wait for others. Or we can go have some adventures. I know a nice little world I think you'll like. At the end of the cycle of birth and death you can go there, with me if you'd like to. Or choose your own company – Vishnu Properties. Choice view lots still available. Fine view of nirvana.

Don't say that no one ever told you. Because no one just did. And if you want to succeed on the path, then for God's sake, commit yourself to the path, with everything that you have and everything that you are. There are no rules, there's spirit. That's what matters. It's heart. It's not through stealth or through techniques. Oh, it's good to have knowledge, but it's heart that is the way. The way is love. The way of self-giving. The way is commitment to the highest ideal that you can perceive without fixating on that ideal. Giving everything that you have to what you think is right. And then tomorrow, if you find that something else is right, or righter, doing that. But it has to be – life has to be lived. You have to pull those layers down that block you. You have to give it your whole heart and your whole mind and your whole being. All the time. That's tantric mysticism. If you do that, how could you fail, how could you have a problem?

Ultimately there's only glory. As the poet [William Wordsworth] says, "Trailing clouds of glory do we come, from God who is our home."

I always liked that stanza from the Roethke poem, "The Waking." I think it really sums up tantric mysticism. "I wake to sleep and take my waking slow. I feel my fate in what I cannot fear. I learn by going where I have to go."

That's the essence of tantric mysticism. It's a field of light. It's a moment in nature. It's a moment with someone you love. It's watching someone die. It's watching someone be born. It's going beyond all of this, through all the different planes, and not judging them by this world. It's experience, it's power, it's light, it's humility.

"I wake to sleep and take my waking slow. I feel my fate in what I cannot fear. I learn by going where I have to go." That's it. That's tantric mysticism. I knew it was in here someplace. It had to be in the tape. I mean the tape does have the name, "Tantric Mysticism." And I wouldn't want you to get a tape that wasn't right. So I guess I saw that in the future and came back in the present and changed the tapes after they'd gone to the manufacturer and been released, just so I could put this part in: "We learn by going where we have to go." That's tantric mysticism.

Nirvana is waiting! Don't keep it waiting too long.

THE BIOGRAPHY OF RAMA -
DR. FREDERICK LENZ

Rama - Dr. Frederick P. Lenz was born on February 9, 1950, in San Diego, California. When he was three years old, his family moved to Stamford, Connecticut. His father worked as a marketing executive and later served as Mayor of Stamford. His mother was a housewife and an advanced student of astrology. His mother told Dr. Lenz that she knew for many months before he was born that he was an exceptional being.

"When I was very young, three, four, five, I used to go into samadhi, a very high state of meditation," Dr. Lenz recalled. "I would be outside in the backyard of my parents' home, and I'd look up at the sky and go away, dissolve, go beyond this world. Naturally, growing up, I never realized that I was essentially different from other children. Of course, I noticed that I was, but I didn't realize that other people didn't see life the way I did."

Dr. Lenz attended schools in the Stamford area. While he described himself as a rebel in high school, he excelled at the University of Connecticut, where he majored in English and minored in Philosophy. While in college, he was inducted as a member of Phi Beta Kappa and graduated Magna Cum Laude. After winning a highly competitive State of New York Graduate Council Fellowship, he received his M.A. and Ph.D. in English Literature from the State University of New York at Stony Brook. His doctoral dissertation on the poet Theodore Roethke was directed by the Pulitzer Prize-winning poet, Louis Simpson, Ph.D.

During the years he pursued his academic education, Dr. Lenz also became deeply involved in meditation and the study of self-discovery. "I started to meditate formally at about 18 and began to go into samadhi right away," he recollected. "I can remember sitting on a mountaintop in Southern California. I had been meditating for maybe six months, just on my own. I'd read a book or two about it. The books reminded me of something, and I would sit out there around twilight and focus on my third eye, and everything would become still. Rings of light would appear, and I'd go through them. Then suddenly, I would be beyond time and space, beyond life and death. I would dissolve for what, an hour, a lifetime, eternity? There are no words.

And I was changed by this experience."

At age 19, Dr. Lenz started formal studies with various meditation teachers. During this period, he wrote two best-selling books based on his own research -- Lifetimes, True Accounts of Reincarnation (1979), and Total Relaxation: The Complete Program for Overcoming Worry, Stress, Tension and Fatigue (1980). While promoting these books, he appeared on numerous national television and radio programs. He taught meditation and yoga at universities around the United States and the world -- representing the teachers he studied with.

As time passed, Dr. Lenz decided it was time to teach on his own. In early 1981, he formed his own school of American Buddhism. Making himself available, sometimes over 200 nights a year, to those interested in living "an uncommonly fine life," he embarked on teaching Buddhist principles and meditation, ultimately to more than 100,000 people.

The Early Years of Teaching, 1981–1988

As a student, teacher and representative of enlightenment, Dr. Lenz described himself as "innately tantric." The Sanskrit term "tantra" means using everything in one's life to grow. It is a sophisticated path where one does not shun experience. Dr. Lenz's body of reaching reflects his classic tantric approach. From his earliest teaching years, he did not restrict himself to imparting a single framework of knowledge. Rather, he presented the best of many teaching traditions and constantly incorporated current American experiences -- books, films, field trips, shopping malls -- into his American Buddhist coursework.

In 1981, when he founded his first school, named Lakshmi after the Indian goddess of harmony and prosperity, the overlying theme was Vedantic philosophy -- the classic paths of Indian yoga: love and devotion, wisdom, action and selfless giving. At the same time, he introduced his students to Tibetan teachings and those of the American mystic, Carlos Castaneda.

In 1982, he adopted a teaching name from the Indian epic, The Ramayana. "Rama is the name of an enlightened warrior who lived thousands of years ago in India," he explained. "I really don't know whether I picked the name or it was given to me. One day I was meditating on a cliff overlooking the ocean in Southern California and I was absorbed in a state of high meditation. As I came out of the meditation and became aware of the sense world, the world around me, I knew that I had a new name. And the name was "Rama."

Throughout 1982, he offered numerous public meditation workshops to ever-larger audiences. Although he had started his teaching career with fifteen students, by 1983 close to one thousand people were enrolled in his teaching seminars. In late 1983, Dr. Lenz scaled back the number of students he worked with directly to less than half but continued to hold frequent, popular public workshops.

Dr. Lenz was a strong believer in advertising. His approach to reaching people and giving them the opportunity to meditate with an enlightened teacher included taking out full-page ads featuring striking photos and text that challenged and awakened minds. Drawn by his mastery of meditation and his unusual ads, often close to one thousand people attended his public lectures.

In 1985, while continuing to teach in Los Angeles and San Francisco, Dr. Lenz journeyed with a number of his students to Boston. Recurrent themes in his talks with his students and to the public were meditation, career success, spiritual balance, the Tibetan rebirth process, psychic development and the enlightenment of women.

By 1986, as Dr. Lenz planned a series of public talks in the San Francisco area, he felt that his eclectic approach to self-discovery most closely resembled Zen Buddhism. Accompanied by one of his students, he traveled to Japan and met with Zen masters in Kyoto. As he described it, "When I go visit my brother monks in Japan and sit down with other Zen masters, and I walk into the monasteries, and I meet the Abbot, drink tea with him and have discussion or silence, they look at my long hair, and they have their shaved heads, and they look at my crazy clothes and my strange expression -- but they feel the power that emanates from my dedication to the practice. So they are comfortable... They don't quite know what to do, yet they find they have to accept me because I'm one with the practice."

Dr. Lenz stared that he himself was the ultimate koan. When he walked onstage in San Francisco wearing black leather clothes, sporting sunglasses, drinking Diet Coke, with a wide ring of curly hair around his head, many minds snapped -- how could a person who looked like that be an enlightened teacher? Throughout his teaching years, those who could not penetrate this koan did not continue to study with him. Those who remained found this koan challenging, intriguing and uplifting.

In early 1988, Dr. Lenz began to shift his seminar program to the East Coast. While he continued to teach on both coasts, by late 1989, he considered himself a New York based teacher.

The Later Teaching Years, 1989 – 1998

With the move to New York came an increased emphasis on career success and absorption in career (particularly computer science) as a form of meditation and mindfulness, while at the same time leading a full, balanced life. By 1990, Dr. Lenz began to emphasize Tantric Zen Buddhism -- an approach inclusive of Vajrayana Buddhism and Tibetan yoga -- as the pathway to enlightenment most suited for Western living.

Dr. Lenz described the 1990s as a time of tremendous freedom. "Just be truthful," he advised. "Determine where you are and where you wish to be, and then use all of your self-effort to make that happen. It's an exciting time. It's a time of battle -- battle and journeys and teaching and learning. But it's an open time. Who could ask for more?"

In early 1992, Dr. Lenz perceived that one of the best ways for his students to grow was to begin teaching on their own, with the option of inviting their students to sit in on one or more of his lectures. Many of the new students subsequently chose to enroll in Dr. Lenz's seminar program. With this, a new generation of students began attending Dr. Lenz's seminars. The new group stepped rapidly into the fast-paced environment of Dr. Lenz's American Buddhist program, balancing meditation with career, travel, and adventure. Adapting his teachings for this new and younger group, Dr. Lenz demonstrated how to balance hard work with play -- scuba diving with his students in islands all over the Caribbean, the Fiji Islands and Hawaii, journeying with his students to Europe, the California deserts and the American Southwest, holding rave dance parties in some of the most elegant settings in Manhattan, including the foyer of the World Financial Center and the Guggenheim Museum. Everyone danced.

During this period, Dr. Lenz also wrote two books about Buddhist teachings – the bestseller *Surfing the Himalayas* (1995, St.

Martin's Press) and a popular sequel, *Snowboarding to Nirvana* (1997, St. Martin's Press).

Dr. Lenz believed that electronic music suffused with the energy of enlightenment could greatly assist the aspiring student. From 1987 to 1994, working with the band Zazen, he co-wrote and produced fourteen musical albums including "Canyons of Light," "Enlightenment," "Cayman Blue" and "Samadhi." These albums featured music geared towards advancing the practice of meditation. Intently listening to Zazen meditation music, focusing on every note, was the equivalent of a "listening meditation."

Dr. Lenz was also a software designer. In conjunction with those working in his companies, he created a wide range of helpful produces. He emphasized the importance of career success for his students, stating, "I define career success as using your work to advance yourself spiritually." He emphasized computer science, "Because if you study computer science, you will find that it will develop your mind. It makes your mind very strong. And it's literally like doing Buddhist exercises all day long." Dr. Lenz was active in the introduction of educational, client/server, networking, medical, banking, trading systems, encryption, internet and internet software and technologies.

Dr. Lenz achieved excellence in a variety of challenging sports. "Sports and athletics are zazen," he said. "They're meditation -- moving meditation. As you are running down that field or shooting that basket, putting that golf ball, caking down your opponent in martial arts or just competing with yourself, there are moments of timelessness and ecstasy and challenge and emptiness." Dr. Lenz himself was an avid runner, a PADI-certified Divemaster and technical scuba diver, a world-class snowboarder, and a black belt in martial arts.

As a philanthropist, Dr. Lenz was a major contributor to National Public Radio in Connecticut and a donor and supporter of the American Civil Liberties Union, the National Cancer Institute, the AIDS Fund, Amnesty International, the National Museum of Women and the Arts in Washington, D.C., Shotokan Karate, the Cousteau Society, and the Audubon Society.

In spite of all his achievements, Dr. Lenz was self-effacing. He said that enlightenment was not "special" but simply "different." A listing of his many achievements belies the fact that his greatest achievement was in consciousness. He attained the highest states of awareness in the midst of numerous obstacles and never wavered in his commitment to teach and help others. He accomplished all tasks with integrity, enthusiasm, and an incredible sense of humor.

Rama - Dr. Frederick P. Lenz passed away on April 12, 1998 in Long Island, New York, giving his students another powerful koan to decipher. He willed the majority of his estate to the Frederick P. Lenz Foundation for American Buddhism for the purpose of supporting Buddhism in America, "in the context as I have taught it."

This image of Lakshmi appeared in the back of the tape set,
"How to Meditate – A 2-Audio Cassette Course" by Rama – Dr.
Frederick Lenz. This set of tapes contained "Introductory and
Intermediate Meditation" and "Advanced Meditation."

CPSIA information can be obtained
at www.ICGtesting.com
Printed in the USA
FSHW04n0503170418
46858FS